Ordoliberalism and European Economic Policy

This volume takes a broad perspective on the recent debate on the role of German ordoliberalism in shaping European economic policy before and after the eurozone crisis. It shows how ordoliberal scholars explain the institutional origins of the eurozone crisis, and presents creative policy proposals for the future of the European economy.

Ordoliberal discourse both attempts to offer political solutions to socio-economic challenges, and to find an ideal market order that fosters individual freedom and social cohesion. This tension between realpolitik and economic utopia reflects the wider debate on how far economic theory shapes, and is shaped by, historical contingencies and institutions.

The volume will be of interest to policymakers as well as research scholars, and graduate students from various disciplines ranging from economics to political science, history, and philosophy.

Malte Dold is an assistant professor in the Economics Department at Pomona College in California. Previously, he spent two years as a post-doctoral fellow at New York University. He holds a master's degree in philosophy and economics from the University of Bayreuth, and received his PhD in economics from the University of Freiburg. His research lies at the intersection of behavioral economics, welfare economics, and political economy. In particular, his research looks at normative and methodological issues in behavioral economics and the historical interdependencies between Austrian and ordoliberal economic thought.

Tim Krieger is the Wilfried Guth Professor of Constitutional Political Economy and Competition Policy at University of Freiburg. He holds a master's degree in economics from the University of Kiel, and received his PhD in economics from the University of Munich. He worked as an assistant and interim professor at the universities of Mainz, Marburg, and Paderborn. His research focuses on economic, social, and education policies in aging and globalizing societies with a special focus national and supranational institutions. In addition, he specializes in the economics of conflict, terrorism, and crime.

Routledge Studies in the History of Economics

216 The Economic Thought of Friedrich List
Edited by Harald Hagemann, Stephan Seiter and Eugen Wendler

217 Economic Crisis and Economic Thought
Alternative Theoretical Perspectives on the Economic Crisis
Edited by Tommaso Gabellini, Simone Gasperin and Alessio Moneta

218 Schumpeter's Capitalism, Socialism and Democracy
A Twenty-First-Century Agenda
Edited by Leonardo Burlamaqui and Rainer Kattel

219 Divine Providence in Early Modern Economic Thought
Joost Hengstmengel

220 Macroeconomics without the Errors of Keynes
The Quantity Theory of Money, Saving, and Policy
James C. W. Ahiakpor

221 The Political Economy of the Han Dynasty and Its Legacy
Edited by Cheng Lin, Terry Peach and Wang Fang

222 A History of Utilitarian Ethics
Samuel Hollander

223 The Economic Thought of Michael Polanyi
Gábor Biró

224 Ideas in the History of Economic Development
The Case of Peripheral Countries
Edited by Estrella Trincado, Andrés Lazzarini and Denis Melnik

225 Ordoliberalism and European Economic Policy
Between Realpolitik and Economic Utopia
Edited by Malte Dold and Tim Krieger

For more information about this series, please visit www.routledge.com/series/SE0341

Ordoliberalism and European Economic Policy

Between Realpolitik and Economic Utopia

Edited by Malte Dold and
Tim Krieger

LONDON AND NEW YORK

First published 2020
by Routledge
2 Park Square, Milton Park, Abingdon, Oxon OX14 4RN

and by Routledge
52 Vanderbilt Avenue, New York, NY 10017

Routledge is an imprint of the Taylor & Francis Group, an informa business

© 2020 selection and editorial matter, Malte Dold and Tim Krieger;
individual chapters, the contributors

The right of Malte Dold and Tim Krieger to be identified as the
authors of the editorial matter, and of the authors for their individual
chapters, has been asserted in accordance with sections 77 and 78 of
the Copyright, Designs and Patents Act 1988.

All rights reserved. No part of this book may be reprinted or
reproduced or utilised in any form or by any electronic, mechanical, or
other means, now known or hereafter invented, including
photocopying and recording, or in any information storage or retrieval
system, without permission in writing from the publishers.

Trademark notice: Product or corporate names may be trademarks or
registered trademarks, and are used only for identification and
explanation without intent to infringe.

British Library Cataloguing-in-Publication Data
A catalogue record for this book is available from the British Library

Library of Congress Cataloging-in-Publication Data
A catalog record has been requested for this book

ISBN: 978-0-367-19381-2 (hbk)
ISBN: 978-0-429-20203-2 (ebk)

Typeset in Bembo
by Wearset Ltd, Boldon, Tyne and Wear

Contents

Notes on contributors	viii
Foreword	xv
WOLFGANG SCHÄUBLE	
Acknowledgments	xix

Ordoliberalism and European economic policy: an introduction	1
MALTE DOLD AND TIM KRIEGER	

PART I
The historical and contemporaneous roots of ordoliberalism   21

1 **Ordoliberalism's embeddedness in the neoliberalisms of the 1930s and 1940s**   23
STEFAN KOLEV

2 **Ordoliberalism and democracy: how the interwar period changed the agenda of German liberalism**   39
GERHARD WEGNER

3 **A new Thirty Years War? Protestant ordoliberalism and the reemergence of the North–South conflict**   58
JOSEF HIEN

4 **Ordoliberalism, social Catholicism, and West Germany's social market economy (1949–1976)**   74
VOLKER BERGHAHN

vi *Contents*

5 **Ordoliberalism and the cross-national disciplinary revolution in liberalism** 91

KENNETH DYSON

6 **Ordoliberalism from the perspective of a US-trained macroeconomist** 108

RÜDIGER BACHMANN

PART II
Ordoliberal explanations of the eurozone crisis 123

7 **Is ordoliberalism institutionally useful for the EU?** 125

WOLF SCHÄFER

8 **The D-mark and the euro: prerequisites for a stable currency** 131

OTMAR ISSING

9 **The commitment problem and the euro crisis** 138

JOHANNES BECKER AND CLEMENS FUEST

10 **Germany and the euro crisis: ordoliberalism in the dock** 151

OLIVER LANDMANN

11 **Ten commandments to overcome the eurozone's many crises: if the EMU is to succeed, it must be developed based on rules** 167

NORBERT BERTHOLD

12 **Ordoliberalism and the future of European integration** 175

MICHAEL WOHLGEMUTH

13 **Ordoliberalism and the eurozone crisis: toward a more perfect market of jurisdictions?** 190

THOMAS BIEBRICHER

Contents vii

PART III
**Advancements of the ordoliberal framework after
the crisis** 205

14 **Toward a European social market economy? The
normative legacy of Walter Eucken, Alexander
Rüstow, and beyond** 207
JULIAN DÖRR, NILS GOLDSCHMIDT, AND
ALEXANDER LENGER

15 **The enigma of German ordoliberalism: is there a
future for a European social market economy?** 223
BRIGITTE YOUNG

16 **The future of German ordoliberalism** 237
LARS P. FELD AND EKKEHARD A. KÖHLER

17 **Ordoliberalism and beyond: economic liberalism for
the 21st century** 246
MALTE DOLD AND TIM KRIEGER

Index 267

Contributors

Rüdiger Bachmann is the Stepan Family Associate Professor of Economics at the University of Notre Dame, where he is also a fellow of the Nanovic Institute for European Studies. He is a research affiliate with the Centre for Economic Policy Research, a CESifo research network fellow and an external research professor at the Ifo Institute in Munich. He also serves as an associate editor for the *Economic Journal* and the *Journal of Economic Dynamics and Control* and is a member of the macroeconomics committee of the German Economic Association. His research area is macro-economics, where he specializes in the macroeconomics of heterogeneous agents. He has published in numerous top journals including the *American Economic Review*, the *Journal of Monetary Economics*, the *American Economic Journal: Macroeconomics*, and the *American Economic Journal: Economic Policy*. Bachmann received undergraduate degrees in economics and philosophy from Mainz University, and a PhD from Yale University in 2007.

Johannes Becker is a professor of economics and director of the Institute of Public Finance at the University of Münster. He is a member of the German Economic Association, an international research fellow at the Ifo Institute, a scientific board member at the Oxford University Centre for Business Taxation, a MATAX Mannheim research fellow, and a CESifo network member of the International Institute of Public Finance. His main research interests are international taxation and European public finance. He coauthored the book, with Clemens Fuest, *The Odysseus Complex: A Pragmatic Approach to Solve the Eurozone Crisis* (in German). His work has been published in renowned international journals, including *Journal of Public Economic Theory, Public Choice, International Tax and Public Finance, Economics Letters*, and *European Economic Review*.

Volker Berghahn is the Seth Low Emeritus Professor of History at Columbia University. He is also a member of the Royal Historical Society. He specializes in modern German history and European–American relations. He previously taught at Brown and universities in England and Germany. He is the author of numerous books and is widely cited in his field. His publications include: *Europe in the Era of Two World Wars* (2006);

America and the Intellectual Cold Wars in Europe (2001); *Imperial Germany* (1995); *The Americanization of West German Industry, 1945–1973* (1986).

Norbert Berthold held the chair of Economics, Economic Regulation and Social Policy at Julius-Maximilians-Universität Würzburg. His research interests include economic and political order theory, social policy, and labor economics. He has been publishing articles on the German ordoliberal tradition for decades. He is the editor of the blog Wirtschaftliche Freihheit, which is the leading forum for ordoliberal thinking in the German-speaking online community. He is also the coeditor of *ORDO*, the yearbook of economic and social order that was established in 1948 by the economists Walter Eucken and Franz Böhm. Berthold sits on the scientific advisory board at the German Federal Ministry for Economic Affairs and Energy.

Thomas Biebricher is a professor of political theory and philosophy at the Goethe University in Frankfurt. He is also a researcher at the Cluster of Excellence "The Formation of Normative Orders" at the Goethe University in Frankfurt and teaches political theory at FU Berlin. He was a visiting assistant professor at Department of Political Science of the University of Florida (2003–2009). Biebricher has published numerous articles on ordoliberalism and neoliberalism. He received his PhD from the University of Freiburg in 2003.

Malte Dold is an assistant professor in the Economics Department at Pomona College in California. Previously, he spent two years as a postdoctoral fellow at New York University. He holds a master's degree in philosophy and economics from the University of Bayreuth, and received his PhD in economics from the University of Freiburg. His research lies at the intersection of behavioral economics, welfare economics, and political economy. In particular, his research looks at normative and methodological issues in behavioral economics and the historical interdependencies between Austrian and ordoliberal economic thought.

Julian Dörr is a research associate at the University of Siegen and a managing director of the Aktionsgemeinschaft Soziale Marktwirtschaft in Tübingen, an ordoliberal think tank that promotes the idea of a social market economy. His doctoral dissertation won the Roman Herzog Research Prize in 2016, which is awarded to outstanding research relating to the social market economy and regulatory issues. He is also a research fellow at the Institute for Normative Societal Foundations at the University of Bonn.

Kenneth Dyson is a visiting research professor of political studies at the universities of Cardiff and Leeds, and an honorary professor of European political economy at the University of Luxembourg. He is also a fellow of the Academy of the Social Sciences, the British Academy, the Learned

x   *Contributors*

Society of Wales, and the Royal Historical Society. His interests lie at the intersection of European integration, comparative and historical political economy, and German studies. He has a long-standing interest in German policies and politics in a European context, especially processes of economic reform. In honor of his scholarly contributions he was awarded the German Federal Service Cross (First Class) for services to Anglo–German relations.

Lars P. Feld holds the chair for Economic Policy and Constitutional Economics at the Albert-Ludwigs-University of Freiburg and is the director of the Walter Eucken Institute. He is an internationally recognized public finance economist with numerous publications in top journals, including the *Journal of Public Economics*, the *European Economic Review*, and the *Journal of Banking & Finance*. He is a member of Leopoldina (the German National Academy of Sciences), the Kronberger Kreis and the Mont Pèlerin Society. He is also a member of the Scientific Advisory Council to the Federal Ministry of Finance, a member of the German Council of Economic Experts as well as a member of the Independent Council of the Stability Council, Germany's Fiscal Council. His research focuses on economic and fiscal policy, political economics, and the economic analysis of law.

Clemens Fuest is professor of economics and director of the Center for Economic Studies (CES) at the Ludwig-Maximilians-University of Munich. He is also the president of the Ifo Institute in Munich and managing director of CESifo. He is also a member of the Scientific Advisory Council to the Federal Ministry of Finance (chair: 2007–2010), program director of the Oxford University Center for Business Taxation, a member of the European Academy of Sciences, and a member of the Scientific Advisory Board of Ernst & Young. He is also a member of the EU's High Level Group on Own Resources and the German federal government's Minimum Wage Commission. His research areas are public finance, public debt, and taxes. Prior to his appointment to Munich, he was a professor at the universities of Cologne, Oxford, and Mannheim. He is the author of numerous books and articles in national and international top journals, such as *International Tax and Public Finance*, *Journal of Public Economics*, and *Public Choice*, as well as commentaries and articles on current economic policy issues in newspapers.

Nils Goldschmidt is a professor of contextual economics and economic education at the University of Siegen. Prior to his appointment to Siegen, he held professorships at the University of Applied Sciences Munich and the Bundeswehr University Munich. His research interests include organizational economics, economic didactics, social policy, the history and methodology of economic thinking, business ethics, and cultural economics. He is chairman of the Aktionsgemeinschaft Soziale Marktwirtschaft, an ordoliberal think tank that promotes the idea of a social market economy, and he is a member of the board of the Wilhelm Röpke

Contributors   xi

Institute, a prominent ordoliberal research group. He is also a member of the board of the Görres Gesellschaft, and an affiliated fellow at the Walter Eucken Institute. He is coeditor of the *Journal of Contextual Economics* and *ORDO*. His research has been published in important journals, including the *Journal of Institutional Economics*, *Constitutional Political Economy*, and the *American Journal of Economics and Sociology*.

Josef Hien is a postdoctoral fellow at the REScEU project. He is interested in the ideational and cultural foundations of European political economies. Hien received his PhD from the European University Institute in Florence and has worked as a postdoc at the Max Planck Institute for the Study of Societies (Cologne), at the Collegio Carlo Alberto (Moncalieri/Turin), and the Berlin Social Science Centre (WZB, Berlin). He has published widely in international scholarly journals on the intersection of religion and economic ideas, and on ordoliberalism in particular. Hien's thesis "Competing Ideas: The Religious Foundations of the German and Italian Welfare States" was awarded the A.SK Social Science Award from WZB in 2014 for its insights in economic government reform.

Otmar Issing was the former chief economist and member of the board of the ECB, and one of the principal architects of the euro. He developed the 'two pillar' approach to monetary policy decision-making that the ECB has adopted. He is currently president of the Center for Financial Studies at the Goethe University of Frankfurt. Previously, he was a member of the executive board of the Deutsche Bundesbank (1990–1998), the central bank of the Federal Republic of Germany. Prior to his appointment to the University of Frankfurt he was a professor at the universities of Erlangen-Nuremberg and Würzburg. His introduction to monetary theory is in its 15th edition. His book *The Euro* has been translated into English and Chinese. His two main research topics are monetary theory and policy and international economic relations.

Ekkehard A. Köhler is an executive research associate at the Walter Eucken Institute in Freiburg. Previously, he was a doctoral fellow at the Friedrich Naumann Foundation for Freedom and an associate of the New Responsibility Foundation in the field of Economic Foresight 2030. His research interests are in the fields of regulatory economics, institutional economics, finance, monetary theory, monetary policy, and the history of economic thinking. Köhler studied economics and business administration, political science as well as modern and recent history at the Friedrich-Alexander-University of Erlangen, the Albert-Ludwigs-University of Freiburg, and the University of Wisconsin, Madison (USA). He received his doctorate from Lars P. Feld at the Walter Eucken Institute in 2015.

Stefan Kolev is a professor of political economy at the University of Applied Sciences in Zwickau and the deputy director of the Wilhelm Röpke

xii *Contributors*

Institute. His research focuses on the history of economic thought, Austrian economics, constitutional political economy, and economic sociology. Kolev's latest book *A Comparison of Neoliberal Notions of the State* (in German, 2017) analyzes the political economies of ordoliberal and Austrian economists of the 20th century. He was visiting researcher at the Bulgarian National Bank, Indiana University Bloomington, and Duke University. He is coeditor of the Journal of Contextual Economics and ORDO. His current projects address the 19th-century origins of these ideas and their revitalization in the 21st century.

Tim Krieger is the Wilfried Guth Professor of Constitutional Political Economy and Competition Policy at Albert-Ludwigs-University of Freiburg. He holds a master's degree in economics from the University of Kiel and received his PhD in economics from the University of Munich. He worked as an assistant and interim professor at the universities of Mainz, Marburg, and Paderborn. His research focuses on economic, social, and education policies in aging and globalizing societies with a special focus on national and supranational institutions. In addition, he specializes in the economics of conflict, terrorism, and crime. He has published in international scholarly journals in both economics and political science, including the *Journal of Public Economics*, the *Journal of International Economics*, the *Journal of Conflict Resolution*, and the *Journal of Peace Research*.

Oliver Landmann is a professor of economics and holds the chair of Economic Theory at the University of Freiburg. He received his PhD from the University of Basel and has held positions at the Swiss National Bank, the Swiss Science Foundation, and the universities of Cologne, Fribourg (Switzerland), and Basel. He has consulted for the Ministry of Economics at the Swiss government, and the ILO at the UN. His major research areas are macroeconomics, international economics, and European monetary integration. He has published numerous articles on the macroeconomics of the EMU.

Alexander Lenger is an interim professor of economics and didactics at the University of Siegen where he codirects (together with Prof. Dr. Nils Goldschmidt) the Moral Development and Economic Understanding research cluster. He is also a research fellow at the Institute of Sociology at the University of Freiburg. His research focuses on socioeconomics, economic sociology, sociology of economics, economics education, and business ethics. Lenger received his PhD from the University of Freiburg in 2012 with a dissertation titled "Notions of Justice, Constitutional Political Economy and Inclusion."

Wolf Schäfer is a former professor of economics and the former vice president of the Helmut Schmidt University in Hamburg. He serves on the board of numerous institutes including the German Economic Association, the Hamburg Institute of International Economics, and the Kiel Institute for the World Economy. He is member of the Brussels Initiative for European Economic Policy and the Working Committee for European Integration. His research interests include the theory and politics of foreign trade and money, European integration, and macroeconomics. In his publications and teaching, Wolf focuses on the EU in the process of globalization and system competition.

Wolfgang Schäuble is one of the architects of German reunification and to many the face of Germany's political response to the euro crisis. He currently serves as president of the German parliament, where he has been a member since 1972. Prior to his appointment as president, he served as the secretary of the CDU/CSU parliamentary group, Federal Minister for Special Affairs, Federal Minister of the Interior, CDU party chairman, and Minister of Finance. He is also the author of numerous books, articles, and chapters covering constitutional law, European integration, migration, national security, finance, and more. He studied law and economics at the universities of Freiburg and Hamburg.

Gerhard Wegner holds the chair of institutional economics and economic policy at the Willy Brandt School of Public Policy at the University of Erfurt. He is the chairman of the Wilhelm Röpke Institute. He is also a member of the German Economic Association, the Hamburg Institute of International Economics, and the social market economy doctoral program at the Konrad-Adenauer-Stiftung. His research interests include economic and political order theory, political and economic liberalism, new institutional economics, and system competition in the EU. He is the author of *Political Failure by Agreement: Learning Liberalism and the Welfare State* (2008) and the editor of several books on the theory of economic policy, including *The Evolutionary Analysis of Economic Policy* (2003), and *Economic Liberalism as Political Theory* (in German, 2002).

Michael Wohlgemuth is the director of the Open Europe Berlin think tank and a professor of political economy at the University of Witten/ Herdecke. He is an affiliated fellow at the Walter Eucken Institute, as well as a leading professor on the postgraduate program 'Social Market Economy' at the Konrad Adenauer Foundation, associate fellow at the Ratio Institute (Stockholm), and member of the Ludwig Erhard Foundation. His research centers on new institutional economics, public choice theory, theories of economic systems, evolutionary economics, social and legal philosophy, and the history of ideas. He holds an MA in economics from the Albert-Ludwigs-University of Freiburg and PhDs from Friedrich Schiller University in Jena and the Private University of Witten/Herdecke. He is the coeditor of numerous books on ordoliberalism including *Social Market Economy* (in German, 2017), *Competition and Rules* (in German, 2008) and *Foundational Texts in the Freiburg School of Constitutional Political*

xiv *Contributors*

Economy (in German, 2008). He has published widely in such peer-reviewed journals as *Constitutional Political Economy*, *Review of Austrian Economics*, and the *Journal for Business, Economics and Ethics*.

Brigitte Young is professor emeritus of international political economy at the University of Münster, as well as an expert adviser to the department of Research and Innovation at the European Commission. She was awarded the Kaethe-Leichter State Prize of Austria for 2016. Her research areas include economic globalization, global governance, feminist economics, international trade, global financial market governance, and monetary policy. She has worked on EU–US financial regulatory frameworks, European economic and monetary integration, and heterodox economic theories. She is the author of many journal articles and books in English and German on the difference between Anglo-Saxon neoliberalism and German ordoliberalism, the European sovereign debt crisis, and the role of Germany and France in resolving the euro crisis.

Foreword

Wolfgang Schäuble

Since the end of the Cold War and with the advent of globalization and the digital age, the dynamics of free markets have gathered huge momentum internationally. This is presenting billions of people with great opportunities for increased prosperity. At the same time, global networking and liberalization of markets also entail risks, and that has been a painful experience. The crisis in the financial markets has seriously shaken the ideal of unregulated markets as a fundamental prerequisite for economic well-being.

We have become aware of flawed developments in the shaping of our economic order, and these have exacerbated the problem of moral hazard – in capital markets and in bank regulation as well as in the sovereign debt crisis with which the euro crisis is linked. They are forcing us to redefine the relationship between the state and the market in order to counteract further instabilities in the realms of economics, currency, and finance. Crises are an opportunity if they enable us to rediscover how important proper incentives, judicious rules, and a realistic regulatory framework are to human action.

This was recognized all of 70-plus years ago by the representatives of ordoliberalism; along with two older rival schools – the 'lectern socialism' associated with the name of Gustav Schmoller on the one hand and Marxism on the other – ordoliberalism is one of three economic schools of thought of German origin that have left a significant mark on economic theory. Their approach to economics is highly value-driven and anthropocentric. In the Freiburg School, as ordoliberalism is also known after the university that was its main center, the human being is at the heart of economic processes. Economic action is not an end in itself, nor should it ever become one. The ultimate aim is human well-being.

At the same time, consideration must be given to the *conditio humana*. As Kant had already realized, humans are endowed for freedom and capable of great things. Their ambitions are an important driving force for economic success and progress. Yet humans are also carved from all-too-crooked timber, can be led astray, are fearful, irrational. They often fail to act for the good of others. This means that politicians must set limits to the market and its players in cases where these might subvert the social values of our economic order and the sources of its legitimacy. It is a matter of curbing its

xvi *Foreword*

overexuberance without discouraging it. For politicians, who seek to do the right thing by people in their weakness as well as in their freedom, it means preserving the difficult balance between too few rules and too many. It is all about a happy medium.

For Alexander Rüstow, Walter Eucken, Franz Böhm, Wilhelm Röpke, and other representatives of ordoliberalism, this is achieved by a market economy with a human face, an economy based on human dignity that takes account of the reality of imperfect human nature. It therefore makes provision for responsible management of freedom within the workings of the market and for corrective elements outside the workings of the market, that is to say limits, rules, and counterbalances, to avert the danger of excesses. Alfred Müller-Armack, one of the intellectual fathers of the social market economy, who was strongly influenced by the ideas of Rüstow and Eucken, put it this way: it was a matter, he said, of "striking a good balance between the ideals of fairness, freedom and economic growth."

In our ever-changing world, this realization is more valid than ever, which means that undiminished importance still attaches to ordoliberalism and its cogent arguments against the illusion that protectionism and demands for equality can create greater fairness. We need to be clear as to what ordoliberalism means in the 21st century and what responses it offers to the challenges of a globalized economy. Further development of the social market economy in the context of increasing global interaction is long overdue. Ludwig Erhard's ideal of 'prosperity for all,' which is just as fitting today as it was then, must be extended to include the fruits of modern schools of thought such as new institutional economics, public-choice theory and behavioral economics. The contributions to this volume provide a host of stimulating ideas in that respect.

All of the subjects addressed here are highly relevant. Chapters are devoted to globalization, the North–South conflict, the future of the social market economy, and, in particular, the still-unresolved eurozone crisis. The fact that its resolution is proving so difficult is due in part to fundamental differences between the economic cultures of Northern and Southern Europe, especially between Germany and France, the two anchor countries of the eurozone. Germany is federally structured, while France has a centralist tradition. Germany tries to avoid crises by means of prudent rules, whereas France places greater trust in ad hoc intervention by a strong central government when crises occur. Such differences are deeply rooted in people's minds, influence mentalities, and limit the options of stakeholders in each country. This makes it difficult to find compromises, and scholars have to bear this in mind when proposing solutions. The authors of the present volume are recognizably committed to a realistic approach and reject economic utopias, as the subtitle of the volume implies. For this and many other reasons, it is to be hoped that the book will enjoy a wide readership.

The editors' decision to publish the work in English ought to contribute to its appeal. For a long time, the reception of ordoliberalism in other

Foreword xvii

countries suffered from the fact that the writings of Eucken, Böhm, and Röpke were not available in the academic lingua franca of the postwar era. Even today, some of their fundamental texts have still not been translated into English. The present representatives of the Freiburg School have overcome this linguistic 'disadvantage' that hampered the first Freiburg School generation and so are helping to boost the study of ordoliberal ideas in other countries, which had already begun to make headway in recent years. Who knows whether the school will even produce Nobel laureates once again in the near future and whether ordoliberalism will hold its own globally with the highly mathematical Anglo-Saxon school, which represents the leading international economic theory of the present time? The 'mathematicians,' probability analysts and risk theorists are important, but they devote insufficient attention to the role of institutions, unduly disregarding the state in particular. The ordoliberals rightly regard this narrow vision as unwise. A strong state that lays down and enforces sensible rules is indispensable, especially in times of crisis. By 'state' I do not necessarily mean nation states. In a context of globalization and interdependence, we need cross-border cooperation and international solutions if we intend to tackle problems really effectively. Accordingly, the state may equally mean a community of states; it may mean Europe or even the global community. But we do need regulation by organizations with political legitimacy.

In the Freiburg School, the state has traditionally been a subject of research, which is why it now enjoys the respect of many who are not actually ordoliberals, including members of such disparate groups as radical marketeers and Marxists. Occasionally there are even usurpation attempts, which can cause problems by generating a tacit "domestication by reinterpretation" (Karen Horn). Nevertheless, the broad reception of ordoliberal thought is striking evidence of the relevance of the output of the Freiburg School. It reaffirms the constitutive principles set out by Walter Eucken by providing the timelessly valid foundations of a prudent competitive system. These include the assets to be guaranteed by the state: private property and freedom of contract, preservation of open markets, consistency of economic policy, and adherence to the principle of liability for actions, which removes the incentive for moral hazard. Even key aspects of the basis of government economic policy in Germany that remains in force today, namely the aim formulated in the Stability and Growth Act of 1967 of achieving, as simultaneously as possible, price stability, a high employment rate, continuous and appropriate economic growth and a trade balance, reflect ordoliberal principles. For decades it has proved to be a pragmatic benchmark for state action based on market economics. The fact that this 'magic foursome' also contains elements of Keynesianism is not a flaw. It lends it the character of a classical compromise between diverse schools of thought. This is also brought out by the authors in this volume, who include both 'classical' ordoliberals and acknowledged Keynes experts who have cast off their predecessors' distaste for ordoliberalism and reflect pragmatically on areas of common ground. They

xviii *Foreword*

thereby show themselves as true heirs to Walter Eucken, who attached more importance to practicable proposals than to theoretical controversies and who once passionately urged that discussion of economic policy should not be about doctrine but about specific regulatory tasks. If today's and tomorrow's decision makers can be repeatedly and effectively reminded of this message from the founding father of ordoliberalism, a message that has lost none of its validity, and can be persuaded to take it to heart, I am confident that the success story of the Freiburg School and the social market economy will continue for a long time to come. In this respect the volume makes a major contribution to present and future economic policy and can serve as a catalyst for further in-depth exploration of ordoliberalism in the age of globalization.

Acknowledgments

This edited volume is the result of the workshop "Der Ordoliberalismus: Chance oder Gefahr für Europa?" held in September 2016 and a subsequent lecture series titled the "Role of Ordoliberalism in European Economic Policy" held during the summer term 2017 at the University of Freiburg. Many scholars who have participated in these two events have further developed their ideas into chapters and for this volume. The editors would like to thank them for their encouragement to publish this volume and for their contributions. They would also like to thank all other authors. The editors are also grateful to Professor Horst Weitzmann and Neue Universitätsstiftung Freiburg, as well as Thorsten Klapproth for financially supporting the above-mentioned events. Finally, we are most thankful to Carl Hase for the considerate editing of the final manuscript, and to Natalie Tomlinson from Routledge for guiding us through the publishing process.

Ordoliberalism and European economic policy

An introduction

Malte Dold and Tim Krieger

Ordoliberalism and the Freiburg School of Economics

Ordoliberalism,[1] which traces its roots to a prolific group of economic and legal scholars at the University of Freiburg's Faculty of Law and Economics in the early 1930s, has proved singularly influential in shaping the social market economy of postwar Germany. Its founding fathers and chief proponents at that time were the economist Walter Eucken (1891–1950) and the jurists Franz Böhm (1895–1977) and Hans Großmann-Doerth (1894–1944). While these scholars were the main proponents of the Freiburg School, Alexander Rüstow (1885–1963), Wilhelm Röpke (1899–1966), and Alfred Müller-Armack (1901–1978) also count among the ordoliberal scholars of the first generation.

At its core, ordoliberalism endorses the idea that a stable legislative – or constitutional – framework is needed to protect both entrepreneurial competition and economic freedom for all private market actors. In fact, ordoliberalism assumes that constitutional choice defines constraints that effectively limit how market participants can pursue their own goals or, more generally, how markets function (Vanberg, 2017). In this respect, a "market order is not a 'natural event' but a legal–institutional order … that requires careful 'cultivation' for its maintenance and proper functioning" (Vanberg, 2017, p. 10).

By emphasizing an economic order that is implemented and maintained by the state, ordoliberalism stands in contrast to laissez-faire liberalism, which sees only a minimal role for the government in economic affairs. At the same time, the role of the government is constrained to improving the economic order only "in an indirect manner, by shaping the rules of the game" (Vanberg, 2017, p. 10). Or, as Sally (1996, p. 239) puts it, "[i]t is incumbent on the state to set up and maintain the institutional framework of the free economic order, but it should not intervene in the mechanisms of the competitive economic process." The state becomes the guardian of the competitive order with the main task of guaranteeing *performance competition* (*Leistungswettbewerb*), thereby creating "conditions under which the 'invisible hand' that Adam Smith had described can be expected to do its beneficial

2 *Malte Dold and Tim Krieger*

work" (Vanberg, 2017, p. 10). Ordoliberalism wants to minimize direct political intervention into the 'playing of the game,' i.e. discretionary economic policies, since they distort the incentives of private actors who usually have better knowledge about which transactions realize their interests.

Ordoliberalism and early European economic integration

Against this backdrop, early European economic integration was a project in line with ordoliberal reasoning. On the one hand, European 'integration through law' started with treaties that followed the 'logic of the market,' today best known for the four basic freedoms of the single market (i.e. the free movement of goods, services, people, and capital across borders). On the other hand, many jurists emphasize that the early jurisprudence of the European Court of Justice (ECJ) transformed the Treaty of Rome into a constitutional charter (see, e.g., Joerges, 2016; Weiler, 1991). Indeed, according to Walter Hallstein (the first president of the Commission), the European Community is a "creation by law, a source of law, and a legal order" (Hallstein, 1979, p. 3, own translation).[2]

Hence, the early European Community set up quasi-constitutional rules from scratch aimed at establishing a competitive market order throughout Europe. In a joint effort, the member states of the European Community developed the rules of the 'economic game' in Europe. The relatively weak position of the European Commission may not have allowed it much influence over the gameplay itself, but its role in enforcing the rules of the game should not be underestimated. To this day, the Directorate-General for Competition (DG Competition) remains the most prominent DG within the Commission, with the explicit goal of making EU markets work better by directly enforcing European competition rules (in close cooperation with the national competition authorities) to the benefit of consumers, businesses, and the European economy as a whole (DG Competition, 2019).[3] Commissioners like Karel Van Miert (1993–1999), Mario Monti (1999–2004), Neelie Kroes (2004–2010), Joaquín Almunia (2010–2014), and, currently, Margrethe Vestager (since 2014) have played an important role in public and political discourse during their terms in office. The ECJ has added to this with a number of decisions (e.g. *Rewe-Zentral AG* v. *Bundesmonopolverwaltung für Branntwein*, better known as *Cassis de Dijon*) that foster competition by removing barriers to the four freedoms.

However, European integration is not merely an economic project; it is also a political one. It has served as a means of overcoming the continental divide between the main adversaries of two world wars and has helped unite against communism. From an ordoliberal perspective, with its emphasis on rules and competition, political integration is acceptable as long as it respects the principle of economic and political – or systems – competition. In fact, ordoliberals have always emphasized the interdependence of the economic, political, and social orders.[4] For political competition in Europe to be efficient, it must be based on the principle of subsidiarity, according to which political issues be dealt with at the most immediate level consistent with their resolution. Since local, regional, and national preferences differ substantially within the EU, following this principle proves central. It ought to preserve the inherent differences between member states, differences fittingly captured in the EU's motto *in varietate concordia* (united in diversity). 'One-size-fits-all' solutions, on the other hand, do not reflect local preferences fully and thus cannot maximize citizens' welfare.

In turn, cross-border spillovers require at least partial policy coordination at the international or supranational level. On the one hand, these spillovers may be unintended and related to an incomplete regulatory framework, such as when national actions affect neighboring countries (e.g. environmental pollution). On the other hand, they may be an intended consequence of the economic and political order itself (e.g. labor mobility). Regarding the latter, enacting the four freedoms necessarily requires coordination between the EU member states. For instance, labor mobility will only work efficiently if pension claims can be transferred between countries.[5] At the same time, illegal immigrants, or even terrorists, can no longer be stopped at the internal borders of the Schengen area due to the lack of border controls, making coordinated European policing efforts necessary (e.g. Mayr, Minter, & Krieger, 2012). In a sense, such supranational policy measures are necessary to protect competition between private economic actors in all EU member states and realize gains from the coordination and harmonization of the political–institutional orders of the member states. Ultimately, such measures should help drive down inefficiencies resulting from national political processes by providing an exit option from unfavorable legislation (e.g. Haupt & Peters, 2003).[6] Correctly understood, the subsidiarity principle in, for instance, the field of social policy ought to rule out the possibilities of both an entirely European system (which is too far from the citizens' interests) and the suppression of national welfare systems in a race to the bottom (which does not meet the demands of risk-averse citizens). Rather, national social policies need to be disentangled from labor migration by disincentivizing welfare migration. Again, this model of a self-constrained European integration process, which emphasizes the importance of competition, is very much in line with ordoliberal thinking.

Ordoliberalism and political and monetary–economic integration in Europe

The actual process of European integration has developed differently than most ordoliberals had wished. The initial aim of economic integration based on the principles of a competitive market order has become increasingly dominated by efforts to integrate Europe in realms beyond the market. As the above example of pension claims shows, some institutional and political

4 Malte Dold and Tim Krieger

integration is an unavoidable consequence of economic integration. However, all too often the intention has been to take much more substantial steps forward. Instead of a relatively loose, confederation-like construct of sovereign member states with a weak central authority for political, economic, or administrative convenience, the aim became a federal system with a relatively powerful central authority. This authority, the European Commission, was to be legitimized democratically at the European level by the European Parliament.[7]

In practical terms, however, the delegation of power to the supranational level has often lacked precisely this democratic legitimization. The European Commission – and to some degree the European Council – enjoys a relatively high degree of independence from the European Parliament. As a result, those in control of decision-making can rarely be held accountable for their actions. Furthermore, the delegation of power often interferes with the principle of subsidiarity and may thus reduce potential efficiency gains from Europe-wide competition. Hence, fears persist of an intrusive European Commission substantially reducing the benefits of the European competitive order. Similarly, a problematic delegitimization of national parliaments has emerged in that the European Council pushes supranational decisions into national legislation, robbing national legislators of discretion in tailoring directives to local circumstances.[8] Consequently, many ordoliberals have turned away from this version of a European Union and expressed their discontent with the Union's move to a legally, politically, and socially integrated federation; for instance, Streit and Mussler (1995, p. 27) state that the "EU Treaty can be summarized to the effect that the Union is likely to develop corporatist structures quite similar to those of the Member States. As such, it will transform itself from a community under the law to a rent-seeking community." At the same time, however, many ordoliberals still embrace the idea of European integration, except that they believe in a European Union based on the principles of both economic competition between private actors in a common European market, and political competition between EU member states. Despite their critique, Streit and Mussler (1995, p. 27, italics added) share – along with many others – the wish for "a return of the European Union to a *community under the law* as a driving force towards an open European society."[9]

Ordoliberal critique of European integration became most pronounced in the context of European monetary integration in the late 1980s, and particularly in the 1990s. The reason was that, in an attempt at large-scale integration,[10] EU member states decided to apply the so-called 'locomotive theory' (favored by France, Belgium, and Luxembourg among the founding six members of the European Union; see, e.g., Bergsten & Kirkegaard, 2012) over the 'coronation theory' (supported by Germany, the Netherlands, and partly Italy). In the first theory, a common currency is introduced early on to act as a locomotive for additional economic and political integration in Europe; in the second theory, the common currency 'crowns' a long process

Ordoliberalism and European economic policy 5

of real economic and political integration in Europe (Bergsten & Kirkegaard, 2012, p. 2).

If anything, German ordoliberals preferred the coronation theory, but the political reality was a different one. In fact, early on, most ordoliberals[11] were concerned that the new common currency could distort incentives for member states of the eurozone, with dominant national interests leading to inefficient outcomes. In particular, it was feared that member states could excessively increase their public debt, knowing that they would be able to shift some of the burden to other members or to get bailed out in case of national insolvency.[12] Anticipating these incentives, the German government, the Bundesbank, and many German ordoliberal economists pushed for a framework to bind member states. They saw this as the minimum requirement to avoid larger political and economic disruptions in Europe in cases of economic crisis, although many ordoliberals remained skeptical as to whether the member states could implement and − if necessary − enforce strong, binding rules. For this reason, they attempted to safeguard the Maastricht criteria (the most important political–legal 'rules' against the problematic incentives of the euro) with additional constraints issued by the German federal constitutional court.[13] However, despite some supportive decisions by the court in the 1990s, the Maastricht criteria remained practically unenforceable. In fact, ordoliberals see the countless breaches of the Maastricht criteria − in particular members' disregard for the deficit criterion, for which Germany and France were the forerunners − as validation of their concerns.

Ultimately, the ordoliberal critique of the 1990s had little impact on the process of European monetary integration in the late 1990s and early 2000s. Although ordoliberals sparked a significant public debate (often in the influential German newspaper *Frankfurter Allgemeine Zeitung*) with open letters signed by many fellow academics who lobbied against the currency union and the allegedly weak Maastricht criteria (Grimm, 2015), the process of European monetary integration proceeded unhindered. When the euro was finally introduced in the early 2000s and heralded as a great success, ordoliberal critics carried the appearance of dogmatic, misguided Cassandras. Until the financial crisis of 2007–2008, the introduction of the single currency led to high growth rates, converging interest rates and − often (e.g. Spain), but not always (e.g. Greece, Italy) − stable public finances in most eurozone member states. Germany proved an exception. It had lost its competitive edge in the late 1990s (due to reunification) and suffered from a reallocation of capital to the more dynamic European periphery.[14] It was only in the mid-2000s that Germany slowly recovered from its economic malaise.

These fierce debates surrounding the introduction of the euro kept the ordoliberal profession occupied and resulted in an increasingly inward-looking perspective. Many ordoliberal scholars became outspokenly political but neglected to keep track of the latest academic developments in theoretical modeling or the application of empirical methods. Consequently, ordoliberals became academically marginalized (in part due to their fight against the

6 *Malte Dold and Tim Krieger*

EMU) and hardly survived the generational change that swept across economics departments at German universities (see, e.g., Feld & Köhler, 2011). What little academic and political influence they had with respect to the pace and form of European integration diminished further. Against this backdrop, today's critique of ordoliberalism as an ideational and practical contributor to the eurozone crisis and its slow resolution requires convincing justification.

The financial crisis, slow crisis resolution, and the critique of ordoliberalism

When the effects of the US subprime mortgage crisis of 2007–2008 eventually spread to Europe, a decade of exceptional economic growth in Europe's periphery terminated abruptly. International investors who had invested heavily in Southern Europe and Ireland suddenly realized that the EMU was not an 'optimal currency area' and that the convergence of interest rates in the eurozone did not translate to a convergence of default risk. In the build-up to the crisis, economies in Europe's periphery had experienced extensive international capital inflows, and high current account deficits. Capital was predominantly channeled into investments in non-tradables (especially in the real estate sector), oversized banking sectors, and – in some (notorious) cases – heavy public debt. Consequently, these countries were soon considered too risky and capital was rapidly redirected to safe havens in Northern Europe.

As a result, the countries on the margins of Europe came under pressure on several levels. Their banks and construction companies collapsed, their economies shrank, and their unemployment rates skyrocketed due to high unit labor costs (relative to Germany), but they could not respond by means of currency devaluations (or increased northbound labor mobility). Their budgets groaned under the burden of bailout funds for the banking sector and increased social spending. This development was especially severe because these countries had failed to implement structural reforms during the boom years after they entered the eurozone.[15] The countries in the central eurozone that did implement structural reforms before the crisis, in particular Germany, benefited from the capital flowing back from the periphery.

It is beyond the scope of this introductory chapter to discuss the root causes and origins of the eurozone crisis in detail. The previous short description indicates, however, that the initial Europe-wide convergence of important macroeconomic variables through the introduction of a common currency ended as a great economic divergence of different groups of member states, most notably a group of declining Southern European countries (plus Ireland) and a group of countries in Europe's core led by a thriving Germany. The resulting asymmetry between these groups and the different perspectives on crisis resolution have shaken the fundamentals of European economic and political integration. In more practical terms, this has resulted in an overly slow process of crisis resolution, which can – in game-theoretic terms – reasonably be explained as a 'war of attrition' (or 'chicken') game (Krieger,

Ordoliberalism and European economic policy   7

2016; Schimmelpfennig, 2015).[16] The main feature of this 'game' is that each player tries to avoid making the first move in order to shift a larger share of the reform costs onto the opponent. For Southern Europe, this means postponing painful economic reforms; for Germany, it means withholding generous support from countries in crisis. However, avoiding reforms continuously accumulates (macroeconomic) costs for all players during the entire game. Unfortunately, the game continues to this day and the crisis remains unresolved. For instance, at the time of writing, Italy is attempting to shift some of its public debt onto its European partners, while at the same time, most of Europe expects Italy to introduce structural reforms in order to return to a stable growth path. Luckily, healthy growth rates in many European countries have helped temporarily ease tensions in the eurozone. Yet, irreconcilable differences remain between northern countries, with their demands for austerity, and their southern counterparts, who vigorously reject these demands – differences that are likely to reemerge during the next economic downturn.

More importantly in our context, however, is how the process of crisis resolution elicited preexisting *Weltanschauungen* and ultimately led to a "battle of ideas" (Brunnermeier, James, & Landau, 2016). Two schools of thought regarding the optimal resolution of a mostly macro-level crisis have clashed, and neither of them is willing to give in. The respective policy conceptions differ markedly; in the words of Brunnermeier et al. (2016, p. 4): "The northern vision is about rules, rigor and consistency, while the southern emphasis is on the need for flexibility, adaptability and innovation. It is Kant versus Machiavelli. Economists have long been familiar with this kind of debate and refer to it as *rules versus discretion*." That the debate on European crisis resolution is largely split along geographic lines lends credence to this theory: the North is afraid of having to support the South, while the South hopes for precisely such support. Interestingly, this debate has played out primarily in international academic macroeconomics, with economists taking sides largely according to their ideological predispositions. The debate mainly concerned whether austerity policies, which aim at improving the supply side of the economy, trump demand-side measures, which necessarily break the rules of the Maastricht Treaty. While German ordoliberals wanted to adhere to the existing rules and therefore sided with the austerity camp, there was no particular ordoliberal dimension to this 'old' battle between rules and discretion.

At the same time, a very different debate took place in other public forums. The leading question in this debate was why Germany was so reluctant to provide support to Southern European countries (e.g. by agreeing to the introduction of Eurobonds that would have shifted some of the burden of the crisis to Germany). Commentators combined this with the question of why Germans did not want to adopt seemingly easy and pragmatic Keynesian solutions to the crisis (i.e. fiscal stimulus) but rather stuck vigorously to the Maastricht criteria. Interestingly, most German ordoliberals

8   *Malte Dold and Tim Krieger*

either missed or deliberately ignored this debate, though some prominent commentators and scholars from the other camp expressed mostly negative opinions on ordoliberals and named them the true culprits for slow crisis resolution.

In his blog post "ordoarithmetic," Nobel Prize winner Paul Krugman (2014) taunts that "in Germany they have their own intellectual tradition," and *Financial Times* associate editor Wolfgang Münchau (2014) scoffs at the "wacky economics of Germany's parallel universe." Mark Blyth believes that "Welcome to Austerity: Kein Kaufen, Nur Sparen!"[17] is a "very ordoliberal/ Austrian slogan" (2015, p. 261) that perfectly describes German policy demands following the outbreak of the crisis. Others refer to the "long shadow of ordoliberalism" in Europe (Dullien & Guérot, 2012) or "Europe's ordoliberal iron cage" (Ryner, 2015); they see a 'strong state' à la Carl Schmitt at work (Bonefeld, 2012) and even go so far as to compare ordo-liberalism to jihadism in that it resembles a kind of religious extremism (van der Walt, 2016).[18] Compared to German ordoliberals' complaints that German and European politicians have consistently ignored their advice since the conception of the EMU in the late 1980s, such harsh critique of ordo-liberalism deserves careful academic investigation. In fact, given these con-flicting views one wonders whether ordoliberalism indeed did, and still does, influence economic policymaking in the eurozone.

Most German economists, only some of whom might consider themselves ordoliberals, would probably deny the critique and point out that ordoliberal scholarship has been marginalized in the profession.[19] They would instead point to pragmatism as an explanation of Germany's economic policy during the eurozone crisis. Germany-based US macroeconomist Michael Burda (2015) points out that "[i]t is not ordoliberal religion, but a mixture of national self-interest and healthy mistrust informed by experience that guides German economic policy today."[20] And even Lars Feld, director of the Walter Eucken Institute in Freiburg, argues that pragmatism trumped 'pure' ordoliberal reasoning during the crisis: "German economic policy was simply a pragmatic response to different crisis phenomena ... German pragmatism during the crisis has caused an unintended break of basic principles of ordo-liberalism – surrendering EMU's de-politicized monetary constitution against the prevention of further fiscal integration on the EU level" (Feld, Köhler, & Nientiedt, 2015). This reasoning is in line with Brunnermeier et al. (2016), who mention the potential influence of ordoliberalism on European politics only in passing, and jokingly downplay its relative importance: "It would indeed be peculiar if a whole country fell prey to a collective ideological imbecilism" (p. 63).

In the course of this debate, renewed interest has emerged in under-standing German ordoliberalism, and more nuanced views have become available. It is the aim of this volume to illuminate ordoliberalism's past, present, and future role in shaping European economic policy. Yet, many open questions remain and careful analysis is required. Is the position of

German politics on the eurozone crisis ordoliberal? If not, then what is the position of German politics on the eurozone? Where does the belief, held by international scholars, that German politics is inherently ordoliberal stem from? What does it mean for a policy to be ordoliberal in the first place? And what are the historical roots of the ordoliberal tradition? Our edited volume explores these questions by taking a broad perspective on ordoliberalism and Germany's influence on European economic policy.

The contributions to this edited volume

The volume begins with a foreword by Wolfgang Schäuble, the former German minister of finance, one of the architects of German reunification and to many the face of Germany's austere response to the eurozone crisis. He reminds us of one of the main tenets of ordoliberalism, that economic action is not an end in itself; rather, the ultimate aim is human well-being. Therefore, he calls for ordoliberals to help build a European economic order with a human face, a market economy based on human dignity that does not neglect its ethical dimension nor economic rationality.

Subsequently, the volume explores ordoliberalism's role in European economic policy in three parts. It highlights the diversity of methodological approaches within ordoliberalism, but also notes important points of criticism from scholars who do not consider themselves ordoliberals. Part I of this volume examines the historical and contemporaneous roots of ordoliberalism from its origins in the 1930s up to the present. Today's discourse of the role of ordoliberalism in European economic policy cannot be understood without the knowledge of its early ideas and their development over time. Part II explores ordoliberal explanations of the eurozone crisis, with chapters from ordoliberal protagonists who first raised concerns about European monetary and political integration as early as the 1990s, but also from scholars of the next generation. The authors in the final part this volume – some more traditional, some more progressive – explore the directions in which ordo-liberalism should develop in the future in order to remain a relevant research program – rather than an oddity from Germany's past.

The historical and contemporaneous roots of ordoliberalism (part I)

The exploration of the origins of ordoliberal thought in Germany begins with chapter 1 ("Ordoliberalism's embeddedness in the neoliberalisms of the 1930s and 1940s") by Stefan Kolev. Kolev argues that ordoliberalism ought to be understood as a German variant of the neoliberalisms that emerged in many western nations in response to a general crisis of liberalism in the 1930s and 1940s. The chapter focuses on Friedrich August von Hayek's role in facilit-ating interaction between ordoliberals and other communities and his contri-bution to their convergence. According to Kolev, portraying ordoliberalism as a 'German oddity' is historically incorrect and conceptually misleading.

10   Malte Dold and Tim Krieger

Rather, ordoliberal thinking had, and still has, its counterparts on both sides of the Atlantic. Hence, Kolev concludes, it is not surprising that recent ordoliberal contributions triggered by the eurozone crisis have to a large extent come from the international community of scholars in political economy that emerged from the early neoliberal discourse.

Chapter 2 ("Ordoliberalism and democracy: how the interwar period changed the agenda of German liberalism") by Gerhard Wegner explores a reoccurring critique of (early) ordoliberals, namely, their lack of unconditional support for democracy. Wegner shows that the rapid move of post-World War I societies toward democratization led to a dysfunctional politicization of the liberal economic order, particularly in the case of the Weimar State. Ordoliberals were not only concerned that democracy might lead to socially harmful and destabilizing economic policies, but they were also confronted with the question of how individual liberty and economic freedom could be brought into accord with the sovereignty of the polity. The ordoliberal research agenda in the 1930s and 1940s was particularly concerned with the unsettled relationship between economic freedom and democratic decision-making. One result of this debate is that ordoliberals proved receptive to politico-economic arguments surrounding European monetary integration and, more generally, in European economic policy.

The third and fourth chapters of this volume are interrelated in that they both explore the role of religion in ordoliberalism. Josef Hien, author of chapter 3 ("A new Thirty Years War? Protestant ordoliberalism and the reemergence of the North–South conflict"), once asked jokingly in a lecture at the University of Freiburg whether ordoliberal ideas for the resolution of the eurozone crisis (with its reemerging North–South conflict) were "Protestant medicine against Catholic dissoluteness." In his chapter, Hien argues that today's ordoliberalism does in fact trace its cultural roots to German Protestantism. Historically, different socioeconomic ideologies in Catholicism and Protestantism led to different socioeconomic institutions that have persisted up to the present, resulting in fundamental disagreement about crisis resolution along the 'Kant versus Machiavelli' lines (Brunnermeier et al., 2016). This may explain why the 'Swabian housewife,'[21] most likely a pietist who never spends more than she saves, has become the symbol of seemingly ordoliberal crisis management characterized by German demands for 'austerity.'

While there is clearly a correlation between religion and demand for austerity in Europe, the German case is not entirely clear. Arguing that German economic and social policy is primarily driven by protestant considerations would not do justice to the (social) Catholic influence on this very policy in the postwar period, as Volker Berghahn explains in chapter 4 ("Ordoliberalism, Social Catholicism, and West Germany's social market economy (1949–1976)"). Berghahn argues that ordoliberalism is only one part of a broader intellectual effort in postwar Germany to answer the 'social question.' While Walter Eucken and the Freiburg School were clearly influential in shaping the German 'social market economy,' in particular with respect to its

Ordoliberalism and European economic policy   11

economic underpinnings, Berghahn shows how social Catholicism has influenced economic and social policy in Germany. This calls for a more nuanced perspective on German recommendations regarding crisis resolution.

Kenneth Dyson's chapter 5 ("Ordoliberalism and the cross-national disciplinary revolution in liberalism") takes a different perspective on ordoliberalism by identifying it as a 'tradition' resulting from a disciplinary revolution in liberalism. Based on its core beliefs in a rule-based economic, political, and social order, ordoliberalism represents an inherently liberal–conservative way of looking at the individual, the market, the state, and their relation to each other. In this respect, it is neither an independent contribution to economic theory nor a distinctly German idea, Dyson argues. As a tradition, ordoliberalism spans the ideological spectrum and caters to liberals and conservatives alike. This has allowed German policymakers to make (rhetorical) reference to ordoliberalism whenever it has proved useful in negotiations on the EMU or eurozone crisis resolution; however, German policy positions in this context were probably not caused by an adherence to ordoliberal principles but by national interest.

In chapter 6 ("Ordoliberalism from the perspective of a US-trained macroeconomist"), Rüdiger Bachmann offers a related perspective on ordoliberalism's role in eurozone crisis resolution. He argues that ordoliberal thinking is almost nonexistent in contemporary German macroeconomics, as scholars in this field are entirely integrated into the international, Anglo-American-dominated scientific community of macroeconomics. Bachmann even denies that ordoliberal thinking resonates in practical politics; rather, it appears more a convenient ideology along the lines of Dyson's argument. Bachmann argues that the lingering influence of ordoliberalism in German society reflects a deep admiration among German intellectuals for the principle-based, formalistic reasoning found in continental law, and skepticism toward the outcome-oriented, pragmatic reasoning in Anglo-American-style economics. He concludes that there is a natural propensity for German culture to admire ordoliberal economics because it resembles the deductive rules- and framework-based thinking found in continental law. In this sense, German citizens regard ordoliberals as good economists because they are in fact lawyers at heart – certainly not a compliment for ordoliberal economists.

Ordoliberal explanations of the eurozone crisis (part II)

While the post-World War II period witnessed the emergence of the German socioeconomic model, as part I of this volume indicates, these events did not occur in a vacuum. Broad, continental political change was underway as major steps were taken toward European integration. Over time, German ordoliberals' initial sympathy for this process gave way to deep skepticism and increasing disappointment, primarily in response to the planning and creation of the EMU. This context forms the backdrop for part II of our book, which explores the positions of German ordoliberals in the 1990s as well as after the

12 *Malte Dold and Tim Krieger*

eurozone crisis which started in 2007/2008. Part II of this volume highlights why ordoliberals believed that the EMU and the euro were doomed to fail, and why they continue to criticize current efforts to solve the crisis. Moreover, part II further illustrates (as in Rüdiger Bachmann's chapter) that many macroeconomists continue to have reservations about ordoliberal positions.

In chapter 7 ("Is ordoliberalism institutionally useful for the EU?"), Wolf Schäfer reflects on how German ordoliberals became increasingly discontent as the pace of European integration accelerated in the 1980s–1990s and culminated in the EMU. Schäfer resorts to the economic theory of institutions in arguing that the state ought to provide democratically legitimized rules with effective behavioral incentives for economic agents and organizations, but all too often sets perverse incentives by discretionary policies. In the institutional context of the EU, the rule of law as the most important institutional anchor for effective societal functioning is violated when the rules of the Lisbon and Maastricht treaties are no longer followed. Against this backdrop, Schäfer postulates reforms based on ordoliberal institutional design; specifically, a market-based functional approach to integration emphasizing subsidiarity and plurality.

Closer inspection of European monetary integration is at the heart of chapter 8 ("The D-mark and the Euro: prerequisites for a stable currency"). Written by Otmar Issing, one of the chief architects of European Central Bank's (ECB) monetary policy, the chapter underscores the relevance of a rules-based, ordoliberal approach in modern political economy. The chapter examines how the Maastricht Treaty provides the anchor for the EMU. The ECB has a clear mandate to maintain price stability and is granted the status of independence in order to conduct monetary policy free from political interference. In this context, the chapter addresses two hotly debated issues that have emerged as a result of the eurozone crisis, namely debt monetization and the no-bailout clause. It makes the case that the prohibition of debt monetization and the no-bailout clause are both important (ordoliberal) elements for the ECB in order to maintain central bank independence.

In chapter 9 ("The commitment problem and the euro crisis"), Johannes Becker and Clemens Fuest summarize the different lines of argument for why the eurozone crisis began in the first place. They review three main narratives on the emergence of the crisis: the "Mundell view," which paints the eurozone as a suboptimal currency union, the "German view," which focuses on sovereign debt, and the "trade deficit" view, which highlights the damaging role of precrisis current account deficits in crisis countries. Similar to Wolf Schäfer, the authors then argue that these narratives ignore fundamental institutional shortcomings that led to a commitment problem, and, in turn, the euro crisis. Any reform of the eurozone would have to create institutions that enable member states to commit to commonly agreed upon positions, strengthen democratic legitimacy, and preserve the congruence of accountability and control in a contemporary application of ordoliberal principles.

Ordoliberalism and European economic policy 13

In chapter 10 ("Germany and the euro crisis: ordoliberalism in the dock"), Oliver Landmann remains skeptical about the potential for reforms in the EMU based on ordoliberal macroeconomic policy. Landmann argues that what divides Germany from the Mediterranean countries is not just a conflict of national economic interests, but a different economic philosophy which resulted in a 'battle of ideas.' In this battle, Germany stands for fiscal rectitude, sound money, and an insistence on binding rules. The Latin European tradition, in contrast, prioritizes flexibility over rigid rules and rejects supranational policy constraints that might hamper crisis management and the pursuit of macroeconomic stability. Landmann concludes that any progress toward a resilient currency union requires difficult trade-offs and political decisions, in which ordoliberal concerns about incentives and liability will have to be weighed against concerns about macroeconomic and financial stability.

Norbert Berthold, in chapter 11 ("Ten commandments to overcome the eurozone's many crises") cautions that the current (2019) economic stability in the eurozone, with no acute crisis meetings, might just be the quiet before the next storm. Important structural reforms are delayed and several macroeconomic factors, such as unemployment or the share of bad loans from banks, are still not favorable in many EU member states. Berthold argues that the relative state of calm provides an opportune moment to reform the EMU from top to bottom. In his ten commandments, he outlines the major lines along which sustainable, rule-bound institutional reform should occur; chief among these is the need to unravel the negative symbiosis between banks and governments.

In chapter 12 ("Ordoliberalism and the future of European integration"), Michael Wohlgemuth follows a similar line of thought. He reminds us of the early ordoliberals' focus on the nation state as their addressee for an 'economic constitution.' Today, key elements of the economic order are located at the supranational level. Wohlgemuth argues that because the political outcome of the 'ever-closer union' project is unsustainable, a clear distinction is needed between policies that should be located at the supranational level of the EU, and policies best left to the national or local level. Based on this differentiation, he presents a model of flexible integration in different policy areas. This would allow for institutional competition and a discovery procedure that can help find the right depth of integration for individual member states.

While the tenor of many of the previous chapters is to call for more ordoliberalism in Europe as a consequence of the eurozone crisis, in chapter 13 ("Ordoliberalism and the eurozone crisis: toward a more perfect market of jurisdictions?"), Thomas Biebricher argues that the outcome of the eurozone crisis was indeed a governance shift toward a more ordoliberal-oriented institutional framework. While many ordoliberals, including Michael Wohlgemuth, deny that post-crisis European economic governance follows the ideal of an economic constitution, Biebricher argues that the crisis response of the

14 *Malte Dold and Tim Krieger*

last few years resulted in a more detailed and tightly arranged regime of competitive federalism among the member states of the eurozone. To him, the result is an economic constitution that approximates the ideal of an order that enables a functioning market of jurisdictions, where only certain forms of competition are possible while others are ruled out. Hence, today's economic European governance represents a significant step in the process of an 'ordoliberalization' of the eurozone.

Advancements of the ordoliberal framework after the crisis (part III)

While the eurozone crisis has sparked a renewed public and academic interest in ordoliberalism, it has also revealed the rich diversity of ordoliberal thought. This diversity provides fertile ground for developing ordoliberalism further and expanding its scope. Therefore, part III of this edited volume asks how ordoliberalism could, and should, advance in the aftermath of the eurozone crisis. What lessons can German ordoliberal economists learn from the criticism levelled by scholars abroad (regardless of whether and how ordoliberalism influenced European institutions)? How, if at all, could Europe benefit from more ordoliberal influence on decision-making in the eurozone?

In chapter 14 ("Toward a European social market economy? The normative legacy of Walter Eucken, Alexander Rüstow, and Beyond"), Julian Dörr, Nils Goldschmidt, and Alexander Lenger ask to what extent ordoliberal politics could contribute to the development of a truly European society despite the growing socioeconomic divide and divergent economic cultures. They call for an advancement of ordoliberalism based on constitutional political economy and Amartya Sen's capability approach in order to legitimize the European order beyond functional characteristics such as the efficient regulation of competition. The authors argue that the legitimacy of an institutional framework stems from the actual consent of the individuals involved. In the EU, such consent can only be achieved if the material and social rights of its citizens are taken seriously, and they are able to exercise their civil liberties. The authors argue that the EU's Cohesion Policy could potentially serve as a kind of *Vitalpolitik* of nations with the goal of anchoring the concept of inclusion at the European level and realizing a transnational social market economy in line with the Freiburg School's ordoliberalism.

Brigitte Young builds on these arguments in chapter 15 ("The enigma of German ordoliberalism: is there a future for a European social market economy?"). Young argues that there is no 'pure ordoliberal school' but rather different branches of ordoliberalism (exemplified by the Freiburg School, Wilhelm Röpke and Alexander Rüstow, and Alfred Müller-Armack). After focusing on austerity, the strong state, and neoliberalism – three highly contested ordoliberal concepts that have contributed to negative stereotypes of German politics in the Anglo-American world – Young turns to the social ordoliberalism of Müller-Armack. She asks whether the idea of a social market economy offers guidance on how to institutionalize a fairer

Ordoliberalism and European economic policy 15

compromise between competitive markets and social solidarity in the EU. She argues that Müller-Armack's social politics gives substance to the rather abstract debate on the European Pillar of Social Rights, introduced by the Commission President Jean-Claude Juncker in 2015.

In chapter 16 ("The future of German ordoliberalism"), Lars Feld and Ekkehard Köhler begin by reminding us of the problem of ideological bias when economists are called upon to evaluate public policies, and of the difficulty of using positive economic analysis for practical purposes while maintaining scientific rigor. Ordoliberals have been criticized for lacking a clear commitment to the claim that the goals of economic policy should be decided upon by the political process rather than the enlightened members of the economics profession. In light of methodological debates that persist to the present day, Feld and Köhler find important lessons for economists (also for its representatives in the Anglo-American world) that can be drawn from discussions of the normative elements in German ordoliberalism. They argue that all too often economists ignore normative elements in their analysis in order to provide practical policy advice. However, such an approach ignores the vast differences in opinion among economists on pressing issues of economic policy as well as the value-laden assumptions implicit in their methods. Consequently, economists are well advised to critically examine the influence of their political and normative commitments on their scientific endeavors.

The volume concludes with chapter 17 ("Ordoliberalism and beyond: economic liberalism for the 21st century") by Malte Dold and Tim Krieger. They carve out some of the core challenges for what they call 'contemporary ordoliberalism.' They identify ordoliberalism as a research program that combines economics with politics, positive insights with normative reasoning, and theoretical idealization with applied policy recommendations. Consequently, they call on ordoliberals to emphasize their foundation in political liberalism and the economics of rules, and see the normativity of ordoliberalism as an actual strength since it explicates and defends the ethical dimension of economic policymaking. They propose that contemporary ordoliberals advance their thinking in connection with international discussions in PPE (philosophy, politics, and economics), as a PPE-oriented ordoliberalism helps analyze and advocate the implicit normative assumptions of economic policy advice. In order to be relevant for academic and political discourse in the 21st century, ordoliberals must also translate their form of economic liberalism into a viable alternative to current populist movements. They must deliver fresh solutions to pressing societal challenges such as inequality and distributional conflicts within and across European nations, the significance of migration for the model of the western welfare state, and the problem of power concentration in the digital economy stemming from rapid technological change and a lack of property rights in data. In all of these areas, ordoliberals can help clarify the advantages of a coordinated Europe that acknowledges the subsidiarity principle in local, national, and supranational policies and the social inclusivity of liberal economic ideas. After decades in which economists

16 Malte Dold and Tim Krieger

neglected fundamental social questions in favor of technocratic details, ordo-liberals can offer an encompassing framework.

Notes

1 In Germany, the term *Ordnungspolitik* is commonly used to describe economic policy inspired by ordoliberal thinking. However, "[t]he term 'Ordnungspolitik' is so typically German, that direct translation into English is almost impossible" (Ordnungspolitisches Portal, 2019). In the following, we will stick to the term ordoliberalism to avoid possible confusion.
2 "Schöpfung des Rechts, Rechtsquelle, und Rechtsordnung."
3 See Articles 101–109 of the Treaty on the Functioning of the EU (TFEU).
4 For instance, Eucken (1952/1990, p. 338) argues that building a new societal order requires that both the political (*Staatsordnung*) and economic (*Wirtschaftsordnung*) order be tackled at the same time because of their interdependence.
5 In general, the EU has little say in social policy issues as social policy is seen as a prerogative of the member states. However, in the early 1970s two highly important Council Regulations were introduced (Nos. 1408/71 and 574/72), which, among other things, allow employees to accumulate contribution time in different countries. This removed a major obstacle to employment in other member states and, thus, fostered cross-border mobility (Krieger, 2005).
6 Note, however, that unconstrained system competition may lead to suboptimal outcomes (e.g. Sinn 1997).
7 Interestingly, Vaubel (1999) proposes the establishment of a directly elected European senate with no powers other than to enforce competition among governments based on qualified minority decisions.
8 As Vaubel (1995, p. 117) states: "Whoever thought that, in a parliamentary democracy, governments are controlled by their parliaments should note that, in the European Community, the national ministers assembled in Brussels jointly control their parliaments."
9 To this day, and with the benefit of hindsight concerning the eurozone crisis, even harsh critics of early European monetary integration like Renate Ohr and Norbert Berthold do not propose abandoning the EMU (*FAZ*, 2017).
10 There is an ongoing debate whether the early introduction of the common European currency, which Germany was not particularly interested in, was the political 'price' to be paid by the country for European – especially French – support for the German reunification (see, e.g., Vaubel, 2002, 2010).
11 One of the few prominent ordoliberal supporters of the Economic and Monetary Union (EMU) of the European Union is Sievert (1993).
12 Arguments like these are reoccurring in the public debate; see, e.g., Henkel (2012); Hankel, Nölling, Schachtschneider, & Starbatty (2001); Ohr and Schäfer (1992).
13 Among the plaintiffs in most of these decisions were typically the jurist Karl Albrecht Schachtschneider and the economists Wilhelm Nölling, Wilhelm Hankel, and Joachim Starbatty (see, e.g., Grimm 2015).
14 At that time, *The Economist* (1999) dubbed Germany the "sick man of the Euro."
15 To be fair, as of 2019, Germany did also not use a decade-long economic boom for any meaningful structural economic reforms. Most likely, the country is ill equipped for the expected downturn in the years to come.
16 This game involves two contestants who compete for a valuable resource, in this case not having to pay the lion's share of the costs of crisis resolution. They do so by resorting to a 'wait-and-see' strategy because the contestant, or government, that moves first and reveals its strategy is fated to be the loser (Dold & Krieger, 2018).

Ordoliberalism and European economic policy   17

17 "Welcome to austerity: no buying, just saving" (own translation).
18 Most founding fathers of German ordoliberalism were Protestants. Some scholars believe that their Protestant ethics explain ordoliberal demands for austerity. For an extensive discussion, see Josef Hien's contribution to this volume (chapter 3).
19 One should note, however, that not only German ordoliberals, but German economists in general were marginalized in the academic discourse on European monetary integration. For instance, Barry Eichengreen's (1993) major review essay on European monetary unification in the *Journal of Economic Literature* contains hardly any references to German economists.
20 The latter remark refers to the experience with Germany's federal structure in which joint liability for each state's debt led to ever-increasing debts.
21 After the collapse of Lehman Brothers in 2008, German Chancellor Angela Merkel stated: "One should simply have asked the Swabian housewife ... She would have told us that you cannot live beyond your means."

References

Bergsten, C. F., & Kirkegaard, J. F. (2012). The coming resolution of the European crisis: An update. PIIE Policy Brief No. PB 12–18.

Blyth, M. (2015). *Austerity: The history of a dangerous idea.* Oxford, UK: Oxford University Press.

Bonefeld, W. (2012). Freedom and the strong state: On German ordoliberalism. *New Political Economy 17*(5) 633–656.

Brunnermeier, M. K., James, H., & Landau, J. P. (2016). *The euro and the battle of ideas.* Princeton, NJ: Princeton University Press.

Burda, M. (2015). Dispelling three myths on economics in Germany. [published on VOX, CEPR Policy Portal] Retrieved from https://voxeu.org/article/dispelling-three-myths-economics-germany

DG Competition. (2019). Competition policy in the European Union, http://ec.europa.eu/dgs/competition/index_en.htm (last retrieved 03.03.2019).

Dold, M., & Krieger, T. (2018). The ideological use and abuse of Freiburg's ordoliberalism. Paper presented at the conference The Freiburg School and the Virginia School: The Research Programs of Ordnungspolitik and Constitutional Political Economy, December 6–9, Freiburg.

Dullien, S., & Guérot, U. (2012). The long shadow of ordoliberalism: Germany's approach to the euro crisis. European Council on Foreign Relations.

Economist, The (1999, June 3). The sick man of the euro. Available at www.economist.com/node/209559 (accessed 18/03/2019).

Eichengreen, B. (1993). European Monetary Unification. *Journal of Economic Literature 31*(3) 1321–1357.

Eucken, W. (1952/1990). *Grundsätze der Wirtschaftspolitik* (6th ed.). Tübingen, Germany: J.C.B. Mohr.

FAZ. (2017, February 7). Wovor die Euro-Kritiker schon früh warnten. *Frankfurter Allgemeine Zeitung.*

Feld, L. P., & Köhler, E. A. (2011). Ist die Ordnungsökonomik zukunftsfähig? *Zeitschrift für Wirtschafts-und Unternehmensethik 12*(2) 173–195.

Feld, L. P., Köhler, E. A., Nientiedt, D. (2015). Ordoliberalism, pragmatism and the eurozone crisis: How the German tradition shaped economic policy in Europe. *Freiburger Diskussionspapiere zur Ordnungsökonomik, No. 15/04.* Inst. für Allg. Wirtschaftsforschung, Abt. für Wirtschaftspolitik, Freiburg i. Br.

18 *Malte Dold and Tim Krieger*

Grimm, R. (2015). The rise of the German eurosceptic party Alternative für Deutschland, between ordoliberal critique and popular anxiety. *International Political Science Review 36*(3) 264–278.

Hallstein, W. (1979). *Die Europäische Gemeinschaft* (5th ed.). Düsseldorf, Germany: ECON.

Hankel, W., Nölling, W., Schachtschneider, K. A., & Starbatty, J. (2001). *Die Euro-Illusion. Ist Europa noch zu retten?* Reinbek bei Hamburg, Germany: Rowohlt Taschenbuch

Haupt, A., & Peters, W. (2003). Voting on public pensions with hand and feet: How young migrants try to escape from gerontocracy. *Economics of Governance 4*(1) 57–80.

Joerges, C. (2016). The overburdening of European law through Economic and Monetary Union. In T. Krieger, B. Neumärker, & D. Panke (Eds.), *Europe's crisis: The conflict-theoretical perspective* (pp. 155–176). Baden-Baden, Germany: Nomos.

Krieger, T. (2005). *Public pensions and immigration: A public choice approach*. Cheltenham, UK and Northampton, MA: Edward Elgar.

Krieger, T. (2016). Any solution in sight to Europe's crisis? Some general thoughts from a conflict theoretical perspective. In T. Krieger, B. Neumärker, & D. Panke (Eds.), *Europe's crisis: The conflict-theoretical perspective* (pp. 27–33). Baden-Baden, Germany: Nomos.

Krugman, P. (2014, October 1). Ordoarithmetics. *New York Times*, https://krugman.blogs.nytimes.com/2014/10/01/ordoarithmetic

Mayr, K., Minter, S., & Krieger, T. (2012). Policies on illegal immigration in a federation. *Regional Science and Urban Economics 42*(1–2) 153–165.

Münchau, W. (2014). The wacky economics of Germany's parallel universe. *Financial Times*. URL: www.ft.com/content/e257ed96-6b2c-11e4-be68-00144feabdc0

Ohr, R., & Schäfer, W. (1992, June 11). Die währungspolitischen Beschlüsse von Maastricht: Eine Gefahr für Europa. *Frankfurter Allgemeine Zeitung*.

Ordnungspolitisches Portal (2019). How to translate "Ordnungspolitik"?, http://ordnungspolitisches-portal.com/home-english (last retrieved 22.02.2019).

Ryner, M. (2015). Europe's ordoliberal iron cage: Critical political economy, the euro area crisis and its management. *Journal of European Public Policy 22*(2) 275–294.

Sally, R. (1996). Ordoliberalism and the social market: Classical political economy from Germany. *New Political Economy 1*(2) 233–257.

Schimmelfennig, F. (2015). Liberal intergovernmentalism and the euro area crisis. *Journal of European Public Policy 22*(2) 177–195.

Sievert, O. (1993). Geld, das man nicht selbst herstellen kann – Ein ordnungspolitisches Plädoyer für die Europäische Währungsunion. In P. Bofinger, S. Collignon, & E. M. Lipp (Eds.), *Währungsunion oder Währungschaos?* (pp. 13–24). Wiesbaden, Germany: Gabler Verlag.

Sinn, H. W. (1997). The selection principle and market failure in systems competition. *Journal of Public Economics 66*(2) 247–274.

Streit, M. E., & Mussler, W. (1995). The economic constitution of the European community: From "Rome" to "Maastricht." *European Law Journal 1*(1) 5–30.

Vanberg, V. J. (2004). The Freiburg School: Walter Eucken and ordoliberalism. *Freiburg Discussion Papers on Constitutional Economics No. 04/11.*

Vanberg, V. J. (2017). Ordoliberalism and Ordnungspolitik: A brief explanation. Aktionskreis Freiburger Schule, Freiburg.

Van der Walt, J. (2016). When one religious extremism unmasks another: Reflections on Europe's states of emergency as a legacy of ordo-liberal de-hermeneuticisation. *New Perspectives* 24(1) 79–101.

Vaubel, R. (1995). Social regulation and market integration: A critique and public choice analysis of the social chapter. *Aussenwirtschaft* 50 111–132.

Vaubel, R. (1999). Enforcing competition among governments: Theory and application to the European Union. *Constitutional Political Economy* 10(4) 327–338.

Vaubel, R. (2002). Geschichtsforschungen zu dem Buch The road to Maastricht von Kenneth Dyson und Kevin Featherstone. *Kredit und Kapital* 35(3) 460–470.

Vaubel, R. (2010). The euro and the German veto. *Econ Journal Watch* 7(1) 82–90.

Weiler, J. H. H. (1991). The transformation of Europe. *Yale Law Journal* 100(8) 2403–2483.

Part I

The historical and contemporaneous roots of ordoliberalism

1 Ordoliberalism's embeddedness in the neoliberalisms of the 1930s and 1940s

Stefan Kolev

Introduction

Until very recently, ordoliberalism was primarily an artefact for historians of economics. When in 2009 the University of Cologne declared its plan to rededicate its chairs for economic policy to macroeconomics and thus symbolically turned away from its postwar ordoliberal tradition of Alfred Müller-Armack, many saw in this new 'battle of methods' (Caspari & Schefold, 2011) the definitive proof that ordoliberalism was academically obsolete and politically irrelevant. The supporters of the university's plan often argued that hardly anybody beyond Germany was interested any more in this very German 'exceptionalism' in economics (e.g. Bachmann & Uhlig, 2009; Kirchgässner, 2009; Ritschl, 2009).

Ten years later, the state of affairs is fundamentally different. Historians of economics are no longer alone in their interest in ordoliberalism, and the burgeoning new literature has been published by the best presses of English-speaking academia, constituting an avalanche of scholarship from disciplines as diverse as macroeconomics, political theory, law, sociology of science, literary studies, or finance (e.g. Beck & Kotz, 2017; Biebricher & Vogelmann, 2017; Blyth, 2013; Bonefeld, 2017; Brunnermeier, James, & Landau, 2016; Commun & Kolev, 2018; Hien & Joerges, 2017; Slobodian, 2018; Zweynert, Kolev, & Goldschmidt, 2016). Most commonly, this interest has been triggered by Germany's fiscal and monetary policy positions in the eurozone crisis, but many authors take the crisis only as a starting point – and either have a closer look at the history of ordoliberalism, or explore whether its intellectual legacy deserves a conceptual revitalization.

For a historian of economics, this literature presents a number of challenges and raises a set of questions. In this exposition, I will examine the diagnosis of ordoliberalism being a 'German oddity' (Beck & Kotz, 2017) or even an 'irritating German idea' (Hien & Joerges, 2017). My central claim will be that the emergence of ordoliberal political economy can be much better understood as a variety of neoliberalism in the context of the general crisis of liberalism and western civilization in the 1930s and 1940s, rather than by only focusing on Germany. To begin with, some conceptual clarifications

24 *Stefan Kolev*

regarding the term 'neoliberalism' are necessary (see next section). The ordo-liberals will be contextualized as an integral part of the neoliberal network of scholars which formed in Vienna, London, and Chicago during the interwar period (third section). While the German roots of ordoliberalism are undeniable (fourth section), they cannot explain the significant parallels between the political economies in Walter Eucken's Freiburg and Wilhelm Röpke's Geneva on the one hand and those in Vienna, London, and Chicago on the other. The Colloque Walter Lippmann in 1938 and the founding meeting of the Mont Pèlerin Society in 1947 show the emerging discourses in the neoliberal 'thought collective' (Mirowski & Plehwe, 2009), with Friedrich August von Hayek playing a special role in building bridges between the ordoliberals and the other communities (Köhler & Kolev, 2013), thus contributing to their convergence (see final section).

Making sense of myths: the multiple meanings of neoliberalism

Neoliberalism is a colorful and embattled term, with its connotations passing substantial transformations over the last decades (Boas & Gans-Morse, 2009). At least three separate meanings are discernible. The most recent one emerged during the 1970s and 1980s, identifying neoliberalism with the set of ideas that inspired political leaders like Margaret Thatcher and Ronald Reagan. Unfortunately, this common interpretation is hardly operational. One can even claim that this understanding of neoliberalism has degenerated into a smear word, void of sufficient analytical clarity and all too often used to label – rather than explain – just about any evil in global politico–economic affairs (Hartwich, 2009, pp. 25–30).

The second meaning of neoliberalism is what I call a 'procedural' take. Google Ngram searches on 'neoliberalism' and 'neoliberal/neo-liberal' show usage of the terms as far back as the 19th century. Debates like those in France around 1820 (Horn, 2018) and exchanges like the one between Maffeo Pantaleoni and Charles Gide in the 1890s (Gide, 1898; Pantaleoni, 1898) as to what 'neo' could mean – only a reformulation of old doctrines or a genuine reconceptualization of those doctrines – are helpful to understand this 'procedural' take. If we broadly subdivide the history of liberalism into n generations of thinkers, we are left with at least $n-1$ neoliberalisms, i.e. attempts by later generations to restate with better methods and higher clarity what constitutes the core of a social order based on liberty. In such a perspective, David Hume and Adam Smith were neoliberals vis-à-vis John Locke. Furthermore, one generation could challenge different previous generations: for example, John Stuart Mill was a neoliberal both vis-à-vis Locke and vis-à-vis the Hume–Smith generation. Finally, different authors within the same generation could (and very often did) wage battles – frequently in different languages – over their contemporaneous reformulations (Kolev, 2018a, pp. 66–68).

Ordoliberalism and 1930s–1940s neoliberalisms 25

The third meaning, which will be the central one for this exposition, I call the 'substantive' take. It is in line with the common narrative in the history of economics which focuses on the 1930s and here on the Colloque Walter Lippmann in 1938 (Burgin, 2012, pp. 70–86; Goodwin, 2014, pp. 233–260; Plickert, 2008, pp. 93–103; Wegmann, 2002, pp. 101–110). 'Neoliberal' in this setting was used to demarcate a substantive difference: the reformist-oriented neoliberals distanced themselves from the 'paleoliberals' whom they viewed as insufficiently willing to reconsider the content of 19th-century liberalism, especially the notion of 'laissez-faire' (Hennecke, 2000, p. 273). If contrasted to the 'procedural' meaning above, the 'substantive' definition stands for *one* particular neoliberalism as formulated during the 1930s and 1940s. This neoliberalism is especially fruitful for historians: the protagonists interacted for decades via publications, correspondence, and live meetings, leaving behind an extensive legacy as to what they envisaged as a liberalism adequate for the 20th century.

Thinking in hubs: Vienna, London, and Chicago as birthplaces of neoliberalism

What is the relationship between neoliberalism and ordoliberalism?

Two very different patterns of connecting these concepts are found in literature. The first constructs a diametric opposition: such comparisons usually use the first meaning of neoliberalism above, claiming that neo-liberalism was above all related to the Thatcher–Reagan policy agenda of the 1970s and the 1980s, and/or to the Chicago School of Milton Friedman, while ordoliberalism is portrayed as a phenomenon of German politico-economic thought of the 1930s and the 1940s (Sinn, 2010; Wagenknecht, 2011). This perspective smuggles a normative connotation: here neo-liberalism is something destructive, guilty of demolishing the 'golden age' of the postwar decades, while ordoliberalism contributed to building that very postwar prosperity by fueling the social market economy in Germany and beyond.

However, if the third meaning of neoliberalism is taken seriously, a very different nexus emerges: here both neoliberalism and ordoliberalism are seen as phenomena of the 1930s and 1940s, and ordoliberalism was an important variety of neoliberalism which emerged along with the other neoliberal varieties. In this interpretation, ordoliberalism was as much a 'German oddity' as it was a product of the European and transatlantic attempts to restate what liberalism means for the embattled western civilization of the 20th century. It is this second approach which will be utilized here, for two reasons. First, it avoids the crypto-normativity of juxtaposing 'bad' neoliberalism to 'good' ordoliberalism and the unnecessary emotionality often involved. Second, this approach allows for a much higher degree of historical precision by analyzing the 1930s and the 1940s as the formative decades of these systems of political economy.

26   *Stefan Kolev*

Embedding Freiburg into the tissue of early neoliberalisms is a complex enterprise. Traditionally, three central birthplaces are mentioned along with Freiburg: Vienna, London, and Chicago (Burgin, 2012, pp. 12–54; Hartwell, 1995, pp. 17–20; Plickert, 2008, pp. 54–86; Walpen, 2004, pp. 66–73; Wegmann, 2002, pp. 135–141; White, 2012, pp. 202–230). Apart from these centers, other important groups developed in France and Italy. More recently, a fifth center has been identified in Geneva (Slobodian, 2018), which will also play a role in this analysis.

The concept of 'schools' which is often attributed to these centers is useful but must be applied with great care. To legitimately describe a group of scholars as a 'school,' three dimensions – substantive, social, and structural – must be critically explored (Blumenthal, 2007, pp. 25–33). Lumping individual theorists together into a 'school' box can blur important substantive differences, but also problematically evoke the connotation of the 'schools' as hermetically isolated entities. This is particularly problematic in the 1930s, a period of frequent migration and intensified live exchange. Also, a pattern often observable at the time is the 'core-satellites' constellation, where single scholars do not tightly belong to a central group but gravitate to it from afar and nevertheless contribute to its evolution. To avoid these 'schools'-related imprecisions, in the following the centers of neoliberalism will be conceptualized as hubs of scholars who interacted 'intramurally' with their local colleagues, but also 'extramurally' across the different groups.

Vienna deserves the first and the most detailed portrayal: this city was the birthplace of one of the oldest still existing traditions in modern economics, spanning over 150 years. Between the 1880s and the 1930s, 'school' is appropriate here, as the geographic focus enabled not only substantive, but also social and structural proximity. The political economy of the different Viennese generations emerged within a series of debates. The founder, Carl Menger, innovated not only in economic methodology by famously initiating the 'battle of methods' (Louzek, 2011): while his subjective value theory (Menger, 1871) was not new within the German tradition, his focus on the consumer as the center of gravity for the entire market system – later to be called 'consumer sovereignty' (Hutt, 1936) – constituted an important reformulation of the role of the individual in society. Still, Menger insisted that markets did not evolve in a vacuum of 'laissez-faire' – rather, he underscored the importance of institutions as a framework for the market (Menger, 1891), among others the state as an indispensable provider of public goods like social security (Dekker & Kolev, 2016). The next generations developed the Mengerian impulse toward a full-fledged system. Eugen von Böhm-Bawerk and Friedrich von Wieser deepened the Viennese understanding of interest, capital, cost, and production theory. Moreover, both were political economists in a twofold meaning: they were active administrators of their Empire, but also embedded their technical economics into a broader theory of social order. Their final pieces addressed the phenomenon of power in its multiple repercussions for economy and society (Böhm-Bawerk, 1914;

Wieser 1926). Menger, Böhm-Bawerk, and Wieser can thus be seen as neo-liberals according the 'procedural' definition covered in the second section of this chapter.

The first Austrian neoliberals in line with the 'substantive' definition covered in the second section were Ludwig von Mises and Friedrich August von Hayek, since they were key figures in the neoliberalism debates of the 1930s and 1940s. Earlier they participated in a series of other debates which were formative for their political economies, most notably the Socialist Calculation Debates and the debates on business cycle policy during the Great Depression (Boettke, 2000; Levy & Peart, 2008; Magliulo, 2016). Just as their teachers, Mises and Hayek took active part in the Viennese debates of the day, most of which took place in the overlapping Vienna Circles across disciplines and ideological lines (Dekker, 2016, pp. 27–45). Starting in 1920, both engaged in a decades-long discussion with proponents of central planning: first during the 1920s with the Austro-Marxists, later during the 1930s and 1940s within Anglo-Saxon academia. These debates sharpened their understanding of the functioning of markets as platforms of mutually beneficial exchange, and – expanding on the Smithian concept of 'division of labour' – of 'division of knowledge' (Hayek, 1945; Mises, 1920). The debates during the Great Depression, famously with Keynes but also within the German-speaking world, focused on the macroeconomic relevance of distortions of the market mechanism (Hayek, 1931; Mises, 1912).

London is not usually attributed the label 'school,' although the London School of Economics and Political Science served as a platform to develop not only substantive, but also social and structural ties (Boettke, 2018, pp. 124–126). That LSE would become a neoliberal bulwark is both substantively and lingually paradoxical. Substantively, because the institution was founded in 1895 by the Fabian Society, an organization dedicated toward piecemeal social change in line with continental social democracy (Dahrendorf, 1995, pp. 3–47). Lingually, because the Fabian agenda was close (but not quite identical) to the so-called new liberalism of Thomas H. Green, Leonard T. Hobhouse, and John A. Hobson, a variety of what would today be called social liberalism (Simhony & Weinstein, 2001). This 'new liberalism' – as personified by LSE's fourth director William Beveridge and his agenda for an encompassing welfare state – clashed in the 1930s and 1940s frequently with Hayek's neoliberalism (Hayek, 1994, pp. 72–76).

Edwin Cannan initiated LSE's neoliberal transformation. Famous in history of economics for his 1904 edition of Smith's *Wealth of Nations*, Cannan led LSE away from its Fabian agenda. From 1929 onward it was Lionel Robbins, a student of Cannan, who largely shaped the faculty and the spirit of LSE economics (Howson, 2011, pp. 166–205; Robbins, 1971, pp. 120–122). Robbins is often described as a 'continental economist' influenced by a series of non-British European economists – most importantly for this analysis, by the Austrian School as embodied in Mises's Viennese Privatseminar which he attended along with other Viennese meetings of economists (Ehs, 2014,

28 *Stefan Kolev*

pp. 711–712). Robbins's *An Essay on the Nature and Significance of Economic Science* can be related to these stays in Vienna and his exposure to the Misesian method later to become known as 'praxeology' (Mises, 1933, p. 19; Robbins, 1932, pp. viii–ix).

Robbins was instrumental in inviting Hayek to deliver in early 1931 his LSE lecture series *Prices and Production* (Hayek, 1931), and in hiring him a few months later in an attempt to build a stronghold against the increasingly influential Keynes (Caldwell, 2004, pp. 170–175). Hayek delved into multiple controversies in economics: the debates about business cycles, the Anglo-Saxon continuation of the Socialist Calculation Debates, as well as the capital theory controversy with Chicago economist Frank Knight. During the same period, he conceived the beginnings of his political economy and social philosophy, and particularly focused on the institutions serving as a framework for the market (Slobodian, 2018, pp. 76–87). In *Freedom and the Economic System* (Hayek, 1939) and in *The Road to Serfdom* (Hayek, 1944), he extensively challenged the wisdoms of 19th-century liberalism. Here Hayek claimed that a nihilistic approach to the state was also responsible for liberalism's steadily declining appeal, and that 'laissez faire' was a non-operational rule of thumb which had misled political economy into a dead end. Instead, he believed the 20th-century political economist should focus on the 'competitive order.' As will be shown below, these Hayekian claims are extremely proximate to the incipient ordoliberal political economies in Eucken's Freiburg and Röpke's Geneva (Kolev, 2015, pp. 432–436).

Chicago is the knot which shows that neoliberalism in the third meaning outlined in the second section was not a purely European phenomenon. The concept of a 'Chicago School' has been at the basis of the antagonistic position between 'good' ordoliberalism based in Freiburg and 'bad' neoliberalism based in Chicago, as depicted above – but there are at least two 'Chicago Schools' which, though interconnected, deserve separate analyses. The 'Old Chicago School' was a phenomenon of the 1930s and 1940s which emerged in opposition to Roosevelt's New Deal, with Frank Knight, Jacob Viner, and Henry Simons at its core, while the 'New Chicago School' emerged in the course of the 1950s and was formative for worldwide economics at least until the 1980s, with Milton Friedman, George Stigler, Aaron Director, and Gary Becker as the key representatives (Buchanan, 2010). For this analysis, Knight and Simons are of special importance. Knight, one of the most influential American economists in the first half of the 20th century, engaged during the 1930s in the abovementioned capital theory controversy with Hayek (Cohen, 2003), but broadly paralleled the political economy incipient in Hayek, Eucken, and Röpke, was one of the first American Max Weber scholars, and played a seminal role in the politico-economic debates during the early decades of the Mont Pèlerin Society (Emmett, 2007). In 1934, Simons, a student of Knight, produced one of the formative pieces of neoliberalism, *A Positive Program for Laissez Faire: Some Proposals for a Liberal Economic Policy* (1934) – a text whose focus on the rule-based approach to any policy domain

Ordoliberalism and 1930s–1940s neoliberalisms 29

and the indispensability of a framework for the market comes as close as one can get to ordoliberalism, as well to Hayek's incipient political economy (Köhler & Kolev, 2013; Van Horn, 2009a, pp. 140–158, 2009b, pp. 209–213). To Hayek's great regret, Simons – one of the key "similarly minded men" (Hayek, 1994, pp. 117–118) – could not join the Mont Pèlerin Society, he unexpectedly passed away in 1946 (Kolev, Goldschmidt, & Hesse, 2014, pp. 15–20). Still, apart from being formative in educating the younger Chicagoan generation of economists and lawyers, Simons's writings provided an important impulse for the emergence of another 'canonic' text of American neoliberalism, Walter Lippmann's *Good Society* (1937; Goodwin, 2014, pp. 243–244).

Ordering liberty: Freiburg and Geneva as cradles of ordoliberalism

The previous section portrayed a number of neoliberalisms as they emerged across time and space, especially those during the 1930s and 1940s on both sides of the Atlantic. This section will juxtapose the emergence of ordoliberal political economy to the processes in Vienna, London, and Chicago. Instead of providing a detailed history of early ordoliberalism (Goldschmidt, 2013; Goldschmidt & Wohlgemuth, 2008; Zweynert, 2013), this analysis focuses on a comparative view between what was endemic in ordoliberalism as a 'German oddity' (this section), and what traits it shared with the incipient Vienna, London, and Chicago neoliberalisms (the next section).

Ordoliberalism did not take shape as a monolithic entity. Instead, it consisted early on of a broad network of scholars: the Freiburg School around Walter Eucken and Franz Böhm as its core, as well as of 'satellites' like Wilhelm Röpke, Alexander Rüstow, and Alfred Müller-Armack. Each of these thinkers had his own intellectual origins and development. And while 'de-homogenization' is certainly an important exercise for historians of economics (Kolev, 2017), some generalizations are nevertheless admissible and helpful for this analysis of the ordoliberals' international embeddedness.

The scholarly socialization of the ordoliberals took place largely in the tradition of the Younger and the Youngest Historical Schools (Rieter, 2002, pp. 154–162), with a different degree of exposure to the technical economics of marginalism, and a different point of time when the emancipation from the Historical School started (Peukert, 2000; Schefold, 2003). In the early decades of their careers, the central debating platform was the meetings of the Verein für Socialpolitik, while conferences beyond the German-speaking world gained importance relatively late. This emancipation from Gustav Schmoller's legacy had already started a generation earlier, with Max Weber as a key figure, and thus Weber's attempts to reconcile abstract theory with empirical work, as well as normativity with positive analysis, were formative for the ordoliberals (Goldschmidt, 2002, pp. 43–65). Eucken in particular lived up to the 'typically German' tendency of spending significant time and

30   *Stefan Kolev*

energy on the problems of methodology and epistemology, with his *The Foundations of Economics* (1940) being a largely methodological book. Eucken's approach used not only Weberian tools like the ideal types, but also elements of Edmund Husserl's phenomenology as epistemological devices for economic theorizing (Goldschmidt, 2013, pp. 135–140).

Another important background for the formation of ordoliberalism – both in Eucken's Freiburg and in Röpke's Geneva – was the reflection and discourse about ethics and Christianity. In the Freiburg context, one manifestation was the founding of the 'Freiburg Circles' as forums of intellectual resistance aiming to design a postwar order of economy and society, beginning with the open atrocities against Jews in 1938 and amid the battles over the relationship between the Protestant Church and National Socialism (Goldschmidt, 2005, pp. 295–306). In the Geneva context, Röpke was perennially willing to engage in debates about the postwar order of economy and society with representatives of the Catholic social teaching (Petersen, 2016, pp. 176–191). The topos of Christian ethics is omnipresent in the ordoliberal writings via the double criterion for evaluating an order: while efficiency is a necessary condition for a 'good' order, it is not a sufficient one – if an order would not allow for a humane life in liberty and justice, this order should be discarded despite its efficiency (Eucken, 1952, pp. 373–374; Röpke, 1944, pp. 80–81).

The ordoliberal topos of power was also related to these ethical considerations. Its overarching normative element of disempowering economy and society by implementing a competitive order can be traced back to ordoliberalism's roots in the Historical School and to Weber, but also, as was shown in the third section, to the debates about the role of power within the Austrian School, especially to Böhm-Bawerk and Wieser. And while it is of course true that the concentration of power was special the German context 1933–1945, the contemporaneous spread of authoritarianisms and totalitarianisms across Eastern and Southern Europe was among the fundamental concerns of all neoliberals discussed in the third section. Franz Böhm played a crucial role in pointing already in the early 1930s to the dire necessity of rethinking the 'economic constitution' with the primary aim to curb power concentration by enabling competition within a competitive order (Kolev, 2018b; Vanberg, 2001). Through Böhm's and Hans Großmann-Doerth's cooperation with Eucken, the Freiburg School was from the very beginning a research group in law and economics (Hansen, 2009, pp. 46–48; Tumlir, 1989, pp. 135–137): within its approach to the economy as sub-order of society with multiple interfaces to the other interdependent societal suborders, the focus on the indispensability of a disempowering legal framework for the market was more pronounced than in the writings of many neoliberal contemporaries.

Coming together: Colloque Walter Lippmann 1938 and Mont Pèlerin Society 1947

While the German specificities in ordoliberalism's emergence are elementary for its DNA, they cannot explain the striking parallels which surface when comparing ordoliberalism to the neoliberalisms in the third section. The 'thinking in orders' – German as it may sound rhetorically – can also be identified in other neoliberalisms. Recognizing the interdependence of the economy to the other societal sub-orders was acknowledged by most, and the necessity to focus on the institutional framework was equally commonplace across the discussed groups. Principles and rules were the preferred tools to design policy, as compared to discretionary case-by-case decisions in an unrestrained democratic process. Even power – as stereotypically German as only order can get – was a recurrent element of the political economies across the Channel and the Atlantic.

How then can those similarities be explained? The five neoliberalisms certainly shared some intellectual roots. The Historical School was not only formative for the ordoliberals, but also indirectly for the Austrians: Vienna was not so dichotomously cut off from Berlin as the textbook version of the 'battle of methods' suggests, with a number of fin de siècle economists serving as 'in-betweens.' In the same period the Historical School was also influential for American economics as embodied in institutionalism, especially in the Midwest. Weber was also formative for the Viennese debates (and thus indirectly also for Robbins), for the Chicagoans (especially for Knight), as well as for the ordoliberals. The intensive exposure of continental students of economics to law (due to the late emancipation of economics as an autonomous university degree) was another formative factor in the scholarly socializations of the neoliberal 'thinkers in order.'

What was at least as important were the discourses across the centers of neoliberalism. Vienna, London, Chicago, Freiburg, and Geneva were not isolated islands – instead, especially since the 1930s an extensive sequence of meetings, conferences and workshops took place, so that live interactions complemented earlier exchanges in publications and correspondence. Geneva and its international institutions became a focal point for these live interactions not only for émigrés like Mises and Röpke, but also for lectures series by numerous other neoliberals like Hayek, Robbins, Viner, or Gottfried Haberler (Slobodian, 2018, pp. 56–76). Germany-based scholars like Eucken and Böhm had increasing problems to travel internationally, but Röpke maintained a vital line between Geneva and Freiburg all the way until the correspondence had to be terminated in 1943 (Hennecke, 2005, pp. 153, 267).

A crucial occasion of live exchange was the Colloque Walter Lippmann (CWL) in Paris in August 1938 (Burgin, 2012, pp. 70–86; Goodwin, 2014, pp. 233–260; Plickert, 2008, pp. 93–103; Slobodian, 2018, pp. 76–85; Wegmann, 2002, pp. 101–110). Fortunately, the records have recently been

32   *Stefan Kolev*

published in an excellent English edition (Reinhoudt & Audier, 2018). Lippmann's *Good Society* (1937) was seen as a manifesto by the neoliberals because of its proximity to the neoliberal political economies described above. As discussed above, the CWL is – historically imprecisely – accredited with having given birth to the term 'neoliberalism,' but it is true that the term was used here and later by that fraction of the rather heterogeneous participants who were more willing to radically criticize 19th-century liberalism and to search for a fundamental reformulation for the 20th century. During the five days of the CWL, many differences and heated debates surfaced among the participants, both on the issues of historically evaluating the legacy of liberalism and on the necessity to conceptually reform it. However, a dichotomous line – as often postulated in literature between 'paleoliberals' like Mises and Hayek and 'neoliberals' like Röpke and Rüstow – is not easy to identify on each issue. It was the allegedly hard-boiled 'paleoliberal' Mises who joined Lippmann in underscoring that the issues "of the possibilities of and of the limits to interventionism" were of prime importance and needed further study and debate (Reinhoudt & Audier, 2018, p. 187).

And while WWII let the CWL pass into the history of neoliberalism as a singular (though fundamental) event, the Mont Pèlerin Society (MPS) – from its foundation in 1947 to this day – has enabled a seemingly endless sequence of debates on practically all topics of political economy and social philosophy. The founding meeting in 1947, but also the Seelisberg meeting in 1949, provide crucial evidence of how the ordoliberals interacted within the neoliberal 'thought collective' (Mirowski & Plehwe, 2009). While solely Röpke and Rüstow represented ordoliberalism at the CWL as Eucken and his Freiburg associates did not participate, the early MPS meetings were heavily influenced by the full breadth of ordoliberals. It might fascinate that, so soon after WWII, a joint session was set up (by Hayek) for a German economist (Eucken) and an American-Jewish economist (Director). And it may be even more striking that, when comparing the three papers by Eucken, Director (stepping in for the deceased Simons), and Hayek in this 1947 session titled "'Free' Enterprise and Competitive Order" – a crystallizing encounter of the political economies of Freiburg, Chicago, Vienna, and London – the mainline of the papers is almost identical (Köhler & Kolev, 2013, pp. 222–224). It was Hayek's intention from the very beginning to integrate the Germans as much as possible into the MPS, and the years until Eucken's passing in 1950 were characterized by an extremely frequent and highly cordial correspondence between Hayek (president) and Eucken (one of the vice presidents) regarding the development of the Society (Kolev, Goldschmidt, & Hesse, 2014, pp. 15–20). Despite the heated debate on competition policy in Seelisberg in 1949 between Eucken and his associate Leonhard Miksch on the one hand, and Mises on the other (Kolev, Goldschmidt & Hesse, 2014, pp. 33–36), Eucken's untimely passing in London – during a lecture series at LSE upon Hayek's invitation – was bemoaned not only by Röpke or Hayek, but also by Mises who expressed the highest appreciation for Eucken's "writings and his exemplary stance during the most difficult times" (Kolev, 2018a, p. 84).

Eucken's personality left behind more than just vivid memories for the young Chicagoans attending the 1947 MPS meeting (Friedman & Friedman, 1998, p. 160; Stigler, 1988, p. 146) or a friendly mention 15 years later in *Capitalism and Freedom* (Friedman, 1962, p. 28). It is intriguing to detect that the very first politico-economic papers of Milton Friedman beyond technical economics were imbued with that very spirit of the 1947 MPS session on the competitive order, the indispensability of frameworks for conducting rule-based policies, and the Freiburg-Chicago-Vienna-London focus on a 'laissez faire within rules' research program (Friedman, 1948, 1951).

Conclusion

The central result of this analysis is that portraying ordoliberalism simply as a 'German oddity' is historically incorrect and conceptually misleading. Rather, the emergence of ordoliberal political economy in the 1930s and 1940s must be seen in the context of the contemporaneously evolving neoliberalisms on both sides of the Atlantic. While it is of course true that the ordoliberals' scholarly socialization took place mostly in Germany, they were never completely isolated from the international politico-economic debates, apart from a very brief period during WWII. Even in the darkest hours of National Socialism, the Freiburg School stayed connected via its 'satellites' – most prominently Röpke and Hayek – to the international students of the embattled western civilization and to their searches for what role liberty would play in the order of economy and society in the 20th century.

From this perspective, it is not surprising that many of the 'trademarks' of ordoliberalism as seen from today can be found in political economies which emerged in Vienna, London, and Chicago, but are also traceable in writings of contemporaneous French and Italian liberals: 'thinking in orders,' founding economic policy on principles and rules, focusing on the indispensability of frameworks (legal and ethical), paying special attention to power relations, searching for new methodological and epistemological foundations of economics very much constituted building blocks of the neoliberalisms of the 1930s and 1940s on both sides of the Atlantic. That these elements became 'trademarks' of ordoliberalism has two causes. First, the ordoliberals were the scholars who weaved these building blocks most explicitly and most coherently into their system of political economy. Second, and perhaps even more importantly, unlike most other groups, the ordoliberals were blessed with having Ludwig Erhard as a political entrepreneur. From 1948 onward, Erhard implemented ordoliberal political economy into concrete policy on a scale not experienced in any other country, popularizing ordoliberalism beyond Germany and legitimizing it by the successes of the social market economy during the 'economic miracle.'

34 *Stefan Kolev*

In the postwar period, the intellectual landscape changed, even though the links of later ordoliberal generations to their international peers remained, among others via the MPS. However, unlike the Austrian economists who, from generation to generation, kept innovating upon the Mengerian origins, the postwar generations of ordoliberal scholars mostly confined themselves to policy consulting, to popularizing the legacy of the Eucken–Röpke–Rüstow generation, and to applying it to policy issues like European integration or the transition in Eastern Europe after 1990. Still, the 'thinking in orders' paradigm kept evolving, but mostly on the other side of the Atlantic. While the broad community of new institutional economics might be the 'chief suspect,' two particular locations of innovation are of special relevance: the Bloomington School around Vincent and Elinor Ostrom, as well as the Virginia School around James Buchanan (Boettke, 2012; Vanberg, 2014). In this sense, it is neither surprising nor paradoxical that the current impulses to ordoliberal political economy triggered by the eurozone crisis have to a large extent come from the international politico-economic community.

References

Bachmann, R., & Uhlig, H. (2009). Die Welt ist nicht schwarz oder weiß. Wer die Wirtschaft verstehen will, muss quantitativ arbeiten. *Frankfurter Allgemeine Zeitung*, 30.3.2009.

Beck, T., & Kotz, H. H. (Eds.). (2017). *Ordoliberalism: A German oddity?* VoxEU.org. London, UK: CEPR Press.

Biebricher, T., & Vogelmann, F. (Eds.). (2017). *The birth of austerity: German ordoliberalism and contemporary neoliberalism*. London, UK: Rowman & Littlefield.

Blyth, M. (2013). *Austerity: The history of a dangerous idea*. Oxford, UK: Oxford University Press.

Blumenthal, K. v. (2007). *Die Steuertheorien der Austrian Economics: Von Menger zu Mises*. Marburg, Germany: Metropolis.

Boas, T. C., & Gans-Morse, J. (2009). Neoliberalism: From new liberal philosophy to anti-liberal slogan. *Studies in Comparative International Development 44*(2) 137–161.

Boettke, P. J. (2000). *Socialism and the market: The socialist calculation debate revisited* (9 vols.). London, UK: Routledge.

Boettke, P. J. (2012). *Living economics: Yesterday, today, and tomorrow*. Oakland, CA: Independent Institute.

Boettke, P. J. (2018). *F. A. Hayek: Economics, political economy and social philosophy*. London, UK: Palgrave Macmillan.

Böhm-Bawerk, E. v. (1914). Macht oder ökonomisches Gesetz? *Zeitschrift für Volkswirtschaft, Sozialpolitik und Verwaltung 23* 205–271.

Bonefeld, W. (2017). *The strong state and the free economy*. London, UK: Rowman & Littlefield.

Brunnermeier, M. K., James, H., & Landau, J.-P. (2016). *The euro and the battle of ideas*. Princeton, NJ: Princeton University Press.

Buchanan, J. M. (2010). *Chicago School thinking: Old and new*. Presentation at the 2010 Summer Institute for the History of Economic Thought, Jepson School of Leadership Studies, University of Richmond, June 2 2010, available online: https://www.youtube.com/watch?v=7_atDse06r4

Ordoliberalism and 1930s–1940s neoliberalisms   35

Burgin, A. (2012). *The great persuasion: Reinventing free markets since the Depression.* Cambridge, MA: Harvard University Press.

Caldwell, B. J. (2004). *Hayek's challenge: An intellectual biography of F. A. Hayek.* Chicago, IL: University of Chicago Press.

Caspari, V., & Schefold, B. (Eds.) (2011). *Wohin steuert die ökonomische Wissenschaft? Ein Methodenstreit in der Volkswirtschaftslehre.* Frankfurt, Germany: Campus.

Cohen, A. J. (2003). The Hayek/Knight capital controversy: The irrelevance of round-aboutness, or purging processes in time? *History of Political Economy 35*(3) 469–490.

Commun, P., & Kolev, S. (Eds.). (2018). *Wilhelm Röpke (1899–1966): A liberal political economist and conservative social philosopher.* Cham, Switzerland: Springer.

Dahrendorf, R. (1995). *LSE: A history of the London School of Economics and Political Science, 1895–1995.* Oxford, UK: Oxford University Press.

Dekker, E. (2016). *The Viennese students of civilization: The meaning and context of Austrian economics reconsidered.* New York, NY: Cambridge University Press.

Dekker, E. & Kolev, S. (2016). Introduction to Carl Menger's "The social theories of classical political economy and modern economic policy." *Econ Journal Watch 13*(3) 467–472.

Ehs, T. (2014). Extra muros: Vereine, Gesellschaften, Kreis und Volksbildung. In T. Olechowski, T. Ehs, & K. Staudigl-Ciechowicz (Eds.). *Die Wiener Rechts- und Staatswissenschaftliche Fakultät 1918–1938* (pp. 701–747). Göttingen, Germany: V&R unipress.

Emmett, R. (2007). Knight's challenge (to Hayek): Spontaneous order is not enough for governing a liberal society. In L. Hunt & P. McNamara (Eds.), *Liberalism, conservatism, and Hayek's idea of spontaneous order* (pp. 67–86). New York, NY: Palgrave Macmillan.

Eucken, W. (1940). *Die Grundlagen der Nationalökonomie.* Germany Jena: Gustav Fischer.

Eucken, W. (1952). *Grundsätze der Wirtschaftspolitik.* Tübingen, Germany: Mohr Siebeck.

Friedman, W. (1948). A monetary and fiscal framework for economic stability. *American Economic Review, 38*(3), 245–264.

Friedman, M. (1951). Neo-liberalism and its prospects. *Farmand,* 17.2.1951, 89–93.

Friedman, M. (1962). *Capitalism and freedom.* Chicago, IL: University of Chicago Press.

Friedman, M. & Friedman, R. D. (1998). *Two lucky people: Memoirs.* Chicago, IL: University of Chicago Press.

Goldschmidt, N. (2002). *Entstehung und Vermächtnis ordoliberalen Denkens: Walter Eucken und die Notwendigkeit einer kulturellen Ökonomik.* Münster, Germany: LIT.

Goldschmidt, N. (2005). Die Rolle Walter Euckens im Widerstand: Freiheit, Ordnung und Wahrhaftigkeit als Handlungsmaximen. In N. Goldschmidt (Ed.), *Wirtschaft, Politik und Freiheit* (pp. 289–314). Tübingen, Germany: Mohr Siebeck.

Goldschmidt, N. (2013). Walter Eucken's place in the history of ideas. *Review of Austrian Economics 26*(2) 127–147.

Goldschmidt, N., & Wohlgemuth, M.. (2008). Entstehung und Vermächtnis der Freiburger Tradition der Ordnungsökonomik. In N. Goldschmidt & M. Wohlgemuth (Eds.), *Grundtexte zur Freiburger Tradition der Ordnungsökonomik* (pp. 1–16). Tübingen, Germany: Mohr Siebeck.

Goodwin, C. D. (2014). *Walter Lippmann: Public economist.* Cambridge, MA: Harvard University Press.

Gide, C. (1898). Has co-operation introduced a new principle into economics? *Economic Journal 8*(32) 490–511.

36 *Stefan Kolev*

Hansen, N. (2009). *Franz Böhm mit Ricarda Huch: Zwei wahre Patrioten*. Düsseldorf, Germany: Droste.

Hartwell, R. M. (1995). *A history of the Mont Pelerin Society*. Indianapolis, IN: Liberty Fund.

Hartwich, M. O. (2009). *Neoliberalism: The genesis of a political swearword*. St Leonards, NSW: Centre for Independent Studies.

Hayek, F. A. v. (1931). *Prices and production*. London, UK: Routledge.

Hayek, F. A. v. (1939). *Freedom and the economic system*. Chicago, IL: University of Chicago Press.

Hayek, F. A. v. (1944). *The road to serfdom*. Chicago, IL: University of Chicago Press.

Hayek, F. A. v. (1945). The use of knowledge in society. *American Economic Review* 35(4) 519–530.

Hayek, F. A. v. (1994). *Hayek on Hayek: An autobiographical dialogue*. Chicago, IL: University of Chicago Press.

Hennecke, H. J. (2000). *Friedrich August von Hayek: Die Tradition der Freiheit*. Düsseldorf, Germany: Verlag Wirtschaft und Finanzen.

Hennecke, H. J. (2005). *Wilhelm Röpke: Ein Leben in der Brandung*. Stuttgart: Schäffer Poeschel.

Hien, J., & Joerges, C. (Eds.). (2017). *Ordoliberalism, Law and the Rule of Economics*. Oxford, UK: Hart.

Horn, K. (2018). Der Neoliberalismus wird achtzig. *Frankfurter Allgemeine Sonntagszeitung*, 12.8.2018.

Howson, S. (2011). *Lionel Robbins*. New York, NY: Cambridge University Press.

Hutt, W. H. (1936). *Economists and the public: A study of competition and opinion*. London, UK: Jonathan Cape.

Kirchgässner, G. (2009). Typisch deutsch! Die deutsche Nationalökonomie darf keinen nationalen Sonderweg gehen. *Frankfurter Allgemeine Sonntagszeitung*, 14.6.2009.

Köhler, E. A., & Kolev, S. (2013). The conjoint quest for a liberal positive program: "Old Chicago," Freiburg, and Hayek. In S. J. Peart & D. M. Levy (Eds.), *F. A. Hayek and the modern economy* (pp. 211–228). New York, NY: Palgrave Macmillan.

Kolev, S. (2015). Ordoliberalism and the Austrian School. In P. J. Boettke & C. J. Coyne (Eds.), *The Oxford handbook of Austrian economics* (pp. 419–444). New York, NY: Oxford University Press.

Kolev, S. (2017). *Neoliberale Staatsverständnisse im Vergleich*. Berlin, Germany: De Gruyter.

Kolev, S. (2018a). Paleo- and neoliberals: Ludwig von Mises and the "ordo-interventionists." In P. Commun & S. Kolev (Eds.), *Wilhelm Röpke (1899–1966): A liberal political economist and conservative social philosopher* (pp. 65–90). Cham, Switzerland: Springer.

Kolev, S. (2018b). Böhm, Franz. In A. Marciano & G. B. Ramello (Eds.), *Encyclopedia of law and economics*. New York, NY: Springer.

Kolev, S., Goldschmidt, N., & Hesse, J.-O. (2014). Walter Eucken's role in the early history of the Mont Pèlerin Society. *Discussion Paper 14/02*, Freiburg, Germany: Walter Eucken Institut.

Levy, D. M. & Peart, S. J. (2008). Socialist calculation debate. In S. N. Durlauf & L. E. Blume (Eds.), *The new Palgrave dictionary of economics*. London, UK: Palgrave Macmillan.

Lippmann, W. (1937). *The good society*. Boston, MA: Little, Brown & Co.

Ordoliberalism and 1930s–1940s neoliberalisms 37

Louzek, M. (2011). The battle of methods in economics: The classical Methodenstreit, Menger vs. Schmoller. *American Journal of Economics and Sociology 70*(2) 439–463.

Magliulo, A. (2016). Hayek and the Great Depression of 1929: Did he really change his mind? *European Journal of the History of Economic Thought 23*(1) 31–58.

Menger, C. (1871). *Grundsätze der Volkswirthschaftslehre*. Vienna, Austria: Wilhelm Braumüller.

Menger, C. (1891). Die Sozialtheorien der klassischen Nationalökonomie und die moderne Wirtschaftspolitik. *Neue Freie Presse*, 06.1.1891 and 08.1.1891.

Mirowski, P. & Plehwe, D. (Eds.). (2009). *The road from Mont Pèlerin: The making of the neoliberal thought collective*. Cambridge, MA: Harvard University Press.

Mises, L. v. (1912). *Theorie des Geldes und der Umlaufsmittel*. Munich, Germany: Duncker & Humblot.

Mises, L. v. (1920). Die Wirtschaftsrechnung im sozialistischen Gemeinwesen. *Archiv für Sozialwissenschaft und Sozialpolitik 47* 86–121.

Mises, L. v. (1933). The task and scope of the science of human action. In *Epistemological problems of economics* (pp. 1–69). Auburn, AL: Ludwig von Mises Institute.

Pantaleoni, M. (1898). An attempt to analyse the concepts of "strong and weak" in their economic connection. *Economic Journal 8*(30) 183–205.

Petersen, T. (2016). *Theologische Einflüsse auf die deutsche Nationalökonomie im 19. und 20. Jahrhundert – drei Fallbeispiele*. Hamburg: Staats- und Universitätsbibliothek, available online: http://ediss.sub.uni-hamburg.de/volltexte/2016/7718

Peukert, H. (2000). Walter Eucken (1891–1950) and the Historical School. In P. Koslowski (Ed.), *The theory of capitalism in the German economic tradition: Historism, ordo-liberalism, critical theory, solidarism* (pp. 93–146). Berlin, Germany: Springer.

Plickert, P. (2008). *Wandlungen des Neoliberalismus: Eine Studie zu Entwicklung und Ausstrahlung der "Mont Pèlerin Society."* Stuttgart, Germany: Lucius & Lucius.

Reinhoudt, J. & Audier, S. (2018). *The Walter Lippmann Colloquium: The birth of neoliberalism*. New York, NY: Palgrave Macmillan.

Rieter, H. (2002). Historische Schulen. In O. Issing (Ed.), *Geschichte der Nationalökonomie* (pp. 131–168). Munich, Germany: Franz Vahlen.

Ritschl, A. (2009). Am Ende eines Sonderwegs: Warum die Ordnungsökonomik sich erschöpft hat. *Frankfurter Allgemeine Zeitung*, 16.3.2009.

Robbins, L. (1932). *An essay on the nature and significance of economic science*. London, UK: Macmillan.

Robbins, L. (1971). *Autobiography of an economist*. London, UK: Macmillan.

Röpke, W. (1944). *Civitas humana: Grundfragen der Gesellschafts- und Wirtschaftsreform*. Erlenbach–Zurich, Switzerland: Eugen Rentsch.

Schefold, B. (2003). Die deutsche Historische Schule als Quelle des Ordoliberalismus. In P. Commun (Ed.), *L'ordolibéralisme allemande: Aux sources de l'économie sociale de marché* (pp. 101–117). Cergy-Pontoise, France: CIRAC/CICC.

Simhony, A., & Weinstein, D. (Eds.). (2001). *The new liberalism: Reconciling liberty and community*. Cambridge, UK: Cambridge University Press.

Simons, H. C. (1934). A positive program for laissez faire: Some proposals for a liberal economic policy. In *Economic policy for a free society* (pp. 40–77). Chicago, IL: University of Chicago Press.

Sinn, H.-W. (2010). Der wahre Neoliberalismus braucht klare Regeln. *Die Welt*, 15.5.2010.

Slobodian, Q. (2018). *Globalists: The end of empire and the birth of neoliberalism*. Cambridge, MA: Harvard University Press.

38 Stefan Kolev

Stigler, G. J. (1988). *Memoirs of an unregulated economist.* New York, NY: Basic Books.

Tumlir, J. (1989). Franz Böhm and the Development of Economic-Constitutional Analysis. In A. Peacock & H. Willgerodt (Eds.), *German neo-liberals and the social market economy* (pp. 125–141). New York, NY: St. Martin's Press.

Vanberg, V. J. (2001). The Freiburg School of Law and Economics: Predecessor of constitutional economics. In *The constitution of markets: essays in political economy* (pp. 37–51). London, UK: Routledge.

Vanberg, V. J. (2014). Ordnungspolitik, the Freiburg School and the reason of rules. *Discussion Paper 14/01,* Freiburg, Germany: Walter Eucken Institut.

Van Horn, R. (2009a). The rise of the Chicago School of Economics and the birth of neoliberalism. In P. Mirowski & D. Plehwe (Eds.), *The road from Mont Pèlerin: The making of the neoliberal thought collective* (pp. 139–178). Cambridge, MA: Harvard University Press.

Van Horn, R. (2009b). Reinventing monopoly and the role of corporations: The roots of Chicago Law and Economics. In P. Mirowski & D. Plehwe (Eds.), *The road from Mont Pèlerin: The making of the neoliberal thought collective* (pp. 204–237). Cambridge, MA: Harvard University Press.

Wagenknecht, S. (2011). *Freiheit statt Kapitalismus.* Frankfurt, Germany: Campus.

Walpen, B. (2004). *Die offenen Feinde und ihre Gesellschaft: Eine hegemonietheoretische Studie zur Mont Pèlerin Society.* Hamburg, Germany: VSA Verlag.

Wegmann, M. (2002). *Früher Neoliberalismus und europäische Integration: Interdependenz der nationalen, supranationalen und internationalen Ordnung von Wirtschaft und Gesellschaft (1932–1965).* Baden-Baden, Germany: Nomos.

White, L. H. (2012). *The clash of economic ideas: The great policy debates and experiments of the last hundred years.* New York, NY: Cambridge University Press.

Wieser, F. v. (1926). *Das Gesetz der Macht.* Vienna, Austria: Julius Springer.

Zweynert, J. (2013). How German is German neo-liberalism? *Review of Austrian Economics 26*(2) 109–125.

Zweynert, J., Kolev, S., & Goldschmidt, N. (2016). *Neue Ordnungsökonomik.* Tübingen, Germany: Mohr Siebeck.

2 Ordoliberalism and democracy

How the interwar period changed the agenda of German liberalism

Gerhard Wegner

Introduction

The tumultuous period of the Weimar State witnessed an intensive intellectual debate in many fields of political and sociological theory, including controversies over the economic order.[1] Several factors eroded confidence in the societal postwar order: The radical move toward mass democracy came along with turmoil after the lost war and an intense struggle for political power – including coups and street fighting between the radical left and right from 1919 to 1923; the economic catastrophes of hyperinflation and mass impoverishment during the Great Depression were new experiences for all contemporaries. The age of institutional security prior to WWI had passed. Indeed, confidence in the future of society, i.e. its proper political and economic order, was shaken.[2] The liberal order had lost its political support, not only among less-privileged social strata. Even liberal politicians and entrepreneurs, such as the first chancellor of the Weimar State, Walter Rathenau, pondered the possibility of a planned economy for Germany as a better alternative to free market capitalism.[3] The socialist calculation debate, which gained momentum after the war, was but one of many fundamental debates about a promising and workable economic order.

A brighter future and greater material well-being suddenly appeared attainable for the majority of society. An upsurge of cultural experimentation followed, perhaps best encapsulated by the Bauhaus movement and its pursuit of aesthetical consumption for the masses. However, the standard of living fell dramatically short of expectations. A glaring discrepancy prevailed between expected well-being and consumption on the one hand, and the gloomy economic reality on the other, a mismatch that was deeply felt by contemporaries. German GDP did not return to its 1913 level during the entire interwar period except for one year. In the end, this failure, among others, robbed the political order of the electorate's support.

The enduring economic crisis of the interwar period formed the empirical background for ordoliberals in search of a workable economic order based on market coordination. However, their framework constituted one of several competing ideas for a preferable economic order. Alternatives ranged from

40 *Gerhard Wegner*

(1) a market order supplemented by state ownership of land, (2) a market order supplemented by large, state-owned enterprises and banks, (3) updated early 19th-century professional orders favored by the Catholic Church in the encyclical letter *Quadragesimo anno*, (4) fascist orders of the Italian and Austrian type which combined a traditional professional order with state control of the economy, (5) conceptions of economic democracy advocated by Naphtali and Social Democrats, and (6) the utopia of a planned society, which Stalin had initiated after the New Economic Policy (NEP) period. In public debate at the time, ordoliberal voices largely fell on deaf ears. This partly reflects that ordoliberalism was still in its infancy – yet, at first glance, a lack of radicalism may also be to blame. In fact, ordoliberalism can be interpreted as an attempt to reestablish the liberal prewar economic order, with modifications focused on dysfunctional elements such as cartelization, and stronger attention to the protective role of the liberal state with regard to industrial workers. The fact that democracy played but a minor role in their reflections led to the charge of authoritarianism (Haselbach, 1991).[4] However, such judgment overlooks the fact that democracy was part of the problem in the Weimar State. Indeed, the ongoing crisis in the Weimar State reflected a greater crisis afflicting the postwar transnational economic order in the western world. In contrast, the prewar economic order in Imperial Germany (Kaiserreich), despite its democratic shortcomings, proved highly successful in terms of economic dynamism. The move from the "half-democracy" (Tooze, 2015) of the Kaiserreich to the full parliamentarianism of the Weimar State went hand in hand with a loss of performance in economic institutions.

Remarkably, participants of the prewar constitutional debate in Imperial Germany anticipated such consequences. While not the sole reason for rejecting French-style full parliamentarianism (France was the only fully-fledged democracy in Western Europe before WWI), the feared loss in economic performance factored heavily in liberals' acceptance of the division of political power between the Kaiser and parliament (Reichstag). The economic performance of the Weimar State confirmed these prewar predictions, which is why it was difficult for ordoliberals to adopt unconditional support for democracy. Specifically, the key question revolved around how individual liberty and economic freedom could be in accord with the sovereignty of the polity. Here, the potential for emergent tension between liberalism and democracy first manifested. The development of ordoliberalism must be understood against this empirical background.

In order to highlight the fundamental change in political and economic order embodied by the Weimar State, I begin with a review of Imperial Germany's political and economic institutions. While the rule of law was guaranteed, the institutional framework fell short of fully-fledged parliamentarianism of the Westminster type. Interestingly, political debates on constitutional reform and full parliamentarianism predicted a loss of stability and economic liberty although the constitutional status quo was generally perceived as an interim solution (the next section). Next, I shift to the Weimar

State, which established democracy but also brought about a new form of politicization of the economic order. Its dysfunctional elements resulted from the erosion of the liberal market order and outweighed potential gains in terms of legitimacy or social security for the lower classes (the third section). Finally, I include the international dimension into the ordoliberal diagnosis of the crisis, with an emphasis on the role of democracy (final section). The chapter ends with a conclusion.

The liberal prewar economic order as a reference

When Eucken wrote his controversial article "Structural Change of the State and the Crisis of Capitalism" in 1932, he drew the course of economic history in large brushstrokes. The difference between the present and the prewar epoch could not have been greater. Unemployment increased to 6 million people in 1932, industrial production fell by 40%, and mass misery followed for both industrial workers and the middle class, including a large number of small and medium–sized farms.[5] Hyperinflation, with its catastrophic consequences for the bourgeois middle class, had occurred less than a decade earlier. The period between 1923 and 1929, sometimes called the "stabilization period" of the Weimar State (in cultural terms the "roaring twenties"), failed to stabilize the economy in a sustainable manner, leading Borchardt to call this period the "crisis before the crisis" as it laid the groundwork for the deep crisis after 1930.[6] One indicator is the rate of investment, which never exceeded 15% of GDP in the interwar period, while 20% was normal in the Wilhelmine period (Plumpe, 2011, p. 47). As a result, investment became more dependent on foreign (mostly US) direct investment. The difficulty to attract foreign investment culminated in the course of the Young plan, which prioritized reparation payments to be paid in foreign currencies without regard to the status of the current account deficit; as a result of their subordination, foreign loans became extremely risky.[7]

Such economic instability was uncommon throughout the decades before the Great War, a period characterized by normal business cycles without dramatic slumps. Rather, the prewar epoch witnessed a period of long-term economic growth. Particularly in the period from 1870 to 1913, the average growth rate of GDP per capita in Germany (together with Switzerland) outperformed the rate of any other economy in Western and Central Europe (Maddison, 2003; Plumpe, 2011, p. 46). Remarkably, the labor market was able to absorb high population growth, causing mass emigration to North America to grind to a halt. Investment rates of 20% of GDP outperformed the European average (15%), whereas investment shifted from the 1870s onwards from railway construction to industry and agriculture (Plumpe, 2011, p. 47). This success story raises the question of the role of the state and the interplay between economic and political institutions.

Earlier judgments of "organized capitalism" in the Wilhelmine state have since proven questionable and have been revised.[8] Rather, despite many

42 Gerhard Wegner

modifications the economy and the state became largely separated from each other. In his review of the development of economic policy in Germany, Eucken concedes that organized groups – industrialists and agricultural interest groups – started to influence the course of economic policy. The *Wirtschaftsstaat* (the state managing its economy), which according to Eucken represented the new economic order after WWI, took its point of departure in the Wilhelmine state. Compared to the postwar order, however, Eucken considered the state as largely independent.

> The state 50 years ago was reluctant to use its power, but its decision-making was independent; conversely, the contemporary state tends to use its power in many places and rigorously, but the real independence of its will is lacking.
>
> ([1932] 1997, p. 14)

A closer look at the type of state activities before WWI reveals that the state resisted market intervention such as price controls. Instead, besides the military, public activities concentrated on the provision of infrastructure, education, and health services. The promotion of the natural sciences encouraged the development of technology-intensive industry. But rarely did the provision of public goods and the adaptation to promising paths of economic development interfere with market coordination. The introduction of statutory social insurance through Bismarck's social reforms already paved the way for a modern welfare state, but remained modest in size. All in all, the prewar economic order met most constituent elements of a liberal free-market order, which Hayek described in his *Constitution of Liberty* decades later: The rule of law was highly developed, the separation of powers was realized, economic freedoms such as the protection of property rights, the freedom of transaction, and the freedom of trade were enforceable rights.[9] These economic freedoms became completely established during the North German Federation in 1867 and were adopted by Imperial Germany a few years later. Wages were generally based on individual private contracts between employers and employees; although collective wage negotiations existed, they were not generally binding. Eucken was aware that this economic order favored entrepreneurs disproportionally and required a rebalancing policy on behalf of industrial workers, e.g. as regards industrial safety protection, as he wrote in his *Grundsätze* published after WWII (Eucken, 2004). But from Eucken's perspective, such policy should be enacted from an enlightened and insightful government disentangled from party disputes and interests. Otherwise, the state would risk losing its impartial view on economic life.

The sharp contrast between the well performing economic order before WWI and the ongoing crisis in the Weimar State has raised the question whether democracy systematically fails to guarantee a liberal economic order, and, if so, which safeguards could remedy these shortcomings. This problem has become a key issue in the liberal debate in succeeding decades to which Hayek, Buchanan, Brennan, and others have made seminal contributions.[10] A tension between democracy and a liberal economic order is widely acknowledged as long as democracy lacks constitutional rules which protect the market order. From the viewpoint of political theory, however, the advocacy of constitutional rules does not suffice since those rules themselves require democratic legitimacy. The latter question, which has turned out to be a complex issue, did not concern the ordoliberals.[11] *Ordnungspolitik*, materialized in the constituent and regulatory principles in Eucken's *Grundsätze*, was designed to secure the liberal economic order and did not refer to a particular political order, be it a democracy or another order.

Eucken was concerned that democracy politicizes the economic order to a hitherto unknown extent, which is chief among the reasons why it became so vulnerable and dysfunctional (see below). Remarkably, this consequence had been predicted even before WWI in political debate among intellectuals, legal scholars, and politicians. The debate was conducted on the question of "constitutionalism versus parliamentarianism" (Hewitson, 2001). This prewar debate is informative because it dealt with real issues of democracy and offers deeper insight into why even liberals eschewed the shift from the imperial political order to parliamentarianism, which was principally possible by changing the constitution of 1871. By constitutionalism the participants of the debate meant the extant political order of Imperial Germany, which included parliament as an important institution, while parliamentarianism was a short name for the political order of the Third Republic in France and the Westminster model in Britain. Pointing to the stabilizing elements of a liberal economic order, even liberal critics of the constitutional monarchy such as Naumann hesitated to advocate parliamentarianism of the English or French style (Hewitson, 2001, p. 734; Naumann, 1908). It was quite natural to interpret the poor performance of the Weimar State against the background of the prewar debate on constitutionalism and to advocate for political principles which could remedy these institutional deficits. Here, German liberals followed liberal thinking at the time, which still took the prewar order as a reference (Raphael, 2011, p. 81).

In order to expound the intrinsic value of constitutionalism that Eucken and others had in mind, some remarks on the political system of Imperial Germany are in order. It defies an unambiguous categorization since it was neither an autocracy nor a democracy. Rather, it can be characterized as a hybrid political order in transition, dominated by a dualism between parliament and the executive branch of government (Kreuzer, 2004). Despite ongoing debate among historians, it is uncontroversial that parliament could increase its significance considerably. The crucial difference to a democracy of the Westminster model was that the government was not elected by parliament but appointed by the Emperor (Kaiser).[12] Unlike Britain, however, elections to the Reichstag took place according to universal and equal, later even secret, suffrage.[13] In comparison to other western countries, which

44 *Gerhard Wegner*

restricted the right to vote far more (France being an exception), this was a fairly universal (male) suffrage. As an important result, class conflict, which high industrialization starting in about 1850 had brought about, became manifest in German parliament. Such representation of all classes was unknown in the elite British democracy, which largely kept industrial workers from parliament. The Marxist Social Democratic Party (SPD), on the other hand, could increase its representation significantly and became the biggest faction in 1912. However, for the SPD, political participation was largely considered an instrument to overcome the capitalist order rather than to improve its performance to the benefit of workers. Together with the Catholic Centre, which likewise rejected the capitalist order (albeit for other reasons), it held the majority in parliament in 1912. It was obvious that full parliamentarianism would have had consequences for the market order – as it turned out in 1919.

At the time, parliament was powerful enough to form legislation because proposals required the majority in parliament. It also held the right to initiate proposals, of which it made ample use. Because legislation also required the majority of the second chamber (Bundesrat), the constitution established a balance of power between the more progressive social forces represented in the Reichstag and the bourgeois–conservative forces which dominated the Bundesrat. This paved the way for an embryonic welfare state but ruled out initiatives for fundamental change in the economic order.

Not only conservatives, but also liberal politicians such as Naumann, who favored full parliamentarianism in principle, saw the advantages of this political order. The government viewed itself as neutral and above the classes, an arbiter as it were; this is exactly the role that Eucken later attributed to *Ordnungspolitik*, competition policy in particular. To be sure, the government's neutral self-image was interrogated by liberal critics such as Theodor Mommsen and others. But despite contemporary criticism, one cannot denounce the self-image as pure ideology; namely, when representation in parliament shifted to the left, government responded to this change, e.g. by including the left-liberal party into the Bülow bloc.[14] The government abandoned its former partisanship for capitalists and took a more neutral stance, e.g. in mass strikes. Generally, government cooperated with the leading factions, and even the SPD could become part of the majority for proposals of the government.

Trade policy exemplifies how the government attempted to find compromises between the farmers (encompassing large landowners in East-Elbian Junkers, but also the great mass of small and medium-sized farmers), industrial workers and industry. However, a shift toward high protectionism, which would have violated the interests of industrial workers but also those of the urban middle class, did not take place; excises on imported luxury goods indicate that the government at least attempted to balance the social cost of tariffs (Dedinger, 2006). Interest groups failed to "capture" the government on a large scale; rather, the government pursued a trade policy of moderate free trade, thereby keeping the general guideline of trade policy of the former decades (Dedinger, 2006). Looking back to the prewar period in the 1940s, Röpke (1945) acknowledged the merits of this prewar policy, which maintained its liberal orientation, even though it had to take the interests of groups into account.

As a result of the "constitutionalism" in the hybrid political prewar order, the government had to deal with groups (classes) and parties in parliament, but was no part of it. In the constitutional debate, conservatives such as Delbrück, but also liberals, were convinced that this "constitutionalism" was superior to parliamentarianism of the French type (Hewitson, 2001). The generally short duration of governments in France and the frequent changes of cabinets were taken as a case in point for political instability to be expected by democracy. Governments that were formed out of parliament were seen as interfering with the separation of powers. References to corruption in French governmental affairs and notorious scandals such as the "Parisian Panama corruption" served as evidence for this thesis (Hewitson, 2001, p. 742). But even socialists such as August Bebel did not want to fight for the French parliamentary system, as it apparently demonstrated the decadence of bourgeois society. Besides, the French system failed to provide better social legislation and social protection for workers than Imperial Germany, which was exemplary in this respect, taking the western industrialized states as a reference (Hewitson, 2001, p. 769).

Even though most parties sought to strengthen the influence of parliament, the government's independence from parties was esteemed as an intrinsic value. The analysis of the consequences of parliamentarianism was comparative, whereby France and Britain served as a reference. The British model was considered inapplicable. Contemporaries claimed that its good performance, and specifically the stable economic and societal development it guaranteed, could not be maintained in combination with universal suffrage in Germany. British parliamentarianism performed well because the two leading parties rooted in the middle and upper class largely agreed on their political convictions. The problem of bridging highly divergent convictions in order to form a coalition did not emerge. In Britain, full parliamentarianism preceded full democratization, while both processes occurred in reverse order in Germany (Kreuzer, 2004). Considering the vast differences occupying the spectrum of Germany's political parties, the economist and social reformer Schmoller predicted the consequences of full parliamentarianism as follows:

> If a feudal–industrial party alternated with a democratic–socialist leadership in our German parliaments, this would mean a changing class regiment, now in favor of the possessing, sometimes in favor of the non-possessing classes. This change would ruin us.
>
> (1912)

46 *Gerhard Wegner*

And he concluded:

> That is why we need a princely public administration over the classes and parties. Everything great that we have done politically is created by this, although of course it also has its downsides. But they are not as big as those of an ultra-democratic constitution.
>
> (1912)

From our present viewpoint the advocacy of political dualism in Imperial Germany looks peculiar; but the transformation of party interests into a public interest poses challenges for any democracy. To this day, and apparently with increasing difficulty, democracies struggle with the problem of transforming pluralism into reasonable policy. Constitutional economics, but also Rawls's political theory, raises the question of how group interests can be refined into "constitutional interests" (Vanberg & Buchanan, 1989), or whether they could form an "overlapping consensus" (Rawls, 1993). Otherwise democracy fails to guarantee the rights of all members of society. As a result, the majority could capture legislation for its own benefit to the detriment of the rest of society. Likewise, any shift in political power, which is the essence of democracy, would generate uncertainty as regards the protection of economic rights. Hence, making democracy align with a liberal order is not a fictitious problem but denotes a real challenge. Contemporaries in the German constitutional debate had not yet developed a solution for this problem and stuck to extant "constitutionalism" as the preferred political regime, supported by a powerful parliament and a critical public (Schmoller, 1912). Eucken's key concern in the Weimar State was "good governance" to be achieved by restrengthening the liberal prewar order. He assumes the principles of a liberal order sufficiently cogent to convince anyone who makes use of his practical reason, to put it in Kantian terms.

The move to permanent crisis in the Weimar State

The dramatic removal of the prewar order after the revolution in November 1918 paved the way for representative democracy in Germany, but also left the future of the economic order uncertain. This became clear to the steel companies when their owners accepted the eight-hour working day in view of the threat of expropriation by the workers' councils (Stinnes–Legien agreement). Even when the shock of revolution was over, with democracy emerging successfully and prevailing in spite of attacks from the right and the left, political power shifted dramatically. As compared to the prewar order, capitalists found themselves in a small minority without control of the course of policy while the unions gained decisive influence. Change of the economic order was enshrined in the Weimar Constitution; its chapter titled "The Economic Life" added socialist elements to a market order and ultimately exposed the economic order to contingent political interference. This generally

Ordoliberalism and democracy 47

confirmed all skeptical conjectures of the prewar debate regarding the transition to a full democracy; exposing the economic (and societal) order to the uncertainty of elections was virtually the nightmare vision of prewar skeptics. The guarantee of property rights lacked its unbounded protection since nationalization became an option. Codetermination of workers in firms could be interpreted as a "democratization" of the capitalist firm, but unionists (such as Naphtali) interpreted it as an interim step toward full control of the workers.

Due to the shift of political power to the detriment of capitalists, corporate taxes and taxes for private companies rose and exceeded taxation in France and Britain (James, 1986, p. 136); tax revenues in relation to GDP were also significantly higher (25% as compared to 20 percent in Britain and 22% in France; James, 1986, p. 138). Lobbying of business associations against excessive taxation of firms was only partly successful. The politicization of the economic order culminated in compulsory wage settlements by the government when unions and employers' associations failed to find a compromise in wage negotiations. As a result, it was rational for unions to capture the Ministry of Labor, since the SPD or the center were part of the ruling coalition. For this reason, employers continued to complain about the "union state," which was not completely groundless. As the SPD, which supported the new democracy, rivalled the Communist Party for voters, it tended to take the side of the unions, thereby disregarding the capacity of firms to bear higher wages. The fact that the Ministry of Labor could impose wages on firms is evidence of the fundamental change of the economic order and the dependence of firms on politics. Without being responsible for the economic consequences of their decisions, policymakers could directly change the profitability of private investment. Against this empirical background, Eucken ([1932] 1997) and his supporters discovered that the market economy requires a disentanglement from politics.

Economic historians have led a controversy about the impact of compulsory wage setting and, in particular, whether it contributed to economic stagnation in the Weimar State. Borchardt (1979) terms the seemingly stable period of 1923 to 1929 as the "crisis before the crisis," pointing to rising unit labor costs and decreasing investment rates. Although this diagnosis has encountered objections, empirical investigations support this view.[15] At the time, Keynes also shared the view that the German economy had lost its competitiveness due to rising real wages. Remarkably, Eucken ([1932] 1997) refuses to place the blame on the unions but takes a broader view which includes productivity as a causal factor for unit labor costs. The key driver for well-being is the ongoing increase of productivity rather than wage policy, Eucken emphasizes. The rise of productivity, in turn, results from free competition. However, competition had come to a halt, Eucken argued, because firms increasingly controlled markets through monopolization and cartels, whereas the state distorted market coordination via price controls. This had been the real cause of economic stagnation and changed the mentality of

48 *Gerhard Wegner*

entrepreneurs who had transformed their spirit from risk-takers to defenders of extant market positions. In fact, this was a unique liberal diagnosis of the causes of the economic crisis.

As a result of the loss of economic dynamism, a vicious circle of politicization and stagnation emerged of which there was no easy escape. Principally, economic growth required structural change, i.e. the reallocation of resources from unproductive ends to more profitable activities. For instance, the dramatic fall in prices of agricultural products brought farmers into an existential crisis and made the relative reduction of employment in the agricultural sector necessary. In the absence of economic growth this could only mean the absolute reduction of employment in this sector. Because job alternatives in the industry or other sectors were still lacking, farmers demanded subsidies (*Osthilfe*). Since the Weimar State faced extreme difficulties in financing its expenditures by borrowing in capital markets, spending cuts elsewhere were necessary. As a result, social policy on behalf of farmers placed high demands on the growing army of unemployed industrial workers, but also on civil servants in the public sector who had to bear extreme salary reductions. Hence, economic stagnation intensified distributional conflicts to a previously unknown extent, and politics was the field on which groups fought the conflict. Chancellor Brüning (who was an economist) cut subsidies for farmers in order to avoid preferential treatment for particular groups at the expense of the rest of society. As a result, however, President von Hindenburg, who sided with the farmers, dismissed him and gave way to the final chapter of presidential cabinets in the Weimar State ultimately leading to Hitler's chancellorship. Brüning's dismissal by von Hindenburg taught him that the withdrawal of subsidies for powerful groups was no option for economic policy oriented toward liberalism. Hitler's party took advantage of Brüning's failure and discovered the considerable voter potential in the countryside, where people had consistently voted for the conservatives previously. Anti-liberal economic policy paid off in elections.

Remarks on the international dimension of the crisis

The German economic crisis was not exclusively a homemade problem. Eucken and his collaborators, Röpke in particular, emphasized the international dimension of ongoing economic stagnation. Again, Eucken emphasized the role of democracy. The failure and unwillingness of western states – combatant and neutral states alike – to restore the international economic order before the war contributed to economic stagnation and the absence of a post-WWII-style economic boom. As for domestic economic policy, Eucken complained about the absence of an "ordering principle" in foreign economic policy. This diagnosis concerned the allied postwar policy toward Germany, which stood in sharp contrast to earlier postwar policies of victorious powers in European wars (Eucken, [1932] 1997, pp. 17–18). The principle of

Ordoliberalism and democracy 49

"distinction between war and peacetime" had been given up, Eucken wrote. In the agreements formed in the Paris suburbs, the victorious powers used their military victory to

> permanently maintain the favorable military situation at the end of the war, instead of creating an order of states to permanently captivate the defeated opponents, thereby creating the strongest tensions, which made overcoming the war impossible as long as the treaties are valid.
>
> (Eucken, [1932] 1997)

The absurdly high reparations spanning many decades (until 1988 according to the Young Plan in 1929) forced recognition, above all, of the war guilt by Germany. A novelty in history, it hampered the establishment of a peaceful postwar order from the outset. However, politicians in the victorious states could not act as rationally as diplomats in previous peace agreements did, e.g. in the Congress of Vienna in 1815. Since they had to justify themselves to their voters and were thus "driven by the masses," they had no incentive for moderation, "but to whip up the mood in their country even more" (Eucken, [1932] 1997).

Eucken attributed the failure of foreign trade policy to the unwillingness of European states to restore a peace order through cooperation. Again, democracy contributed to the problem because it boosted interest groups who opposed free trade (Eucken, [1932] 1997, p. 18). In a letter to Alexander Rüstow, Eucken complained about this failure of democracy:

> All democracies are pursuing an incoherent protective tariff policy. The implementation of free trade requires a sense of coherent economic policy, but this sense of coherence is lacking in all areas of democratic economic policy. Monarchies or aristocrats are systematically pushing either protectionist or free trade policies – democracies are unsystematic in both strategies ... Free trade was never carried out by democracies: In Germany it was [implemented] by the Prussian Kings ... in France by Napoleon III against Parliament, [and] in England by the bourgeoisie. Democratic countries are always unsystematic protectionists.... We are now sliding into this miserable protectionist policy and we will have it as long as we have democracies, which will certainly be the case for several decades to come.[16]

The "modern economic state" (*Wirtschaftsstaat*) tended to break the rules of free markets and confiscate assets from foreign investors, which is why direct foreign investment became risky. Röpke shared Eucken's view and stressed the overall liberal character of the prewar economic order. He did not over-look tendencies toward protectionism before the war but emphasized the stable institutional framework of moderate tariffs. In particular, the unpredict-ability of trade policy in nations that unilaterally erected trade barriers

50 *Gerhard Wegner*

accounted for volatile trade flows and short-term horizons for foreign inves-tors (Kindleberger, 1989; Röpke, 1942, p. 50). The dissolution of the Habsburg Empire and the founding of new nations in Eastern and Central Europe intensified economic disintegration, especially since the newly founded nations also subscribed to economic nationalism.[17] Once a large, coherently integrated region, Europe was now fragmented. The benefits of large-scale production, which had been boosted after the war and would have required larger markets, could hardly be exploited.

Generally, the need for a stable international economic order was widely acknowledged and its implementation through a multinational agreement was attempted. But while the (moderately) liberal international order was set up from below before the Great War, i.e. through numerous bilateral trade agreements which enclosed the most-favored nation clause, multinational trade agreements turned out to entail far greater complications after the war. At the World Economic Conference in Geneva in 1927 nation states failed to agree on lower tariffs even though the necessity to restore the international economic order was accepted in principle. But European nations that stayed out the war were also not able to complete trade agreements. Kindleberger reports on a failed agreement between Belgium, Sweden, the Netherlands, and Norway which could only agree on giving notice if one of the partners was going to raise tariffs unilaterally (Kindleberger, 1989, p. 169). The United States was not alone in resorting to high protectionism during the Great Depression, as European nations adopted similar measures; e.g. France increased its average tariffs from 23 to 38% and Czechoslovakia's increase was from 31 to 50% (Raphael, 2011, p. 177). Great Britain's attempt, in turn, at its own trading region with its dominions in the Ottawa treaties, could not compensate for the collapse of the international economic order.

Again, ordoliberals appreciate the intrinsic value of a stable institutional framework even if it falls short of free trade. The interwar economic order was far from achieving such a framework. The German economy was more dependent on a workable international economic order because reparations had to be paid in foreign currencies while the reparation regime required the maintenance of the gold standard. Otherwise, competitiveness for exports would have necessitated deflationary policies that entailed social hardship. But even in the absence of reparations, the restoration of the international eco-nomic order was key in order to overcome the stagnation of the interwar period. The simultaneous erosion of the liberal international order and the domestic order reinforced each other: The lack of international competition in the domestic market gave effect to cartels which, in turn, sought to pre-serve protectionism. Protectionism, however, also found support by voters outside of interest groups. Therefore, a workable international order could at least have weakened the effectiveness of cartels and monopolies. With hind-sight, the international economic order could have turned out to be an effective instrument to limit the adverse impact of cartels and monopolies on productivity growth.

Remarkably, ordoliberals did not regard economic stagnation as something natural or as a new phase of capitalism that society would have to accept. Rather, economic stagnation was interpreted as the result of a new economic order that had come about after the state had undergone "structural change" (Eucken). A return to the economic momentum of the prewar period was, at least in principle, considered possible. This explanation of the causes of the persistent crisis differed remarkably from contemporary diagnoses of other economists or sociologists, who favored mixed orders including the nationalization of industries, land, and the banking sector. Eucken, however, stressed that the monopoly problem could not be solved by nationalization because nationalized monopolies would likewise fail to produce competitive results. The weakness of investment activity had no secular causes, as many such as Emil Lederer speculated.[18] Technical progress was not viewed as a problem for society but as the solution to the problem of economic stagnation. The fact that entrepreneurs withheld long-term investment did not originate from a "savings glut" or the lack of investment opportunities. It would therefore be no solution if the government tried to fill the private investment gap with public investment (Eucken, 2004, p. 288).[19] Rather, entrepreneurs shied away from the risk of long-term investment because the course of economic policy led to uncertainty in terms of the returns they could expect on their investment; instead they preferred short-term portfolio investments which could quickly be made liquid and withdrawn from particular settings.

Ordoliberals resisted conceptualizing a radically new economic order or a "third way" between capitalism and socialism – any such self-description is misleading. Instead, they offered a "past-oriented utopia" which sought to update the institutional performance of the prewar economic order without turning the political order back to the imperial period. It was intended to build on the liberal prewar tradition but at the same time overcome the weakness that was already emerging as a result of monopolization and cartelization. Likewise, consideration of workers had become much more important than ever before in a liberal conception, perhaps with the exception of Mill. This reorientation toward a liberal economic order was unique in the political debate of the interwar period where anti-capitalist criticism set the tone. Eucken's principles were directed to constitutionalize economic policy and protect the economic order from distributional struggles of interest groups. The role of the state as an "arbiter" which implements and supervises the rules independently from vested interests parallels the constitutionalist self-image of the government (*Reichsleitung*) before the war and its defense in the constitutional debate (see above). Now, the role of the government is carved out from analyzing the working conditions of a market order. Without ignoring the requirement of regulations in many fields, e.g. in order to protect workers from the imbalance of power relations, the ordoliberal conception offers first priority to the establishment of competition.

It is no coincidence that Eucken termed his policy guidelines "constituent principles" (supplemented by regulatory principles). They responded to

52 *Gerhard Wegner*

political failures committed in the Weimar state. Monetary policy avoiding inflation, the protection of property rights or the freedom of transaction ceased to be automatically guaranteed by politics that discovered legislation as an instrument for income creation. Above all the "principle of constant economic policy" added a new element previously unknown in the liberal agenda. The "lacking atmosphere of trust" which Eucken complained about called for predictable economic policies (Eucken, 2004, p. 288). This principle specifically takes issue with the procedural norms of democracy. Since political power is contestable and uncertain for powerholders, the outcome of economic policy is intrinsically uncertain as well. Otherwise, political rivals would have to find agreement on issues which constitute their competitive edge. It is therefore difficult to bring stable and predictable economic policy in harmony with political competition. At least at the time, Eucken's proposal for rule-oriented policy could be considered as a challenge to democracy because it constrained discretion more than any government was willing to accept. Eucken, however, was more concerned about the recovery of the German economy and considered the sentiments of the "masses" and their political representatives foremost as an obstacle to overcome.

Conclusion

Ordoliberalism went far beyond the old prewar liberalism, redefining the role of the state, which considerably gained in importance. The ideal of the state was maintained and still viewed as the "representative of a common morality," to put it in Hegelian terms. The necessity to adopt this "higher morality" even increased as the state faced new anti-competitive forces that challenged its role as an arbiter. As it turned out, competition was not naturally predetermined but required political ambition to realign the institutional framework. The stance against nationalization directly ensued from this understanding of the state: If the economy requires the state as the "arbiter" for competition, the state must not be an economic "player" at the same time. The credibility of the role of the state hinges on the disentanglement of the market economy from the state as an economic actor. The 'depoliticization' of the market economy was thus the first priority, expanding on the rule of law and the division of power in the liberal state.

The economic thinking of ordoliberalism that emerged from the interwar period had several typical patterns that have been outlined here. (1) The national and international orders are seen as coexisting in a reciprocal relationship. If the essentially liberal world economy of the prewar order had supported the liberal economic order in the domestic economy, then the reverse was true for interwar interventionism. (2) In retrospect, and despite several shortcomings, the prewar order remained a reference model for a well-performing economic system; with modification, this held true even for the first decade after WWII. (3) The comprehensive approach of 'thinking in orders' distanced itself from national biases and sensitivities, emancipating itself from national conservative attitudes. Protectionism, too, was regarded as an international phenomenon rather than assigning priority to particular powers ("nostra maxima culpa" in a formulation by Röpke). (4) In addition to interventions distorting competition, instability and unpredictability were declared to be major causes of the national and international economic crisis, which were in turn attributed to the uncertainty of political competition. (5) Unlike the liberalism of the 18th and 19th centuries, the lack of an optimistic belief by ordoliberals at the time is striking. The permanence of crisis is a novel background in the history of liberalism; a return to the economic momentum at the time of high industrialization, which was to become a reality after WWII, was only considered as theoretically possible. (6) In view of the severity of the crisis, ordoliberals included a social dimension, namely social disintegration in their analysis. They distrusted social integration occurring through economic progress and prosperity, exploring ethical 'anchors' for society, with Christianity playing a special role. (7) The position of liberalism was regarded as expert opinion which lacked any chance to survive in political competition. This explains why ordoliberals did not reflect on the compatibility of liberal principles with democracy and remained skeptical of the ability of democracy to bring about 'good governance.'

Politically speaking, liberalism's standing was in disrepute. At the beginning of the Weimar State, the two liberal parties (the more conservative pro-business DVP party and the social–liberal DDP party) won more than 20% of the vote. Even later their joint share was about 15%. When economic depression culminated in 1932, they dropped to less than 3% and ceased to exist in political life. Liberal ideas had no chance of finding acceptance by voters. At the time (but even today) it was a conventional diagnosis that the economic crisis of the interwar period resulted from a failure of capitalism per se rather than from its institutional deficits. This diagnosis supported radical Marxist but also fascist answers to the crisis. That the politicization of the economic order caused the crisis rather than capitalism as such, which had ceased to exist in its well-performing form, was the new message. At the same time, ordoliberals integrated new elements into a holistic concept for society. In so doing, ordoliberalism expanded on the intellectual heritage of 19th-century liberalism.

Notes

1 For a comprehensive study, see Hacke (2018).
2 Peukert (2014) coined the term "crisis of classical modernity."
3 See Gall (2009).
4 For a careful consideration see Nientiedt and Köhler (2016).
5 For a concise overview see Balderston (2002).
6 See Borchardt (1982); Holtfrerich (1984) opposes Borchardt's argument; Ritschl's (2002) comprehensive study lends credence to Borchardt's key arguments.
7 See also James (1986).
8 See Hentschel's (1978) critique of Wehler (1973).

54   *Gerhard Wegner*

9 See Hayek (1960/1991, pp. 246–263).
10 Pars pro toto, see Brennan and Buchanan (1985) or Hayek (1960/1991).
11 Brennan and Buchanan (1985) shift attention to this issue by applying the idea of a social contract among citizens which include principles and norms for in-period economic policy.
12 For an overview of the debate, see Kühne (2005).
13 Anderson (2009) describes how secret voting became effectively established.
14 The Bulow bloc was an electoral alliance between conservatives and liberals and can be regarded as the predecessor of coalition government.
15 For a comprehensive overview and detailed investigation, see Ritschl (2002).
16 Unpublished letter to Alexander Rüstow from March 21, 1930, Eucken-Archive, Jena.
17 For interwar trade policy in Czechoslovakia, see Krpec (2015).
18 For a review, see Allgöwer (2001).
19 The *Grundsätze der Wirtschaftspolitik*, originally published in 1952, reflects on the economic crisis of interwar period.

Bibliography

Acemoglu, D., & Robinson, J. A. (2012). *Why nations fail: The origins of power, prosperity, and poverty.* New York, NY: Crown

Allgöwer, E. (2001). Emil Lederer: Business cycles, crises, and growth. Universität St. Gallen, Discussion Paper no. 2001–13.

Ambrosius, G. (2005). *Regulativer Wettbewerb und koordinative Standardisierung zwischen Staaten. Theoretische Annahmen und historische Beispiele.* Berlin, Germany: Franz Steiner.

Ambrosius, G. (2009). *Liberale vs. institutionelle Integration von Wirtschaftspolitiken in Europa. Das 19. und 20. Jahrhundert im systematischen und historischen Vergleich.* Baden-Baden, Germany: Nomos.

Anderson, M. L. (2009). *Lehrjahre der Demokratie. Wahlen und politische Kultur im Kaiserreich.* Berlin, Germany: Franz Steiner.

Balderston, T. (2002). *Economics and politics in the Weimar Republic.* Cambridge, UK: Cambridge University Press.

Barth, B. (2016). *Europa nach dem Großen Krieg. Die Krise der Demokratie in der Zwischenkriegszeit 1918–1938.* Frankfurt, Germany: Campus.

Blackbourn, D., & Eley, G. (1980). *Mythen deutscher Geschichtsschreibung. Die gescheiterte bürgerliche Revolution von 1848.* Frankfurt am Main u. a.

Boch, R. (2004). *Staat und Wirtschaft im 19. Jahrhundert.* Munich.

Böhm, F. (1933). *Wettbewerb und Monopolkampf. Eine Untersuchung zur Frage des wirtschaftlichen Kampfrechts und der rechtlichen Struktur der geltenden Wirtschaftsordnung.* Berlin. Reprint: Köln 1964.

Böhm, F. (1966). Privatrechtsgesellschaft und Marktwirtschaft. Ordo 17, 75–151.Borchardt, K. (1979). Zwangslagen und Handlungsspielräume in der großen Weltwirtschaftskrise der frühen dreißiger Jahre: Zur Revision des überlieferten Geschichtsbildes. *Jahrbuch der Bayerischen Akademie der Wissenschaften, 1979*, 85–132.

Borchardt, K. (1982). *Wachstum, Krisen, Handlungsspielräume der Wirtschaftspolitik. Studien zur Wirtschaftsgeschichte des 19. und 20. Jahrhunderts.* Göttingen.

Bösch, F. (2009). Grenzen des "Obrigkeitsstaates". Medien, Politik und Skandale im Kaiserreich. In S. V. Müller & C. Torp (Eds.), *Das Kaiserreich in der Kontroverse* (pp. 136–153). Göttingen, Germany: Vandenhoek & Ruprecht.Brennan, G., &

Buchanan, J. M. (1985). *The reason of rules: Constitutional political economy.* Cambridge, UK: Cambridge University Press.

Brunnermeier, M., James, H., Landau, J.-P. (2016). *The euro and the battle of ideas.* Princeton, NJ: Princeton University Press.

Congleton, R. (2011). *Perfecting parliament: Constitutional reform, liberalism and the rise of western democracy.* Cambridge, UK: Cambridge University Press.

Dedinger, B. (2006). From virtual free-trade to virtual protectionism: Or, did protectionism have any part in Germany's rise to commercial power 1850–1913? In J.-P. Dormois & P. Lains (Eds.), *Classical trade protectionism 1815–1914* (pp. 219–241). London, UK: Routledge.

Eucken, W. ([1932] 1997). Staatliche Strukturwandlungen und die Krisis des Kapitalismus. In *ORDO 48* (1997) 5–24. [reprinted as: Weltwirtschaftliches Archiv, Bd. 36, 1932, 297–321]

Eucken, W. (2004). *Grundsätze der Wirtschaftspolitik.* Tübingen, Germany: UTB.

Friedman, M. (1962). *Capitalism and freedom.* Chicago: Chicago University Press.

Gall, L. (2009). *Walter Rathenau. Portrait einer Epoche.* Munich: Beck.

Grant, O. (2005). *Migration and inequality in Germany 1870–1913.* Oxford, UK: Clarendon Press.

Grimmer-Solem, E. (2003). *The rise of historical economics and social reform in Germany 1864–1894.* Oxford, UK: Clarendon Press.

Hacke, J. (2018). *Existenzkrise der Demokratie. Zur politischen Theorie des Liberalismus in der Zwischenkriegszeit.* Frankurt: Suhrkamp.

Hallerberg, M. (1996). Tax competition in Wilhelmine Germany and its implications for the European Union. *World Politics 48* 324–357.

Haselbach, D. (1991). *Autoritärer Liberalismus und Soziale Marktwirtschaft. Gesellschaft und Politik im Ordoliberalismus.* Tübingen, Germany: Nomos.

Hayek, F. A. v. (1960/1991). *Die Verfassung der Freiheit* (3rd ed.). Tübingen, Germany: Mohr Siebeck.

Hentschel, V. (1978). *Wirtschaft und Wirtschaftspolitik im wilhelminischen Deutschland. Organisierter Kapitalismus und Interventionsstaat.* Stuttgart, Germany: Klett-Cotta.

Hewitson, M. (2001). The *Kaiserreich* in question: Constitutional crisis in Germany before the First World War. *The Journal of Modern History 73* 725–780.

Holtfrerich, C.-L. (1984). Zu hohe Löhne in der Weimarer Republik? Bemerkungen zur Borchardt-These. *Geschichte und Gesellschaft: Zeitschrift für historische Sozialwissenschaft 10* 122–141.

James, H. (1986). *Deutschland in der Weltwirtschaftskrise 1924–1936.* Stuttgart, Germany: Deutsche Verlags-Anstalt.

Keynes, J. M. (2002). *The economic consequences of the peace.* Amherst, NY: Skyhorse.

Kindleberger, C. (1989). Commercial policy between the wars. In P. Mathias & S. Pollard (Eds.), *The Cambridge economic history of Europe from the decline of the Roman Empire* (pp. 161–196). Cambridge, UK: Cambridge University Press. doi:10.1017/CHOL9780521225045.003

Knortz, H. (2010). *Wirtschaftsgeschichte der Weimarer Republik.* Göttingen, Germany: UTB.

Kreuzer, M. (2004). Und sie parlamentarisierte sich doch: Die Verfassungsordnung des Kaiserreichs in vergleichender Perspektive. In M.-L. Recker (Ed.), *Parlamentarismus in Europa: Deutschland, England und Frankreich im Vergleich* (pp. 17–40). Munich: De Gruyter.

56 Gerhard Wegner

Kroll, F.-L. (2013). *Geburt der Moderne. Politik, Gesellschaft und Kultur vor dem Ersten Weltkrieg*. Berlin-Brandenburg, Germany: be.bra.

Krpec, O. (2015). Czechoslovakian trade policy after World War I (1918–1927): Nationalism and capitalism. Working paper presented at the GERG conference, Geopolitical Economy of the 21st Century World, Winnipeg, Canada. http://gergconference.ca/wp-content/uploads/2015/09/Krpec-paper-Czechoslovak-Trade-Policy-in-1920s-2.pdf (last accessed: 09. 02. 2017).

Kühne, T. (2005). Demokratisierung und Parlamentarisierung: Neue Forschungen zur politischen Entwicklungsfähigkeit Deutschlands vor dem Ersten Weltkrieg. *Geschichte und Gesellschaft 31* 293–316.

Lawson, R. A. & Clark, J. R. (2010). Examining the Hayek–Friedman hypothesis on economic and political freedom. *Journal of Economic Behavior & Organization 74*(3) 230–239.

Maddison, A. (2003). *The world economy: Historical statistics*. Paris, France: OECD.

Naumann, F. (1908). Die Umwandlung der deutschen Reichsverfassung, *Patria* 81–105.

Nientiedt, D., & Köhler, E. (2016). Liberalism and democracy – A comparative reading of Eucken and Hayek. *Cambridge Journal of Economics 40*(6) 1743–1760.

North, D. C., Wallis, J. J., & Weingast, B. R. (2009). *Violence and social orders: A conceptual framework for interpreting recorded human history*. Cambridge, UK: Cambridge University Press.

Olson, M. (1982). *The rise and decline of nations: Economic growth, stagflation and social rigidities*. New Haven, CT and London, UK: Yale University Press.

Peukert, D. (2014). *Die Weimarer Republik*. Frankfurt, Germany: Suhrkamp.

Pierenkämper, T., & Tilly, R. (2004). *The German economy during the nineteenth century*. New York, NY and Oxford, UK: Berghahn Books.

Plumpe, W. (2011). Eine wirtschaftliche Weltmacht? Die ökonomische Entwicklung Deutschlands von 1870 bis 1914. In B. Heidenreich & S. Neitzel (Eds.), *Das Deutsche Kaiserreich 1890–1914* (pp. 39–60). Schöningh, Germany: Ferdinand Schöningh.

Raphael, L. (2011). *Imperiale Gewalt und mobilisierte Nation: Europa 1914–1945*. Munich, Germany: Beck.

Rawls, J. (1993). *Politischer Liberalismus*. Frankfurt: Suhrkamp.Reckendrees, A. (2003). From cartel regulation to monopolistic control? The founding of the German "steel trust" in 1926 and its effect on market regulation. *Business History 45*(3) 22–51

Reckendrees, A. (2015). Weimar Germany: The first open access order that failed? *Constitutional Political Economy 26*(1) 38–60.

Ritschl, A. (2002). *Deutschlands Krise und Konjunktur 1924–1934. Binnenkonjunktur, Auslandsverschuldung und Reparationsproblem zwischen Dawes-Plan und Transfersperre*. Berlin, Germany: Akademie.Röpke, W. (1942). *International economic disintegration, with an appendix by Alexander Rüstow*. London, UK: W. Hodge.

Röpke, W. (1945). *Internationale Ordnung*. Zurich, Switzerland.

Schmoller, G. (1906). Das Verhältnis der Kartelle zum Staate. *Schriften des Vereins für Socialpolitik, 116, Verhandlungen der Generalversammlung in Mannheim*, 237–271.

Schmoller, G. (1912). Demokratie und soziale Zukunft. *Soziale Praxis und Archiv für Volkswirtschaft XXII*. Jahrg., Nr. 6, vom 7. November 1912. Sp. 145–151, http://gutenberg.spiegel.de/buch/zwanzig-jahre-deutscher-politik-1897-1917-10115/11

Spoerer, M. (1994). German net investment and the cumulative real wage position, 1925–1929: On a premature burial of the Borchardt debate. *Historical Social Research 19* 26–41.

Spoerer, M. (2004). *Steuerlast, Steuerinzidenz und Steuerwettbewerb. Verteilungswirkungen der Besteuerung in Preußen und Würtemberg (1815–1913)*. Berlin, Germany: De Gruyter.

Tooze, A. (2015). *Sintflut. Die Neuordnung der Welt 1916–1931*. Munich, Germany: Siedler.

Torp, C. (2009). Erste Globalisierung und deutscher Protektionismus. In S. O. Müller, & C. Torp (Eds.), *Das Kaiserreich in der Kontroverse* (pp. 422–440). Göttingen, Germany: Vandenhoek & Ruprecht.

Vanberg, V., & Buchanan, J. M. (1989). Interests and theories in constitutional choice. *Journal of Theoretical Politics 1* 49–62.Wegner, G. (2015). Capitalist transformation without political participation: German capitalism in the first half of the nineteenth century. *Constitutional Political Economy 26* 61–86.

Wegner, G. (2016). Defensive modernization in Germany and in the Habsburg Empire – A historical study of capitalist transformation. *Journal of Institutional Economics 12* 443–469.

Wehler, H.-U. (1973). *Das Deutsche Kaiserreich 1871–1918*. Göttingen, Germany: Springer

Wehler, H.-U. (2008). *Deutsche Gesellschaftsgeschichte; Vol. III. Von der "Deutschen Doppelrevolution" bis zum Beginn des Ersten Weltkriegs 1849–1914*. Munich, Germany: Beck.Weingast, B. (1995). The economic role of political institutions: Market preserving federalism and economic development. *Journal of Law, Economics and Organisation 7* 1–31.

Wischermann, C., & Nieberding, A. (2004). *Die institutionelle Revolution. Eine Einführung in die deutsche Wirtschaftsgeschichte des 19. und frühen 20. Jahrhunderts*. Stuttgart, Germany: Franz Steiner.

3 A new Thirty Years War?

Protestant ordoliberalism and the reemergence of the North–South conflict

Josef Hien

Introduction

The Protestant origins of ordoliberalism have been well established. Yet, we know little of the implications of this Protestant background for European integration, and especially the handling of the euro crisis. Looking at the split between crisis and non-crisis countries, it seems at first glance that the crisis countries are all Catholic or Orthodox while the non-crisis countries overwhelmingly share a Protestant background. The split between Catholic/Orthodox and Protestant countries also goes together with other classifications such as creditors vs debtors or import vs export countries. In a 2011 newspaper article about the Troika, a Greek minister stated that "we are dealing here with idiots and Protestants, hence there is no solution" (cited in Makrides, 2015, p. 373).

Are we witnessing a new Thirty Years War in Europe? The cultural and ethical rooting of German ordoliberalism and the reliance of German politicians on the concept helps German politicians approach the crisis as a morality tale of northern saints and southern sinners (Hien, 2017). In this chapter I explore the roots of divergence between capitalist market economies in Northern and Southern Europe that made the crisis such a vexing problem. In particular I will focus on how the different socioeconomic ideologies of Catholicism and Protestantism led to different socioeconomic institutions that persist till today. For this purpose, the chapter picks two exemplary cases of the North–South divide in Europe that opened through the European crisis and that is largely congruent with the cultural influence zones of Protestantism and Catholicism: Germany and Italy. This focus on culturally informed economic ideas that split Europe into North and South opens up a new perspective on the European crisis which I call cultural political economy.

After introducing the concept of cultural political economy (the following section), the chapter lays out the socioeconomic points of divergence between Catholic and Protestant thought as they developed from the 1930s onwards in Germany and Italy (third section). It also explores how much of this socioeconomic thought found its way into the institutional reform of both countries in the 1950s and 1960s and traces the evolution of the two doctrines and the institutions they informed to the present (fourth section).

The dominant approaches within political economy to the crisis

What does a cultural–economics approach to the European crisis look like? In this section I lay out the epistemic background of the dominant approaches in political economy toward the European crisis: the varieties-of-capitalism approach, the growth model approach, the ideational approach, and the cultural–political economics approach.

The varieties-of-capitalism approach has dominated comparative political economy for almost 20 years (Hall & Soskice, 2001). Putting the firm, business networks, and their interaction with the (welfare) state at the center of the analysis, varieties-of-capitalism scholars argue that market economies cluster into coordinated and liberal market economies. Coordinated market economies rely on diversified quality production. They orient their production toward market niches where quality and customization are important. A state-run vocational training system ensures the supply of skilled labor and high employment protection creates incentives to invest in specific skills. The system is coordinated through strong employer and employee organizations. In the original account of the varieties of capitalism and in most follow-up literature, Italy and Germany are classified as coordinated market economies.

During the 2000s, the varieties-of-capitalism approach reigned supreme. According to Google Scholar, the introductory chapter of the Hall and Soskice book *Varieties of Capitalism* has been cited 11,522 times. The theory got seriously challenged through the shockwaves that the financial crisis sent through Europe's coordinated market economies (Hall, 2014; Johnston & Regan, 2016). The crisis drastically showcased a strong 'variety within the variety' of European market economies between Northern, Southern, Central, and Eastern Europe (Armingeon, Guthmann, & Weisstanner, 2015; Höpner & Lutter, 2017).

Prior to the crisis, authors like Streeck, Baccaro, and Svallfors had already criticized varieties of capitalism for not accounting for the far-reaching processes of neoliberalization that all of these national economies have undergone since the 1990s. The decline in union density and corporatist arrangements, as well as wage dispersion and dualization of the labor markets, eroded the equilibrium that the coordinated marketed economies had found before the 1980s (Streeck, 2009, Baccaro & Howell, 2011; Svallfors, 2016). The different ways in which these liberalizations were executed contributed to significant shifts in the configuration of GDP growth in Germany and Italy. This is the gist of the new research paradigm in the comparative political economy approach: the growth model perspective. It emphasizes that in the 1990s Germany turned from a growth model that was equilibrated between domestic demand and exports, to an export-led economy. The share

60 *Josef Hien*

of exports in German GDP growth doubled in the 1990s and 2000s (Baccaro & Pontusson, 2016, p. 189). To support the export competitiveness of price sensitive German manufacturing goods, domestic demand (household consumption) was suppressed through wage depression. Unions in the manufacturing sector agreed to wage restraints and the rest of the labor market was deregulated (Baccaro & Benassi, 2017).

Italy displays no clearly identifiable pattern of growth model throughout the same period and illustrates that "persistent stagnation is always an option" (Baccaro & Pontusson, 2016, p. 187). For the proponents of the growth model perspective and the preceding liberalization scholars, the German model runs at the expense of the southern political economies of the eurozone which are geared toward demand-led growth. Germany's proposed and enforced solutions to the euro crisis must also be seen in this light. The interests of the German export coalition provide the underlying motivation for the austerity policies the German government set as a precondition for loans and rescue packages. These austerity measures risk being counterproductive because they stifle domestic demand, which has traditionally been the key driver of growth in southern European economies. In the literature on the European crisis, this features as a cleavage dividing Northern and Southern Europe between importer vs exporter states, and it sometimes also appears as a cleavage between debtor vs creditor states.

A third explanatory framework for the euro crisis is based on ideas. The ideational turn in comparative political economy has demonstrated the power of economic ideas in politics (Blyth, 2003; Carstensen & Schmidt, 2016). Idiosyncratic national economic ideologies like ordoliberalism or French dirigisme have experienced an unexpected explosion of public and scholarly interest during the euro crisis because they link expert ideas with a common national tradition concerning how the economy should be run (Amable, 2017; Blyth, 2013; *The Economist*, 2015; Hien & Joerges, 2017; Nedergard & Snaith, 2015). In particular, the clash between French and German economic ideas has been blamed for the prolonged stalemate between the countries on the right crisis policy (Brunnermeier, James, & Landau, 2016).

The varieties of capitalism, the growth model perspective, and the ideational accounts exist largely independent from one another. The reason can be found in the different epistemological points of departure. Varieties of capitalism is anchored in a rational–efficiency–oriented institutionalism. The growth model perspective relies ultimately on an interest coalition between segments of capital and labor in the export sector. The ideational approach relies on the power of ideology to serve as the blueprint for socioeconomic actions and institution building. They do not incorporate a historical evolutionary perspective. Moreover, they are apolitical since they leave electoral considerations and the anchoring of different economic strategies in the population by the wayside.

Arguably, there exists a fourth explanatory strand for the euro crisis which so far has lived in the shadow. Here, historical evolutionary pathways are at the center of attention, allowing for a more integrative epistemic perspective. Economic historians have developed the idea of different economic cultures (Abelshauser, 2003; Abelshauser, Gilgen, & Leutzsch, 2013). This strand tracks the embeddedness of the economy in national cultures, traditions, and prevalent economic ideas within a nation-state (Dyson, 2017). Here, the crucial role of 'meaning-making' in reducing complexity in the economy is emphasized. Cultural political economy promises a "dialectic of discursivity and materiality" (Jessop, 2004, p. 164). The concept highlights the importance for contemporary actors of economic imaginaries that use past evolutionary trajectories of the economy as reference points (Best & Paterson, 2015; Esch & de Jong, 2017; Jessop & Sum, 2017). In contrast to standard ideational accounts, which are usually limited to elite ideas, it is a temporally integrated view on meaning-making in the economy of elites and the public.

The concept of cultural political economy has so far only appeared on the fringes of debates on comparative political economy. For the rest of social science, culture as an explanatory variable is (often not unfoundedly) accused of being a residual category that gets evoked when all other explanations fail (Staricco, 2017). However, when applied properly its strength is to integrate the interplay of elite and mass ideas and overcome the trichotomy between material, ideational, and institutional accounts that currently divides the study of political economy and the euro crisis.

Catholic and Protestant reactions in socioeconomic concepts to the crisis of 1930

Language and religion are two major carriers of culture. This chapter focuses on religion and traces how different socioeconomic doctrines of religious institutions left their imprint on post-World War WII ideologies and institutions. Our story starts with the world economic crisis of the 1930s that reformed the dominant strands of socioeconomic thought in Europe. The ordoliberal project as it evolved in Germany from the late 1920s onward was the reaction of Protestant social thought to the upheavals of Weimar that cumulated in the world economic crisis.

Eucken, the founding father of the ordoliberal school, had already commented in the 1930s that loosening ties with the church had facilitated people turning to secularisms in the Weimar period, and that "religion had increasingly lost the power to provide individuals' lives, and thus also their economic activity, a context of meaning" (1932, p. 306). Numerous "explicitly normative–anthropological deliberations" of the ordoliberals were derived from Protestantism and "the strong affinity of a liberal ethos [was] largely influenced by Protestantism" (Jähnichen, 2010, pp. 11, 13).

The "deep Protestant grammar" (Manow, 2001) of ordoliberalism was no accident. All the key figures of the first ordoliberal generation were Protestants. In a 1942 letter to Rüstow, Eucken wrote: "I could neither live nor work if I did not believe that God exists" (Lenel, 1991, p. 12). The

62 Josef Hien

ordoliberal project that developed in the late 1930s and early 1940s in the Freiburg circles was therefore a genuinely Protestant attempt to design an economic order. The project was meant as an antidote to the social–Catholic, the Keynesian–welfare-state, and the neoclassical Austrian–Anglo-Saxon approaches. The key figure was the Protestant theologian Dietrich Bonhoeffer. Between 1938 and 1944, he brought Protestant theologians (Otto Dibelius, Constantin von Dietze), Protestant economists (Walter Eucken, Leonard Miksch, Adolf Lampe), Protestant jurists (Franz Böhm, Hans Großmann-Doerth), and Protestant historians (Gerhard Ritter) together in the Bonhoeffer Kreis and the Arbeitsgemeinschaft Erwin von Beckerath, the two most important ordoliberal circles in Freiburg (Goldschmidt, 1997).

The Freiburger Denkschrift, which originated from these circles and was to be the blueprint for postwar reconstruction, laid out the first coherent Protestant economic and social ethics. Its underlying values clearly differentiate ordoliberalism from 19th-century laissez-faire liberalism and the post-Keynesian Anglo-Saxon neoliberalism which has become the dominant ideational paradigm since the late 1970s. Although self-interest induces people to give their best, it can also bring them to manipulate competition to their own benefit. Just as in Protestantism, ordoliberalism considers people to be "neither angels nor devils" (Dietze, 1947, p. 26), but rather "justified and sinners at the same time; that is why it is decisive to place them within an order that disciplines the *peccator*" (Reuter, 2010, p. 3). In his work, Eucken seeks a compromise between "a Calvinist theocracy with its near identity of church and state and the Lutheran two-kingdoms doctrine with its separation of the spiritual and secular spheres" (Petersen, 2008, p. 23). His concepts mirror Bonhoeffer's "authoritative–paternalistic ... thinking" that "trusts an order and authority based on law and responsibility more than individual freedom" (Falcke, 2011, p. 382). Ordoliberalism's notion of society is not paternalistic, even though the state's ability to provide order is so important to it. The state is supposed to hold back and limit itself to setting underlying conditions for the social order. Ordoliberals reject social transfer payments as false incentives. Unconditional transfers for reasons of solidarity would in the end result in a "total catastrophe for state and society" and make citizens "slaves of the state" (Röpke, 1949, p. 257). Instead, the state should limit itself to ensuring equal opportunity and creating the conditions for helping people to help themselves. This is what sets ordoliberal ideology apart from the Keynesian and Beveridgean welfare state concept that aim at equality in society on the one side and social–Catholic welfare concepts that emphasize a male breadwinner-centered corporatist transfer heavy welfare state on the other side.

Eucken saw social policy as something that would, in the long run, kill all individual self-responsibility. He emphasized that it would "foster collectivization, create coercion and dependency that diminish self-responsibility and endanger the unfolding of the powers which strive in the individual human being for fulfillment" (Eucken, 1949, p. 113). Müller-Armack, who later

Ordoliberalism and the North–South conflict 63

became state secretary in the ministry of the economy, opined as early as 1947 that, in any case, "the social policy results ... have been quite poor" (1947, p. 130). Kaufmann notes that for Ludwig Erhard, later to become finance minister and the single most prominent Christian Democratic exponent of ordoliberalism, "economic policy was the best social policy" (cited in Kaufmann, 2003, p. 131).

Due to their Protestant religiosity, ordoliberals searched for a political home in the Christian Democratic Party (not in the Liberal Party). Böhm was minister in Hessen and became a member of the federal parliament, Erhard was minister and later became chancellor, and Müller-Armack was state secretary. However, these Protestant ordoliberals faced a mighty opponent within the Christian Democratic Party: the social Catholic faction. At the same time as the ordoliberals, and also as a reaction to the crisis of the late 1920s, the social Catholics had developed socioeconomic ideas that ran in most points exactly the opposite from the Protestant ordoliberals. Their ideology was based largely on the social encyclical *Quadragesimo anno*, which like the *Ordo Manifesto* had been issued as a response to the world economic crisis of the 1930s. The prime target of criticism in *Quadragesimo anno* is the current "economic dictatorship" brought about by a rampant system of free competition which had led to the "virtual degradation of the majesty of the state" (p. 109). According to *Quadragesimo anno*, "the free market has destroyed itself" (p. 109).

The encyclical stresses that its socioeconomic concept is neither neoliberal nor socialist, but instead represents a third, distinctly Catholic set of ideas. In contrast to Socialism, private property remains central but, unlike neoliberal conceptions, all private property has to be subject to the advancement of the common good. *Quadragesimo anno* is of the view that "the right order of economic life cannot be left to a free competition of forces" (p. 87). The judgment is harsh: "free competition ... clearly cannot direct economic life" as "it cannot curb and rule itself" (*Quadragesimo anno*, p. 88). Unrestricted free market competition would be directed by the "evil individualistic spirit" spread by "the errors of individualist economic teaching" stemming from a "poisoned spring" (*Quadragesimo anno*, p. 88). Instead, the papal letter puts forward that economic life must again be "subject to and governed by a true and effective directing principle" (*Quadragesimo anno*, p. 88).

Quadragesimo anno marks a new step in Catholic social thinking. Catholic social thinking is now no longer limited to social welfare institutions that engage in repair work after capitalism has brought social dislocation and hardship by destroying the old social order. Instead, its plea for corporatism takes a step toward actively shaping capitalism. The encyclical promotes a specific type of neo-corporatism in which the state only intervenes as a last resort. Christian Socialism emphasizes the importance of collective organization for the common good (*Quadragesimo anno*, p. 85). Employers and employees should be organized in mutual associations depending on the sector of activity. These mutual associations should grant a stable and smooth running of

64   *Josef Hien*

the economy which would avoid strikes on the one hand, and wage depriva-tion on the other. The encyclical notes that "both workers and employers with united strength and counsel can overcome the difficulties and obstacles and let a wise provision on the part of the public authority aid them" (*Quad-ragesimo anno*, p. 73). Wages should be negotiated fairly in bipartite negoti-ations and, in case of stalemate or dissatisfaction, the state should intervene. Workers should be protected by ample work protection legislation that would regulate maximum work hours as well as female and child labor. Codetermi-nation should reduce industrial conflict and give the employed a say in the administration of the firm. In general, "the riches that economic–social developments constantly increase ought to be so distributed among individual persons and classes that the common advantage of all, which Leo XIII had praised, will be safeguarded" (*Quadragesimo anno*, p. 75). The prime aim of the economy is to increase aggregate wealth instead of individual riches. This shared wealth should be generated not only through the payment of a "just wage" and the regulation of working hours and conditions, but also through a system of redistribution. Therefore, "we must strive that at least in the future the abundant fruits of production will accrue equitably to those who are rich and will be distributed in ample sufficiency among the workers" (*Quadragesimo anno*, p. 61). With its emphasis on corporatist organization of socioeconomic relations and the transfer–heavy male breadwinner model the encyclical reads like an anti–manifesto to Protestant ordoliberal claims.

Thus, ordoliberalism distinguished itself clearly from Catholic social ethics and this is largely due to the different conceptions of the human being that Catholics and Protestants loaded into social Catholicism and ordoliberalism (Hien, 2012). Catholicism assumes that individuals are not equipped with the same intellectual, moral, and physical capabilities. For this reason, ensuring fair and equal starting conditions and opportunities (level playing field), as ordoliberals do, would not suffice for Catholic social ethics; instead, society must also guarantee a certain amount of redistribution (*Quadragesimo anno*, p. 75).

The mutual distrust between both camps was tangible up into the 1960s. In 1963, the leading figures of German Catholic social teaching (von Nell-Breuning, Gundlach) and ordoliberalism (Röpke and Rüstow) met secretly in a hotel in Augsburg to discuss whether the social Catholics could be won over for the term social market economy that the ordoliberal Müller-Armack had coined. One of the participants later commented that this was a highly delicate meeting (Emunds, 2010, pp. 1–2). It had to be kept secret because of widespread skepticism in both camps toward collaboration. The Catholics were later reported to have rejected the term and concept of a social market economy since it contained too much ordoliberal Protestant thinking.

The ordoliberals joined the Christian Democratic Party out of electoral considerations. With German partition the denominational balance had shifted to roughly 50% Catholic and 50% Protestant in West Germany. Since Protestants voted not only Christian Democrat but also Liberal and Social

Ordoliberalism and the North–South conflict 65

Democrat (but almost all Catholics voted Christian Democrat) they needed the Catholics to form an electoral coalition to get at least some of their points through. However, given the differences in socioeconomic ideology, Social Catholics worked as an effective counterweight to ordoliberal ideas in the early years of the republic. On the other hand, ordoliberalism also balanced social Catholicism toward a moderate position away from its hard-core corporatist standpoints of the 1930s. Such a moderation effect did not exist in Italy. Here, mono-confessionalism pampered through the softer version of fascist totalitarianism led to a less clear-cut break with the past and a generally easier embrace of corporatist and Social Catholic (even Christian Socialist) ideas.

In contrast to the West German Christian Democratic Party (CDU) the Italian Democrazia Cristiana (DC) was all Catholic. The DCs founding father De Gasperi is portrayed by historiography as a pragmatic realist politician (Cau, 2009, p. 431), a governor interested in organizing with little or no stake in ideology or doctrine. Newer historiographic research shakes this picture, pointing to the early formative experience of De Gasperi and his training as a Catholic sociologist and Catholic militant in Vienna (Pombeni & Nobili Schiera, 2009). De Gasperi emphasized in his early writings the centrality of the Catholic corporatism of *Quadragesimo anno* and its connection to the personalist concepts of Emmanule Mounier and Heinrich Pesch. The independence of organizations was "a natural consequence of personal freedom" since they were "natural organs of civil society" (Cau, 2009, p. 441). While De Gasperi and Adenauer were similar regarding their ability to reconcile ideological positions and political ambitions, the Italian Catholic left was arguably much more to the left than its German counterpart.

To the left of De Gasperi stood the 'dossetians' who were recruited from a circle of young university researchers around Giuseppi Dossetti – a professor and social philosopher at the Catholic University of Milan. Two other central figures in his faction were Giorgio La Pira, who later became mayor of Florence, and Giuseppe Lazzati, who became rector of the Catholic University of Milan (Masala, 2004, p. 101). Dossetti's social thinking drew heavily on personalism, inspired by the philosophy of Christian Democracy championed by the Frenchmen Emmanuel Mounier and Jaques Maritain. Like Pesch's and Nell-Breuning's personalism in Germany, the emphasis was more on the view that "the human personality unfolds through organic belonging to the successive communities" (La Pira cited in Acanfora, 2007, p. 312). In contrast to De Gasperi's insistence on interclassism and mediation, which bears relics of more conservative Austrian Catholic Vogelsangian thought, it aimed at getting rid of classes all together.

In 1942 and early 1943, in a series of clandestine meetings that rotated among the homes of several of its members, the first programmatic party manifesto of the DC emerged bearing a strong imprint from the Catholic left. The program had a strong Christian Socialist leaning inspired by the encyclical *Quadragesimo anno*. The most remarkable prescription of the program is for

66 Josef Hien

the establishment of two parliamentary chambers, of which one would be elected while the other would serve as a forum for corporatist interest representation. This "assembly of the organized interests" (DC, 1943, p. 1) should be "founded foremost on the elected representatives of the organized professions" (DC, 1943, p. 1). This represented an almost word-for-word incorporation of the provisions of the social encyclical *Quadragesimo anno* into the Christian Democratic program. The concept was one of a "liberal Christian idea of a free organic collaboration of all means of production" (DC, 1943, p. 2). In line with the provisions of *Quadragesimo anno*, the state should be confined to a role of "vigilance" (DC, 1943, p. 2) that guarantees the functioning of the neo-corporatist model. Regarding the issue of social security, the program spelled out that "social insurance should be extended, simplified, its organization decentralized and its management put into the hands of the people that it concerned" (DC, 1943, p. 2) reflecting the subsidiarity clauses of *Quadragesimo anno*. In Germany, such corporatist positions can only be found in the Ahlen manifesto of the CDU, an internal concession to the left-Catholic party wing by Adneauer in the 1940s, quickly quashed and replaced through the Protestant liberal conservative Düsseldorfer Leitsätze in 1949. Another difference between Italian and German social Catholicism was that the DC could count on the backing of a strong Catholic union movement ('Gronchians' headed by the influential union leader Giovanni Gronchi), while in Germany the Catholic unions were subsumed under the roof of the Deutscher Gewerkschaftsbund and pulled into the orbit of the Social Democrats (Schroeder, 1992).

Impact of Catholic and Protestant doctrines and institutions

Under De Gasperi the Catholic left remained contained and the socio-economic policy was dominated by the liberal linea Einaudi, but once De Gasperi resigned the Christian Socialist Amintore Fanfani became the leading figure of the party. Corporatism started to be reinstated wholesale. Fanfani, student of Dossetti, was a leftist reformer for whom, in the words of the leader of the Catholic union wing in the party in 1952, "the battle of the DC has to be fought ... on the territory of social justice, on the recognition of the new rights of the new status of work" (Gronchi cited in Vecchio, 1979, p. 182). Gronchi and his union wing pressed for a comprehensive social policy program and the integration of the lower classes as the "resistance to Bolshevism, in doctrine as well as in social political regime, does not compensate for blocking the working classes in their aspirations for more justice" (Gronchi cited in Vecchio, 1979, p. 181). Under the leadership of Fanfani, the party's left wing, with its connections to farm leagues and Catholic unions, gained considerable strength within the party.

Fanfani started with the countryside by ordering Paolo Bononi to build up a dense network of rural savings banks and peasant leagues, the so-called

Ordoliberalism and the North–South conflict 67

Coldiretti. They not only gave out loans to farmers but also became a strong interest group within the DC (Ginsborg, 1990, p. 171). In order to anchor in the urban areas, Fanfani promoted the expansion of a huge network of Christian Democratic *circoli* (social organizations) which usually consisted of a venue with an alcohol license in the center of the town or neighborhood in which Catholic workers could gather. At the end of the 1950s, these ACLI (Associazioni cristiane dei lavoratori italiani) *circoli* boasted over one million members. In order to acquire more members, Fanfani initiated large-scale membership subscription campaigns that were held in festival-like atmospheres where prizes were handed out for inscription. This led to a shift of the socioeconomic background of DC members in favor of working-class members (Galli, 1978, p. 178).

By contrast, German Catholicism was pulled in a liberal direction by the ordoliberals and Protestants after WWII, and therefore away from stronger corporative thinking. The new corporatist strategy entailed that the DC tightened its grip on the existing state entities and created yet more new ones. The party also had to simultaneously distance itself from the liberal employers association, Confindustria, in order to increase its financial autonomy (Galli, 1978, p. 72). The prime means for this were the creation of the ministry of state holdings (Ministro delle partecipazioni statali) which was approved by parliament after prolonged and fierce debate on December 22, 1956. One year later, on January 11, 1957, the law on fossils (*legge idrocarburi*) followed, which gave the state company ENI (Ente Nazionale Idrocarburi) a monopoly on research and exploitation in that sector. The strategy to curb the power of business over the party, and society in general, was completed by the withdrawal of all IRI (Istituto per la Ricostruzione Industriale – a large state holding) companies from Confindustria only a year later on January 1, 1958. Galli notes that, from this point on, "the party that used to be the prince of the industrial complex controlled progressively the means of production, which are the source of true power" (1978, p. 180). The ENI, a huge oil and gas company founded in 1953, is exemplary of this process. The Christian Democrat Enrico Mattei "a man of few principles and great entrepreneurial skill" (Ginsborg, 1990, p. 163) became its restless president. Starting with the state petrol company AGIP, Mattei built up an industrial empire in the state sector that within a few years encompassed industries as diverse as petrochemicals, highway construction, synthetic rubber production, contract engineering, construction, and nuclear research (Ginsborg, 1990, pp. 164–165). Despite the rampant clientelism and often corrupt practices within ENI, it was – together with IRI, the second largest state holding – a key driver of Italy's after war economic miracle. The flipside of this success was that it tightened the state's, and therefore the party's, grip on society and created a class of politico-economic Christian Democratic barons, making it increasingly hard to judge whether their motivations were fueled by left Catholic ideology or pure rent-seeking for themselves and their party faction.

68 *Josef Hien*

Fanfani had intended to build a party with electoral ties independent of the Vatican, the Allies, or Confindustria. He wanted to do this with a strong left corporatist program. But, owing to Italy's regional disparities, this played out in different ways in different parts of the country. While the North saw the construction of a strong Christian Democratic subculture based on a Christian Democratic worldview, the South witnessed the establishment of a gigantic clientelist party machine. The party was Catholic–Christian Democratic in the North and clientelist–corrupt in the South. In the same way, some of the large state holdings became synonymous with the rampant favoritism and clientelism of the DC. The special blend of corporatism that Fanfani had elaborated in his 1948 book *Economia* was too vulnerable to corruption and clientelism. The transformation of the DC under Fanfani into a corporatist party was, especially in the South, coupled with a drift toward a clientelist party.

In the Italian case, the initial social Catholic motivations for a specific and distinctive model of corporatist capitalism were gradually replaced after the 1960s by vote and rent-seeking interests. However, ideology and interests reinforced one another in the model for spoils distribution, thereby contributing to its stability and making reform difficult, a fact laid bare in the euro crisis. The Christian Democratic left was similarly instrumental to the early setup of institutions in Germany, yet due to the balancing effect between ordoliberal protestants and social Catholics, the outcome was much less corporatist than in Italy.

Social Catholics also had the upper hand in Germany, but only as long as their subculture and political connections remained strong. The reinstallment of the Bismarckian welfare state in Germany was a key social Catholic project. The pension reform of 1957 was an enormous popular success. The ordoliberals fought it where they could but were defeated. A public opinion survey from the Allensbach Institute found that Germans ranked it as the "Most popular event in the eight year long history of the Federal Republic" (Conze, 2009, p. 169). The reform contributed immensely to Adenauer's landslide victory in the next election. The year 1957 was not only that of Adenauer's big pension reform, but also that of the "Conceptual final stroke of the social market economy" (Schulz cited in Conze, 2009, p. 169). As compensation, an "interconfessional compromise" (Manow, 2001), the core ordoliberal projects of an independent federal central bank (Bundesbank) and the cartel law, which led to the formation of an independent cartel agency, were finally enacted. The same year was also the endpoint of another often-unnoticed struggle between ordoliberal Protestants and Social Catholics: the introduction of a corporatist interest mediation institution (*Bundeswirtschaftsrat*). It should guarantee a democratization of the economy by establishing a second forum for representation of capital and labor interests, next to parliament, as foreseen in *Quadragesimo anno*. This idea was pushed by the unions and social Catholics but heavily opposed by the ordoliberals. Ludwig Erhard (ordoliberal, Protestant, minister of the economy, and later chancellor) could not fully erase the plans, but he managed to postpone and transform them.

Ordoliberalism and the North–South conflict 69

Seven years later and seven legislative proposals later the result was the establishment of an expert committee that is still of central importance in German economic affairs today. It is dubbed the council of the five sages of the economy, and has since its establishment been a hotbed of ordoliberal economic expertise that counsels the federal government on matters of political economy. Hence, the reinstallment of socioeconomic institutions in Germany in the 1950s and 1960s was heavily influenced by social Catholic ideas, but it did not come to a wholesale influence of Catholic corporatism ideology due to the counterweight of the ordoliberal faction within the CDU. On the other hand, central elements of Germany's socioeconomic system never had an ordoliberal imprint. After the stagflation crisis Germany slowly began to embark on a reform trajectory inspired by ordoliberal ideas. This process, which picked up speed but met much resistance from a still strong social Catholic wing within the CDU, accelerated with German reunification.

Reunification brought huge economic problems. During the 1990s, Germany underwent a transformation from being regarded as the strongman to being regarded as the sick one. This was the chance for an ordoliberal comeback. The neoliberal reform agenda, with its emphasis on deep welfare cuts, privatization, equal starting conditions, individualization of social risks and equality of opportunity, came against the backdrop of skyrocketing unemployment, debt, and sluggish economic growth. This made it ever the more politically attractive. Reunification also opened an enormous practical laboratory for neoliberal politics. Approximately 14,600 formerly state-owned companies with 4 million employees, together with 2.4 billion hectares of land and a huge public housing stock, were to be privatized according to the "principles of the social market economy" (Deutsche Demokratische Republik, 1990, §2). However, these "principles of the social market economy" were now interpreted more liberal than ever before. Additionally, reunification altered the electoral map of Germany. With the addition of the eastern states, 16 million citizens from a Protestant cultural background joined the German electorate and decreased the importance of the Catholic vote for the Christian Democratic Party (Hien, 2013).

After German partition, West Germany became 45.8% Catholic and 50.6% Protestant. In East Germany (GDR) the 1950 census showed 85% Protestants and 10% Catholics. Through a strong policy of de-Christianization, the GDR brought these figures down to 25% Protestants, 5% Catholics and 70% unaffiliated on the eve of reunification in 1989 (Pollack & Pickel, 2003). West Germany experienced only a slight drop in church affiliation up to reunification (though church attendance dropped remarkably). In 1987, 42.9% were Catholic while Protestants, whose numbers dropped to 41.6%, became a minority for the first time. The number of unaffiliated had risen from 3.6% in 1950 to 11.4% in 1987 (FOWID, 2011). Through the strong decrease in church affiliation in the East, reunification boosted the "non-members of a statuary religious corporation," as the census of 2011 put it, to

70   *Josef Hien*

33% in the same year. Catholic Church membership sunk to 31% of the population and Protestant church membership to 30.8%.

Social Catholicism had already lost much of its political clout in the Christian Democratic Party in the 1980s when the Christian Democratic Employees' Association lost members and influence. Angela Merkel, the daughter of an East German Protestant Priest, became the symbol of the (neo-) Protestantization of the German Christian Democrats, a party that had, for most of its post-WWII history, been more Catholic than Protestant in its program, membership, and electorate. Norbert Blüm, the last prominent "heart-Jesus-Marxist" (Herz-Jesu-Marxist), ended his last term as welfare minister in 1998 and got hissed at the party congregation of Leipzig in 2003 for his critique of the new neoliberal party program (Zeit, 2003). The Protestant Finance Minister Wolfgang Schäuble represented a restrengthened ordoliberalism. This enabled a series of welfare reforms in the 1990s and later the Agenda 2010, which was hammered out by the red–green coalition under Chancellor Schröder but was espoused and passed with the votes of the Christian Democratic Party. Chancellor Merkel stated the following when assuming office in 2005: "I want to thank Chancellor Schröder personally for bravely opening a door with the Agenda 2010" (Merkel, 2005).

Conclusion

The Agenda Reform was the 'homework' that Germany demanded from the crisis countries in exchange for fiscal solidarity. Due to the mono-confessional layout of Italy, a similar reform process and trajectory never happened, and this is the key to understanding the sharp divergence in the positions of the two economies. It is very hard to reform the Italian political economy from the outside as most northern Protestant countries in the eurozone demand, because it is anchored so strongly in the cultural background of the country. The approach of cultural political economy to the European crisis taken here suggests that there are no quick fixes to be expected through structural reforms. Instead, it has shown how political economies like the German and Italian ones evolved over almost a century and that institutions, ideas, and interests interacted in setting their pathway, providing a highly durable complex of relations that is hard to break up, especially from the outside.

References

Abelshauser, W. (2003). *Kulturkampf: Der deutsche Weg in die Neue Wirtschaft und die amerikanische Herausforderung*, Berlin, Germany: Kadmos.

Abelshauser, W., Gilgen, D., & Leutzsch, A. (Eds.). (2013). *Kulturen der Weltwirtschaft*, Göttingen, Germany: Vandenhoek & Ruprecht.

Acanfora, P. (2007). Myths and the political use of religion in Christian Democratic Culture. *Journal of Modern Italian Studies 12*(3) 307–338.

Ordoliberalism and the North–South conflict 71

Amable, B. (2017). Dirigisme and modernism vs ordoliberalism. In J. Hien & C. Joerges (Eds.), *Ordoliberalism, law and the rule of economics* (pp. 13–22). Oxford, UK and Portland, OR: Hart.

Armingeon, K., Guthmann, K., & Weisstanner, D. (2015). How the euro divides the union: The effect of economic adjustment on support for democracy in Europe. *Socio-Economic Review 14*(1) 1–26.

Baccaro, L., & Benassi, C. (2017). Throwing out the ballast: Growth models and the liberalization of German industrial relations. *Socio-Economic Review 15*(1) 85–115.

Baccaro, L., & Howell, C. (2011). A common neoliberal trajectory: The transformation of industrial relations in advanced capitalisms. *Politics & Society 39* 521–563.

Baccaro, L., & Pontusson, J. (2016). Rethinking comparative political economy: the growth model perspective. *Politics & Society 44*(2) 175–207.

Best, J., & Paterson, M. (2015). Towards a cultural political economy – Not a cultural IPE. *Millennium: Journal of International Studies 43*(2) 738–740.

Blyth, M. (2003). Structures do not come with an instruction sheet: Interests, ideas, and progress in political science. *PS: Political Science and Politics 1*(4) pp. 695–706.

Blyth, M. (2013). *Austerity: The history of a dangerous idea*. Oxford, UK: Oxford University Press.

Brunnermeier, M., James, H., & Landau, J.-P. (2016). *The euro and the battle of ideas*. Princeton, NJ: Princeton University Press.

Carstensen, M., & Schmidt, V. (2016). Power through, over and in ideas: Conceptualizing ideational power in discursive institutionalism. *Journal of European Public Policy 23*(3) 318–337.

Cau, M. (2009). Alcide De Gasperi: A political thinker or a thinking politician? *Modern Italy 14*(4) 431–444.

Conze, E. (2009). *Die Suche nach Sicherheit*. Munich, Germany: Siedler.

DC. (1943). *Le Idee Ricostruttive della Democrazia Cristiana*. Rome, Italy.

Deutsche Demokratische Republik. (1990). Treuhandgesetz, www.gesetze-im-internet.de/treuhg/index.html

Dietze, C. (1947). *Theologie und Nationalökonomie*. Tuebingen/Stuttgart, Germany: Furche.

Dyson, K. (2017). Ordoliberalism as Tradition and as Ideology. In J. Hien & C. Joerges (Eds.), *Ordoliberalism, Law and the Rule of Economics*. Oxford: Hart Publishing.

Economist, The (2015, May 9). German ordoliberalism has had a big influence on policymaking during the euro crisis.

Emunds, B. (2010). Ungewollte Vaterschaft. Katholische Soziallehre und Soziale Marktwirtschaft. *Ethik und Gesellschaft* 1/2018.Eucken, W. (1932). Staatliche Strukturwandlungen und die Krisis des Kapitalismus. (1997) [1932] 48 *ORDO: Jahrbuch für die Ordnung von Wirtschaft und Gesellschaft* 5–25.

Eucken, W. (1949). *Die Sozialpolitische Frage*. Heidelberg, Germany: Weber.

Esch, F. v., & Jong, E. d. (2017). National culture trumps EU socialization: The European central bankers' views of the euro crisis. *Journal of European Public Policy*. doi:10.1080/13501763.2017.1391862

Falcke, H. (2011). Welche Ansätze Für Eine Wirtschaftsethik finden wir bei Dietrich Bonhoeffer? *Evangelische Theologie 71* 376–95.

Fanfani, A. (1948). *Economia*. Brescia, Italy: Morcelliana.

72 Josef Hien

FOWID, Religionszugehörigkeit Bevölkerung 1970–2011, https://fowid.de/meldung/entwicklung-religionszugehoerigkeiten-nach-bundeslaendern-1950-2011

Galli, G. (1978). *Storia della democrazia cristiana*. Bari, Italy: Editori Laterza.

Ginsborg, P. (1990). *A history of contemporary Italy*. London, UK: Penguin.

Goldschmidt, N. (1997). Die Entstehung der Freiburger Kreise. *Historisch-Politische Mitteilungen: Archiv für Christlich-Demokratische Politik* 1–17.

Hall, P. A. (2014). Varieties of capitalism and the euro crisis, *West European Politics* 37(6) 1223–1243.

Hall, P. A., & Soskice, D. (2001). *Varieties of capitalism: The institutional foundations of comparative advantage*. Oxford, UK: Oxford University Press.

Hien, J. (2012). *Competing ideas: The religious foundations of the German and Italian welfare states*. Florence, Italy: Cadmus, European University Institute.

Hien, J. (2013). Unsecular politics in a secular environment: The case of Germany's Christian Democratic Union family policy. *German Politics* 22(4) 441–460.

Hien, J. (2017). The religious roots of the European crisis. *Journal of Common Market Studies*. Early view. http://onlinelibrary.wiley.com/doi/10.1111/jcms.12635/abstract

Hien, J., & Joerges, C. (Eds.). (2017). *Ordoliberalism, law and the rule of economics*. Oxford, UK and Portland, OR: Hart.

Höpner, M., & Lutter, M. (2017). The diversity of wage regimes: Why the eurozone is too heterogeneous for the euro. *European Political Science Review* 10(1) 71–96.

Jähnichen, T. (2010). Die Protestantischen Wurzeln der Sozialen Marktwirtschaft. *Ethik und Gesellschaft* 49–58, at 11, 13.

Jessop, B. (2004). Critical semiotic analysis and cultural political economy. *Critical Discourse Studies* 1(2) 159–174.

Jessop, B. & Sum, N.-L. (2017). Putting the Amsterdam School in its rightful place: A reply to Juan Ignacio Staricco's critique of *Cultural Political Economy*. *New Political Economy* 22(3) 342–354.

Johnston, A., & Regan, A. (2016). European Monetary Integration and the incompatibility of national varieties of capitalism. *Journal of Common Market Studies* 54(2) 1–19, 318–336.

Kaufmann, F.-X. (2003). *Sozialpolitisches Denken*. Frankfurt, Germany: Suhrkamp.

Lenel, H. O. (1991). Walter Eucken's Briefe an Alexander Rüstow. 42 *ORDO: Jahrbuch für die Ordnung von Wirtschaft und Gesellschaft* 11–14, at 12.

Makrides, V. (2015). Hat Die Orthodoxie Mit Der Tiefgreifenden Finanzkrise in Griechenland Seit 2009 Etwas Zu Tun? In R. Floghaus & J. Wasmuth (Eds.), *Orthodoxie Im Dialog*. Berlin, Germany: De Gruyter.

Manow, P. (2001). Ordoliberalismus als ökonomische Ordnungstheologie. *Leviathan* 29 179–98.

Masala, C. (2004). Born for government: The Democrazia Cristiana in Italy. In M. Gehler & W. Kaiser (Eds.), *Christian democracy in Europe since 1945* (vol. 2). London, UK: Routledge.

Merkel, A. (2005, November 30). Regierungserklärung von Bundeskanzlerin Dr. Angela Merkel vor dem Deutschen Bundestag. Bulletin 93–1. Retrieved from www.bundesregierung.de/breg-de/service/bulletin/regierungserklaerung-von-bundeskanzlerin-dr-angela-merkel-795782

Müller-Armack, A. (1947). *Wirtschaftslenkung und Marktwirtschaft*. Hamburg, Germany: Kastell.

Ordoliberalism and the North–South conflict   73

Nedergaard, P., & Snaith, H. (2015). "As I drifted on a river I could not control": The unintended ordoliberal consequences of the eurozone crisis. *Journal of Common Market Studies 53* 1094–1109.

Petersen, T. (2008). Die Sozialethik Emil Brunners und ihre Neoliberale Rezeption. *HWWI Research Paper No. 5–6*, 2008, 1–27.

Pollack, D., & Pickel, G. (2003). De-institutionalization of religion and religious individualization in Eastern and Western Germany. *KZfSS Kölner Zeitschrift für Soziologie und Sozialpsychologie 55*(3) 447–74.

Pombeni, P., & Nobili Schiera, G. (2009). Alcide de Gasperi: 1881–1954 – A political life in a troubled century. *Modern Italy 14*(4) 379–397.

Quadragesimo anno, Pius XI (1931). available at: http://w2.vatican.va/content/pius-xi/en/encyclicals/documents/hf_p-xi_enc_19310515_quadragesimo-anno.html, 75 (accessed 22/08/2017).

Reuter, H.-P. (2010). Vier Anmerkungen zu Philip Manow Die Soziale Marktwirtschaft als interkonfessioneller Kompromiss? Ein Re-Statement. *Ethik und Gesellschaft 1* 1–22.

Röpke, W. (1949). *Civitas humana: Grundfragen der Gesellschafts- und Wirtschaftsreform* (3rd ed.). Erlenbach–Zurich, Switzerland: Eugen Rentsch.

Schroeder, W. (1992). Katholizismus und Einheitsgewerkschaft. Bonn: Dietz Verlag.

Stariccio, J. I. (2017). Putting culture in its place? A critical engagement with cultural political economy. *New Political Economy 22*(3) 328–341.

Streeck, W. (2009). *Re-forming capitalism: Institutional change in the German political economy*. Oxford, UK: Oxford University Press.

Svallfors, S. (2016). Politics as organised combat – New players and new rules of the game in Sweden. *New Political Economy 21*(6) 505–519.

Vecchio, G. (1979). *La democrazia christiana in Europa (1891–1963)*. Milan, Italy: Mursia.

Zeit (2003). Blüms Erben: Kulturkampf in der CDU. www.zeit.de/2003/43/CDA

4 Ordoliberalism, social Catholicism, and West Germany's social market economy (1949–1976)

Volker Berghahn

Introduction

The current state of the American model of capitalism and its future have recently generated plenty of research and argument among the social sciences. On the one hand, there are those who continue to insist on the viability and dynamism of this model, whose roots are generally traced back to the late 1970s and 1980s and the shift toward neoliberal economics under presidents Jimmy Carter and Ronald Reagan, reinforced by Thatcherism in Britain. As a result, we have seen the introduction of policies of deregulation, privatization, financialization, regressive taxation, accompanied by public expenditure cuts in welfare, health provision, transportation infrastructure, and education. In the 1990s, these policies partially spilled over into the European economies after the collapse of the Soviet bloc. Finally, and under the impact of digitalization, neoliberalism began to morph in this century into a network and platform capitalism that – it is argued – continues to set the pace of change in the international economy.[1] In short, the United States is, in this view, still seen as the global leader of socioeconomic change. Convinced of its superior dynamic, its protagonists usually downplay the progressive degrading not only the environment but also of the living conditions of most of humanity in favor of an unprecedented accumulation of wealth in the hands of a few.

On the other hand, there are those for whom America is fast losing its early postwar capacity and power to shape the structures of the world because it is increasingly stymied by its neoliberal values and practices that have set the country on a path of self-erosion and serious crisis. As a result, they have begun to look at other capitalisms and believe that, instead of promoting a neoliberal 'rugged individualism,' societies should prioritize policies of achieving greater social justice and solidarity with those who, after decades of stagnation or even downward mobility, have been manifestly forced into poverty. No longer convinced that American capitalism offers a viable and humane path to the future, the skeptics refuse to throw their arms up in despair when scrutinizing Uber's and Amazon's platform business models and thrust. To them it is more fruitful to look for alternatives that would 'bend' capitalism toward greater equality. They see the way forward in the ideas of the

Social Catholicism and social market economy   75

varieties-of-capitalism paradigm, first advanced in 1991 by the French social scientist Michel Albert who identified two divergent capitalisms: the Anglo-American type and another one that he called "Rhenish" (Albert, 1991). Ten years after Albert, this categorization was taken up and reconceptualized by Peter Hall and David Soskice (2001).[2] To them it was not Albert's notion of a dualism that opened up new possibilities for the study of contemporary market economies. Instead they and others extended Albert's comparison to a whole range of capitalisms, including Swedish, French, or even Chinese ways of running a modern industrial and commercial economy.

In other words, instead of assuming that this is still the age of the post-1945 Pax Americana, it is held to be more insightful to study alternative paths taken by countries that, having come to doubt the superiority of the 'American way,' are trying to find approaches and solutions to the socio-economic problems that their countries face both at home and in their dealings with their partners and competitors in the international system. This is where current debates on Germany's 'social market economy' come in, and on which this chapter is focused. Written by a historian, it has a starting point that differs from that of social scientists. It argues that discussions on Germany's social market economy covered in the other contributions to this volume cannot be understood without reconstructing their origins in the early postwar period. Accordingly, and as a first step, I go back to the Freiburg School of economics. Even though the concept of social market economy itself is deemed to have been coined in 1947 by Alfred Müller-Armack, at first a close adviser of Economics Minister Ludwig Erhard and later state secretary in the Federal Economic Ministry, I am putting Walter Eucken at the center of the first section, widely assumed to have been one of the key founders of the Freiburg School. After an examination of Eucken's life, ideas, and influence in shaping Erhard's social market economy, the chapter will turn in a quite different direction and look at the role of social Catholicism in shaping the West German political economy. In this sense it tries to complement the initial analytical framework of Josef Hien's contribution to this volume, which deals with the Protestant roots of ordoliberalism, before he links them to the reemergence of the North–South conflict.

Walter Eucken and the Freiburg School of Economics

Walter Eucken was born on January 17, 1893 into an upper-middle-class family. His father Rudolf was a professor of philosophy at Jena University.[3] His mother, Irene Eucken, hailed from a bourgeois family in Bremen. While she made a name for herself as a painter, her husband achieved one of the highest honors when he was awarded the Nobel Prize in Literature in 1908. Although Rudolf's pre-1914 work was concerned with the intellectual and cultural life of the Wilhelmine monarchy, he, like so many other German academics, became politicized during World War I (WWI) and supported the German monarchy's expansionist war aims. The family stayed in Jena after

76   Volker Berghahn

1918 and their home became a center of intellectual life. Famous men visited them and Irene became the founder of the Society of the Friends of the Arts of Jena and Weimar. It seems that this milieu left a profound impression on Walter, but instead of studying philosophy and theology, he decided to embark on a career as an economist. After receiving his doctorate, he completed his *Habilitation* in 1921 and, after a brief spell as a full professor at Tübingen University, was offered a chair in economics at the University of Freiburg in 1927 where he stayed until his death in 1950.

One reason for making Freiburg his home was that it was well out of the way from the centers of power when Hitler established his dictatorship in 1933. An anti-Nazi of the first hour, he continued to lecture and also vigorously criticized Martin Heidegger, then Freiburg's rector, for his policies of Nazification of the university and his dismissal of Jewish academics, with the famous philosopher Edmund Husserl, a friend of the Euckens, being among those who lost their jobs. It is probably fair to say, instead of leaving Germany, Walter Eucken went into 'inner emigration.' This meant that he did not fall completely silent. He continued to give his lectures at Freiburg; in 1939, he published his *Grundlagen der Nationalökonomie*, essentially a comparative study of different forms of national economic management. It ranged from an analysis of the highly centralized Nazi economy to more liberal ones and was such a dry read that the Nazis apparently saw no reason to censor or even ban it. In 1940 he accepted a temporary position as an adviser to the Reich Economics Ministry in Berlin. One reason for Eucken's cautious maneuvering seems to have been that his wife, Edith Erdsiek-Eucken, had a Jewish mother, and as the Nazi regime stepped up its policies of discrimination and ultimately the mass murder of the Jewish populations of Europe in the 1940s, both women were increasingly threatened by deportation. Uncertain if Edith's mother was safe with the Euckens in Freiburg, she eventually moved to her son in provincial Celle to the north-east of Hannover and survived. Meanwhile her daughter remained in Freiburg, protected by her 'Aryan' husband.

It is important to try to imagine the psychological impact that rumors of the Holocaust that were circulating in Germany by 1943 had on the Euckens. So, it took some courage when by 1944 Walter decided to join a circle of Freiburg academics who met privately not only to express their opposition to the Hitler regime, but also discuss Germany's future once it had become clear that the Allies would sooner or later defeat the Nazi dictatorship.[4] After the failure to assassinate Hitler in July 1944, some of Eucken's colleagues, such as the historian Gerhard Ritter, were arrested and imprisoned. Eucken was interrogated by the Gestapo, but let go. So, when the war finally ended and the University of Freiburg reopened its lecture halls to students, Eucken, given his proven anti-Nazi record, was able to resume his teaching. At the same time, he and his colleagues decided to establish an academic yearbook with the aim of helping shape socioeconomic policymaking and theory during the period of Allied occupation and, after 1949, in the emergent

Federal Republic of Germany. Some of his lecture manuscripts survived and were later published. But instead of examining these and other early postwar statements by Eucken, I propose to focus on two articles that he published in 1948 and 1949 in the first and second issues of *ORDO. Jahrbuch für die Ordnung von Wirtschaft und Gesellschaft.*

The first one harkened back to his book of 1939 in which he had analyzed the transition from early modern family economy to the more dynamic industrial economies of the modern period.[5] Having surveyed the divergent ways in which these economies had historically been structured and organized through the mid-1940s, he wrote approvingly of Allied attempts to ban cartels and syndicates that had been the hallmark of the German system even before the Nazi regime and its brutal policies of centralizing and 'synchronizing' for the war effort what was still a capitalist economy based on private ownership. Like the American occupation authorities in particular, Eucken, too, wanted to destroy concentrations of power, whether dominated by state agencies or by private individuals and large corporations. In short, he was opposed to both the 'overweening power of the economic state' (*Übermacht des Wirtschaftsstaates*) as well as the no less suspect *Übermacht* of the private employer. This concern over great accumulations of power and influence raised the question of the constitutional framework within which a modern industrial economy was supposed to function. What he had in mind was an 'order' that provided freedom, but explicitly also set strict limits against the misuse of liberties granted by the constitution. It is important that Eucken highlighted the link between economic liberties and a modern political constitution at the time when the so-called Basic Law of the Federal Republic was drawn up in 1948 and finally ratified in 1949.

How Eucken envisioned his economic constitutional order emerged more specifically from his second article in the 1949 issue of the Yearbook (Eucken, 1949). Pointing to the existence of private 'power groups' that had allied themselves in WWI with the bureaucratic apparatus of the monarchical state, he concluded that the public and private economic systems that emerged from this during the interwar years were marked by so many flaws that there was only one type of socioeconomic order that allowed both enterprises of all sizes and households to plan and act in freedom in the marketplace: 'perfect competition' (*vollständiger Wettbewerb*). Eucken stressed that this form was not to be equated with laissez-faire liberalism of the 19th century. Nor did it have anything to do with the struggles of monopolies and oligopolies among each other that would merely promote a type of economy designed to hinder competition or inflict damage on a competitor. What he envisioned was a system that was guided by a performance-based competition (*Leistungswettbewerb*). Time and again Eucken returned to the threat that private and public concentrations of power posed to economy and society that ultimately could only be kept in check by a monopoly authority. The tasks that this authority was supposed to fulfil were in his view similar to the role of a constitutional court in a parliamentary democracy: it had to guarantee the civil liberties

78 Volker Berghahn

enshrined in the constitutional document, but also to supervise the limits set by it. For him, the monopoly authority was to be mandated to dissolve monopolies that were avoidable and to monitor strictly those that were 'unavoidable.' Ultimately, his ordoliberal economy was decentralized and dominated not by large corporations but by medium-sized enterprises.

If Eucken gave a fairly detailed exposition of the market economy he had in mind in his *ORDO* articles and also in his other book *Grundsätze der Wirtschaftspolitik*, published posthumously in 1952, his early death in 1950 prevented him from expanding on another principle that was also indispensable to his vision of economy and society: the importance of the social, i.e., the obligation to provide welfare. Next to his concern to create a competitive economy, there was – as he put it – nothing else that was not also "important in social terms." When introducing the social, he, like many other West Germans, evidently had before his eyes those millions of war widows and orphans, refugees and expellees from the East, returning soldiers, often physically mutilated and psychologically traumatized or both, and finally those who had lost everything in Allied bombing raids. It was clear that they could not be exposed to the harsh winds of 'perfect competition.' It was not only inhuman to do this, but also dangerous in a constitutional system based on the right to vote as part of the universal suffrage, reestablished in the Basic Law and the constitutions of the *Länder*. There had to be a safety net that these millions would be able to rely on or the stability of the existing constitutional order was feared to be threatened by the power held by ordinary citizens via the ballot box. If the experience of the ill-fated Weimar State held any lessons for West Germany, it was that a working democratic order was inseparable from the functioning capitalist economy based on *Leistungswettbewerb* and vice versa.

Perhaps the most concise statement of this interdependent system is to be found in the Düsseldorfer Leitsätze that the Christian Democratic Party (CDU) issued on July 15, 1949, a few weeks before the official founding of the Federal Republic.[6] These guidelines defined the "social market economy" as "the socially anchored law for the industrial economy, according to which the achievements of free and able individuals are integrated into a system that produces the highest level of economic benefit and social justice for all." The aim was effectively to combine "monetary, credit, trade, customs, tax, investment and social policies, as well as other measures" in order to create "an economy that serves the welfare and needs of the entire population, thereby fulfilling its ultimate goal," including the mandate to also meet "adequately … the needs of those parts of the population suffering hardship." The Guidelines also promised to "create social peace and grant each individual the freedom and opportunity to participate in the economic process and secure a political democracy by means of social and economic democracy."

If the notion of social market economy as presented in the Düsseldorfer Leitsätze and hence also in the vision of Alfred Müller-Armack, his boss, Economics Minister Ludwig Erhard, and last but by no means least of Eucken at

Social Catholicism and social market economy 79

the Freiburg School, it is important to remember that the CDU was founded in 1945 as an alliance of North and Southwest German Protestants, on the one hand, and Rhenish Catholics, on the other. Both wings wanted to establish a parliamentary democracy and a social–liberal, private enterprise market economy without cartels and monopolies. But while the protagonists of the former were rooted in the principles of a Lutheran Protestantism that, after the fall of Nazism, had seen a revival both in terms of its theological and ethical principles and of West Germans professing them, Rhenish Catholicism had different foundations. However, whereas there is an extensive scholarly literature on Erhard's social market economy, the contribution made by Rhenish Catholicism to its initial shaping and later evolution is much less well known and underappreciated. This is why the rest of this chapter is devoted to the Catholic input into the kind of social market economy that emerged in West Germany after 1949. However, for reasons of space, my analysis will be confined to two prominent Catholics, the professor of theology and later Cardinal Joseph Höffner and to the professor of theology Oswald von Nell-Breuning, S.J.

Nell-Breuning is remembered in the context of Rhenish left Catholicism and the Sozialkommissionen der Christlich-Demokratischen Arbeitnehmerschaft (Social Commissions of the Christian-Democrat Workers (CDA);[7] Höffner has been forgotten by a wider public and is mostly studied by academic historians of the Catholic Church in Germany and its activities. However, Norbert Trippen (2009, pp. 7–8) drew attention some years ago to the significant role that Höffner played in the thinking and "construction of Social Catholicism after 1945 and the social legislation of the Federal Republic after 1949"; he was "a central figure of Catholicism and of German social history" between 1951 and 1962.[8] His 900-page biography of Höffner is particularly useful in that he quotes extensively from his letters and reminiscences. Much of what follows is therefore based on these two massive volumes.

Joseph Höffner and Germany's social market economy

Höffner was born on December 24, 1906 in Horhausen near Neuwied in the Rhine Valley. His parents Paul and Helene came from the region in which both their families had been involved in agriculture for several generations. Although Paul expected his son to take over the farmstead, he excelled in primary school and later in high school and, with his *Abitur* certificate in his pocket, decided to train for the priesthood and was offered a place to study at the papal Gregoriana University in Rome. Apart from theology, he became particularly interested in law and economics and was influenced by the teachings of two pastors, Artur Vermeersch and Oswald von Nell-Breuning. It appears that he also studied the encyclical *Quadragesimo anno* that Pope Pius XI had published in 1931 and that was to gain great importance for the subsequent development of social Catholicism. This encyclical was the Vatican's

80　Volker Berghahn

attempt to offer, at the height of the Great Depression, an alternative to socialism and communism to working-class Catholics who, it was felt, must not be left during this period of mass unemployment and social distress without the spiritual and material support that the Church felt compelled to provide both for reasons of the Christian faith, but also of politics. Exposed to all these currents, Höffner became a broadly educated theologian and social scientist who received his doctorate in July 1929 and was ordained three years later.

Although he was no friend of the Nazis, he responded cautiously to the pressure that the Hitler regime began to exert on the Catholic Church and its organizations from January 1933 onwards. Like many other Catholics, Höffner left it to the Conference of Bishops to manage relations with Hitler and concentrated on receiving an Italian theological doctorate which he successfully defended in the summer of 1934. It was devoted to the theme of social justice and social love, which seems to be a telling theme at a time when the Nazi dictatorship became ever more arbitrary and brutal. Interestingly enough, he sent a copy of the manuscript to Nell-Breuning who did have some critical comments on it. Having completed his academic training at least for the time being, Höffner assumed responsibility for a parish in Saarbrücken, whose inner city was divided into three districts. This gave him an opportunity to make contact with local labor associations, but also with working-class inhabitants of the run-down areas around the railroad station and the canal harbor. Appreciating that he had grown up in an intact family, he went into the working-class neighborhoods in which he experienced very directly the miserable conditions of life in the backyards. When the Saarland was integrated into Nazi Germany in 1935 and the Gestapo appeared on the scene, political discussion in these quarters became confined to those who knew and trusted each other.

In November 1935 the teacher of religion at the local Oberrealschule fell ill, and Höffner was asked to take up his position. It did not take long for the education department of the regional government to become suspicious of his teaching. In May 1936 he mentioned to Nell-Breuning that he was interested in deepening his legal and social science training. Nell-Breuning recommended that he should go to Berlin, even though Höffner preferred Freiburg. As the Nazis did not recognize his Italian degree, he opted for a German doctorate in theology and decided to do both. In January 1938 he defended this dissertation, followed a year later by a diploma in economics. This paved the way for another doctorate – this time in economics – at the University of Freiburg, under none other than Walter Eucken. His topic was very much one that also interested his mentor: "The Struggle over Monopolies in the 15th and 16th Centuries." Nell-Breuning, who also read the manuscript, was more impressed this time than by his earlier work and the two began to discuss scholarly as well as social–political questions. Höffner stayed in Freiburg until June 1942 to submit his theological *Habilitation*, with Theodor Müncker, professor of moral theology, and Eucken as referees, though it took

Social Catholicism and social market economy   81

another two years before he was able to deliver the obligatory inaugural lecture before the faculty to obtain his *venia legendi*, the right to offer lectures. In 1941 he took charge of a parish in the suburb of Berlin-Schlachtensee before returning to the Trier Seminary in April 1943. It was during this period that he persuaded a local farmer in Kail on the Moselle River to hide a young Jewish woman whom he had apparently known in Berlin. At his behest, his sister provided a refuge for a Jewish physician and her husband. In short, throughout the war Höffner took considerable risks in rescuing victims of the regime who would otherwise have been deported and murdered. He also involved himself in a group of Catholic laypeople who began to ponder the shape of a Germany after the defeat of the Third Reich.

The insights that he gained from his years as an anti-Nazi priest and rescuer would profoundly influence not only his work as a clergyman, but also his sociopolitical activities after the war. It is significant that, having gained a professorship at his seminary, he immediately offered a course on social ethics. But he was anxious to teach larger numbers of students at a secular university and after more detours, Höffner was given a chair in Christian social sciences at Münster University. He was also successful at obtaining funding from the ministry of education and culture in Düsseldorf for an Institute of Christian Social Sciences that also received external support from the Bund Katholischer Unternehmer (BKU) (Association of Catholic Entrepreneurs). But instead of pursuing larger research projects, he devoted himself to the students who flocked to his lectures and seminars. He took them on excursions to visit factories and confronted them with the problems of modern industrial societies and the situation of workers and employers in the emergent Federal Republic. He also accepted many invitations to speak before associations and civic groups. Thus he also gave the keynote speech on the occasion of the founding of the BKU on March 27, 1949 titled "The Catholic Entrepreneur in the Coming Economic Order." He also issued a pastoral letter in which he stressed the importance of finding a solution to the social question. He invited Nell-Breuning as a speaker but, no less significantly, also Eberhard Welty, of the Dominican Walberberg monastery. He had been involved in the drafting of the Ahlen Program of the CDU in 1947 that had been quite critical of German capitalists and their role in the Third Reich. Among the other invitees were also representatives of the Deutsche Gewerkschaftsbund (DGB) as well as businessmen.[9]

It is at this point that a link must be made to the question of West German codetermination and the long debate that it unleashed. As is well known, in 1947 the British occupation authorities had supported the DGB's quest to introduce what came to be termed *paritätische Mitbestimmung* (codetermination based on the principle of parity between capital and labor) in the coal and steel industries of the Ruhr.[10] It provided for an equal representation between 'capital and labor' on company supervisory boards, chaired by a neutral person who, in case of a tie, had the decisive vote. Moreover, a 'worker director' was added to the management board with an equal voice. With the

82 Volker Berghahn

founding of the Federal Republic, legislative powers were transferred to the government and parliament in Bonn, and it did not take long for the trade unions to demand an expansion of coal and steel codetermination to all large corporations; the Ruhr coal and steel industrialists by contrast wanted to abolish it altogether. The subsequent political struggle ended in a sort of compromise: *paritätische Mitbestimmung* was upheld in the Ruhr industries, but not introduced in other large manufacturing companies. To soothe the DGB, a Works Constitution Act was passed in 1952 that established works councils with consultative rights, though no decision-making powers, as existed in the coal and steel industries.

What is significant here is that the BKU took up the debate in October 1949, but it led to major disagreements among its members. One of the BKU motions in October caused the greatest consternation, arguing that "the human being stands at the center of any perspective of the national or company economy. The right to co-determination is being recognized in social, personnel and economic questions."[11] This right, it was added, was part of natural law within a God-given order and is thus to be supported just like the right to property. Not surprisingly, putting codetermination on the same level as property rights upset not only many participants at the meeting but also Höffner who attended it. Just a few days later he therefore wrote to the BKU executive director, asking for "urgent" conversation on the motion. Certainly an "unlimited" codetermination was a formula that, as he put it very diplomatically, was not "quite fortunate." He added that a "somewhat more measured" formula had been found in another of the conference's working groups relating to the "re-ordering of property" and chaired by him.

Word of such radical tendencies also seems to have reached Cardinal Joseph Frings, the Archbishop of Cologne, even before the BKU meeting. He had become so alarmed by these tendencies that he put out a statement. In it, he praised the "openness" of Catholic entrepreneurs, but felt that the situation was too complicated to be dealt with in a "summary and general" fashion. It required a commentary to "avoid misunderstandings." He did not wish to reject out of hand codetermination in the "social, personnel and economic sphere." But this did not mean that it should be expanded to all three and without limitations. "Economic reason," if nothing else, demanded this. Business had to be transacted independently by a company's leadership if the enterprise was to be "operational and gainful," also for the employees. However, in Frings's view, employees should be given a primary right to have a say (*Mitspracherecht*) when a company was to be closed down, "jeopardizing the livelihoods of hundreds and thousands of employees." The introduction of codetermination by law could not be completed "by tomorrow," but had to be the terminus of a longer development in the course of which the forms and repercussions for the three spheres (and also for different size firms) would be tested in times of prosperity and recession.

With this letter the cardinal had delineated the scale and scope of the discussion of codetermination among most West German Catholics. If the

Social Catholicism and social market economy   83

protagonists of a social Catholicism that wanted to reorganize labor relations in the post-Nazi era had high hopes in the late 1940s, they were sorely disappointed. Two days after Frings's letter, on September 20, 1949, the BKU president wrote to Höffner that the motion was causing him "considerable headaches." He felt that it promised the workers too much and put a burden of responsibility on the entrepreneur that he could not assume. Especially the justification that codetermination was part of an order based on God's will and should be accepted on the same basis as the right to property went too far. This is why he suggested that he would like to talk to Höffner about these issues.

However, there were other, more leftist Catholic circles who wanted to broach the shaping of labor relations with a number of CDU deputies and to bring them together in a working circle to study Catholic social teaching in greater depth and to prepare them for the legislative task ahead of them. Such a group of Christian deputies was indeed formed after the 1949 elections. Its members either belonged to the world of enterprise or stood close to it. Höffner was invited to give a lecture before this circle. Beyond this, it was now sufficiently clear that both the Church and the BKU had no wish to introduce a right of codetermination that was founded in Catholic theology and natural law. There would be no shift in the power balance between the two sides of industry and even the 1976 reforms of codetermination law did not adopt the coal and steel model. Rather the task was to enshrine the property guarantee in the Basic Law as one of the foundational principles of the socioeconomic order of the Federal Republic that could not be changed. The owners continued to occupy the dominant position, and in this respect it did not matter whether they were running a family enterprise themselves or were merely shareholders in a major West German corporation.

In the 1950s, Höffner endeavored to explain this position inside and outside the BKU, knowing that there were still quite a few who wanted to abolish *paritätische Mitbestimmung* in coal and steel. Accordingly, he used his Institute of Christian Social Sciences to publish the ideas of his more conservative vision of labor relations. He continued to lecture to students and also accepted invitations to speak before companies, such as the Buderus Works or the china manufacturer Villeroy & Boch. On November 27, 1953 he addressed a meeting of the Bundesvereinigung deutscher Arbeitgeberverbände (BdA) (Employers' Federation) with the telling title "The Mensch as the Center of the Social Order." Its presidents, Walter Raymond and Constantin Paulssen took a 'soft' approach as far as labor relations were concerned that was partially inspired by German models of the 1920s related to the discovery by psychologists of the 'worker's soul' and by the American model of 'human relations' that appeared in West Germany in the early 1950s.[12] Höffner now held up this 'social order' to his audiences as a commandment of social justice and Christian love, but also as a need to preserve the social peace, with the memory of the much more conflictual industrial relations of the Weimar years constantly hovering in the background. He also promoted the schooling

84 *Volker Berghahn*

of Christian trade unionists so that they were thoroughly familiar with the institutions and practices of labor relations and bargaining. His aim was not only to generate solidarities within the framework of the unfolding social market economy, but also to encourage self-responsibility. With the exception of the communists, he was in touch with virtually all organizations and political parties, but also remained conscious of his pastoral duties that he had fulfilled before 1945 in parishes in Saarbrücken, the Rhineland and in Berlin. He acted as an adviser to the Catholic weekly *Rheinischer Merkur*, and joined various committees set up by the ministerial bureaucracy to investigate current issues of family and youth policy. It was only in the 1960s that he was forced to reduce these activities when he was inaugurated as bishop of Münster in September 1962 before being installed as Frings's successor as Archbishop of Cologne in April 1969.

There can be little doubt that Höffner was one of the most important representatives of the social Catholic wing in West Germany. He was familiar with the ideas of social market economy, having studied both theology and economics. As a former student at Freiburg, he also had close knowledge of ordoliberalism and thus provided a striking and often overlooked link between postwar Protestant economic thought and practice and Rhenish social Catholicism. But it is time to move on to Nell-Breuning, the other major figure in the Catholic camp without whom the evolution of the social market economy cannot be understood and who must be integrated into current discourses about the German model of running a modern industrial economy and society. He is a particularly interesting figure on the Catholic side of the themes covered in this chapter and this anthology because he adopted the most poignant criticism of the weaknesses of social market economy and the most radical positions with regard to worker participation and codetermination.

Oswald von Nell-Breuning and the 'bending' of capitalism

Oswald von Nell-Breuning was born in the old Roman town of Trier on March 8, 1890 as the son of Arthur von Nell and his wife Bernharda von Breuning.[13] They tended a wine-growing and wine-making estate not far from the Moselle river and Arthur expected Oswald to inherit and continue the enterprise. But his wealthy parents also valued education and sent their son to the Friedrich-Wilhelm Gymnasium in Trier where he learned ancient Greek and Latin and received a humanistic *Bildung*. Having completed his *Abitur*, he first decided to study the sciences, but after several moves between the universities of Kiel, Munich, Strasburg, and Berlin, as was quite common in those days, he finally opted for philosophy and theology in 1910 and entered the Jesuit order two years later. He continued his training at the Jesuits' high school near Maastricht in the Netherlands. After further theological studies he was ordained in 1921 and finally completed his doctoral dissertation at the University of Münster titled "Basic Outlines of the Morality of the Stock Market" in 1928. In other words, he had become particularly interested in ethical questions of modern economics.

A few months later, he was fortunate enough to be appointed to a professorship of Church law, moral theology, and social sciences at the Philosophical-Theological High School of Sankt Georgen in Frankfurt. Both his dissertation but also a book that he published in 1930 titled *Labor Law and Morality* caught the attention of the Vatican and Pius XI invited him to participate in the preparation of the *Quadragesimo anno* encyclical. Subsequently, Nell-Breuning published a commentary on this document that he titled "The Social Encyclical," but returned to Germany and experienced the repression of the Hitler dictatorship. He was banned from writing and publishing in 1936 and was sentenced during the war to two years of penitentiary for currency dealings in which he was allegedly involved, but was spared from serving his term. It was not difficult to demonstrate his anti-Nazi positions to the Allies and, like Eucken, he resumed his lectures at Sankt Georgen and, from 1948, also at Frankfurt University. In the same year he was appointed to the Scientific Advisory Council of the Verwaltung für Wirtschaft, the Allied precursor of the Federal Economics Ministry under Ludwig Erhard. He also worked on housing problems, and in 1950 the Ministry for Urban Reconstruction and Housing made him the vice chair of its council of experts. Like Höffner, Nell-Breuning was therefore not just a teacher but also involved in practical policymaking that gained him national recognition.

In trying to understand his attitudes toward post-Nazi reconstruction, it is important that in the 1920s he came under the intellectual influence of the Archbishop of Cologne, Cardinal Schulte. Both of them accepted the reality of a capitalist–industrial economy, but rejected the mentalities of an 'unrestrained greed' that was deemed 'mammonistic.' This meant that he also distanced himself from 'the romanticizing proclivities' among the Catholic clergy and lay movement. Later he added that capitalism was "basically moral" and "good as well as useful" so long as it was embedded in the social order "as it should be." There were corporatist elements in his thinking at the time of the 1931 encyclical that he later regretted espousing. In 1968 he confessed to being "totally upset" when he discovered that Pius XI had called the proto-fascist Austria of 1934 under Chancellor Engelbert Dollfuss a "Quadragesimo-anno State." It seems therefore that Nell-Breuning was influenced by *ständestaatliche* ideas in the 1930s, but shed them once the true face of fascism had become abundantly clear to him so that after 1945 he firmly identified with the democratic parliamentarism and the principles of social market economy, except that he hoped to transform the Erhardian model, with the help of the trade unions and the SPD, into a more finely balanced political economy.

His positions on these issues must be seen against the background of another insight that he had gained from the past. On the one hand, he went back to the early social Catholicism of Adolf Kolping and W. E. von Ketteler,

86   Volker Berghahn

both of whom postulated that the Church had a more general obligation toward the emerging working class and the distressing socioeconomic conditions under which they had to live in the German Empire (Nell-Breuning, 1990).[14] Thus the Volksverein für das katholische Deutschland took the path of offering tangible help to Catholic workers. But the Volksverein continued to be opposed by the 'integralists' who insisted that the Church's mission and contemporary politics had to be kept separate. Nell-Breuning was among those who, in retrospect, defended the controversial policies of the Catholic Center Party during the interwar years, but criticized the 'integralists' as a movement that stood in the way of a modernization of Catholicism. So, to him there was a lot of ballast to be thrown overboard after 1945, and he insisted that it was within the powers of the Church "to stop mistakes that it had committed against the working class in the past und to prevent their repetition and hence further damage" in the future. For this reason, Nell-Breuning also favored a relaxation of tensions that had arisen between West German Catholicism and the DGB. As Wolfgang Schroeder put it, he made this reconciliation "a central concern" and thus moved the interpretation of Christian social thought "farthest in the direction of unionist and Social Democrat policy."

Over time, Nell-Breuning developed good contacts with Hans Böckler and other DGB leaders. He gave lectures to young trade unionists and was invited in 1973 to contribute an article to *Gewerkschaftliche Monatshefte* titled "The Catholic Church and the Trade Unions" (Nell-Breuning, 1990, pp. 82–96). He admitted that the Church had treated the unions for a long time without much understanding. Its representatives witnessed the misery of the workers, but had vigorously opposed their Marxist class analysis. Accepting in principle that Germany had been a class society, he thought it legitimate that German workers should struggle to change it. At the same time he believed that the time had come for transcending class differences. After all, Pius XI, too, had spoken in his 1931 encyclical against an "Either-Or" and for an "As-Well-As." He thus felt no reluctance to criticize entrepreneurs who were denouncing priests devoted to social welfare in industrial cities as "Hetzkapläne."

There is another article by Nell-Breuning, titled "Gewerkschaften" that is even more important for an understanding of Nell-Breuning's views of capitalism and codetermination (Nell-Breuning, 1990, pp. 69–81). It began in a rather Marxist vein in that he started with the interaction of two social classes, among which one disposes over the means of production and the other, while lacking such ownership, offered its labor to be deployed by the owners of the means of production. But the use of Marx's ideas provided, in Nell-Breuning's view, at the same time a chance to cast off the ideological and economic errors that Marx had made. After all, the goal was, as had already been mentioned in *Quadragesimo anno*, to construct a just societal order. It was the Christian profession of God's justice that demanded a commitment to social justice in this world and to take sides with parts of the population that

Social Catholicism and social market economy   87

lived under oppression. What Nell-Breuning required was a "new definition of a Christian societal ethic." The question was, though, what would happen if the divergent class interests clashed. Did the owners still have the upper hand? Frings and Höffner sided with the owners which meant that – as Nell-Breuning put it in another article "Property and Co-determination" – that the two were irreconcilable. But he also envisioned a constellation in which one side put in its capital, with the other side providing its personal labor so that they could wield their authority jointly. They found themselves in a position of shared responsibility. While Nell-Breuning thought that it would be difficult to balance the two sides in smaller and medium-sized enterprises, he envisioned the possibility of a different solution for large anonymous corporations. This alternative was that the director of the enterprise, rather than being installed by the shareholders alone, could just as well be authorized by those who provide the capital *jointly* with those who proffered their labor. Codetermination was thus a system in which capital and labor together nominate the directors of the firm and put them into their entrepreneurial positions to manage the company.

All this sounded rather abstract but gains greater transparency if we connect it with paritetic codetermination in which capital and labor were equally represented on the supervisory board and headed by a neutral chair, with the day-to-day decision-making authority laid into the hands of the management board with a labor director among them. What Nell-Breuning ultimately had in mind was not to 'break' a capitalist market economy as the Marxists kept demanding, but to 'bend' (*umbiegen*) it in the direction of the employees. This arrangement was to put the owners under the obligation to bear the interests of the employees constantly in mind. And once this mechanism had been established within the corporation, it would also make certain that a consciousness of social responsibility and the need for social justice would affect the ethos of the national industrial economy as a whole.

It is against the backdrop of these calculations that Nell-Breuning returned to the social market economy and took on Müller-Armack by asking in another article "How 'Social' Is the Social Market Economy?" (Nell-Breuning, 1990, pp. 222–238). Nell-Breuning admitted that Müller-Armack's edifice of ideas had been exceptionally attractive. Its success during the boom years of the 1950s had facilitated the expansion of the West German welfare state in a whole range of social programs. But, as Nell-Breuning quoted the father of social market economy, this social progress had been achieved with measures that were "*marktkonform*," i.e., they did not touch the capitalist property structures. Thus, prosperity and greater social justice could be pursued, but only for as long as the gains were large enough to also finance social policies. Once this was no longer the case the older class conflicts would resurface and, in the absence of a *paritätische Mitbestimmung* framework, would be all the more difficult to resolve.

This became of course abundantly clear in the prolonged economic crisis of the 1970s, whose causes lay, inter alia, in the disastrous American war in

88 Volker Berghahn

Southeast Asia. Its escalating costs unhinged the international currency system of Bretton Woods, followed by the enormous hikes in the price of oil in 1973. It was at that point that West Germany's employers were relieved that they had always refused to accede to union demands for an expansion of *paritätische Mitbestimmung*; the DGB on the other hand came to regret that it had not pushed much harder for this expansion to secure a system of social justice that could not be reversed, as it subsequently was with the advent of neoliberalism in the 1980s.

This new phase in the evolution of capitalism was decidedly not social, as Reaganism and Thatcherism began to dismantle the postwar welfare state, cut public expenditure, privatized the public sector enterprises, gave tax breaks to the rich, reinforced the power of the owners and shareholders and moved the western economies in the direction of greater social injustice, and the impoverishment of ever larger sections, especially of the American and British populations. This is why it is useful to recall not only Eucken, Müller-Armack, and Erhard, but also Höffner and Nell-Breuning and the social Catholic tradition of the social and economic system of the Federal Republic, and to study the larger context of the varieties of capitalism that make up an increasingly multipolar international economy. To understand the contemporary shape of the German variant, looking back on the history of the social market economy is quite illuminating. Even more importantly perhaps, this retrospective reminds us of the social responsibilities that Germany's economic, political, and cultural elites felt during the early postwar decades and that these elites would ignore today only at their peril. After all, in the past, social market economy has always been more than organizing and running a modern economy efficiently and profitably in which the winners take all. Rather, it is an edifice grounded in social and ethical imperatives. Today, the term social market economy is often invoked, but with various definitions. For this reason, it seems prudent to remember the definition that Erhard offered after the war, but also to reconstruct the thoughts of Eucken, Hoeffner, and Nell-Breuning on the subject.

Notes

1 For a most helpful and critical assessment of recent developments in American capitalism, see Rahman and Thelen (2018). I would like to thank the authors for making this paper available to me.

2 See also Berghahn and Vitols (2006).

3 To limit the number of notes for this article, this analysis is based on: von Klinckowstroem (2000), Heinemann (1989), Ptak (2004), Dathe and Goldschmidt (2003). To be sure, Eucken was not the only economist to belong to the 'Freiburg Circles,' see, e.g., Blumenberg-Lampe (1973). To avoid confusion, it seems important to differentiate Eucken's 'neoliberalism' from its usage today to describe the current Anglo-American type of capitalism that is different from 'ordoliberalism' and German social market economy, as it was defined in the 1950s and is today.

4 See, e.g., Goldschmidt (2005) and Maier (2014).

Social Catholicism and social market economy 89

5 See Eucken (1948). See also the article by his wife, Edith von Erdsiek-Eucken (1948). She provides a good insight into the attitudes and intellectual and psychic climate prevalent in the Eucken household after the end of the Nazi dictatorship and the physical destruction around them, from which Freiburg was not spared at the very end of the war, not to mention their sense of moral catastrophe that was also widespread in West Germany during the late 1940s.

6 Reprinted in Flechtheim (1973, pp. 162–163).

7 These Social Committees had been founded after 1945 and became a powerful voice of social Catholicism within the CDU. Its early leader was Jakob Kaiser, who had been a member of the Catholic Center Party and the Christian trade unions during the Weimar State. After the Nazi seizure of power, he cooperated with the Social Democrat Wilhelm Leuschner. While Leuschner was arrested, tried and executed after the failed July 1944 plot to assassinate Hitler, Kaiser survived and went into hiding in Potsdam. After 1945, Kaiser was at first active in the CDU of the Soviet zone, but escaped to the West after East Germany became Stalinized. As deputy chairman of the Western CDU, many viewed him as Konrad Adenauer's counterpart, in whose government he became Minister for All-German Questions. Karl Arnold was not as prominent as Kaiser before 1933. Persecuted by the Nazis, he joined the Rhenish CDU and became Kaiser's successor of the CDA Social Committees. Later, Norbert Blüm, born in 1935, emerged as the most influential social Catholic politician, first as the executive director of the CDA committees and from 1977 as their chair.

8 See Trippen (2009) and Trippen (2012). I would like to thank Dr. Arnd Küppers for drawing my attention to Cardinal Höffner on whom I subsequently found Trippen's two-volume study. The details of his biography and professional work are taken from Volume I seriatim without specific page references to save space.

9 The Ahlen Program of the CDU of the British Zone was adopted at their meeting on 1–3 February 1947. Reprinted in Flechtheim (1973, pp. 157–162). Welty is another important cleric in the context. Apart from theology, he had studied economics and sociology. He joined the Dominican High School at Walberberg in 1930 and taught Ethics and Moral Theology. After the war he became an advocate of "Christian Socialism" which is reflected in the Ahlen Program. Although he did not become as well known as Höffner, he was close to the Social Committees of the CDU and also talked to the SPD when its reformist wing drew up the Godesberg Program of 1959.

10 This arrangement concerned the composition of the supervisory board, and also placed a 'worker director' on the management board as an equal member. See, e.g., Berghahn and Karsten (1987, pp. 104ff., 140ff.).

11 On these debates within the BKU and the Catholic Church see Trippen (2009, pp. 165ff.).

12 On the BdA and its ideology under Raymond and Paulssen see, e.g., Berghahn (1986, pp. 230ff.).

13 For concise biographical and professional information with a list of further literature, see Wikipedia contributors (2018, November 16). See also Nell-Breuning (1980).

14 As indicated by the sub-title this is an excellent collection of Nell-Breuning's most important writings.

References

Albert, M. (1991). Capitalisme contre capitalisme. *Politique étrangère 56*(4) 980–981.

Berghahn, V. (1986). *The Americanisation of West German industry, 1945–1973*. New York, NY: Berg.

90 *Volker Berghahn*

Berghahn, V., & Karsten, D. (1987). *Industrial relations in West Germany*. Oxford, UK: Oxford University Press.

Berghahn, V., & Vitols, S. (2006). *Gibt es einen deutschen Kapitalismus? Traditionen und globale Perspektiven der sozialen Marktwirtschaft*. Frankfurt, Germany: Campus.

Blumenberg-Lampe, C. (1973). *Das wirtschaftspolitische Programm der Freiburger Kreise*. Berlin, Germany: Duncker & Humblot.

Dathe, U., & Goldschmidt, N. (2003). Wie der Vater, so der Sohn? Neue Erkenntnisse zu Walter Euckens Leben und Werk anhand des Nachlasses von Rudolf Eucken in Jena. *ORDO. Jahrbuch für die Ordnung von Wirtschaft und Gesellschaft 54* 22–53.

Erdsiek-Eucken, E. v. (1948). Chaos und Stagnation. *ORDO 1* 3–15.

Eucken, W. (1948). Das ordnungspolitische Problem. *ORDO 1* 56–90.

Eucken, W. (1949). Wettbewerbsordnung und ihre Verwirklichung. *ORDO 2* 1–99.

Eucken, W. (1952). *Grundsätze der Wirtschaftspolitik*. Tübingen, Germany: Mohr Siebeck.

Flechtheim, O. K. (1973). *Die Parteien der Bundesrepublik Deutschland*. Hamburg.

Goldschmidt, N. (Ed.). (2005). *Wirtschaft, Politik und Freiheit. Freiburger Wirtschaftswissenschaftler und der Widerstand*. Tübingen, Germany: Mohr Siebeck.

Gräfin von Klinckowstroem, W. (2001). Walter Eucken. Eine biografische Skizze. In L. Gerken (Ed.), *Walter Eucken und sein Werk. Rückblick auf einen Vordenker der sozialen Marktwirtschaft* (pp. 53–115). Tübingen, Germany: Mohr Siebeck.

Hall, P., & Soskice, D. (2001). *Varieties of capitalism: The international foundations of comparative advantage*. Oxford, UK: Oxford University Press.

Heinemann, A. (1989). *Die Freiburger Schule und ihre geistigen Wurzeln*. Munich, Germany: VVF.

Maier, H. (Ed.). (2014). *Die Freiburger Kreise. Akademische Widerstand und Soziale Marktwirtschaft*. Paderborn, Germany: Ferdinand Schöningh.

Nell-Breuning, O. v. (1980). *Arbeitsmarkt und Menschenwürde*. Münster, Germany: Aschendorff.

Nell-Breuning, O. v. (1990). *Oswald von Nell-Breuning. Den Kapitalismus umbiegen. Schriften zu Kirche, Wirtschaft und Gesellschaft. Ein Lesebuch*. H. Hengsbach (Ed.). Düsseldorf, Germany: Patmos.

Ptak, R. (2004). *Vom Ordoliberalismus zur Sozialen Marktwirtschaft*. Opladen, Germany: Springer.

Rahman, K. S., & Thelen, K. (2018). Broken contract: The rise of the networked firm and the transformation of 21st-century capitalism. *CES Papers*, Cambridge, MA.

Trippen, N. (2009). *Joseph Kardinal Höffner (1906–1987), Vol. I: Lebensweg und Wirken als christlicher Sozialwissenschaftler bis 1962*. Paderborn, Germany: Ferdinand Schöningh.

Trippen, N. (2012). *Joseph Kardinal Höffner (1906–1987), Vol. II: Seine bischöflichen Jahre, 1962–1987*. Paderborn, Germany: Ferdinand Schöningh.

Wikipedia. (2018, November 16). Oswald von Nell-Breuning. Retrieved January 24, 2019, from https://de.wikipedia.org/w/index.php?title=Oswald_von_Nell-Breuning&oldid=182233683

5 Ordoliberalism and the cross-national disciplinary revolution in liberalism[1]

Kenneth Dyson

Introduction

The main significance of ordoliberalism does not lie in its independent contribution to economic theory or in its being a distinctively German idea. It stems from representing a certain way of looking at the individual, the market, and the state and at how they relate to each other. It has, in short, the hallmarks of a tradition (see Dyson, 2017). The ordoliberal tradition is associated with a certain mindset. It is grounded in a hybrid liberal–conservative ideology; in a distinctive set of ethical commitments when thinking about political economy; in a rejection of both collectivism and the laissez-faire liberal state; in a recognition that the chief danger to liberalism can come from within; in opposition to a naturalistic conception of the market as a self-correcting mechanism that enshrines competition; and in the belief that a flourishing and sustainable liberal order requires a disciplinary framework of binding precommitments. Economic, financial, and monetary policies must be, first and foremost, principle-based and be the responsibility of public institutions with the authority to safeguard these principles. Not least for reasons connected to its conservative–liberal ideological character, the ordoliberal tradition remains embattled. It is dismissed as a historical museum piece or castigated as authoritarian and rooted in Old Testament justice.

This chapter examines the nature of ordoliberalism as a tradition; its embeddedness in a wider cross-national disciplinary revolution in liberalism; the distinctive roots of this disciplinary revolution in aristocratic liberalism, in ethical philosophy, and in religion; and the significance of ordoliberalism, using Germany as a case study.

The chapter shows, on the one hand, that ordoliberalism has borrowed heavily from US-based economics and has had a resonance well beyond Germany: and, on the other, how it has remained highly contested, not just internationally but even within Germany. Ordoliberalism endured in Germany because it offered a rhetorical device to justify strategic positioning as a creditor state in European and international negotiations (see Dyson, 2014). As a rhetorical device it owed much of its substantive content as macroeconomic theory to taking on board post-1970s US-based credibility

92   Kenneth Dyson

and time-consistency theory. Credibility and time-consistency theory was consistent with the conservative–liberal mindset of ordoliberalism.

The nature of the ordoliberal tradition

A tradition does not begin with a name. The term ordoliberalism dates from the year of Walter Eucken's death (Moeller, 1950). However, as the next section shows, the lineaments of the tradition stretch further back to before the Great Depression of the 1930s. They are manifested in Britain, France, Italy, and the United States, as well as in Germany. Moreover, its German manifestation borrows heavily from earlier non-German sources, notably in the early Chicago School (Köhler & Kolev, 2011). Equally, a tradition does not just emerge from borrowing through personal networking, crossreferencing, and citations. It exists in the form of correspondence in the ways in which, independently of each other, thinkers respond to their own experiences. Shared experience in times of existential crisis serves as the trigger for the emergence of a tradition. Common ideological outlook shapes the correspondence in how thinkers respond. In short, material and ideational factors collude in the formation of a tradition.

The lens of tradition helps in avoiding a reductive view of ordoliberalism as a certain school, as a certain set of formal texts, and as having a single authentic form. This kind of view reduces ordoliberalism to the Freiburg School, to Walter Eucken's *Grundsätze der Wirtschaftspolitik* (1952) and to the Eucken School's publications as they appeared from 1934/1935 to 1952. It decontextualizes ordoliberalism in space and in time. It excludes non-Germans as at best peripheral, as well as many Germans who are held to be imperfect fits (like Alfred Müller-Armack) or to have departed from the authentic tradition (like the Austrian Friedrich Hayek). The contributions of Eucken and the early Freiburg School to the formalized knowledge of the ordoliberal tradition remain enormously important. However, the tradition is far richer than this narrow and Germanic perspective captures.

The ordoliberal tradition's character is defined by three features.[2] First, it takes the form of tacit as well as explicit knowledge. Being part of the tradition does not necessarily depend on having read certain formal texts and acting to implement their prescriptions. Few German officials who reveal ordoliberal preferences have read ordoliberal foundational texts. These texts tend to be read, selectively and instrumentally, by the speech writers who seek to justify a certain set of policy positions.[3] Teaching of German economics and law offers limited, often no, direct exposure to ordoliberal foundational texts. And yet, German officials who have graduated in these subjects are accused of pursuing an ordoliberal agenda for the European Union (EU) and the euro area. This paradox resolves when one notes that the ordoliberal tradition has been absorbed into the taken-for-granted background knowledge of certain German institutions. It has been absorbed in this way because of its instrumental value in safeguarding certain German vital national and

Ordoliberalism and revolution in liberalism 93

institutional interests. Ordoliberal rhetorical referencing is part of strategic positioning in the practice of negotiating complex domestic and EU economic and political relations. Certain texts were not the primary cause of German officials adopting policy positions that corresponded with ordoliberal principles. Rather, they were drawn on selectively to justify national and institutional interests.

Second, the ordoliberal tradition is held together by crosscutting and criss-crossing features, not all of which are necessarily present in those who feel a sense of belonging. A tradition manifests the variety that accompanies family resemblance (see Wittgenstein, [1953] 2009). The lens of family resemblance casts light on two characteristics of the ordoliberal tradition: its open and porous borders; and the way in which some thinkers are more akin to 'natives' of the tradition and others are 'migrants.' Its porous borders are evident in its relations with the Austrian tradition, especially as represented by Hayek. The Austrians and the ordoliberals were in broad agreement in their diagnosis of the causes of the Great Depression in the 1930s. They adhered to the same monetary theory of the business cycle. Similarly, the monetarism of the Chicago School from the 1960s, and later US-based work on credibility and time-consistency, resonated within the monetary policy thinking of ordoliberalism (Janssen, 2006). They gave intellectual support to the principles of price stability and consistency.

Similarly, the tradition was a complex mixture of a few natives and many migrants. The star Italian economist Luigi Einaudi's migration into the tradition dated from 1942 when he was 68 (Giordano, 2006). The ordoliberalism of the French economist Jacques Rueff and of the philosopher Louis Rougier dated from the Lippmann Colloquium in Paris in August 1938 (Audier, 2012). Hayek's belonging to the precepts of the Eucken School lasted from around 1935 to around 1948 (Köhler & Kolev, 2011). Figures like Einaudi, Hayek, Rougier, and Rueff were too intellectually inquisitive and too long-lived to count as pure natives of the ordoliberal tradition.

Third, ordoliberalism was a tradition in the making. It was reinvented in the face of changing circumstances and challenges by successive generations of thinkers. In the process the relationship of the ordoliberal tradition to its intellectual roots became attenuated. Over time, the Freiburg School evolved. Freiburg 1 was the Eucken School, the morphological method of thinking about orders, and the constructivist conception of the state as market-maker (Eucken, 1940, 1952). Freiburg 2 reflected the arrival of Hayek and the evolutionary conception of markets as a discovery procedure (Hayek, 1967; Hoppmann, 1988). Freiburg 3 involved a relaunch as 'constitutional economics,' as developed by the US economist James Buchanan (1991). It was grounded in methodological individualism and in public choice theory, demystifying the state of Eucken (Vanberg, 2011). Certain features recurred, but Freiburg 1 and Freiburg 3 exhibited marked differences.

More generally, the crisis of the 1970s – the collapse of the Bretton Woods system, the oil-price shocks, and inflation with high unemployment –

94   Kenneth Dyson

generated new thinking in mainstream US-based economics that helped to reinvigorate the ordoliberal tradition. First, Chicago-style monetarism and later credibility and time-consistency theory added intellectual power to the principles of price stability and of long-term consistency in economic policy. They entered the mainstream at a time when the debate about European monetary integration and union was intensifying. In the process they helped to reestablish the relevance of ordoliberalism to the negotiations about Economic and Monetary Union (EMU) and its reform. However, this attributed significance of ordoliberalism in EMU hid a substantive content that was non-Germanic in origin.

The lens of invented tradition throws light on the processes of memorizing and forgetting in ordoliberalism. Later thinkers and commentators 'cherry-pick' past texts. The effects are apparent in the reputation of Wilhem Röpke. In the 1920s–1930s he was a much more respected economist than Eucken both in Germany and abroad; in the 1940s–1950s he was more widely read than Eucken; and he enjoyed much closer relations with Ludwig Erhard and with Luigi Einaudi when they were preparing stabilization programs in postwar Germany and Italy than did Eucken. And yet, when it came to the definition of German policy positions on the design of the euro area, and on its reforms in the context of the post-2007 financial, economic, and sovereign debt crises, the reference was to Eucken. Röpke's sociological ordoliberalism did not serve as a reference point. What was forgotten was Röpke's insistence on the moral limits on competitive markets and his fears that a market fundamentalism could 'poison' society and threaten social solidarity (Röpke, 1942, 1958). Röpke's position was shared by other ordoliberals: Rougier and Rueff in France; Einaudi and Costantino Bresciani-Turroni in Italy; and Müller-Armack and Alexander Rüstow in Germany, not to mention many Catholic social thinkers like Götz Briefs and Luigi Sturzo.

What then are the shared features that bind ordoliberalism as a tradition? In answering this question, one must bear in mind that – other than a common, hybrid liberal–conservative mindset – one unifying feature is not necessarily found in all who identify with the tradition.

- an austere and ascetic view of civic virtue;
- intellectual hostility to utilitarianism, to materialism, and to philistine elites and publics;
- attachment to law, order, morality, and personal conscience;
- the need for social hierarchy and for respect for authority;
- the sacrosanct nature of private property, qualified by lack of equal regard for all kinds of property, notably unproductive capital;
- distaste for many 'unhealthy' middle-class values, notably the dominance of the commercial spirit;
- respect for the independently minded, creative artisan, for family businesses, for the free professions, and for the balance and solidity of farming and rural communities;

Ordoliberalism and revolution in liberalism   95

- the interdependence of the social, legal, economic, and political orders;
- the strong but limited state – strong in the face of mass politics and limited to 'market-conforming' intervention;
- an educated, cultivated, and disinterested elite that rules in the name of the general interest as servants of the community;
- a cautious approach to democracy that protects both individual rights and public virtue from the political demagogue and the excesses of public opinion;
- the need for sources of influence that are independent of government: for instance, via decentralization and via non-majoritarian institutions, notably the law, academia, central banks, and regulators of competitive markets;
- a juridical, rule-based market order; rejection of untrammeled private market power; competitive markets as a safeguard of individual liberty;
- price and financial stability as preconditions of a liberal order;
- profound skepticism that history is an unfolding of moral and intellectual progress.

The embedded nature of the ordoliberal tradition

The ordoliberal tradition's porous boundaries were evident not just in relation to other traditions of political economy. They were apparent in cross-national terms. Ordoliberalism was one – major – manifestation of a wider disciplinary revolution in liberalism. This cross-national disciplinary revolution took the form of the belief that historical laissez-faire liberalism had failed and had left space within which collectivist – socialist, communist, and fascist – forms of political economy could gather political support. The lesson of the interwar crisis, notably the Great Depression and the rise of fascism, was that the renovation of liberalism was necessary. Liberalism had to be saved from its past errors.

The cross-national foundational event was the Lippmann Colloquium in August 1938. This colloquium was convened by the French philosopher Louis Rougier in Paris to debate Walter Lippmann's *The Good Society* (1937) and to launch a cross-national network to renew liberalism. It was the precursor of the postwar Mont Pèlerin Society (Plickert, 2008). Lippmann's critique of the experimentalism of the US New Deal under President Roosevelt had been inspired by Frank Knight's ethical critique of laissez-faire liberalism and Henry Simons's advocacy of a rule-based monetary and credit policy (Knight, 1935; Simons, 1936). Knight and Simons were the two leading figures in the establishment of the Chicago School in the 1930s (Emmett, 2009). Walter Eucken – in part through his student Friedrich Lutz – was influenced by Simons's critique of discretionary monetary policy. The early Chicago School had a major influence on the economic theory-building of the German ordoliberals. Later, the constitutional economics of Freiburg 3 (see above) drew on these early Chicago roots, via the medium of Buchanan,

96 *Kenneth Dyson*

who had been a student of Knight. Buchanan (1991) was a critic of the later Chicago School's fundamentalist conception of markets as perfectly efficient and self-correcting.

In interwar Britain the main advocate of disciplinary liberalism was the treasury economist Ralph Hawtrey. Like Knight, Hawtrey (1926) advocated an ethical renewal of liberalism based on rules. He was also a staunch critic of his Cambridge colleague John Maynard Keynes. Hawtrey supported external discipline through the gold standard; an independent central bank; tight restrictions on credit; and rule-based fiscal policy. In the 1920s he was more cited than Keynes in the economics literature and in the top 10 for citations over the period 1920–1944 (Deutscher, 1990). His influence was marked in the United States. Before and during the Bretton Woods negotiations, Hawtrey opposed Keynes's proposals for international credit provision as likely to encourage lax behavior by debtor states. In the case of Hawtrey, there is no evidence of contact with German ordoliberals. Nevertheless, his work on the nature and implications of the interwar crisis revealed a marked correspondence in thinking.

In the case of interwar France, the main disciplinary liberals were Charles Rist at the Banque de France, Jacques Rueff, the inspector of finance and senior treasury official in the 1930s, and the philosopher Louis Rougier. Rougier and Rueff went further than Rist in attempting to systematize their thinking about the renovation of liberalism from the late 1930s, especially after the Lippmann Colloquium. Rougier was, above all, the prewar intellectual entrepreneur of the renovation of liberalism in France and internationally. His economic thought drew heavily on Michel Allais and on Rueff (Rougier, [1938]/1949). Rueff's monumental *L'Ordre social* (1945) called for firm external exchange-rate discipline; for an end to fiscal deficits; and for the creation of new, independent international and national bodies to monitor and sanction fiscal positions. The book closes with a fierce denunciation of the fiscal profligacy of governments. Rueff went much further than Eucken in elaborating the institutional arrangements and rules for fiscal policy. His proposals bore a close correspondence with the EU Stability and Growth Pact (SGP) of 1997 and the fiscal compact treaty of 2011. In 1958 Rueff was called on by the new French President Charles de Gaulle to produce measures to stabilize the franc. He also proposed major liberalization reforms. However, Rougier and Rueff proved marginal figures within French economic thought (Denord, 2007). Unlike Einaudi in Italy and Eucken and the Freiburg School in Germany they lacked the postwar association with resistance to Nazi tyranny and, in their case, were compromised by links to the Vichy regime.

The two main representatives of disciplinary liberalism in postwar Italy were Einaudi (1942) and Bresciani-Turroni ([1945] 2006), both star technical economists. Their approach to postwar stabilization and reconstruction in 1944–1947 ran counter to the international mainstream. They advocated the domestic 'house-in-order' approach. Einaudi – as budget minister and as

Ordoliberalism and revolution in liberalism   97

governor of the Banca d'Italia – pressed for immediate deflation, with tight monetary and credit policies and public spending cuts. In contrast, Bresciani-Turroni recommended a more gradual approach that would minimize and equalize social sacrifices by accepting a measure of foreign aid to cover the external deficit (Bini, 1992; Costabile, 2010).

Beginning in 1942, Einaudi deepened his friendship with Röpke, arranging for the publication of his *Die Gesellschaftskrise der Gegenwart* (1942) in Italian, giving it a lengthy and very positive review, and later inviting Röpke to meetings of the new Italian Liberal Party (Einaudi 1942). Röpke's work was taken up by numerous Italian liberal intellectuals, including Einaudi, Panfilo Gentile, Ernesto Rossi, and Dom Luigi Sturzo. It struck a chord with the strong tradition of Christian humanism in Italy, with its intellectual roots in classical philosophy, the Renaissance, and the Enlightenment. A major reason for this reception was the shared belief with Röpke in the moral limits of the market and in the need to ensure that economic outcomes did not endanger the social solidarity that was the necessary basis for a sustainable liberal order. The Italian reception was essentially of sociological ordoliberalism, not Eucken's variant.

Disciplinary liberalism remained an embattled tradition in France and Italy. Nevertheless, both states possessed a small, technocratic elite that retained a commitment to a rule-based stabilization tradition. These traditions were legitimated by reference to domestic historical memories. In the case of France, the reference points were the stabilization of the French franc in 1926–1927 under Raymond Poincaré (in which Rist and Rueff had been closely involved) and the stabilization of the franc in 1958 (when again Rueff had been involved). In the case of Italy, the reference point was the 'Einaudi experiment' in 1944–1948, notably during the Italian crisis in 2011–2013. The technocratic elites who identified with disciplinary liberalism in France and Italy were pessimistic about the quality and the effectiveness of their domestic political classes. The Italian central banker and later treasury minister Guido Carli (1993) summarized the approach as persuading political elites to embrace an external constraint (*vincolo esterno*). The domestic house could be put in order through an external discipline (Dyson & Featherstone, 1996). Till 1971 to 1973 the instrument had been the Bretton Woods system; from 1979 to 1999 it was the European Exchange Rate Mechanism (ERM); and from 1993 it was the Maastricht Treaty and the completion of monetary union in 1999.

For this reason, the rule-based approach to EMU is not to be understood as simply a German-imposed ordoliberal settlement. It was grounded in a wider cross-national elite commitment to using a disciplinary liberalism in Europe as a counterweight to the irresponsible behavior of domestic politicians, employers, and trade unions. This commitment, and the shared mindset behind the EMU settlement at Maastricht, was grounded in US-based credibility and time-consistency theory. This post-1970s theory helped rejuvenate disciplinary liberalism across Europe, including in Germany, and to place

98 Kenneth Dyson

central bank independence and rule-based fiscal policy at the heart of EMU. More broadly, credibility and time-consistency theory reinforced a conservative disposition in macroeconomic theory that affected Keynesians as well.

The roots of the disciplinary revolution in Europe

The social roots of the disciplinary revolution in liberalism were firmly planted in the intellectually cultivated middle class (the *Bildungsbürgertum*), either by birth or by socialization and self-identification (see Dyson 2021). There was a firm sense of an intellectual aristocracy: humanistic in its learning; ethical in its social, economic, and political commitments; and fundamentally disinterested in its judgments. Its mindset was represented by figures like Johann Wolfgang von Goethe (the most cited by Müller-Armack, Röpke, and Otto Veit); the cultural historians Jakob Burckhardt and Johan Huizinga (cited by Einaudi and Röpke); the philosopher George Santayana (the mentor of Lippmann); José Ortega y Gasset (universally cited); the philosophers Rudolf Eucken and Edmund Husserl (who deeply influenced Walter Eucken); and Lord John Acton and de Tocqueville (whom Hayek took as his chief inspiration from the 1940s).

The disciplinary revolution in liberalism has three intellectual roots: in aristocratic liberalism; in ethical philosophy; and in religion. Aristocratic liberalism informs its social and political philosophy. In elaborating his thinking about a postwar relaunch of liberalism, Hayek (1945) proposed the title of the Acton–Tocqueville Society. His book *The Road to Serfdom* (1944) was named after a phrase in a speech by Tocqueville on the right to work. Acton and Tocqueville represented the twin fears of disciplinary liberals: the anarchy that would be unleashed by 'unlimited democracy'; and the servitude that would follow from the growth of state centralization, competences, and power. The constitutional ordering of the political and the economic orders was the best safeguard against these dangers. Democracy required a disciplinary framework of rules if it were to be made compatible with a liberal order. Burckhardt was another influential figure, notably in the work of Röpke and Einaudi. He feared that the materialism of commerce and the centralization of power in militarized states were undermining respect for civilized values. Burckhardt looked to the decentralized character of his native Switzerland and its culture of the artisan as a model. These themes were strongly represented in the thinking of Einaudi, Rougier, and Röpke about a renovation of liberalism.

A second characteristic of disciplinary liberalism was its roots in ethical philosophy, the basis of its economic humanism. *Die Tatwelt*, the interwar journal of the Eucken Association (Euckenbund), gave prominence to four philosophers – Rudolf Eucken, Nicolai Hartmann, Husserl, and Max Scheler. They represented different variants of Kantian idealism, emphasizing the importance of moral and spiritual values as a distinct domain. This emphasis went along with a critique of contemporary civilization. This philosophical literature formed the basis for the ordoliberal rejection of the naturalistic

Ordoliberalism and revolution in liberalism   99

approach to economics. Economics was making itself irrelevant by claiming to be a science on the model of physics. It was above all grounded in moral values. The intellectual enemies were materialism and positivism. This critique originated not just from Kantian idealism. It was also linked to Christian humanism within Italian economics. In France, by contrast, positivism had long played a role in elite economics training, represented by the 'engineer-economists.' Rougier and Rueff argued that economic science justified the superiority of disciplinary liberalism over both laissez-faire liberalism and collectivism. The latter two were dismissed by Rougier as *mystiques*. In addition, Rougier and Rueff pointed to the differences between the natural and the social orders. Drawing on classical mythology, they emphasized the Promethean creative power of the individual to remake the social order and prevent the entropy by which the natural order was afflicted.

Religion was the third intellectual root of the disciplinary revolution in liberalism. There was a striking correlation with adherence to Lutheran and Reformed Protestant religious tenets. This correlation helps to explain why disciplinary liberalism has a strong presence in Switzerland, Germany, the Nordic and Baltic states, the Netherlands, and in certain milieus of the United States (see Gorski, 2003). In Germany, Lutherans dominated ordoliberalism (Manow, 2001). They included Franz Böhm, Erhard, Eucken, Müller-Armack, Röpke, and Veit. The wartime Freiburg resistance circles of ordo-liberals were based around the Confessing Church (Bekennende Kirche), which opposed the incorporation of the Lutheran Church in the Nazi order (Blumenberg-Lampe, 1991).

Even in a secularized age, the religious tenets of Lutheranism and Reformed Protestantism retained a social presence (Hien, 2017). They emphasized an austere and ascetic attitude to life, the importance that is attached to the inner moral conscience, personal responsibility, and the respect that attaches to hard work, to a frugal, prudent, and sober lifestyle, and to good neighborliness. Ordoliberalism and the wider disciplinary liberalism as a cultural tradition are impregnated with these secularized religious tenets.

The Lutheran and Reformed Protestant roots help explain the difficult relationship that ordoliberalism has had with Roman Catholic economic and social teaching as it has evolved since the mid-19th century and with the secularized Christian humanism that helps shape southern European culture. Christian humanism argued that economic policy must be adapted to the needs of the poor and disadvantaged. It was driven by a profound concern for social outcomes of economic policy. Rule compliance was a secondary consideration. Catholic social teaching favored corporatist forms of economic and social organization and extensive mechanisms of social support. In contrast, ordoliberals argued that there was a heavy price to pay in not allowing the competitive market to enhance both individual opportunities and standards of living. The price was lock-in of economic and social standards.

100 *Kenneth Dyson*

The significance of ordoliberalism in Germany: case studies

Skepticism about the influence of ordoliberalism within Germany is far from new. Pierre Mendès-France, a leading figure within the French non-communist left, claimed in an article in *Le Monde* in 1954 that the success of the 'Erhard method' derived from the way in which the currency reform of 1948 and Marshall Aid had reactivated the powerful prewar and wartime German production system. France lacked this inheritance. The French economist André Piettre (1962) pointed to the German paradox. The ordoliberal discourse and policy approach contrasted with economic, financial, and industrial structures that were far from liberal, with high levels of concentration and concertation within both banking and industry. The close bank–industry nexus was to provide an important part of the structure of a coordinated market economy which encompassed collective bargaining, vocational training, and technology transfer (Hall & Soskice, 2001). For both Mendès-France and Piettre there was a striking continuity in structure and functioning of the German economy.

Key triggers of the postwar German economic miracle could not be attributed to ordoliberalism (Abelshauser, 1987). Marshall Aid, followed by the London Debt Agreement of 1953, were part of the fortuitous circumstances that favored the success of the 'Erhard method.' The Debt Agreement provided a significant boost for German public finances, helping to make possible high levels of public investment. Even the 1948 currency reform and the establishment of central bank independence owed more to US thinking than to German ordoliberalism. The German contribution to the currency reform was essentially technical (Meardon, 2014). The minutes and papers of the council of the Bank deutscher Länder show that the debate about central bank independence bore no trace of ordoliberalism. It dealt with the US Federal Reserve Model and with the experience of the Reichsbank.[4] Eucken himself was equivocal at best on central bank independence as the precondition for price stability (Bibow, 2013). The main evidence of ordoliberal contribution was the important role that Leonhard Miksch, a former student of Eucken, played in the liberalization reforms that accompanied the currency reform. However, his role was short-lived (Dathe, 2015). Eucken's contributions to discussions about postwar reconstruction were regarded by Erhard as too abstract (Wünsche, 2015).

Röpke (1958, pp. 49–51) was soon expressing his deep disappointment with progress toward a market economy in Germany. He noted the strong counter-pressures in social policy, housing, agriculture, capital markets, and public finances. There was, in his words, a "collectivist mine-field" within the market economy. He noted the failings in anti-trust and competition policies, in tax reform, and in welfare-state reform. Externally, he pointed to two failings: monetary policy was not mitigating the risks of imported inflation; and Germany had signed up to a process of 'European mis-integration'

Ordoliberalism and revolution in liberalism 101

with the European Coal and Steel Community (ECSC) and the European Economic Community (EEC). Ordoliberals faced three major setbacks in 1957: the long-debated anti-trust law exempted key sectors from its provisions; the pension law was judged to be collectivist and to entrench the old Bismarckian welfare-state provision; and the Treaty of Rome built trade integration around a small rather than a large Europe.

Christian democratic ascendancy in the 1950s proved a very imperfect political vehicle for ordoliberalism. The political logic of the commitment of the two sister parties, the Christian Democratic Union (CDU) and the Christian Social Union (CSU), to becoming a 'catch-all' party (Volkspartei) was strategic positioning as a bridge across the traditional confessional divide between Lutherans and Catholics. The ordoliberal tradition was Lutheran in its social ethics. Reaching out to the large Catholic populations in the Rhineland – the home of the first, long-serving Federal Chancellor, Konrad Adenauer – and in southern Germany meant taking seriously Catholic thinking about social and economic policies (Manow, forthcoming). The federal ministry for labor and social affairs became a fiefdom of Catholic thinking. It pursued and protected corporatist ideas in corporate governance and in the governance of social policies. In consequence, Erhard often found himself embattled and overruled. The pensions law of 1957 was a clear defeat.

Ordoliberalism faced another difficulty. Speedy German reconstruction depended on the federal government finding partners who could help provide large amounts of capital speedily and make efficient use of it. The state became locked into working with the big commercial banks; with the large coal, iron, and steel companies, automobile companies, engineering companies, chemical companies, and energy providers; as well as with the banking, industrial, and employer associations and trade unions. This was not the neutral, disinterested, and 'strong' state that ordoliberals had envisaged. It created privileges as well as competition, two features of a market economy that were far from compatible. There was a privileged access to federal and to state political power; subsidies and exemptions; and a revolving door between the state and the private sector. The consequences were made clear in the diluted form in which the anti-trust law of 1957 emerged and in later scandals like that engulfing the German automobile sector in 2017.

The question of the significance of German ordoliberalism for European integration, and of European integration for ordoliberalism, is fraught with complexity. In one main respect, the Treaty of Rome in 1957 was a success for German negotiators. The EEC took on competence in antitrust and competition policies. Moreover, from the first European Commission German officials played a leading role in the competition directorate-general. It soon became clear that the EEC could help push the agenda of domestic reform in German anti-cartel and competition policies. However, from the 1980s ordoliberal thinking was displaced within the competition directorate-general by ideas taken from the new Chicago School. Economic efficiency rather than the safeguarding of individual rights became the prime measure in EEC

102 Kenneth Dyson

competition policies. With the single market program, European integration empowered domestic competition policy reform in Germany but less obviously on ordoliberal terms. Despite these pressures from European integration, resistance to liberalization measures remained conspicuous in the three-pillar German banking system, the energy sector, and the wider service sector.

The process of Economic and Monetary Union (EMU) was a similar tale of complexity. This process fell within the Commission's directorate-general for economic and financial affairs, where German presence was less strong. From the outset, deep suspicion characterized the relationship between, on the one hand, the German economics and finance ministries and the Bundesbank and, on the other, the Commission. Erhard opposed the Commission's Action Programme for the Second Stage in 1962 as *dirigiste*. The period 1966–1972 proved different in that the new Federal Economics Minister, Karl Schiller, a Social Democrat, shifted German economic thinking closer to the international mainstream by embracing Keynesian countercyclical thinking. In consequence, the German government was able to agree on the principle of parallel progress in fiscal and in monetary integration in the Werner Plan on EMU in 1970. Progress was impeded by the French government's unwillingness to cede sovereignty in fiscal policy, not by German opposition.

The collapse of the Bretton Woods system in 1971–1973 had two consequences. First, freed from the exchange-rate constraint, the Bundesbank was newly empowered and revised its monetary policy strategy. The historical papers make clear that the ordoliberal option, presented by Robert Gocht, for a strict rule-based monetary and credit policy (akin to the Chicago Plan of the 1930s) received little support (Gocht, 1975). The revised monetary policy strategy followed the thinking of Milton Freedman and the new Chicago School in focusing on money supply targeting.[5] Second, the reestablishment of exchange-rate stability in Europe with the ERM in 1979 reflected in its basic design the views of the newly empowered Bundesbank. The domestic statutory requirement to "safeguard the currency" came before the new external commitment.

From 1979 German attitudes to ERM reform and German policy positions on EMU were anchored, first and foremost, in the national interest in minimizing the exposure of Germany to external risks. The priority was to price stability and to international competitiveness, two objectives that were deemed complementary. The Bundesbank, and German federal government negotiators, sought to ensure that Germany did not become liable for the failure of other EU member states to put their own houses in order. Hence, in the drafting of the Delors Report on EMU in 1988–1989, and in the negotiation of the Maastricht Treaty provisions on EMU in 1990–1991, the stress was on a treaty-based monetary union that established a strictly independent European Central Bank (ECB) with a single objective of price stability; on rule-based fiscal policy coordination that left member states responsible for their own debts; and on softer modes of coordination in

Ordoliberalism and revolution in liberalism 103

economic policies. Rule-based fiscal policy coordination – later through the SGP and then the fiscal compact treaty – was preferable to a fiscal transfer union and to a form of banking union which would expose Germany to risks created by others.

These German attitudes and policy positions may have corresponded in substantial part with ordoliberalism. They were not caused by ordoliberalism. They followed logically from national interest in reducing risk exposure in EMU. They were the thinking of the biggest creditor state in the EU. It was a mode of thinking common to big creditor states in other international monetary arrangements (Dyson, 2014). Rhetorical references to ordoliberalism served to help justify strategic positioning by German negotiators. Moreover, the substantive content of German position-taking was primarily driven by alignment with a new post-Bretton Woods cross-national consensus on credibility and time-consistency as the chief requirements of effective macroeconomic policies. This new consensus gave a conservative rule-based character to international liberal economic thought from the 1980s through to the financial and economic crisis post-2007.

French and Italian technocratic elites colluded in the idea of a rule-based EMU that would bind the hands of domestic political classes in whose governing competence they had serious doubts. Their collusion had nothing to do with German ordoliberal thought and everything to do with US-based credibility and time-consistency theory. Guido Carli (1993) wrote of the value of an external constraint (*vincolo esterno*) in breaking the domestic vicious circle of inflation, competitiveness problems, and currency depreciation. EMU was to function as an external discipline that would force fiscal, labor market, and wage-negotiation reforms (Dyson & Featherstone, 1996). This kind of thinking had earlier featured in French Prime Minister Raymond Barre's thinking about the ERM (Howarth, 2016). Domestic inflation and competitiveness problems – along with political inertia – encouraged disciplinary liberals in France and Italy to back a rule-based EMU.

Mitigating risk to German interests as a creditor state was the central theme that ran through German debates about the euro area crisis from 2010 onwards and about the reforms that were required to the governance framework of EMU. It ran as a thread through the strengthening of the SGP, through the asymmetrical construction of the new Macroeconomic Imbalances Procedure (MIP) so that onus was placed on adjustment to imbalances by states in current account deficit; the establishment of the European Stability Mechanism (ESM) as an intergovernmental body that gave Germany a veto on rescue programs; the strict rules of the fiscal compact treaty on budgetary balance and on debt reduction; and the priority to effective banking supervision over the bank resolution mechanism and over the deposit guarantee mechanism in building European banking union. The extent to which these risk-mitigation achievements corresponded with ordoliberal principles does not imply that the latter caused the former.

104   Kenneth Dyson

Ordoliberals were characteristically very critical of the effectiveness of the German government in mitigating liability (e.g. Koerfer, 2017). Germany's own rule-observance proved to be flexible in the face of changing circumstances. When the competitiveness and fiscal problems of the German economy became apparent in 2001–2003, the German government had precipitated a crisis of the SGP and sought a relaxation of its rules. This breach horrified German ordoliberals (Heipertz & Verdun, 2010). Similarly, many of them regarded the ESM, European banking union, and not least the special crisis-fighting monetary policy measures of the ECB as evidence of the erosion of the sound principles on which the Maastricht Treaty had been based. German ordoliberals were increasingly doubtful of the correspondence between their thinking and the way in which the EU, the euro area, and the ECB were developing. Huge sovereign bond purchases by the ECB had breached the principle of separation between monetary and fiscal policies (e.g. Issing, 2011; Sinn, 2014; Stark, 2013).

The problems inside the euro area were not so much caused by German ordoliberalism, which was only partially influential in Germany itself and, in the view of ordoliberals, in retreat in the EU and the euro area. They stemmed from the construction of a much larger and more heterogenous monetary union than had been envisaged by its architects (Dyson & Maes, 2016). The architects had expected a monetary union of five or six member states, with Italy a questionable starter. Such an expectation meant that optimum currency area (OCA) theory seemed of questionable value at the time of the Maastricht negotiations. However, the later scale and heterogeneity of the euro area reveals its deficiencies as an OCA and its vulnerability to asymmetric shocks. Keeping a deficient OCA in existence placed enormous economic and political strains on creditor and debtor states alike. Too few creditor states and too many debtor states created the context in which populists could exploit negative and ugly feelings in both sets of states. The outcome was that ordoliberalism felt embattled and marginalized in the biggest creditor state, while simultaneously being attacked in many debtor states as the basis of a German imperial policy in Europe.

Notes

1 This chapter examines some of the questions considered in Dyson (2021).
2 These features are further developed in Dyson (2021).
3 Based on elite interviews in the German federal economics ministry, the finance ministry, and the Bundesbank.
4 Research conducted by the author in the Historical Archive of the Bundesbank.
5 Based on the author's research in the Historical Archive of the Bundesbank.

Bibliography

Abelshauser, W. (1987). *Die Langen Fünfziger Jahren: Wirtschaft und Gesellschaft der Bundesrepublik Deutschland 1949–1966*. Düsseldorf, Germany: Schwann.

Audier, S. (2012). *Le Colloque Lippmann: Origines du néo-libéralisme*. Paris, France: le Bord de l'eau.

Bibow, J. (2013). On the origin and rise of central bank independence in West Germany. *European Journal of the History of Economic Thought 16*(1) 155–190.

Bini, P. (1992). *Costantino Bresciani Turroni. Ciclo, moneta e sviluppo*. Civitanova Marche: Otium.

Blumenberg-Lampe, C. (1991). Oppositionelle Nackriegsplanung: Wirtschaftswissenschaftler gegen den Nationalsozialismus. In E. Johns, B. Martin, M. Mück & H. Ott (Eds.), *Die Freiburger Universität in der Zeit des Nationalsozialismus* (pp. 207–220). Freiburg, Germany: Ploetz.

Bresciani-Turroni, C. ([1945] 2006). *Liberalismo e Politica Economica*. Bologna, Italy: Il Mulino.

Buchanan, J. (1991). The economy as a constitutional order. In J. Buchanan, *The economics and the ethics of constitutional order* (pp. 29–41). Ann Arbor, MI: University of Michigan Press.

Carli, G. (1993). *Cinquant'anni di vita Italiana*. Rome, Italy: Editori Laterza.

Costabile, L. (2010). Costantino Bresciani Turroni and the Macroeconomics of Reconstruction. *Rivista Italiana degli economisti 3* 403–432.

Dathe, U. (2015). Leonhard Miksch (1901–1950): Leben und Werk. In L. Feld & E. Köhler (Eds.), *Wettbewerbsordnung und Monopolbekämpfung: Zum Gedenken an Leonhard Miksch (1901–1950)* (pp. 7–35). Tübingen, Germany: Mohr Siebeck.

Denord, F. (2007). *Néo-libéralisme version française: Histoire d'une idéologie politique*. Paris, France: Demopolis.

Deutscher, P. (1990). *R. G. Hawtrey and the development of macroeconomics*. London, UK: Macmillan.

Dyson, K. (2014). *States, debt and power: Saints and sinners in European history and integration*. Oxford, UK: Oxford University Press.

Dyson, K. (2017). Ordoliberalism as tradition and as ideology. In J. Hien & C. Joerges (Eds.), *Ordoliberalism, law and the rule of economics* (pp. 87–99). Oxford, UK and Portland, OR: Hart.

Dyson, K. (2021). *Disciplinary liberalism and Ordoliberalism: a conservative challenge to economic and political thought and practice*. Oxford: Oxford University Press.

Dyson, K. & Featherstone, K. (1996). Italy and EMU as "vincolo esterno": Empowering the technocrats, transforming the state. *South European Society and Politics 1*(2) 272–299.

Dyson, K. & Featherstone, K. (1999). *The road to Maastricht: Negotiating Economic and Monetary Union*. Oxford, UK: Oxford University Press.

Dyson, K. & Maes, I. (Eds.). (2016). *Architects of the euro: Intellectuals in the making of European Monetary Union*. Oxford, UK: Oxford University Press.

Einaudi, L. (1942). Economia di concorrenza e capitalismo storica. La terza via tra i secoli xviii e xix. *Rivista di storia economica 7*(2) 49–71.

Emmett, R. (2009). *Frank Knight and the Chicago School in American economics*. London, UK: Routledge.

Eucken, W. (1940). *Grundlagen der Nationalökonomie*. Berlin, Germany: Springer.

Eucken, W. (1952). *Grundsätze der Wirtschaftspolitik*. Tübingen, Germany: Mohr Siebeck.

Giordano, A. (2006). *Il pensiero político di Luigi Einaudi*. Genova, Italy: Name.

Gocht, R. (1975). *Kritische Betrachtungen zur nationale und internationalen Geldordnung*. Berlin, Germany: Duncker & Humblot.

106 Kenneth Dyson

Gorski, P. (2003). *The disciplinary revolution: Calvinism and the rise of the state in early modern Europe*. Chicago: Chicago University Press.

Hall, P. & Soskice, D. (2001). *Varieties of capitalism: The institutional foundations of comparative advantage*. Oxford, UK: Oxford University Press.

Hawtrey, R. (1926). *The economic problem*. London, UK: Longman.

Hayek, F. (1944). *The road to serfdom*. London, UK: Routledge.

Hayek, F. (1945). Memorandum on the proposed foundation of an international academy for political philosophy tentatively called "the Acton–Tocqueville Society." In IWP, papers of Albert Hunold.

Hayek, F. (1967). Grundsätze einer liberalen Gesellschaftsordnung, *ORDO 18* 11–33.

Heipertz, M. & Verdun, A. (2010). *Ruling Europe: The politics of the Stability and Growth Pact*. Cambridge, UK: Cambridge University Press.

Hien, J. (2017). Ordo-liberalism and the quest for sacrality. In C. Joerges & J. Hien (Eds.), *Ordoliberalism, law and the rule of economics* (pp. 261–270). Oxford, UK and Portland, OR: Hart.

Hoppmann, E. (1988). *Wirtschaftsordnung und Wettbewerb*. Baden-Baden, Germany: Nomos.

Howarth, D. (2016). Raymond Barre: Modernizing France through European monetary cooperation. In K. Dyson & I. Maes (Eds.), *Architects of the euro: Intellectuals in the making of European Monetary Union* (pp. 75–92). Oxford, UK: Oxford University Press

Issing, O. (2011). Perversion von Solidarität, interview, *Der Spiegel* 12, 21 March, p. 82.

Janssen, H. (2006). *Milton Friedman und die "monetarischen Revolution" in Deutschland*. Marburg, Germany: Metropolis.

Knight, F. (1935). *The ethics of competition and other essays*. New York, NY: Harper.

Koerfer, D. (2017). Der verlorene Kompass – Angela Merkels Abkehr von Ludwig Erhard und die Sozialen Marktwirtschaft. In P. Plickert (Ed.), *Merkel: Eine kritische Bilanz* (pp. 73–83). Munich, Germany: Finanzbuchverlag.

Köhler, E. & Kolev, S. (2011). The conjoint quest for a liberal positive programme: "Old Chicago," Freiburg and Hayek. HWWI Research Paper 109. Hamburg, Germany: Hamburg Institute of International Economics.

Lippmann, W. (1937). *The good society*. New York, NY: Grosset & Dunlap.

Manow, P. (2001). Ordoliberalismus als ökonomische Ordnungstheologie, *Leviathan 29*(2) 179–98.

Manow, P. (forthcoming). *Social protection, capitalist production – The Bismarckian Welfare State in the German political economy, 1880–2015*.

Meardon, S. (2014). On Kindleberger and hegemony: From Berlin to MIT and back. *History of Political Economy 46* 351–374.

Moeller, H. (1950). Liberalismus. *Jahrbücher für Nationalökonomie und Statistik, 162*(3) 214–420.

Piettre, A. (1962). L'économie allemande est-elle vraiment libérale? *Revue économique 13* 339–354.

Plickert, P. (2008). *Wandlungen des Neoliberalismus. Eine Studie zu Entwicklung und Ausstrahlung der "Mont Pèlerin Society."* Stuttgart, Germany: Lucius and Lucius.

Röpke, W. (1942). *Die Gesellschaftskrise der Gegenwart* (4th ed.). Erlenbach–Zurich, Switzerland: Eugen Rentsch.

Röpke, W. (1958). *Jenseits von Angebot und Nachfrage*. Erlenbach–Zurich, Switzerland: Eugen Rentsch.

Rougier, L. ([1938] 1949). *Les mystiques économiques* (2nd enlarged ed.). Paris, France: Librairie de Médicis.

Rueff, J. (1945). *L'ordre social* (2 vols.). Paris, France: Recueil Sirey.

Simons, H. (1936). Rules versus authorities in monetary policy. *Journal of Political Economy 44*(1) 1–30.

Sinn, H.-W. (2014). *The euro trap: On bursting bubbles, budgets and beliefs.* Oxford, UK: Oxford University Press.

Stark, J. (2013). Es gibt keine rote Linie mehr. *Handelsblatt Wirtschafts- und Finanzzeitung,* 26 July.

Vanberg, V. (2011). Liberal constitutionalism, constitutional liberalism and democracy. *Constitutional Political Economy 22* 1–20.

Wittgenstein, L. ([1953] 2009). *Philosophical investigations* (4th ed.). Oxford, UK: Wiley-Blackwell.

Wünsche, H. (2015). *Ludwig Erhards Soziale Marktwirtschaft. Wissenschaftliche Grundlagen und politische Fehldeutungen.* Reinbeck–Munich, Gemany: Lau Verlag.

6 Ordoliberalism from the perspective of a US-trained macroeconomist

Rüdiger Bachmann

The personal

Rejection. My first real encounter with ordoliberalism was personal, was one of rejection. "Politically uninterested careerists"[1] – called Hans Willgerodt, professor emeritus of *wirtschaftliche Staatswissenschaften* at Cologne University and doyen of German ordoliberalism, people like me in an op-ed, titled "From Being Free of Values to Being of No Value"[2] and published in the important German daily *Frankfurter Allgemeine Zeitung*. How did this happen? In 2008, the Department of Economics at Cologne University decided to use six professorial vacancies, previously occupied by professors of an ordoliberal leaning, to form a US-style macroeconomics group through an attempt at cluster hiring. I was offered one of these positions. Professor Willgerodt, whose former chair was one of the six vacancies, together with his colleague Christian Watrin, also professor emeritus at Cologne University and also a staunch ordoliberal, tried to torpedo this attempt, first through the distribution of internal memos, and later publicly through the press, mainly the *Frankfurter Allgemeine Zeitung*. The German business daily *Handelsblatt* called this affair the "Cologne emeritus uprising."[3]

As another part of their campaign, professors Watrin and Willgerodt wrote two open letters (Watrin & Willgerodt, 2009a, 2009b) claiming that (1) US-style macroeconomics had recently failed in a catastrophic manner, as if the US financial crisis had anything to do with the academic quality of the newly offered professors at Cologne, only half of whom had ever held positions in the United States; (2) macroeconomists could not be entrusted with researching and teaching questions of economic policy relevance; (3) macroeconomics was much narrower than the German-style (ordoliberal) economic policy that was taught and researched at Cologne University theretofore; (4) there was too much mathematical formalism in macroeconomics, a standard claim without establishing what "too much" actually means; and (5), indirectly, that people like me who publish in highly recognized international journals but without monographs are ultimately not sufficiently serious academics to be deserving of a professorship at Cologne University.

Ordoliberalism: a US macroeconomics perspective 109

The invectives of professors Watrin and Willgerodt were shared much more broadly, culminating in a public manifesto, published again by the *Frankfurter Allgemeine Zeitung* and signed by 83 economics professors, alleging that anything other than German-style economic policy was a mere exercise in logical deduction without any basis in reality, and could not possibly contribute fruitfully to economic policy debates (*Frankfurter Allgemeine Zeitung*, 2009).[4]

The German press more generally also echoed a pro-ordoliberalism stance: Michael Hüther, head of the business-financed think tank Institut der deutschen Wirtschaft, published an *Ordungspolitischer Einspruch* (ordoliberal objection) in the *Handelsblatt* (Hüther, 2009b; see also Hüther, 2009a). Hans Barbier, perhaps the most important journalist advocate of German ordoliberalism and then the head of the Ludwig-Erhard-Stiftung, a major networking group for ordoliberals, came out very strongly in support of the manifesto of the 83 (Barbier, 2009). Specifically, he uses the German cash-for-clunkers program at the time as an example of how the neglect of ordoliberal thinking leads to bad economic policy, as if modern macroeconomics does not know anything about durable good cycles. By contrast, Barbier appears to have no notion that durable good cycles may look different in economies with underutilized resources, a form of state dependence with which ordoliberalism seems unfamiliar. He even goes so far as to hint that the government should intervene to keep German ordoliberalism alive at universities, a remarkable statement for someone preaching non-interventionism as his most important creed. More public support for ordoliberalism came from Viktor Vanberg (2009), then the head of the Walter Eucken Institute at The University of Freiburg, another important ordoliberal think tank, who suggested that economics was not a second physics; the then still-extant conservative-Christian weekly *Rheinischer Merkur* (Balling & Linneweber, 2009); and from the *Süddeutsche Zeitung*, known for its pro-ordoliberal business and economics section (Goldschmidt & Zweynert, 2009).

These pro-ordoliberalism op-ed forays are important because, as I will argue below, ordoliberalism's impact has been felt strongest not so much in German economics departments nor even always and everywhere in concrete German economic policy, but rather in German intellectual life as a strong and influential movement and network that promotes a particular social philosophy. And this network sprang into action, when in 2009 an ordoliberal stronghold at Cologne University was about to be supplanted and the ensuing *Neuer Methodenstreit* left ordoliberalism on the defensive.

The remainder of this story can be told in brief: starting with op-eds and interviews in defense of modern (macro)economics (e.g. Bachmann & Uhlig, 2009), I eventually coorganized, jointly with Dirk Krüger and Harald Uhlig, a counter-manifesto with 188 signatories, published in the *Handelsblatt*, stating the obvious for anyone at least tangentially familiar with the issue: modern US-style economic research is overwhelmingly highly empirical and highly policy-relevant. It is the old German divide of economic theory versus

110   Rüdiger Bachmann

economic policy, with a separate and special role for public finance, that is ultimately anti-empirical thus hardly policy-relevant, because data and statistical tools for their analysis often did not play a role in either.

The general

The 2009 German *Methodenstreit* abated rather quickly and made way for a number of separate if related methodological debates in economics, for instance a rekindled heterodox attack on mainstream economics blaming it and its alleged monism to be responsible for the financial crisis and the Great Recession. There was also a more specific debate about the usefulness of dynamic stochastic general equilibrium models in both academic and central bank macroeconomics. And, finally, an attack on German (ordoliberal) macroeconomics and macroeconomic policy was launched from both outside (Krugman, 2013a–f; Wren-Lewis, 2013, 2015, 2016; Yates, 2015), that is, mostly the Anglo-Saxon world, and from inside Germany (Bofinger, 2016). The claim was that ordoliberalism was one of the main culprits for the backwardness and insularity of German macroeconomic policy. "Ze Germans" did not appreciate or even understand the importance of expansionary fiscal policy in stabilizing aggregate demand crises, their monetary policy view was too obsessed with inflation, and they hailed trade surpluses as a sign of national economic strength rather than a destabilizing factor in a currency union. German economic policymakers were essentially accused of mercantilism, sometimes mocked as "Merkelantilism."

I found this attack unfortunate,[5] because it led to four misunderstandings: (1) Anglo-Saxon economics, in the eye of the public, was being equated with Keynesianism; (2) Anglo-Saxon *macro*economics became associated with Keynesianism; (3) economics in Germany was being equated with ordoliberalism; (4) German economists, especially those using ordoliberal arguments during the euro crisis, whether they were actually part of the ordoliberal school of old or not, were denounced as somehow behind the curve, outright bad economists. While the Anglo-Saxon onslaught was indeed led by prominent and public Keynesians (Krugman, Wren-Lewis, Yates, and DeLong), their position has never been a consensus position in US academic economics: for example, macroeconomists from Chicago, such as John Cochrane (2009), are just as ardent skeptics of expansionary fiscal policy and large-scale monetary policy as German ordoliberals. I have personally overheard a US economist defending then Finance Minister Wolfgang Schäuble's micromanagement of the Greek government, decried even by conservative German economists at the time, as the natural outcome of and rational solution to a political economy problem: if internal reforms lead to massive distributional conflicts an outsider must be used as a scapegoat to justify these reforms. I have called this a McKinsey effect (Bachmann & Braunberger, 2015). This means, by extension, that US-style macroeconomics is of course much more pluralistic than Keynesianism, especially the simple Keynesianism in undergraduate

Ordoliberalism: a US macroeconomics perspective 111

textbooks. US-style macroeconomics is a big tent: there are proponents of largely real factors as drivers of the business cycle, macroeconomists emphasizing financial issues, and Keynesian macroeconomists of many colors: from modern Neo-Keynesianism to Paleo-Keynesianism. Conversely, it is downright ludicrous to equate German macroeconomics with ordoliberalism or decry it as insular (more on this below). Finally, has it ever occurred to the Anglo-Saxon critics that German economists were perhaps not oblivious to the effects and benefits of aggregate demand management, yet still might have thought of political economy problems as the empirically more relevant issue? Or that they had experience with some of the pathologies of the German federal redistribution and insurance system between richer and poorer *Länder* within Germany (James, 2017; Schmidt, 2017)? It would be beyond the scope of this chapter to take a side in this debate, but I hope it has become clear that scoring ideological rather than academic points seemed to have been a high priority on both sides.[6]

How influential, then, was and is ordoliberalism? In the following, I will break this question up into four parts: (1) How influential is ordoliberalism in German macroeconomics today? (2) What are possible examples of influential academic ordoliberals? (3) How influential was ordoliberalism in the postwar history of German economics academia? (4) How influential has ordoliberalism been for German economic policy? The short answer: not so much, certainly less than one might think.

Today German macroeconomics is well integrated into the international, Anglo-Saxon-dominated scientific community of macroeconomics. Its most important representatives publish in the best international journals, go to the same conferences as Anglo-Saxon macroeconomists, and they teach from the same textbooks (Bofinger, 2016 explicitly recognizes this). None of the members of the macroeconomics committee, the Ausschuss für Makroökonomik, of the Verein für Socialpolitik, Germany's most important professional association of economists, certainly none of the active members, appear to be known ordoliberals; rather, there is a great variety of methodological and, to the extent that this can be known, economic policy stances.[7] This committee is meant to gather the leading academic macroeconomists based in the German-speaking countries. Consequently, there appears to be absolutely no influence of ordoliberalism on German macroeconomics today beyond what one would find also in US macroeconomics.

Second and without striving for completeness, there are Lars Feld, Volker Wieland, and Clemens Fuest who are academically influential German economists more broadly and whom perhaps the general public might perceive as heirs to ordoliberal doctrine. All three are members of the Kronberger Kreis, a special group within the influential Stiftung Marktwirtschaft, again a network with ordoliberal roots.[8] All three are influential in German public discourse: professors Feld and Wieland are members of the Sachverständigenrat, the German Council of Economic Experts and the institutional equivalent of the Council of Economic Advisers to the President of the

112 Rüdiger Bachmann

United States. In addition, Professor Feld is the current head of the afore-mentioned ordoliberal think tank Walter Eucken institute, and Professor Fuest heads the Munich-based Ifo Institute, arguably one of the top two German economic policy institutes, as president. However, each has achieved their academic reputation with mainstream economics research that has little to do with old-school ordoliberalism. Professor Wieland is an internationally recognized expert in new Keynesian dynamic stochastic general equilibrium models and their use for monetary and fiscal policy,[9] issues and a methodo-logical framework that would have been of little interest to professors Watrin and Willgerodt. Professors Feld and Fuest are internationally recognized applied public finance economists, the former with at least four publications in the *Journal of Public Economics*, the top field journal of public finance, and the latter with at least nine such publications. In addition, as Braunberger (2012) points out, Professor Feld has been very critical of the old ossified ordoliberal research program. And Professor Fuest was part of the search committee that planned the creation of a macroeconomics group at Cologne University that then led to the ordoliberal uprising. To summarize: while each of them are influential voices in German economic policy discourse, and often might advocate what might be considered traditional ordoliberal posi-tions, they certainly have not gained their academic standing with an ordolib-eral research program of the kind that professors Watrin and Willgerodt envisioned in Cologne after their retirement. And to the extent that the public influence of the three is shaped by their ordoliberal positions, these positions would be nothing that would not be considered part of US main-stream as well (see Feld, Köhler, & Nientiedt, 2017). In addition, all three have achieved mainstream academic success with their research.

Third, we can ask whether ordoliberalism had historically an important influence on German academic economics. Jan-Otmar Hesse, in his magis-terial monograph on the development of German economics from 1945 to the 1970s, makes it very clear that this was not the case (for example in Hesse, 2010, p. 49).[10] Hesse (2010, pp. 115, 290) also describes how the very influ-ential economic theory committee, the Theoretische Ausschuss, of the Verein für Socialpolitik used to be a hotbed of Keynesianism in Germany. Its inau-gural chairman, Erich Schneider (1953–1962), essentially brought Samuelso-nian Keynesianism to Germany with his popular four-volume textbook *Einführung in die Wirtschaftstheorie*. The committee's first meetings had arch-Keynesian topics such as "*Löhne, Preise und Beschäftigung*," "*Kontroverse Fragen der Multiplikatortheorie*," and "*Beschäftigungsgrad und Einkommensverteilung*" on the program.[11] The economics department at Bonn University, arguably one of the most internationally visible and academically influential in German economics, started out somewhat ordoliberal with Fritz Meyer, another important figure in German ordoliberalism, receiving an endowed chair pro-fessorship in 1949. Yet, certainly by attracting Wilhelm Krelle to an endowed chair professorship in 1958, Bonn had shed its ordoliberal past. Professor Krelle, like few others, shaped the Bonn economics department and postwar

Ordoliberalism: a US macroeconomics perspective 113

German economics more broadly. A similarly prominent role can be attributed to Heinz König, the doyen of empirical economics in Germany, and the builder of the international visibility of the Mannheim economics department, the second internationally competitive powerhouse in German academic economics. Heinz König, being an applied econometrician, had arguably no intellectual connection to ordoliberalism. This means, in summary, that the two academically most influential departments in German economics had decidedly non-ordoliberal professors as their modern founders. In addition, Bofinger (2016) is right when he calls Walter Eucken's insights, on which German ordoliberalism squarely rested for much of postwar history, "almost trivia": a functioning price system, primacy of the monetary order, open markets, private property, freedom of contract, liability, and continuity of economic policy (see also Beck & Kotz, 2017a).[12] It seems, therefore, small wonder that aspiring young economists in Germany after the war were not excited about ordoliberalism as the foundation of a research program. And to the extent that some ideas of ordoliberalism were fruitful as foundational elements of research programs, they were often imported to Germany in the form of public choice, institutional and constitutional economics, political economy, and mechanism design, etc.

The question remains whether ordoliberalism had a *political* influence even if it had little *academic* influence in Germany. The first impression has to be in the affirmative.[13] German ordoliberals had a network of think tanks that connected academia and the (conservative and liberal-in-the-European-sense) political sphere: the Ludwig-Erhard Stiftung, the Stiftung Marktwirtschaft, and the Kronberger Kreis, and almost unlimited access to write opinion pieces in the *Frankfurter Allgemeine Zeitung*. There were many ordoliberals in the Wissenschaftliche Beirat beim Bundeswirtschaftsministerium (academic council of the Federal Ministry of Economic Affairs):[14] Franz Böhm, Walter Eucken, Alfred Müller-Armack, Elisabeth Liefmann-Keil, Leonhard Miksch, and Fritz Meyer; and there are still some left: Norbert Berthold, Charles Blankart, and Christian Watrin. Bofinger (2016) identifies "three pillars" of German macroeconomic policy that smack of ordoliberalism: balanced-budget fixation, price stability, and flexible prices to solve unemployment problems. However, the de facto influence of ordoliberalism has historically always been dependent on whether the center-right (more influence) or the center-left (less influence) governed. For example, in the late 1960s, and certainly in the 1970s, Keynesian ideas were politically very influential in Germany (see Burda, 2017). Karl Schiller, a member of the Social Democratic Party of Germany (SPD) and a leading German Keynesian academic economist, was not only a member of the Wissenschaftliche Beirat essentially all his academic life, but also the Federal Minister of Economic Affairs from 1966 to 1972 (in addition to being the Federal Minister of Finance from 1971 to 1972).[15] Traditional Phillips curve thinking was ingrained in economic policymaking at the time: Chancellor Helmut Schmidt, also from the SPD, (in)famously quipped in 1972, then the Minister of Economic Affairs and

114   *Rüdiger Bachmann*

Finance (and Karl Schiller's successor), that he would prefer 5% inflation over an unemployment rate of 5%. It should be of little surprise that Keynesian thinking, after its perceived failures in the 1970s – Chancellor Schmidt was embattled by both unemployment and inflation, as predicted by the academic critiques of Keynesianism – not only fell into academic disrepute but also politically so, leading to the 1980s conservative turn in Germany, not only in terms of economic policy, but in politics and society more broadly.[16] Jumping to the most recent economic history, where (see above) Germany was criticized for imposing too much austerity on the European South during the euro crisis, and, thus, for not following Keynesian orthodoxy, it is also difficult to sustain the claim that German economic policy followed ordoliberal orthodoxy. As has been shown, the aforementioned German cash-for-clunkers stimulus program was decried by staunch ordoliberals; bailing out major German banks was heavily criticized as an original sin, but (conservative) German politicians did it anyway (Beck & Kotz, 2017b); and the ordoliberal's criticism of too lax a monetary policy by the ECB was hardly ever picked up by important conservative politicians in Germany. It seems that German policymakers use ordoliberal traditions and principles if they perceive a need to academically justify economic policy measures that simply happen to align with ordoliberalism but were already decided on independently from ordoliberal considerations. Instead, German policymakers appear to follow much more the principle of economic nationalism (see Burda, 2017; Zettelmeyer, 2017) – that is, they pursue what they perceive as an economically good policy for Germany – than traditional ordoliberalism would allow for and the general pro-European rhetoric of German politicians would suggest. To sum up: even ordoliberalism's political influence, while certainly stronger than its academic influence, has been mixed at best.

A thesis and a paradox

Still, ordoliberalism's political and intellectual success needs an explanation, as indeed Germany seems to have embarked on a partial *Sonderweg*, an idiosyncratic path, in embracing it. And why has it taken so long for international mainstream macroeconomics, be it of the Keynesian, New Keynesian, or the more neoclassical variety, to have an academic breakthrough, if not yet fully in the political sphere?[17] More specifically, how did ordoliberalism establish itself as an important social philosophy, ultimately its enduring success? And why did Germany, after the failures of simple Keynesianism in the 1970s, not take the Anglo-Saxon route toward neoclassical macroeconomics that ultimately led to another synthesis in the form of New Keynesianism, but rather turned to ordoliberalism? These questions demand answers.

From a certain perspective, the success of ordoliberalism as a social philosophy in early postwar Germany is not surprising: (1) It correctly identified the disasters of Nazi economic management, in addition, of course, to the other atrocities of the regime, and vehemently pushed for a democratic, rules-based, "individual freedom and property rights"-respecting, competition-driven economic system. Of course, it also ignored the failure to implement Keynesian insights during economic crises times, that is, the infamous austerity policies by Chancellor Heinrich Brüning, as one of the reasons the Nazis came into power in the first place.[18] Germany and the United States thus started their postwar experiences from a very different point in terms of economic policy paradigm:[19] the disaster of a state-run, monopoly-capitalist economy in Germany versus the prosperity–experience of the New Deal in the United States. (2) Germany experienced a so-called *Wirtschaftswunder* (economic miracle) from the 1950s on, with an avowed ordoliberal, Ludwig Erhard, the Federal Minister of Economic Affairs, at the helm, so that, rightly or wrongly, ordoliberalism could claim that it worked in practice. (3) And this is a bit of an academic reason, but it should not be underestimated: Ordoliberalism could be viewed (and it viewed itself as such, see Hesse, 2010, p. 51) as an intellectual mediator in the older *Methodenstreit* in German social sciences which pits the description and analysis of historical contingency against seeking (eternal) laws of society and the economy.[20] Eucken saw ordoliberalism firmly grounded in the microeconomic theory of his time but, at the same time, Eucken's idea of *Wirtschaftsordnungen* (economic orders) can be viewed as a successor to the *Wirtschaftsstil* paradigm (economic styles) of the German historical school of economics.

However, while these historical developments might have some plausibility in explaining the immediate success of ordoliberalism after the war, I find them insufficient to explain the staying power of ordoliberalism, in the sense of ordoliberal ideas appearing to have periodical recurrences, as in the early 1980s or during the euro crisis. Ordoliberalism appears like a German intellectual zombie. In my view, this can only be understood through a systematic history of thought, rather than a mere historical argument: German political philosophy since at least the 19th century had a tendency to conceive of the state as an entity sui generis. This idea could take on an enlightened form, as with Georg Friedrich Wilhelm Hegel, in that the state represented the general, the rational above the private idiosyncrasies of its members. It could also come in anti-enlightenment, romantic forms, where the state was perceived as a metaphysical body consisting of organs that, like living organisms, have grown naturally into codepending on each other. The Austrofascist economist Othmar Spann would be an example of this strand. In both varieties, the liberal Anglo–Saxon idea that the state is a pragmatic means of free people to organize themselves so as to interact with each other in a prosperous and peaceful coexistence is absent. This metaphysical rather than pragmatic view of the state (see Beck & Kotz, 2017) is still deeply ingrained in German culture. Economics, for a long time, has been viewed as a *Staatswissenschaft*, an academic discipline whose purview it is to understand the organism that is the (rational) state, rather than an (empirical) social science.[21] Of course, the "queen" of the *Staatswissenschaften* in Germany is jurisprudence, as derived from political, social, and legal philosophy. Compare this to the

116   *Rüdiger Bachmann*

Anglo-Saxon world, where economics appears to be widely recognized as the "queen" of the social sciences, often bemoaned by its critics as economic imperialism. Economists, as social scientists, never had much influence in German public and political discourse, it has always been lawyers and social philosophers who had the ear of the decision makers and the public.[22] In Germany, it is not unusual for a philosopher to weigh in on the European Monetary Union (see, for example, Habermas, 2011), and have more public impact than any economist might command. There is a deep admiration among German intellectuals for the principle-based, formalistic reasoning found in continental law, and a skepticism toward the outcome-oriented, pragmatic reasoning in Anglo-Saxon-style economics (and business). The word *Krämerseele*, denoting a small-minded person, is derived from an old-fashioned German word for businessman (*Krämer*). The bottom line of this argument is: there is a natural tendency for German culture to accept, perhaps even admire, ordoliberal economics, because it is a type of economics that is close to continental law: rules- and framework-based. Put even more succinctly: ordoliberals are viewed as good economists because they really are like jurists.[23] The tendency of Anglo-Saxon economists to measure, to gather data, to calculate and simulate, to use statistical reasoning rather than formalistic reasoning, comes as horror to many German intellectuals:[24] a side-by-side op-ed by Roland Vaubel,[25] one of the strongest public voices in favor of the *Frankfurter Allgemeine Zeitung* manifesto, and myself (Bachmann & Vaubel, 2009), was titled by the *Financial Times Deutschland* with "*Berater oder Rechenkünstler?*" ("Advisers or Number Crunchers?"), invoking the image of economic professors as wise state advisers compared to the shady number crunchers ("*Rechenkünstler*" has a pejorative undertone in German) that are the Anglo-Saxon economists and their German followers.[26]

In this view, it is the strong position of ordoliberalism as a social philosophy that made its various comebacks in German postwar history possible: unlike in the United States where academic economics did not give up, in fact intensified the quantitative nature of its inquiries after the Keynesian problems in the 1970s, German economic policy economists of an ordoliberal bent succeeded in equating quantitative economics with discredited Keynesianism, and, more generally, with leftist politics. The same revisionist narrative played a role in the German reaction to the euro crisis.

Moreover, the strong position of ordoliberalism as a social philosophy had palpable, if indirect structural consequences for German academic economics: (1) From an Anglo-Saxon perspective, public finance has played an outsized role as a subfield of economics in Germany (see also Hesse, 2010, p. 55). Whereas public finance in an Anglo-Saxon economics department is a subgroup within applied microeconomics, public finance was much more elevated in the traditional German tripartite division of economics into economic theory, economic policy, and public finance.[27] (2) While, as we have seen above, economic theory during the early years of German postwar economics meant macroeconomic Keynesian theory, with the discrediting

Ordoliberalism: a US macroeconomics perspective   117

of Keynesianism, economic theory in Germany became what we call economic theory today: price and general equilibrium theory, and later game theory. The nature of the meetings of the *Wirtschaftstheoretischer Ausschuss* of the Verein für Socialpolitik has radically changed since the heydays of Keynesianism. Notice, however, that it was not the new neoclassical, quantitative macroeconomics from the Anglo-Saxon world that supplanted Keynesianism in the most prestigious committee. That type of macroeconomics was essentially homeless in Germany until 2000, when the Ausschuss für Makroökonomik was founded. In other words, the partial turn to ordoliberalism in the economic policy sphere was paralleled in the academic sphere by a return to mathematical microeconomic theory, a step which is itself a reflection of the social philosophy behind ordoliberalism: the pure study of the organic economic system, not to be muddied with economic policy considerations. The focus on microeconomics, if not mathematical methods, is entirely consistent with ordoliberal ideas (see Hesse, 2010, p. 53). With the prestige that economic theory has always enjoyed in German economics academia (see Hesse, 2010, p. 261) this meant: (3) a long-lasting dearth of applied macroeconomic theory and empirical macroeconomics in Germany, of which German economics has only recently begun to recover: while there are now a few strong macroeconomic research centers in Germany, the US situation, where most leading economics departments have a sizeable macroeconomics group and where macroeconomics is part of the core curriculum of any PhD education, has still no broad parallel in Germany. In addition, because most of the researchers in these macroeconomic groups are still relatively young in their academic life cycle – they are essentially a product of the 2000s – and are thus naturally underrepresented in German policy advising, macroeconomic expertise to the very day is both relatively less available to and sought out by policymakers compared to the United States.

I only need to explain the following paradox now: Why is it that the state-admiring, even statist (see Hesse, 2010, p. 54) German ordoliberal economics is skeptical about interventionist economic policies, whereas the non-statist Anglo-Saxon economics has no qualms about interventionism, if and when the situation calls for it? The answer to this paradox is fundamentally *dialectic*: when the state is viewed as an entity sui generis, superior to the economic realm, its organic function is to guarantee the functioning of the economy through rules and principles, but not through politically and economically expedient interventions, which could be subject to manipulation from (irrational) idiosyncrasies and particular interests, and would also mean that the state would have to react to stimuli from an inferior realm.[28] Conversely, for Anglo-Saxons the state is ultimately so unimportant that one might as well use it as a means to make the economy and the civil society more generally function better. The dialectic movement is thus: the important becomes unimportant if used frivolously, the unimportant becomes important if used sensibly.

118　*Rüdiger Bachmann*

A US-trained German economist ending with a dialectic argument: What more evidence do you need for the main thesis of this chapter?

Notes

1 "Politisch desinteressierte Karrieristen" (see Willgerodt, 2009).
2 "Von der Wertfreiheit zur Wertlosigkeit" (see Willgerodt, 2009).
3 "Der Kölner Emeriti-Aufstand" (see Storbeck, 2009).
4 It should be noted that this manifesto was also signed by a small number of non-ordoliberals, such as Fritz Helmedag and Rudolf Hickel, both lifelong adversaries from the left to German ordoliberalism, which is why the manifesto carefully avoids any allusion to ordoliberalism. It is clear, however, from the majority of the signatories that, at least for this majority, defending economic policy at German universities meant defending ordoliberalism at German universities.
5 And myself, somewhat surprisingly, often on the defending side of German macroeconomics and macroeconomic policy (Bachmann & Braunberger, 2014, 2015), including on points that might have been traditionally associated with ordoliberalism.
6 Frankel (2017) is another example where an American mainstream economist does not follow Krugman-style agitation but rather lays out where the pros and cons were in the arguments between German (ordoliberal) economists and American (Keynesian) pragmatists with regards to the euro crisis.
7 The same, by and large, appears to hold true also for the monetary theory and policy committee. For the non-German readers: think of the macroeconomics committee as roughly the equivalent of the economic fluctuations and growth group and the monetary theory and policy committee as roughly the equivalent of the Monetary Economics Group at the National Bureau of Economic Research.
8 "Diese marktwirtschaftliche Stimme wird in Deutschland auch in Zukunft benötigt. Deswegen wollen wir uns als Kronberger Kreis weiterhin mit ordnungspolitisch fundierten und zugleich praktisch umsetzbaren Politikvorschlägen einmischen." Lars Feld on the webpage of the Kronberger Kreis: www.stiftung marktwirtschaft.de/inhalte/kronberger-kreis (March 1, 2018).
9 Professor Wieland is the lead author of the new *Handbook of Macroeconomics* chapter titled "New Methods for Macro-Financial Model Comparison and Policy Analysis" (see Wieland et al., 2016).
10 And this despite the starting advantage vis-à-vis Keynesianism that ordoliberalism and its disciples had through being linked in with the international neoliberal Mont Pèlerin Society and thus important US economists (see Hesse, p. 162).
11 "Wages, prices and employment," "Controversies in multiplier theory," and "Employment level and income distribution"; https://sites.google.com/view/theoretischer-ausschuss/home/tagungen
12 In fairness to Walter Eucken, many of these principles were violated during the Nazi regime and even before in the Weimar State, and were perhaps in danger of being violated again in the young Federal Republic of Germany, so he had good reasons to insist on them. The other potential defense of Walter Eucken lies in the insularity of German economics during the war and right after it, which meant that he simply could not follow much of the international academic debate of his time (see Bofinger, 2016, quoting Viktor Vanberg for this claim). Hesse (2010, p. 45), on the other hand, disagrees with this insularity thesis and claims that Keynes's work was being read in Germany even before the war, certainly immediately after.
13 Hans Werner Sinn thinks so, too, in his recent autobiography; see Sinn (2018, p. 239).

Ordoliberalism: a US macroeconomics perspective 119

14 See Hesse (2010, pp. 123, 127) on the preeminence and importance of this council.

15 Karl Schiller was also one of the leading authors of the 1967 *Stabilitäts- und Wachstumsgesetz*, essentially a political implementation of Keynesian thinking at the time and very influential for German macroeconomic policy ever since.

16 It should be noted, of course, that this German conservative turn at the time was not idiosyncratic to Germany but mirrored the developments in the Anglo-Saxon world.

17 Currently, the Sachverständigenrat has two macroeconomist members, professors Bofinger and Wieland, but never in recent history has the chairman been a macroeconomist. Of the large *Wirtschaftsforschungsinstitute* (German economic think tanks) only the Berlin-based DIW institute has a macroeconomist as its head, Marcel Fratzscher.

18 Eucken was so horrified by the Nazi experience that he likened stabilization policies in reaction to aggregate demand crises to Hitler's employment policies (Landmann, 2017).

19 Of course, in addition to everything else that was different for the two countries.

20 It is probably no exaggeration to claim that this debate was just never as virulent in Anglo-Saxon social sciences.

21 The aforementioned Cologne professors were Professors für wirtschaftliche Staatswissenschaften (professors of economic state sciences). The economics department at Bonn University, for example, is part of the Rechts- und Staatswissenschaftliche Fakultät (see also Hesse, 2010, p. 72).

22 Wolfgang Schäuble, the European austerity czar, a lawyer by training, is rumored to not have been very open to economic arguments during internal debates in the Federal Ministry of Finance.

23 Harold James (2017) calls this phenomenon "Kant versus Machiavelli," although he refers with this distinction to the intra-European divide between the desire for "rules, rigor, and consistency" in the North, and the desire for "flexibility, adaptability, and innovation" in the South.

24 As one example, take Schirrmacher (2013), a coeditor of the *Frankfurter Allgemeine Zeitung* and a leading cultural intellectual in Germany since the 1990s, criticizing the number and calculation obsession of (financial) markets to the detriment of the organic functioning of the state.

25 Relatedly, Professor Vaubel once hypothesized that the reason why Samuelson, Solow, and Arrow turned to mathematics and were politically relatively on the left was their poor family background and, because of that, their relatively weaker verbal skills, compared to their mathematical ones; see Braunberger, 2013, for the corresponding quote.

26 The Austrian economists Ludwig von Mises and Friedrich August von Hayek were clearly influenced in their skepticism toward data and empiricism by a broader German cultural mentality.

27 This elevated status of public finance as determining structure is vanishing and converging to the Anglo-Saxon model, but, because of long tenure lags in the German civil service, this is a slow process.

28 It is important to note that, unlike its Anglo-Saxon non-statist sister social philosophy, the Chicago School of Economics, which absorbed many Austrian economists, ordoliberalism did argue for a very strong role of the state as a rule and framework setter (see Hesse, 2010, p. 52).

References

Bachmann, R., & Braunberger, G. (2014). Deutsche und amerikanische Ökonomen leben nicht in getrennten Welten. Interview Fazit Blog, *Frankfurter Allgemeine Zeitung online* November 23.

Bachmann, R., & Braunberger, G. (2015). Gespräche mit Ökonomen (9): Es gibt keinen angelsächsischen Block gegen Deutschland. Interview Fazit Blog, *Frankfurter Allgemeine Zeitung online* July 23.

Bachmann, R., & Uhlig, H. (2009). "Die Welt ist nicht schwarz oder weiß." *Frankfurter Allgemeine Zeitung* p. 10.

Bachmann, R. & Vaubel, R. (2009). Berater oder Rechenkünstler? *Financial Times Deutschland* July 2, p. 24.

Balling, S., & Linneweber, S. (2009). Vom Sockel gestoßen. *Rheinischer Merkur* No. 8, p. 13.

Barbier, H. (2009). Der Ruf der dreiundachtzig. *Frankfurter Allgemeine Zeitung online* May 4.

Beck, T. & Kotz, H.-H. (2017a). Introduction. In T. Beck & H.-H. Kotz (Eds.), *Ordoliberalism: A German oddity?* (pp. 11–23). VoxEU.org. London, UK: CEPR Press.

Beck, T., & Kotz, H.-H. (2017b). Banking union: Rules versus discretion? In T. Beck & H.-H. Kotz (Eds.), *Ordoliberalism: A German oddity?* (pp. 107–119). VoxEU.org. London, UK: CEPR Press.

Bofinger, P. (2016). German macroeconomics: The long shadow of Walter Eucken. VOXEU column, June 7.

Braunberger, G. (2012). Aufruhr in der Ordnungsökonomik! Lars Feld kritisiert Altvordere und formuliert ein Programm. *Frankfurter Allgemeine Zeitung online* January 1.

Braunberger, G. (2013). Ruinieren die Bildungsfernen die ökonomische Wissenschaft? *Frankfurter Allgemeine Zeitung online*, April 2

Burda, M. (2017). Ordnungsökonomik or Teutonomik? In T. Beck & H.-H. Kotz (Eds.), *Ordoliberalism: A German oddity?* (pp. 53–62). VoxEU.org. London, UK: CEPR Press.

Cochrane, J. (2009). Fiscal stimulus, RIP. November 9, 2010. http://faculty.chicago booth.edu/john.cochrane/research/papers/stimulus_rip.html

Feld, L., Köhler, E., & Nientiedt, D. (2017). The "dark ages of German macroeconomics" and other alleged shortfalls in German economic thought. In T. Beck & H.-H. Kotz (Eds.), *Ordoliberalism: A German oddity?* (pp. 41–52). VoxEU.org. London, UK: CEPR Press.

Frankel, J. (2017). German ordoliberals vs American pragmatism: What did they get right or wrong in the euro crisis? In T. Beck & H.-H. Kotz (Eds.), *Ordoliberalism: A German oddity?* (pp. 135–144). VoxEU.org. London, UK: CEPR Press.

Frankfurter Allgemeine Zeitung (2009). Rettet die Wirtschaftspolitik an den Universitäten! April 24, p. 12.

Goldschmidt, N. & Zweynert, J. (2009). Gute alte Zauberformel. *Süddeutsche Zeitung* May 9.

Habermas, J. (2011). Der Konstruktionsfehler der Währungsunion. Blätter für deutsche and international Politik, May 2011, 64–66.

Handelsblatt (2009). Baut die VWL nach internationalen Standards um! June 8, p. 9.

Ordoliberalism: a US macroeconomics perspective 121

Hesse, J.-O. (2010). Wirtschaft als Wissenschaft. Die Volkswirtschaftslehre in der frühen Bundesrepublik. *Campus Forschung Volume 947.*

Hüther, M. (2009a). Die Krise als Waterloo der Ökonomik. *Frankfurter Allgemeine Zeitung* March 16, p. 12.

Hüther, M. (2009b). Die Verantwortung der Ökonomen. *Handelsblatt online* February 13.

James, H. (2017). Rule Germania. In T. Beck & H.-H. Kotz (Eds.), *Ordoliberalism: A German oddity?* (pp. 25–30). VoxEU.org. London, UK: CEPR Press.

Krugman, P. (2013a). German surpluses: This time is different. The conscience of a Liberal [blog]. *New York Times online* November 3.

Krugman, P. (2013b). France 1930, Germany 2013. The conscience of a Liberal [blog]. *New York Times online* November 2.

Krugman, P. (2013c). Sin and Unsinn. The conscience of a Liberal [blog]. *New York Times online* November 2.

Krugman, P. (2013d). Defending Germany. The conscience of a Liberal [blog]. *New York Times online* November 2.

Krugman, P. (2013e). More notes on Germany. The conscience of a Liberal [blog]. *New York Times online* November 1.

Krugman, P. (2013f). The harm Germany does. The conscience of a Liberal [blog]. *New York Times online* November 1.

Landmann, O. (2017). What's wrong with EZ: Conflicting narratives. In T. Beck & H.-H. Kotz (Eds.), *Ordoliberalism: A German oddity?* (pp. 123–134). VoxEU.org. London, UK: CEPR Press.

Schirrmacher, F. (2013). *Ego: Das Spiel des Lebens.* Munich, Germany: Karl Blessing.

Schmidt, C. (2017). Don't shoot the messenger: About the diversity of economic policy conclusions in the face of severe identification issues. In T. Beck & H.-H. Kotz (Eds.), *Ordoliberalism: A German oddity?* (pp. 63–78). VoxEU.org. London, UK: CEPR Press.

Sinn, H. W. (2018). *Auf der Suche nach der Wahrheit.* Freiburg, Germany: Herder.

Storbeck, O. (2009). Der Kölner Emeriti-Aufstand. *Handelsblatt Online* February 18.

Vanberg, V. (2009). Die Ökonomik ist keine zweite Physik. *Frankfurter Allgemeine Zeitung* April 14, p. 10.

Watrin, C., & Willgerodt, H. (2009a). Das Fach Wirtschaftspolitik an der Universität zu Köln. Undated open letter.

Watrin, C., & Willgerodt, H. (2009b). Letter to Carl Christian von Weizsäcker from 29 March 2009, forwarded to the Verein für Socialpolitik Committee on Economic Policy, April 17.

Wieland, V., Afanasyeva, E., Kuete, M., & Yoo, J. (2016). New methods for macro-financial model comparison and policy analysis. In J. Taylor & H. Uhlig (2016). *Handbook of macroeconomics* (vol. 2) (pp. 1241–1319). Amsterdam, the Netherlands: Elsevier.

Willgerodt, H. (2009). Von der Wertfreiheit zur Wertlosigkeit. *Frankfurter Allgemeine Zeitung* February 27, p. 12.

Wren-Lewis, S. (2013). The real problem with German macroeconomics policy [mainly macro blog], November 3.

Wren-Lewis, S. (2015). What is it about German economics? *mainly macro* blog, 9 June 2015.

Wren-Lewis, S. (2016). German macroeconomics revisited. [mainly macro blog], July 19.

Yates, T. (2015). Proximate roots of German monetary and fiscal conservatism [longandvariable blog], February 20.

Zettelmeyer, J. (2017). German ordo and eurozone reform: a view from the trenches. In T. Beck & H.-H. Kotz (Eds.), *Ordoliberalism: A German oddity?* (pp. 155–166). VoxEU.org. London, UK: CEPR Press.

Part II

Ordoliberal explanations of the eurozone crisis

7 Is ordoliberalism institutionally useful for the EU?

Wolf Schäfer

Ordoliberalism as modern institutional economics

Ordoliberal economics could be looked at as a special part of the general theory of institutions. What has become known as ordoliberalism of the Freiburg School was originally founded in the 1930s at the University of Freiburg in Germany by economists and jurists. Ordoliberal theory implies that public policy should stimulate a competitive market economy through creating a set of rules as credible institutions (Vanberg, 2008). Thus, it could be described as an institutional middle path between laissez-faire liberalism and socialism. In this respect, it is principally distinct from classical liberalism – though classical liberalism decidedly represents the fundamental departure for ordoliberal economics (Starbatty, 2016).

The basic idea behind ordoliberalism is to promote a strong state in order to effectively set the institutional environment in which the market process should be framed. The state should be seen as a powerful referee but not the playmaker in the political–economic game. It should strictly care about the players respecting the rules of the game. Therefore, the state should avoid attempting to directly steer the everyday business of the economy. The enforcement of incentive-oriented rules as being effective institutions of an economic and social system is one of the prime objections of the theoretical concept of ordoliberalism.

Ordoliberalism: rules rather than discretion

Ordoliberalism implies the idea of creating 'good rules' (ordo) for policy-makers and economic agents: rules rather than discretion. Therefore, ordo-economics is pure institutional economics. It should be seen as an integral part of the *new institutional economics* approach implying, by all means, a modern theoretically and politically relevant substance to open the floor for a broad variety of research in the field of current international, and particularly European, affairs.

With some differentiations, ordoliberal thinking principally shaped Germany's *social market economy* (SME) conceptual approach after World War II.

126 *Wolf Schäfer*

The most important figures in the development of this concept include Walter Eucken, Wilhelm Röpke, Alexander Rüstow, Franz Böhm, Alfred Müller-Armack (who coined the term SME), and Ludwig Erhard who, as Minister of Economic Affairs, was named 'father' of the postwar German *Wirtschaftswunder*. The Freiburg faculty included law as well as economics providing a conductive ordo-framework for a combined legal and economic perspective.

Ludwig Erhard was deeply convinced that economic policymaking along the ordoliberal *good rules* was the best way to create "wealth for all" (Erhard, 1957), as he personally put it. There is no denying the fact that the splendid postwar economic recovery in Germany in the 1950s and early 1960s was proof that his ordoliberal approach was highly successful. But subsequent developments in Germany have led policy astray by abandoning the spirit of SME and its original principles and core values, e.g. individual responsibility, which means subsidiarity; balance of rights and responsibilities; low levels of regulation and intervention. Instead, the focus has been collective and corporate responsibility, which means more centrality; (re)distribution policy; high and ever-increasing levels of state regulations including extended welfare state arrangements. Put simply: In Germany, the spirit of SME has been fading away, and market economy thinking has lost its general reputation and public acceptance. In comparison with the primary ordoliberal and SME–spirit Germany has become an overregulated country.

The EU: breathing the spirit of ordoliberalism?

How about the European institutional landscape in the light of ordoliberalism? It is interesting to look at the constitutional objectives of the European Union (EU). Article 3(3) of the Lisbon Treaty (TEU) explicitly says that the Union "shall establish an internal market which shall work as a highly competitive social market economy." Before this SME approach was integrated in the Treaty there had been controversial discussions between the EU members about whether or not to principally follow the example of the primary German ordoliberal approach. Constitutionally speaking, the internal market approach could be seen as a kind of ordoliberal imitation representing the core basics of market economy thinking: the internal market needs *good rules* to function adequately. The *rule of law* is the most important institutional anchor for an effective functioning of societies and integration areas.

The same is true for institutionally operating the single currency area: introducing the euro within an economically and politically heterogeneous club of member states without having state-equivalent constitutional arrangements for the euro area is effectively functioning only under a system of *good rules* such as have been fixed, e. g., in the Maastricht Treaty. These rules principally breathe the spirit of ordoliberalism. But the main problem is that the (basic) rules of the Maastricht Treaty are not observed by the national governments and more often than not by the Commission when and if they find them incompatible with their own political goals. Under these circumstances the introduction of the euro is more destructive than constructive for the EU.

This is one of the reasons why the spirit of ordoliberalism in the Maastricht rules has been largely replaced by a growing body of ordo-averse institutional mechanisms in order "to rescue the euro" as the political phraseology puts it. Furthermore, a spirit of extended communitization of risks and liabilities in addition to enlarged redistributional transfer payments have governed the politico-economic spirit of the EU. This implies an institutional anchoring of collective responsibility and therefore of centrality and harmonization. It deeply contradicts the institutional approach of subsidiarity which has been voiced as one of the most effective institutional arrangements of societies and integration areas. Thus, the EU needs broad institutional innovations along ordoliberal lines. This especially applies to the concept of subsidiarity. Therefore – and for reasons of brevity – I concentrate the analysis on dealing with the fundamental ordo principle of subsidiarity.

The principle of subsidiarity

In the Lisbon Treaty, the subsidiarity concept is explicitly codified in Article 5(3) as a general principle of action for the EU regarding the institutional task sharing within the Union. In particular, this task sharing is related to the competences of the member states in relation to the Community. Despite its importance, the principle of subsidiarity is not clearly defined in economic or legal terms. From an economic point of view, it appears appropriate to identify the subsidiarity principle as the institutional manifestation of the general principle of comparative advantage that applies in societies based on the division of labor, i.e. the division of labor within a community should take place in such a manner that a particular institution be entrusted with those tasks for which it has a comparative advantage over other institutions. Comparative advantages should be identified pertaining to their proximity to citizens' preferences and cost-efficiency. In this respect there is need for concrete institutional competence catalogues (Kirchner, 1997).

The interpretation of the modern ordoliberal theory of the state associates the principle of subsidiarity with limiting state power and safeguarding individual freedom and self-responsibility. In this context it is first assumed that responsibility should rest on the private rather than the state level, and second on the lower rather than the higher state level. This implies that the state's task of allocation entails providing incentives for the efficient production of goods in the private economy and in the case of purely public goods to supply these in accordance with citizens' preferences. One example of a purely public good within the EU as a whole is the realization of the single market with its four freedoms and *good rules* which significantly correspond to ordoliberal thinking.

Ordoliberal politico-economic approaches are cognate to the theory of federalism, which says that the subsidiarity principle is regarded as a rule for

128   *Wolf Schäfer*

establishing responsibility within a multitiered state structure. The principle inherent predilection for tasks to be allocated on a decentralized basis is fueled by the aim of satisfying citizens' preferences to the greatest extent possible. The more heterogenous these preferences are, the less capable homogeneous public services provided by central bodies are of living up to this heterogeneity. Rather, the supply of public services has to be geared toward their different users who should then also provide their financing. This addresses the principle of fiscal equivalence which is assigned to the principle of subsidiarity within the framework of fiscal federalism.

A decentralized form of task sharing between administrative bodies should not only satisfy citizens' heterogeneous preferences in optimal fashion, but also – by means of the vertical and horizontal competition between government institutions initiated by it – produce incentives for innovation among public suppliers. This refers to the Hayekian view of competition as the best discovery procedure for future solutions which are unknown at present (Hayek, 1968). This addresses the fruitful dynamic component of the principle of subsidiarity. Thus, it becomes clear that subsidiarity corresponds to the organizing principles of the market economy and its institutional manifestation is inherent to competition forces.

Running counter to subsidiarity: centralization

Increasing centralization and harmonization activities of the EU Community's bodies which run counter to the principle of subsidiarity are taking hold of more and more areas of policy – even though it is the fundamental principle for action in the Union. The EU has been postulating an increasing number of Community responsibilities, i.e., in social, structural, tax, environmental, employment and wages, health, industrial, transport, technology, research, and education policy. These are policy areas which lie almost exclusively within the competence of the member states and primarily belong there. Policy developments running counter to the principle of subsidiarity are weakening the institutional potential of the EU. The presumably decisive reasons for straying from the subsidiarity principle in the EU are more likely to be derived from the domain of politico-economic explanation approaches: The Community's bodies are striving to strengthen their power by extending their area of activity. This is equally true for the Commission, the European Parliament, and the European Court of Justice.

However, national governments have an interest in political cartelization in the form of harmonization because they want to use it to avoid institutional competition and consequently the principle of subsidiarity. The interest in harmonization is greatest where, in institutional competition, governments have a comparative disadvantage in the relevant policy areas and therefore have an interest in a strategy of *raising rivals' costs*. This leads to the question of how to respond to the creeping loss of importance ascribed to the subsidiarity principle.

The German Council of Economic Advisers proposes the installation of a European Subsidiarity Court to preside over charges related to the distribution of competences between the EU and its member states and whose judges are appointed from the highest national courts. However, since it is the citizens in the member states who presumably have the greatest interest in the subsidiarity principle one could demand the establishment of an additional parliamentary chamber as a European Senate for Political Competition whose members are directly elected by the citizens of the EU (Vaubel, 1999). The notion that political cartels – in similar fashion to economic cartels – can be contracts to the detriment of third parties and thus require political competition regulation – again in the same way that we have economic competition regulations – has yet to become generally accepted. In the EU *good competition rules* for political agents to prevent detrimental effects through the abolition of political and institutional competition should be installed. International political and institutional competition plays the basic role for what is called the "New Systems Competition" (Sinn, 2003).

Alternative subsidiarity-linked concepts of integration

The subsidiarity principle demands new institutional concepts of integration in the EU. It should be pointed out that the Commission's 'roadmap' for deepening the Economic and Monetary Union as well as its proposals for a European Deposit Insurance Scheme of November 2015 and its reflection paper on the deepening of the Economic and Monetary Union of May 2017 definitely cannot be identified as adequate institutional innovations that match the subsidiarity principle – quite the contrary (European Institutional Group, 2018). But there exist some prominent theoretical approaches which have been discussed in the literature on European integration. The basic differences in the concepts have to do with the goals and time path of the integration process. In the multi-speed concept (Pop, 2017) the same goal is set for all participants in the process, but the amount of time that individual members are allowed to reach the goal differs. Further, participants are allowed to set their own time frames for reaching the common goal. The concentric circle approach (Lavenex, 2011) is closely related to the multi-speed concept. In this approach there is a highly integrated core surrounded by numerous rings of continually less integrated countries. Participants are dealt with according to their willingness or economic ability to complete certain stages of integration. In the partial membership approach (Bieler, 2002), which does not require that member countries participate in a comprehensive integration, there is limited participation with regard to individual areas such as common foreign and defense policies, anti-terrorist policies, and asylum policies.

Finally, there exists the concept of overlapping integration areas which is nearest to the subsidiary concept. This is based on considerations of the theory of clubs (Buchanan, 1965; Casella & Frey, 1992). The basic premise of this concept is that integration areas can be considered to be clubs which

130 *Wolf Schäfer*

provide club goods to the club members. These goods are club-public goods: They are subject to the exclusion principle and are partially rivalrous. Non-members are excluded as a matter of principle. Under conditions of institutional competition members can join and quit a club. Changing clubs does not necessarily mean changing places of residence but refers equally to functional mobility. As a concept of functional integration the borders of a country or integration area lose their strict delimiting function: Integration areas overlap internationally and functionally whereby optimum integration areas are thus no longer defined politically. Consequently, optimum currency areas are today no longer consistent with optimum security areas, legal jurisdiction areas or social policy areas (Schäfer, 1995).

This market-based functional approach of integration implies a *bottom-up* rather than a *top-down* strategy and is, in this respect, the incarnation of subsidiarity. The key vision should not be a Europe of centralized equality, but a Europe of subsidiarity, of plurality in differentiation. This means EU institutions reconciling with the spirit of ordoliberalism.

Bibliography

Bieler, A. (2002). *Globalisation and enlargement of the European Union: Austrian and Swedish social forces in the struggle over membership.* London, UK: Routledge.

Buchanan, J. M. (1965). An economic theory of clubs. *Economica 32* 1–14.

Casella, A. & Frey, B. (1992). Federalism and clubs: Towards an economic theory of overlapping political jurisdictions. *European Economic Review 36* 639–646.

Erhard, L. (1957/1964). *Wohlstand für alle.* Düsseldorf, Germany: Econ-Verlag.

Hayek, F. A. v. (1968). Der Wettbewerb als Entdeckungsverfahren, *Kieler Vorträge* (vol. 56). Kiel.

European Institutional Group. (2018). Open letter to the president of the European Commission. In *Wirtschaftliche Freiheit* April 5.

Kirchner, C. (1997). Competence catalogues and the principle of subsidiarity in a European constitution. *Constitutional Political Economy 8* 71–87.

Lavenex, S. (2011). Concentric circles of flexible European integration: A typology of EU external governance relations. *Comparative European Politics 9*(4).

Pop, V. (2017). Once scorned, "multispeed Europe" is back. *Wall Street Journal*, March 1.

Schäfer, W. (1995). Overlapping integration areas. In F. P. Lang & R. Ohr (Eds.), *International economic integration* (pp. 49–64). Heidelberg, Germany: Physica.

Schäfer, W. (2006). Harmonisation and centralisation versus subsidiarity: Which should apply where? *Intereconomics. Review of European Economic Policy 42* 246–249.

Sinn, H.-W. (2003). *The new systems competition.* Oxford, UK: Blackwell.

Starbatty, J. (2016). *Die englischen Klassiker der Nationalökonomie.* Stuttgart, Germany: Kohlhammer.

Vanberg, V. J. (2008). *Wettbewerb und Regelordnung.* Tübingen, Germany: Mohr Siebeck.

Vaubel, R. (1999). Enforcing competition among governments: Theory and application to the European Union. *Constitutional Political Economy 10* 327–338.

8 The D-mark and the euro

Prerequisites for a stable currency

Otmar Issing

Current problems – underlying divergences

Looking back upon its 20 years of existence, the euro is firmly established as a stable currency with an average annual inflation rate below 2%. To put this into perspective, the equivalent figure for the D-mark from its birth in 1948 until its demise in 1998 amounts to 2.8%, suggesting that the euro is even more stable than the D-mark, which counted (together with the Swiss franc) as the most stable currency of the post-World War II era.

However, drawing such a strong conclusion based on this comparison of inflation rates alone would be premature and superficial: Premature, because 20 years make for a very short appraisal period in the life of a currency; superficial, because a currency reflects and represents the totality of the political and economic history of its country.

Before the start of the European Monetary Union (EMU) there was an intense and widespread debate as to what extent the euro could become a currency as stable as the D-mark, and the European Central Bank (ECB) would emerge as a supranational central bank following in the footsteps of the Bundesbank. Especially on the latter issue there were those, mostly in Germany, who hoped for this to happen, and others who were rather afraid of this perspective. On a related question during my hearing before the European Parliament on May 7, 1998 I responded:

> I don't see the ECB as a Bundesbank clone. In the law it looks like it in many respects – independence, price stability, a central bank council – it would certainly appear so; and yet they are in part completely different. The ECB Governing Council is composed of governors from countries with different tax systems, welfare systems and labour market conditions, all forming a stark contrast to the German situation. The task is substantially different. While working at the Bundesbank, I rested on the shoulders of the past, and lived off the reputation that this institution had built over time. The ECB is a new institution that has yet to gain people's trust. It already enjoys an early vote of confidence by the markets; this is evident from the low long-term interest rates. But it needs to justify that

132   *Otmar Issing*

confidence through its policy, both through transparency and wise decision making. We all need to be aware that this is a difficult phase.

(Issing, 2008, p. 42)

Experience collected in the meanwhile shows that divergences in economic and social policies between member countries of the EMU have anything but disappeared and have caused and continue to cause tensions which are a heavy burden for the monetary policy of the ECB and for member countries.

If one digs deeper, those divergences are the expression of fundamentally different positions and traditions:

> The basic elements of the contrasting philosophies can be delineated quite simply. The northern vision is about rules, rigor, and consistency, while the southern emphasis is on the need for flexibility, adaptability and innovation. It is Kant versus Machiavelli. Economists have long been familiar with this kind of debate and refer to it as *rules versus discretion*.
>
> (Brunnermeier, James, & Landau, 2016, p. 4)

But all these countries signed the Maastricht Treaty, abandoned their national currencies, and subscribed to the euro as their common currency and to the ECB as their supranational central bank. And we should not forget that the stability of the D-mark was the designated model to follow.

Why is it that the D-mark and the Bundesbank became a standard not only in the European context? And to what extent was it not simply sufficient to transfer sovereignty for monetary policy to the European level? To provide an answer to these questions one has to go back to the time when the D-mark was created.

The birth of the D-mark

Twice in one generation had the German people suffered from the total destruction of their currency – in 1923 due to hyperinflation and in 1948 in the course of the so-called stopped inflation when controls prevented prices from rising and undermined the Reichsmark's capacity as a medium of exchange.

The currency reform of 1948 was organized by the Allies, the Federal Republic of Germany was established only one year later. German experts, however, had started long before to reflect on how policies should ideally be designed to deal with the tremendous challenge of restoring Germany economically from the ruins left by a totalitarian regime and a lost war.

The newly established Council of Economic Advisers brought together leading academics. In their report from April 1, 1948, they argued in favor of removing (most) price controls[1] (Der Wissenschaftliche Beirat beim Bundesministerium für Wirtschaft, 1973). The following statement is remarkable and representative of the economic line of reasoning prevailing in postwar Germany:

> The currency reform only makes sense if it is combined with a fundamental change in the current management of the economy. As an isolated, purely technical measure it would be worthless, if not dangerous.
>
> (1973, p. 1)[2]

A member of the group, Walter Eucken, also a member of the resistance against the Nazi regime, was one of Germany's leading professors of economics. His ideas had great influence on German economic policies after the war. In his influential book, he specified what had been written before in the council's report:

> All efforts to establish a market economy are futile as long as a certain stability of the currency is not secured. Currency policy therefore possesses primacy for the market economy.[3]
>
> (1955, p. 256)

For Ludwig Erhard, who as Minister of Economics became the architect of the German economic renaissance, the ideas of 'ordoliberalism,' developed by Eucken and others, formed the theoretical basis for his policy. He also subscribed to the primacy of stability of the currency. He saw a stable value of the currency as the fundament for civil society (Erhard, 1964).

It was the Allies – to be precise the Americans – who 'imposed' the independence of the central bank system on the Germans. Against the resistance of Chancellor Adenauer, independence of the central bank also became a key element of the law on the Deutsche Bundesbank in 1957. This independence from politics and the mandate to 'safeguard the currency' were the cornerstones of the monetary policy of the central bank. On this institutional foundation, the Bundesbank conducted its policy of maintaining price stability, remaining imperturbable even in times of external shocks like the oil price crises (Issing, 2005a) or German unification (Issing, 2005b). Monetary targeting began in 1975 and can be interpreted as a rules-based approach for the conduct of monetary policy. It has contributed to the success of the central bank in preserving the stability of the currency.

This is not the place to cover monetary policy in Germany from 1948 to 1998, the year when the D-mark episode ended. In this short contribution, two aspects deserve special attention. One is the fact that stability of the currency was always seen in the context of the economy as a whole and society in general (Issing, 1989). Stability of the currency is not only a fundamental prerequisite for the proper functioning of markets, but confidence in the stability of the D-mark was also the basis for long-run saving decisions, which is a key determinant for an individual's ability to provide for retirement – an important factor in a 'country of savers.' Fiscal solidity should also go hand in

134 *Otmar Issing*

hand with monetary stability. The other fundamental element of the D-mark regime is the institutional arrangement. The Bundesbank law of 1957 is based on two pillars: the goal of price stability[4] and the status of independence.

What was widely seen as a kind of constitutional basis was, however, a simple law which could have been changed anytime by a one-vote majority in the federal parliament. But, throughout this period, the potential fragility of this legal basis was never tested. The reason for this abstinence was not that all politicians were in favor of the independence of the central bank, but none of them saw any chance to gain in popularity by questioning the statute of the Bundesbank (Issing, 1993).

This is in sharp contrast, for example, to the situation in the USA. Between 1979 and 1990, 200 initiatives were started containing 307 proposals of which 56 pertained to monetary policy. Although none of these initiatives succeeded, the number alone demonstrates that politicians saw such attacks as a means to get (positive) public attention. And this attitude has not changed since.

To summarize: Against the backdrop of the total destruction of two currencies in one generation, the stability of the D-mark by itself was an extraordinary experience and at the same time a fundamental element of overall stability in postwar Germany. Jacques Delors is often quoted as having said: "Not all Germans believe in God, but all believe in the Bundesbank" – exaggerated as it may sound, it reveals the important role the central bank – or rather the stability of the D-mark – played in postwar Germany and how it represented a key element in the concept of the *Soziale Marktwirtschaft*.

The birth of the euro

When the European Monetary System (EMS) was established in 1979, it soon became apparent that, against early intentions, the system was based on its strongest currency, the D-mark. The following period of this exchange-rate regime was characterized by the anchor role of the D-mark and the Bundesbank's monetary policy. Accordingly, there was, e.g., a notion in France that 'our monetary policy is now made in Frankfurt.' For obvious reasons this situation was seen as unsustainable. On the other hand, when it came to deciding the format of the future EMU, there was a common conviction that the euro should become a currency as stable as the D-mark.

An obvious consequence was to design a statute for the future ECB which would emulate that of the Bundesbank. As a matter of fact, during the Maastricht negotiations, a global consensus had emerged that central bank independence combined with a clear mandate for price stability or low inflation would constitute the optimal statute for a central bank. Therefore, it is not surprising that the number of central banks which were given independence on a worldwide scale rather exploded (Masciandaro & Romelli, 2017).

However, without the track record of the Bundesbank it might have been impossible to achieve a unanimous accord to endow the ECB with the status of independence at a time when no other national central bank in Europe enjoyed this freedom fully.

To sign an agreement on such a statute is one thing; to stand behind it with complete conviction is a different matter. The fact that not all countries were enthusiastic about this decision became obvious when, e.g., in the run-up to the French referendum on the Maastricht Treaty, President Mitterrand declared in a televised debate on September 3, 1992:

> The Central Bank, the future Central Bank ... does not decide ... The technocrats of the Central Bank within the monetary sphere are charged with implementing the decisions of the European Council which are taken by the 12 heads of state and government, i.e. by the politicians that represent their people ... Everywhere I hear people say ... that this European Central Bank will be the master of decisions! This is just not true! The monetary policy belongs to the European Council and the implementation of the monetary policy belongs to the Central Bank within the limits of the decisions of the European Council.

One could argue at length whether this statement is representative – of the opinion in France and beyond – or not. What can hardly be denied is the fact that many member countries of the EMU did not comply with the consequences that the euro as a stable common currency would entail. The Stability and Growth Pact was designed to close the gap in the area of fiscal policies. This pact was violated time and again. A former president of the Commission even declared the pact as 'stupid.' The point here is not about the details of this arrangement, but the need to conduct solid public fiscal policy in the context of a stable single currency.

The same is true for structural policies to fulfil the flexibility criteria which would guarantee that the single monetary policy fits all (see Issing, 2008). According to the Lisbon Treaty, Article 3(3) now has a new reference:

> The Union shall establish an internal market. It shall work for the sustainable development of Europe based on balanced economic growth and price stability, a highly competitive social market economy, aiming at full employment and social progress, and a high level of protection and improvement of the quality of the environment. It shall promote scientific and technological advance.

Again, it is not so difficult to agree on such a wording, but it is extremely demanding to implement reforms which are conducive for an economy consistent with the prerequisites of a stable euro.

136   *Otmar Issing*

Concluding remarks

As a member of the Board of Directors of the Bundesbank and in reference to the objective of the EMU, I wrote in 1993:

> All experience goes to show that, while the independence of the central bank is a *necessary* condition, it is by no means a *sufficient* condition to ensure the maintenance of the value of money. It would therefore be illusory to believe that it would suffice for a society to transfer this task, as it were in a once-for-all effort, to an institution which is independent – and then to continue to overburden the real potential with excessive demands.
>
> (Issing, 1993, p. 35)

The statute of the ECB contains a clear mandate – priority of the maintenance of price stability – and endows the institution with independence from political pressure to allow for a monetary policy that can reach that goal. The convergence criteria provided that countries had to qualify for entry into EMU, but were – insufficient as they have been – not binding for conducting appropriate national structural and macroeconomic policies thereafter. The Stability and Growth Pact failed miserably to guarantee solid national fiscal policies.

Permanent and sometimes almost fatal problems of the EMU originate in the fact that policies in a number of member states ran counter to a single monetary policy aimed at achieving price stability. The source of this defect goes back to different underlying economic philosophies (see Brunnermeier et al., 2016), which seem not to have changed in substance during the years since the start of the euro. This is a fundamental threat to the proper functioning of monetary union and could even risk the cohesion of the present membership.

The experience of the D-mark episode demonstrates how an independent central bank can preserve the stability of the currency in the context of policies which are consistent with such an institutional arrangement. The statute for the central bank could be transferred to the European level. Mainly triggered by crises, structural reforms in some countries were implemented which are conducive to a better functioning of the overall system. However, there is still a wide gap between national policies and the prerequisites for a common stable currency.

And, finally, Germany itself is raising concerns that it is departing from the model which more or less existed during the D-mark time (Issing, 2015).

Notes

1 This was the view of the majority. Before the establishment of a German government these reports were directed to a preliminary institution.
2 Translation by author of this chapter.

3 The German text refers to *Wettbewerbsordnung* – literally translated as "the order of competition." What is meant is a rules-based framework for an economy grounded in competition in markets.
4 As already mentioned, the wording in the law is "safeguarding the currency" which would include also stability of the external value (i.e. the exchange rate) which unavoidably would be inconsistent in a global inflationary environment. The Bundesbank throughout the course of time was successful in convincing the policymakers that its mandate was the domestic stability of the D-mark.

References

Brunnermeier, M., James, H., & Landau, J.-P. (2016). *The euro and the battle of ideas.* Princeton, NJ: Princeton University Press.

Der Wissenschaftliche Beirat beim Bundesministerium für Wirtschaft. (1973). Sammelband der Gutachten von 1948 bis 1972. Göttingen, Germany: Bundesministerium für Wirtschaft.

Erhard, L. (1964). *Wohlstand für Alle.* Düsseldorf, Germany: Econ-Verlag.

Eucken, W. (1955). *Grundsätze der Wirtschaftspolitik,* 2. Auflage, Tübingen, Germany: Mohr Siebeck.

Issing, O. (1989). Primat der Währungspolitik, *ORDO: Jahrbuch für die Ordnung von Wirtschaft und Gesellschaft 40* 351–361.

Issing, O. (1993). Central bank independence and monetary stability. Institute of Economic Affairs, Occasional Paper 89, London, UK.

Issing, O. (2005a). Why did the Great Inflation not happen in Germany? *Federal Reserve Bank of St. Louis Review 87*(2).

Issing, O. (2005b). Monetary policy in uncharted territory. In O. Issing, V. Gaspar, O. Tristani, & D. Vestin, *Imperfect knowledge and monetary policy.* Cambridge, UK: Cambridge University Press.

Issing, O. (2008). *The birth of the euro.* Cambridge, UK: Cambridge University Press.

Issing, O. (2015). Ludwig Erhard – überall und nirgendwo. *Ludwig-Erhard-Initiativkreis, Schriftenreihe,* Heft 4, Fürth.

Masciandaro, D., & D. Romelli. (2017). Ups and downs of central bank independence from the Great Inflation to the Great Recession: Theory, institutions and empirics. *Financial History Review 22*(3), 259–289.

9 The commitment problem and the euro crisis

Johannes Becker and Clemens Fuest

The euro: promise and disappointment

In 1999, 11 countries abandoned their national currencies and created the eurozone. It all began so promisingly. Credibly pegged to the hard-currency countries in the North, interest rates in Southern Europe fell to heretofore unknown levels. Huge volumes of international capital flowed into these countries, were invested or consumed, and boosted nominal GDP. As late as 2009, Jean-Claude Trichet – the ECB President at the time – was hailing the euro as a historic success and a significant achievement. But the downturn had already begun. A full 18 months before, several banks in the United States had got into difficulties as a result of falling real estate prices. This had triggered a general loss of confidence, which assumed global proportions when the US investment bank Lehman Brothers filed for bankruptcy in mid-September 2008. However, all of this still seemed to have nothing to do with the euro. It was only when Irish banks also started to wobble and the Greek government reported a much-higher-than-expected deficit in mid-October 2009 that the crisis broke loose in the euro area. International investors' confidence evaporated and the crisis-hit countries' bond yields shot up. The southern European countries suffered massive capital outflows. Even countries with healthy public finances, such as Ireland and Spain, were hit by debt crises because their national economies – fueled by real estate booms – collapsed, banks went bust and the bailout of financial institutions stretched public finances to breaking point. Eurozone governments, acting under considerable time pressure, managed to conjure up a bailout mechanism that was immediately put to use. First Greece, then Ireland, Portugal, and Spain received financial assistance to ensure that they could meet their current liabilities; private investors were no longer prepared to lend money to these countries on reasonable terms. Even Italy teetered on the brink of bankruptcy. A sense of calm was restored only when the European Central Bank (ECB) assured markets in mid-2012 that it would, if necessary, purchase unlimited amounts of crisis countries' government bonds – a promise which many observers believe overstepped the ECB's mandate.

How did the euro project go so badly wrong? Why has the eurozone fallen so low after such a promising start? And how can we prevent the crisis from being reignited? These questions are crucial to the future of the euro area.

Institutional failure

Any reform of the eurozone is only as good as the underlying analysis of the root causes. Since its peak in the period from 2010 to 2012, there has hardly been a topic more intensely discussed among experts but less agreed upon as why the eurozone has become mired in crisis.

Some commentators claim that the euro crisis can be attributed to the high levels of sovereign debt in Southern Europe.[1] Others blame the high levels of private debt and point to the loss of competitiveness and persistent current-account deficits being run by the crisis countries (Gros, 2015). Although this diagnosis of excessive debt is correct, it does not explain the root cause: one would be equally justified in concluding that the reason why a football team has suffered a defeat is that it has not scored enough goals. Any analysis of the root causes must do more than merely describe the symptoms of the crisis. Other observers, e.g. the German tabloid *Bild*, blame the mentality of the people in the crisis countries. According to this view, Greeks are simply incapable of budgeting properly or unwilling to do so. Even if we ignore the unsavory chauvinistic subtext that is often implied in such comments, this approach is not convincing either. A country's budgetary policies should be a matter between the electorate, government, and creditors; it is not clear why these policies should cause the eurozone to fail. What's more, Greece was running a chronic budget deficit even before it joined the euro. Its situation was clear for all to see at the time the eurozone was set up. Moreover, if a country whose GDP accounts for less than 2% of the eurozone as a whole can sink an entire continent because its public spending was a few billion too high, then it may just be that the single currency area has a few other problems anyway. Finally, some commentators (Baldwin et al., 2015) blame international capital flows because they initially entered Southern Europe in their eager quest for higher investment returns, suddenly changed their mind and left economic chaos and damaged welfare systems in their wake. But even if this characterization is correct – and even if international capital is fickle, volatile, and cruel – it is unlikely to undergo a personality change any time soon. Unless we intend to manage without international capital permanently, we need to build a eurozone that can accommodate such difficult guests. Analysis of root causes should first address the issues that we can really change.[2]

We think that the actual cause of the euro crisis is institutional failure. Banking regulation prior to the outbreak of the crisis was inadequate, and no one took the rules on sovereign debt seriously. Once the crisis hit, it became obvious that there was an almost total lack of effective procedures for dealing with crises.

140 *Johannes Becker and Clemens Fuest*

Banking regulation was inadequate in all European countries. In the crisis countries in particular it was simply accepted that banks took unsustainable risks. In Ireland it was not unusual at times to take out a mortgage loan that amounted to more than 100% of the purchase price of the house concerned. What appears to be incomprehensible in hindsight can be understood if we take ourselves back to the years shortly after the euro was launched. The countries on the periphery of the euro area had joined the single currency with the desire and ambition of catching up with the economies of core member states such as Germany and France. The massive reduction in interest rates when the euro was introduced seemed to fire the starting gun and, as it turned out, the periphery countries (except for Portugal and Italy) experienced an economic boom. Given the expectation that all of these prosperity gains would last, all caution was abandoned. Certain that wages and incomes would rise, people in these countries went on a shopping spree. In Ireland and Spain they bought expensive houses, while in Greece the government financed pay increases by borrowing. The lenders in all these cases were banks, which succumbed to the general mood of euphoria and were not prevented from doing so by the national regulatory authorities. Ten years after the euro's introduction, this euphoria gave way to disillusionment, and the banks were weighed down with mortgage loans (Ireland and Spain) and government bonds (Greece and Portugal). The losses on these bonds and the inevitable write-downs on mortgage loans sent shock waves through the banking system. Smart regulation could have prevented the housing market excesses and ruled out the possibility that individual banks would be so severely affected by a trend reversal in these markets. The banks in Ireland and Spain were bailed out, which turned the banking crisis into a sovereign debt crisis.

A further institutional weakness was the ineffective rules on government debt. These rules were introduced back in 1992 as part of the Maastricht Treaty and were originally designed to apply only during the lead-up to the euro. At Germany's insistence, however, they were later extended to remain in place after the euro's introduction. Even the drafting of these rules casts an unfavorable light on this regulatory framework. The debt ceiling set in 1992 roughly corresponded to the average for the founding member states. The deficit rule of no more than 3% was built on the logic that the debt ceiling of 60% of GDP could be maintained indefinitely as long as the budget deficit remained at 3% and GDP grew at a nominal rate of 5%. Even then, this growth rate had little to do with reality. However, this objection was always dismissed with the argument that the '3%' rule was only intended to act as an upper limit on the deficit. In reality, though, 3% became more of a benchmark for some countries rather than a ceiling. Even in the years prior to the euro's launch these criteria were regularly flouted. Germany was soon forced onto the defensive here because in 1995 it assumed one-off liabilities from its Treuhandanstalt privatization agency and therefore had to report a higher deficit. Greece submitted incorrect figures, and Italy only met the Maastricht criteria because its interest rates – in anticipation of the euro – had fallen sharply from 1997 onward. This picture did not change after the euro had been introduced: only in some countries did governments reduce their debt levels significantly, among them Ireland and Spain – to 25% and 35% respectively. Public spending in Greece, Portugal, and Italy exceeded revenues every year despite the healthy economic environment. France and Germany also flouted the Maastricht criteria and – to add insult to injury – even opposed the excessive deficit procedure stipulated by the Maastricht Treaty for dealing with such cases. Because both Jacques Chirac and Gerhard Schröder faced domestic political pressures and resisted implementing spending cuts, the Stability Pact's institutional framework – which had been weak at the best of times – was effectively abandoned and exposed to ridicule.

A lack of effective procedures to deal with crises completes the list of shortcomings. Caught up in the euphoria of low interest rates, and without any constraining banking regulation or sovereign debt rules, the eurozone hurtled headlong into the abyss before realizing much too late that it had no parachute to arrest its freefall. The eurozone had taken no precautions for the eventuality that a country – let alone a whole group of countries – would be hit by a crisis. Here is Commission President Romano Prodi, who in 1999 – shortly after the euro had been launched – said: "I am sure the Euro will oblige us to introduce a new set of economic policy instruments. It is politically impossible to propose that now. But some day there will be a crisis and new instruments will be created" (Prodi, 2000). Indeed – a small, manageable crisis soon after the introduction of the euro could have fundamentally changed the course of history. The institutional shortcomings would have been clearly revealed without a global economic crisis raging at the same time. Given the necessary time and effort, the eurozone could have built the institutions that were so badly missing from 2009 onwards. But this crisis did not materialize – nor did the improvements to the institutional framework.

However, it would be too easy simply to blame the lack of any crisis management precautions on basic omissions. The German view was that there were no such shortcomings initially: after all, there was the Stability and Growth Pact plus the Maastricht criteria, compliance with which would prevent any serious crises. And, if a crisis were to arise, the EU's no-bailout clause would apply anyway. The countries hit by a crisis would therefore be able to call the IMF, as could any non-eurozone country. One could, if one wanted, see this as a form of rescue mechanism. The only problem was that this view was not shared by the other member states. The Romano Prodi quote above illustrates the point that some countries at least were pinning their hopes on other institutions that had yet to be created. The lack of any euro-specific crisis management strategy created a vacuum. Because no new institutional mechanisms or reforms materialized even after 1999, it was left to the discretion of those involved to fill this vacuum. We do not know whether the banks and countries of Southern Europe thought about this question at all and, if they did, what they thought. Whatever they thought, they behaved as though they either never expected to see another downturn (erroneously believing the familiar line that 'this time is different') or as though, if and when a crisis arose, they could rely on the northern eurozone countries to spontaneously provide assistance.

When the crisis storm crossed the Atlantic in 2008, it was met with a sense of astonishment followed by fear. The banking sector and public finances were geared toward the expectation that the good times would continue. When things suddenly took a turn for the worse, there were no financial buffers and no reserves – and no crisis management precautions. But straight-forward bankruptcy was not an option either. First, the French simply blocked this idea and held a protective hand over 'their' Mediterranean region and their banks, which had accumulated considerable exposure to Southern Europe. And, second, Lehman's bankruptcy, with its devastating impact on the global economy, had spooked all stakeholders. No one wanted to be responsible for a second, European Lehman bust.

The euro crisis was caused by overly lax banking regulation, ineffective sovereign debt rules, and a lack of institutions able to deal with crises. So, we have now identified the problem – job done, one might think. But these shortcomings are not so easy to rectify. Rather, they are symptomatic of a more fundamental issue associated to the governance structure in the eurozone.

The eurozone's commitment problem

The crucial problem here is that the eurozone is suffering from the inability of its member states to commit themselves. For purpose of illustration, take Odysseus who lashed himself to the mast so he could resist the siren calls. The eurozone member states cannot bind themselves, and they consequently succumb to the siren calls of higher debt and postponing unpopular reforms indefinitely. The ceilings of 3% of GDP for current deficits in public finances and of 60% of GDP for national debt have never been adhered to by all member states at any time since the euro was introduced. Germany has broken these rules as well.

Politicians have reacted to this situation by making it easier to impose sanctions on those who flout the rules, while on the other hand agreeing a number of additional rules and exemptions from these rules. In addition to fiscal policy, many other indicators – such as current account surpluses and deficits – are now included in coordination efforts at European level. None of this solves the problem of the eurozone being unable to bind itself. On the contrary, the tendency to extend coordination to more policy areas is likely to dilute commonly agreed positions and make them less transparent. The fact that it is easier to impose sanctions does not in any way mean that these sanctions will actually materialize if agreements are not honored. A qualified majority on the European Council can block sanctions demanded by the European Commission. Large countries such as France and Germany will

The commitment problem and the euro crisis 143

organize the necessary majorities if push comes to shove. Given this, the deterrence effect of sanctions cannot work.

But has the financial crisis not brought about a change of mindset here? The eurozone's shortcomings are, after all, obvious for all to see. And it is indeed true that the member states have promised to regulate their banks better, pursue responsible budgetary policies, respond swiftly and decisively to future crises, and so on. However, this is simply not credible. When the crisis hits, Europeans will revert to being Germans, French, or Italians who have to listen to their domestic electorates. This is already being demonstrated by the ongoing unwillingness of the Italian elites to comply with European fiscal rules and in Eastern Europe where even commonly agreed policies on refugees are being nonchalantly abandoned so that national governments do not frighten their own electorates.

What Austrian political satirist Werner Schneyder once said is quite true: "Europe consists of countries that do not want to be told to do what they themselves have jointly decided."

In order to approach a solution to this problem, it is worth taking a closer look at the structure of the commitment problem.[3] In period 1, while Odysseus is still out of earshot of the sirens, he does not want to succumb to them because he knows that this would have fatal consequences. In period 2, when he hears the sirens, he wants to succumb to them. If he were not tied to the mast, he would now capsize and drown. What Odysseus wants therefore changes over time, and he foresees this change. He uses the opportunity in period 1 to take precautions so that in period 2 he does not get what he wants. He ties himself to the mast.

Politicians, too, regularly face the problem of binding themselves. Generally speaking, governments want to pursue responsible budgetary policies that do not impose a burden on subsequent generations. They want to invest in the future, in education, and infrastructure. They want to implement fundamental reforms and equip the country for the future. They want to keep the promises they have made to their European partners. But every year something gets in the way – elections, coalition feuds, or poor opinion poll ratings. So governments give in, succumb to the siren song, hand out short-term gifts to the voters and kick necessary reforms into the long grass. The task of balancing the budget is postponed because pension increases have to be funded first. And one can always argue that stimulating demand is more important than limiting government debt.

Fortunately, there are a few areas where politicians have succeeded in binding themselves credibly. We can use these cases as a template for resolving the euro crisis. The problem of politicians binding themselves is especially pronounced in the realm of monetary policy. Consumers and businesses must be able to rely on price stability. But those printing the money have a huge incentive to print more than agreed in return for the seemingly reasonable price of modest inflation. In order to resolve this monetary policy issue, countries used to promise to exchange banknotes for gold (or silver) if required. But even this promise must, of course, be credible. Today's monetary systems tend to rely more on independent central banks. Under this approach, democratically elected institutions define the central bank's mandate, thereby restricting their own powers or those of the incumbent government. This is why the central bank takes no instructions from the government – it is independent. The central bank's leadership is appointed for a fixed term, but this is often a lengthy period and there is no possibility of reappointment. This is designed to reduce the incentive for incumbents to pursue accommodative monetary policies in order to be appointed for a second term. Once the leadership has been appointed, politicians have virtually no influence over the central bank. In the days when Germany still had the D-mark, this meant that even chancellors such as Helmut Schmidt lost out in their power struggles with the Bundesbank. This was just one of the reasons why the Bundesbank was regarded as the template for independent institutions in managing to resolve the credibility problem in monetary policy. It is no coincidence that the ECB has been modelled on the Bundesbank and, despite the criticisms levelled here, has the potential to follow in its footsteps.

At national level it is the democratic political process that helps to mitigate the commitment problem. Politicians of all parties have a huge incentive prior to elections to make manifesto commitments that they cannot – or do not want to – honor afterwards. The political process (media coverage, public debate, oversight exercised by parliament and constitutional courts) and, in particular, the threat of being punished by voters at the next election limit the scope for making political capital out of unrealistic promises. In Germany, for example, this is illustrated by the fact that no political party went into the last general election campaign with plans to cut taxes significantly. This has not always been the case and it is not everywhere. In general, it is a matter of political culture. In the Netherlands, for example, the parties have agreed to have their economic policies audited by a research institute in the run-up to elections in order to provide voters with impartial information about the consequences of their plans. This form of (self-)regulation does not always work in countries where the state and political parties are less well respected. If voters believe anyway that all politicians are liars, those campaigning have no incentive to ensure that they are being truthful with their promises.

At the European level it is the independence of technocratic institutions, and at the national level the democratic process, that successfully mitigate the problem of politicians binding themselves. What does not work, on the other hand, is agreements and promises made at the intergovernmental level during EU summits in Brussels – as we will argue in the following.

Democratic legitimacy

Due to the absence of a strong central eurozone government, the heads of national government and the ministers concerned seek solutions in the form of multilateral agreements. These have, as discussed, no permanence when push comes to shove because of the national voters' resistance. In this section and the next we will discuss two important causes for this resistance – the erosion of democratic legitimacy and the disintegration of accountability and control – both of which have proven important in the euro crisis.

Agreements struck at meetings of the Council of Ministers or at EU summits enable national politicians to distance themselves: the resultant measures are, after all, decided not by them personally but by Brussels; they really only agree reluctantly. In doing so, national governments refuse to take political responsibility or, consequently, to bear the cost in terms of electoral popularity. The medium- and long-term damage inflicted on the political culture is considerable because the general public inevitably gets the impression that it is being governed remotely from Brussels.

This is already the case where agreements among equals are concerned, i.e. when all countries are in a similar situation and are trying to agree on a common strategy. Things become truly problematic in asymmetric situations where those present are dealing with countries that are flouting European rules or deviating from European norms in some other way. The usual procedure in such cases within the EU and eurozone is for heads of state, heads of government, and ministers to appeal directly to the populations of the recalcitrant countries and to pay them state visits during which they both admonish and woo them and argue the case for policy changes. Meanwhile, the political leaders in deviant countries are able to side with their reluctant populations and oppose the seemingly outrageous demands being made by Brussels.

Nations do not want to relinquish their sovereignty. All member states are having a political debate about the right course of action here. Every party is trying to convince the voters that its proposals will indeed improve the country's well-being. If one of these parties receives backing from Brussels, its chances of success are – as things currently stand – more likely to suffer. There is nothing wrong with Brussels pooling information, identifying cases of best practice, or drawing comparisons in order to promote competition among institutions in Europe. But it is unrealistic to expect that coordination and supervision at the European level will prevent member states from implementing other policies if the national governments or voters want to do so.

Member states can only be forced to implement policies against their will if they can be put under massive pressure. That happened to some countries during the eurozone crisis. One example is Ireland, which was forced, against its will, to agree to a bailout of its banking system. Another example is Greece, which was forced to make swinging cuts in welfare and public spending, at least in the early phase of the first adjustment program. We are not claiming that these measures were economically wrong; it was the nature of the decision-making that inflicted the greatest damage here. The ECB played its part in the process. Former ECB President Trichet telephoned the Irish prime minister in person to persuade him of the need for a bailout; otherwise,

146 Johannes Becker and Clemens Fuest

Trichet claimed, the ELA credit facility would be cancelled, which would have pushed Ireland's banking sector into the abyss. His successor, Mario Draghi, decided – given politicians' inability to get the crisis under control – to announce massive interventions in markets for government bonds of the crisis countries. The objective was to reduce their borrowing costs and to maintain their access to credit. All of these decisions lacked sufficient democratic legitimacy.

One possible objection to this view might be that democracy can sometimes get in the way during times of crisis. But things that have not been legitimized are not regarded as legitimate and therefore have no political support when it is needed. And institutions that lack political support are not credible. For example, the promise not to allow Greece to go bankrupt is not very credible for international investors if serious conflicts are being waged in all creditor countries and the majority of electorates express their strong opposition to any bailouts.

This damage is currently reflected in the spread of Euroskepticism and in the resurgence of populist right-wing and left-wing parties across Europe. Many people are not necessarily against reforms and do not oppose fiscal consolidation measures and even painful spending cuts – they just want to decide these things for themselves. Those taking part in the angry protests against the Troika and 'German occupation' included people who agreed with the direction of the reforms but simply felt that the way in which they were being implemented amounted to extortion and coercion.

Agreements between countries negotiated in Brussels that are not endorsed by national decision makers at home, policy recommendations made by the EU Commission which are perceived as undemocratic, and crisis management in the form of threats and overstepped mandates – all of these have undermined political support for European integration and have damaged the reputation of European institutions. Europeans need to learn a lesson that has long been a consensus view in international development aid: the ability to influence sovereign states' policies from outside is very limited, despite the fact that EU membership is meant to imply a form of shared sovereignty.

The aim must be to construct a eurozone where, in policy areas relevant to monetary union, there are either strong incentives to behave well or, alternatively, effective limits are placed on the scope for national decision-making. Nation states should remain sovereign in all other areas. If another member state then adopts reforms that lower its productivity, raise unemployment, and jeopardize its prosperity, Germany should be able to simply shrug its shoulders and say that it would have done things differently but that it respects the decision of other countries and does not need to worry about them because it will not be forced to pay for the consequences.

Liability and control

Democratic sovereignty of nations only makes sense if countries are accountable for their own decisions.[4] This principle has increasingly been abandoned in recent years – at both a governmental and private level. Banks and their creditors do not bear the full consequences of their actions because, when push comes to shove, they are bailed out by taxpayers. Governments' budgetary policies, which permit high deficits even during boom years, are partly subsidized by other countries if these countries finance bailouts. And, if some politicians in Brussels, Paris, and Rome get their way, this principle will be extended further. Transfer union and joint liability are just some of the terms used to describe the complex and overlapping relationships between control and accountability that are set to evolve in Europe.

But those who control things for which they are not accountable become careless; and those who are held accountable for things that they do not control become angry. Above all, however, the divergence between accountability and control creates the necessity for precisely the kind of agreements in Europe which, because of the commitment problem, do not work. Nonetheless, the objective of reforming the eurozone should be to create a community of equality – a genuine form of fiscal federalism – in which each country, within the limits of its responsibility to the single currency area, has a certain freedom of action and is alone fully accountable for the consequences of its policies. In such a world, a country would have the freedom to make poor economic policy decisions. If some government wants to nationalize large swathes of industry and the people have given it a mandate to do so, then the principles of democracy and sovereignty demand that no Troika should intervene and that no European institutions should protest and try – using more or less subtle means – to dissuade the government from implementing these plans, provided they do not violate basic rules like those of the European internal market. However, such freedom exists only in a system without joint liability.

This has a direct equivalent in the economic freedom in a market economy, which also presupposes that there is a close link between accountability and control. Further improvements are required here as well. If private companies or consumers sign loan agreements with banks, the consequences must be borne by these two parties – even in the event of a crisis.

It has to be conceded, however, that the principle of linking accountability and control cannot be perfect. There are spillovers across national borders – if one European country experiences an economic crisis, this will unavoidably affect its neighbors. In a monetary union these spillovers imply that we cannot totally exclude the possibility that risks are mutualized in certain situations, as is explained further below. However, this scenario should be limited to the unavoidable.

A close link between accountability and control does not rule out redistribution within Europe. Redistributive policies have long been pursued on a

148 *Johannes Becker and Clemens Fuest*

large scale in agriculture and through the structural and social funds – although democratic legitimacy is weak here as well. It is important to note, however, that redistribution becomes problematic if it undermines incentives to pursue sound economic policies. If a government knows that the eurozone countries will provide assistance if private capital markets refuse to grant new loans, this weakens the incentive to pursue responsible budgetary policies. These are not merely theoretical considerations: Germany's fiscal equalization scheme (*Länderfinanzausgleich*) provides decades of pertinent experience (Feld & Thushyanthan, 2010), while Italy's chronically underdeveloped and subsidized South offers another example.

Reforming the eurozone

The process of reforming the eurozone should start with its institutions. It should create institutions that mitigate the commitment problem as much as possible. It should strengthen democratic legitimacy and preserve the congruence of accountability and control. It should make the eurozone appealing to those EU countries that have not yet joined the euro – especially Sweden, Denmark, and Poland. Germany in particular has a considerable interest – both economically and culturally – in maintaining close relationships with these countries. Some of the suggestions that have been put forward would widen the gap between the eurozone and these countries.

Any successful reform of the eurozone must – first – respect Europe's past and facilitate its future without trying to force it. It is, after all, still the nation states that claim to exercise sovereignty and the key decision-making powers on behalf of their peoples. And yet the economic, cultural, and personal ties between them are so strong that any reversal of European unity would be out of the question. Second, there are cultural differences between the member states that give rise to conflicts in many contexts in which common solutions are being sought. Consequently, priority should be given to the principle of subsidiarity, and common solutions should only be sought in cases where there is only one way (e.g. in monetary policy) and coordination is essential. And, third, this coordination is being made more complicated by the fact that it is impossible to make binding agreements in the eurozone as it is currently constituted. We believe that reforms which take account of these three restrictions could well succeed.

A credible, functioning eurozone must rely only on rules and agreements that are solid enough to withstand crises. We therefore suggest that as few material operational decisions as possible should be taken during night-time negotiations between governments in Brussels. Decision-making powers should either remain with the nation states or be assigned to European technocratic institutions. The latter should have precisely defined guidelines that are laid down in the European treaties and have been legitimized by the competent democratic institutions, i.e. primarily the national parliaments. The mutualization of risks would be restricted to disasters; in such cases the member states should be able to provide significant assistance through the European Stability Mechanism (ESM). Beyond this, we do not see the need for further risk sharing (whether in the form of a European unemployment insurance scheme or in any other way). This is not to say that these risk-sharing mechanisms cannot be beneficial. One day there may be a political majority in favor of introducing a pan-European system of social security or a fiscal equalization scheme. But the euro will manage to survive without any such schemes. The eurozone will be equipped to ensure that each country bears the consequences of its own policies and thus, to a certain degree, regains its freedom of action. In areas such as banking supervision there will be European authorities that monitor and implement democratically adopted guidelines. If, within these parameters, a country decides to pursue bad economic policies, it should be able to do so. The principle of democratic self-determination and sovereignty implies, in extreme cases, that countries should be allowed to damage their own economies – if that is the will of the people.

The next time that Greece, Italy, or another eurozone country gets into a fiscal crisis, the other countries should be able to show genuine empathy with the fate of the people affected, quite apart from their concerns about the financial risks that Northern Europe will be shouldering as the crisis unfolds. There should then be little need for ad hoc coordination or conflict between the finance ministers and heads of government in Brussels. Political activity should then be mainly focused on the crisis states and be primarily restricted to politicians from these countries. There should be sovereign, democratically legitimized decisions that lead countries out of the crisis and are paid for and controlled by the voters of those same crisis countries and their creditors.

Notes

1 This view is often referred to as the 'German view' since the German government has repeatedly put emphasis on high sovereign debt levels as a cause of the euro crisis. For an academic (and much more differentiated) example, see Feld et al. (2015).
2 Alternative views on the root causes of the euro crisis are discussed e.g. in Demosthenes et al. (2015).
3 The commitment problem was pioneered by Grossman and Hart (1986) as well as Hart and Moore (1988).
4 The role of liability has also been stressed by Jens Weidmann, Chair of the Bundesbank (2014).

References

Baldwin, R. et al. (2015). Rebooting the eurozone: Step 1 – Agreeing a crisis narrative. *CEPR Policy Insight No. 85*. https://voxeu.org/article/ez-crisis-consensus-narrative
Demosthenes, I., Leblond, P., & Niemann, A. (2015). European integration and the crisis: Practice and theory. *Journal of European Public Policy 22* 155–176. doi:10.1080/13501763.2014.994979

150 *Johannes Becker and Clemens Fuest*

Feld, L., Schmidt, C., Schnabel, I., & Wieland, V. (2015). Divergence of liability and control as the source of over-indebtedness and moral hazard in the European monetary union. In R. Baldwin & F. Giavazzi (Eds.), *The eurozone crisis – A consensus view of the causes and a few possible solutions* (pp. 185–200). A VoxEU.org eBook.

Feld, L., & Thushyanthan, B. (2010). Federalism, budget deficits and public debt: On the reform of Germany's fiscal constitution. *Review of Law & Economics* 6(3) 365–393.

Gros, D. (2015). The eurozone crisis and foreign debt. In R. Baldwin & F. Giavazzi (Eds.), *The eurozone crisis – A consensus view of the causes and a few possible solutions* (pp. 121–128). A VoxEU.org eBook.

Grossman, S., & Hart, O. (1986). The costs and benefits of ownership: A theory of vertical and lateral integration. *Journal of Political Economy* 94(4) 691–719.

Hart, O., & Moore, J. (1988). Incomplete contracts and renegotiation. *Econometrica* 56 755–785. doi:10.2307/1912698

Weidmann, J. (2014). Market economy principles in monetary union. Speech at the Wolfram Engels Prize ceremony, Kronberg, Germany, March 28.

10 Germany and the euro crisis
Ordoliberalism in the dock

Oliver Landmann[1]

> Who is responsible for the eurozone crisis? The simple answer: Germany.
>
> Simon Wren-Lewis (2015)

> The Germans have a name for their unique economic framework: ordoliberalism.
>
> Wolfgang Münchau (2014)

Introduction: ordoliberalism and the "battle of ideas"

When the imminent default of the Greek government sparked a crisis of the European Monetary Union (EMU) in May 2010, the management of the crisis and of the subsequent recovery gave rise to bitter disagreements over the proper conduct of economic policy, over the binding force of the agreed rules of the eurozone, and over the amount of political integration required to make the EMU viable in the long term. These controversies flared up again when newly elected French President Emmanuel Macron proposed far-reaching reforms to deepen European integration, reforms which Germany has been rather reluctant to embrace. What divides Germany and some of its northern neighbors from the Mediterranean countries along the southern rim of the eurozone is more than just a conflict of national economic interests. More fundamentally, it is, as Brunnermeier, James, and Landau (2016) have put it, a "battle of ideas." In this battle, Germany stands for responsibility and accountability, fiscal rectitude, sound money, and an insistence on binding rules. The Latin European tradition, in contrast, prioritizes flexibility over rigid rules and rejects any constraints that might hamper crisis management and the pursuit of macroeconomic stability. It is in the context of this deep ideological divide that the German set of policy views has come to be branded 'ordoliberal' by its critics – the epithet often being used in a similar way as the more common 'neoliberal': with a pejorative overtone and with little regard for the precise meaning or origin of the term (Young, 2017).

This sudden prominence of ordoliberalism has revived academic interest in the doctrine and triggered an outpouring of publications explaining it to a broader public and exploring its significance to the current political debate in

152 *Oliver Landmann*

Europe (Beck & Kotz, 2017; Biebricher & Vogelmann, 2017; Hien & Joerges, 2017). Three questions stand out in this debate:

1   It is widely acknowledged that Germany played a dominant role in the process of creating the EMU, leaving its imprint on the Maastricht Treaty of 1992 which defined the rules of the game for the new currency. To what extent were German views on the governance of the EMU inspired by ordoliberalism in the sense of the set of policy prescriptions associated with the Freiburg School of Economics?
2   What role did Germany play in the string of events that led to the crisis of the eurozone and, subsequently, in the management of the crisis? And again: Were pertinent German policy decisions guided by ordoliberalism in any meaningful sense?
3   As the attention of European policymakers begins to shift from the immediate concerns of crisis management toward the longer-term issues of institutional reform, what are the lessons to be drawn from the failures of the original set of rules? Does ordoliberalism provide any guidance?

The present chapter cannot possibly do justice to these wide-ranging questions. What it does attempt, however, is to add some sober macroeconomic perspective to a debate which at times has become highly emotional, both inside and outside Germany.

Are German views on the governance of the EMU inspired by ordoliberalism?

To answer the question about the influence of ordoliberalism on Germany's preferences regarding the governance of the EMU, it is useful to remember that ordoliberalism was not founded as a doctrine to guide the design of a currency area. Rather, it was a response to the malfunctioning economic and political system of the Weimar State and the authoritarian decadence of the Nazi regime which had held the principles of individual freedom and free markets in contempt. The early ordoliberals thus focused on a set of rules that would guarantee the smooth operation of free competitive markets and they emphasized the absolute precedence of these rules over the discretion of policymakers as a necessary precaution against the abuse of power of any sort.

Remarkably, for a doctrine that reflected on Germany's sorry experience of economic depression, political dictatorship, and war, ordoliberalism never paid much attention to the subject of macroeconomic stability. The sole macroeconomic element of ordoliberalism is its insistence on the 'primacy of monetary policy,' i.e. on the principle of sound money. This postulate was motivated by the experience of the collapse of monetary exchange brought on by the 1922–1923 hyperinflation as well as that of the deflation during the Great Depression. But why did the mass unemployment of the Great

Depression not leave more of an imprint on the ordoliberal doctrine? Eucken never warmed to Keynesian economics. In line with Austrian business cycle theory, he believed that recessions were purgatory periods of adjustment in the wake of excessive credit expansion and overinvestment.

Eucken decisively rejected fiscal "full employment policy," both in his principal monograph *Grundsätze der Wirtschaftspolitik* (1952) and in his London lectures, delivered in London shortly before his death in 1950 (Eucken, 2001). It is somewhat disingenuous, therefore, to argue that he "was not generally opposed to expansionary fiscal policy," simply because in 1931, in the darkest hours of the Great Depression, he put his weight behind the Lautenbach plan for fiscal stimulus (Feld, Köhler, & Nientiedt, 2017, p. 43). As Eucken (2001, p. 46) explained himself, he did so not because he would have subscribed to a Keynesian diagnosis of the depression, but rather out of desperation in the face of the collapse of the democratic order and the imminent power grab by Hitler's NSDAP. He never accepted macroeconomic stabilization as an integral element of economic policy in a market economy, on an equal footing with the prevention of market concentration or the protection of property rights. His hostility toward the concept of full-employment policy was strongly shaped by his observation of how the initial job creation schemes of the Nazi regime quickly morphed into a system of extensive price controls and other oppressive interventions into markets. Eucken concluded that any full employment policy was incompatible with a free market system. He did not live to see this generalization proven wrong by the further history of business cycles and demand management in the second half of the 20th century.

With its rejection of Keynesian macroeconomics, German ordoliberalism followed a track quite different from the Anglo-Saxon mainstream, which quickly embraced the necessity of countercyclical macroeconomic stabilization, not as an alternative to the principle of free markets, but rather as a framework suitable for understanding how the stability of a market economy can be sustained. The complementarity of macroeconomic stabilization policy and the efficiency of free markets was the core idea of Samuelson's (1955) 'neoclassical synthesis.' In contrast, ordoliberalism is philosophically more in line with the Chicago tradition of economics with which Eucken was in close contact (Feld et al., 2017). The more modern variants of the Chicago School, from Friedman's quantity-theoretic approach to money and the rational expectations revolution down to real business cycle theory, share the ordoliberal skepticism toward Keynesian economics and its interventionist flair, but differ from the Freiburg School in their acceptance of neoclassical general equilibrium theory as the analytical foundation for the analysis of economic dynamics.

As German economics gradually caught up with the international mainstream after the war, Keynesian macroeconomics spread in academia and found its way into the realm of practical policymaking for the first time when countercyclical stimulus was applied in the fight against the first major

154   *Oliver Landmann*

postwar recession in 1967. In German universities, macroeconomics is taught with the very same textbooks that are in use across the globe. Ordoliberalism may be covered as one strand of thought on economic policy in general, but certainly not macroeconomic policy. Still, the attitude toward the principle of macroeconomic stabilization policy remained ambivalent in Germany. When the financial crisis had caught up with Germany in the autumn of 2008, the German finance minister grandiosely ruled out that Germany would emulate "the crass Keynesianism" of the British stimulus package which at the time was already under way. Only a few weeks later, Germany had cobbled together its own, rather extensive stimulus package. But, then again, when the eurozone embarked on generalized fiscal austerity long before its deep recession was over, another German finance minister denied that this would have much of an effect on economic activity. In short, there is simply no such thing as a consistent doctrine guiding Germany's stance on macro-economic policy.

The same lack of consistency characterizes Germany's approach toward the governance of the eurozone. Pragmatism and the imperatives of domestic politics have regularly prevailed over the rule-bound 'steadiness' of economic policy favored by ordoliberalism. Germany was among the first eurozone members to violate the deficit limit as early as in 2003 when it suffered from anemic growth and high unemployment. A few years later, when the imminent default of Greece shook up the eurozone, Germany quickly gave in to the demands of France and the European Central Bank (ECB) and agreed to a bailout, throwing the no-bailout clause of the Maastricht Treaty overboard. The main concern at the time was the risk of contagion, i.e. of the speculative pressure spreading from the bonds of the Greek government to those of other highly indebted countries in which French and German banks were invested to the tune of several hundred billion euros. Thus, the breach of the Maastricht rules was pure national self-interest, or perhaps rather domestic political expediency: Neither the French nor the German governments felt their voters and taxpayers were prepared to pay up for another bailout of banks only two years after the financial crisis, let alone to commit the money needed to ring-fence the bonds of governments that were fundamentally solvent, but at risk of becoming the target of a speculative attack nevertheless. Simply to follow the rules was not an option under these circumstances.

Germany's cavalier way with the rules of the Maastricht Treaty is all the more remarkable as these very same rules had been put in place at Germany's insistence. When the Treaty was negotiated, a large body of academic research on "optimum currency areas" (Mundell, 1961) could have provided guidance. This research had emphasized the vulnerability of a currency union to macroeconomic instability once member states had handed over their monetary policy autonomy to a common central bank. But these were not the issues the architects of the Maastricht Treaty had in mind when they crafted the rules of the game. What mattered instead was the need to allay the deep-seated skepticism of German public opinion toward the prospect of having to give up the beloved D-mark.

Germans were worried about two issues in particular: First, would a new currency, resulting from a merger of the D-mark with notoriously soft currencies, be as stable as the mark has been historically? In 1992, 62 German professors of economics circulated a manifesto criticizing the Maastricht Treaty on the grounds that the ECB would not achieve price stability as the diverse interests of national decision makers would not allow it to muster the will to do so. The second objection concerned the moral hazard of governments abusing a common currency to free-ride on others. Thus, the threat of a European 'transfer union' turning Germany into the paymaster of the eurozone loomed large. As a consequence, Germany insisted on building safeguards into the Maastricht Treaty strong enough to guarantee a stable currency and to prevent any resource transfers on which it did not have a veto. A long list of rules can be traced to these two German concerns. The strict mandate and the independence of the central bank, the prohibition of the monetization of government debt, the ceilings on debts and deficits, the no-bailout clause: they were all designed to win the trust of the German population.

As it happens, the rules Germany insisted on including in the Treaty of Maastricht are in line with two fundamental principles of ordoliberalism: The principle of sound money and the liability principle, the latter demanding that decision makers be held accountable and bear the consequences of their own actions. What Eucken regarded as necessary constraints on the actions of individual households and firms in the marketplace, Germany attempted to impose on governments sharing a common currency.

To sum up: Ordoliberalism has provided guidance in crafting rules for the EMU intended to protect Germany against inflation and fiscal exploitation, while neglecting the elementary preconditions of macroeconomic and financial stability. Nevertheless, whenever these rules collided with German self-interest once they were supposed to be applied, German policymakers did not hesitate to put discretionary self-interest above compliance with the rules.[2]

Germany's role in the eurozone crisis

When the global financial crisis engulfed the eurozone in 2008, it came as much as a surprise as anywhere else. Only three months before the bankruptcy of Lehman Brothers in September 2008, the European Commission (2008) had hailed the euro as "a resounding success." Clearly, the turmoil that was brewing on Europe's financial markets was not widely appreciated. Initially, the financial crisis and the subsequent slump of economic activity in the eurozone did not appear to differ much from that in the United States. But the eurozone was much less prepared to face a crisis of this sort and scale than the United States. As Rodrik (2010) aptly put it early in the crisis

156　*Oliver Landmann*

Europe's bad luck was to be hit with the worst financial crisis since the 1930's while still only halfway through its integration process. The euro-zone was too integrated for cross-border spillovers not to cause mayhem in national economies, but not integrated enough to have the institutional capacity needed to manage the crisis.

The lack of institutional capacity was most visible in banking policy where fragmented national regulators hesitated to act forcefully to clean up the financial sector and where national resources were strained to the limit by the rescue of troubled banks. Fiscal policy was fragmented as well, with each government constrained in its countercyclical actions by the openness of its economy, the deficit rules of the Maastricht Treaty, and the threat of losing access to the capital market. In the absence of a fiscal capacity at the center of the system, no one was in charge of the aggregate stance of fiscal policy for the eurozone as a whole, let alone of fiscal policy coordination. This left the ECB as the only player in the economic policy arena with clout and a sense of responsibility for keeping the eurozone on track. But even the ECB was severely hampered by controversy surrounding most of the measures it took in the face of multiple threats to the financial and macroeconomic stability of the eurozone.

These institutional weaknesses were mainly responsible for the sluggish recovery of the eurozone which trailed that of the United States by a substantial margin. Domestic demand, in particular, hardly got off the ground, held back by the long-lasting slump of investment and harsh fiscal austerity. Sustained growth of eurozone GDP did not set in before 2015 while it took domestic demand a full ten years until 2017 merely to recover its precrisis level, which is to say that all of the growth of GDP attained in the decade since the onset of the crisis was owed to the growth of net exports. Put differently, the eurozone did not add any steam of its own to the recovery of the world economy from the Great Recession, but merely sailed on the coat-tails of the more dynamic regions of the world. No doubt, this lopsided recovery fueled the protectionist sentiment confronting Europe's export industries in recent years.

Where does Germany come into this story, and why is Germany so widely held responsible for the depth of the crisis? To answer this question, one has to go back to the first decade of the EMU, the one declared a "resounding success" by the European Commission in 2008. Below the surface of that success, the potential for trouble was continuously growing due to rapidly increasing current-account imbalances between the core and the periphery of the eurozone. Germany's export surplus was mirrored by a corresponding import surplus in the periphery while German excess savings were happy to fund these imbalances. At the same time, price levels and unit labor costs drifted apart, rising significantly above the eurozone average in the periphery and falling below this same average in Germany. When the periphery suffered a sudden stop of capital inflows in the wake of the financial crisis, it faced the triple challenge of a collapse of domestic demand, a

Germany and the euro crisis   157

large overhang of foreign debt, and a loss of competitiveness resulting from years of excessive inflation.

Narratives about this sequence of events differ widely. The prevailing view in Germany is that the periphery was having a party for a decade, living beyond its means on borrowed money and now had to tighten its belt, bring down its mountain of debt, and catch up on delayed structural reform in order to recuperate its competitiveness and to revive economic growth. Outside Germany, and with some critical minds in Germany as well, the narrative suggesting that the travails of the periphery had nothing to do with Germany did not go down well. An alternative narrative rather maintained that Germany's success story was largely built on a beggar-thy-neighbor strategy of lowering unit labor costs. According to this narrative, Germany's export surplus was not so much the result of its industrial prowess as of its wage policies undercutting the European trading partners. Some critics suspect an intentional mercantilist industrial strategy designed to advance German interests at the expense of foreign economies (Cesaratto, 2010).

There is a grain of truth to this alternative narrative in that German workers, with very few exceptions, have been keenly aware of the significance of wages for the international competitiveness of German manufacturing. This is particularly true for the postwar *Wirtschaftswunder*, but continues to apply more recently. It is incorrect, however, to identify this sensitivity to competitiveness with a conscious mercantilist policy. Wage growth is not decided by any policymaker, but is negotiated on an industry-by-industry basis between employers and unions and as such is subject to exogenous influences on labor market conditions that may have their origin in policies of the German government as well as in developments abroad. Germany had its rude awakening to globalization earlier than other western countries in the early 1990s when the Iron Curtain fell and German manufacturing was suddenly confronted with low-cost competitors right at its doorsteps. German employers, unions, and work councils responded by increasing the flexibility of wage setting, taking into account threats to employment literally down to the firm level (Dustmann, Fitzenberger, Schönberg, & Spitz-Oener, 2014). Later, the flexibility of Germany's labor market was further enhanced by the much-heralded Hartz reform of 2005. But an inspection of the data reveals that the downward trend of Germany's real exchange rate vis-à-vis the rest of the eurozone set in as early as 1994, years before the start of EMU, and persisted until about 2010.

This German wage flexibility contributed to a fall in the equilibrium unemployment rate and hence boosted the production capacity of the economy. Elementary economic principles suggest that any expansion of the supply capacity of an economy should lower the relative price of domestic goods in terms of foreign goods – which amounts exactly to the real depreciation experienced by Germany over some 15 years. The downward trend of the relative price of German goods was reinforced when the convergence of interest rates in the run-up to the EMU acted as a strong asymmetric shock

158   *Oliver Landmann*

on the eurozone, boosting the periphery and pushing up prices there, as described above. The handling of this asymmetric shock was the first instance where the deficiencies of the eurozone's German-inspired institutional design became apparent. The ECB, setting its policy rates with a view to the average condition of the eurozone, could not do anything about the increasing disparity of cyclical conditions in the eurozone. By design, there can only be a single monetary policy stance for the entire eurozone, which was much too loose for the needs of the periphery and somewhat too tight for Germany under the circumstances prevailing at the time. The asymmetric counter-cyclical policies that would have been required to contain the destabilizing effects of the asymmetric shock simply did not exist in the playbook of the EMU. Since most periphery economies – with the notable exception of Greece – were well below the debt and deficit limits of the Maastricht Treaty, there was no pressure on them to tighten their fiscal policies to cool their booming economies.

Thus, the increase of the German current-account surplus from near zero at the beginning of the EMU to more than 8% of GDP by 2017 can be explained as the combined outcome of a textbook-like response to well-understood exogenous forces and the lack of countercyclical stabilizers in the architecture of the EMU. No conscious German strategy of wage dumping, let alone mercantilism was at work. The notion, put forward by some of Germany's critics that a currency union "should" have roughly uniform inflation rates and that countries are under an obligation, therefore, to keep the growth of their unit labor costs aligned with the inflation target of the common central bank is both *dirigiste* and at odds with elementary market logic. When the determinants of fundamental real equilibrium exchange rates change, there should be enough breathing space for inflation differentials to bring about the required adjustment. If such adjustment is deemed to strain the adjustment capacity of the currency union, the appropriate policy action should focus on the underlying disturbance, e.g. by adjusting fiscal policies. Heavy-handed intervention in the wage-setting mechanism, in contrast, would merely address a symptom while leaving the underlying problem unresolved.

Where Germany's critics do have a point, however, is with regard to the handling of the crisis management once the sudden stop of capital flows had occurred. The order of the day was to restore financial and macroeconomic stability as quickly as possible. The initial response – slashing interest rates, providing liquidity to the financial sector, and fiscal stimulus – was correct, largely uncontroversial, and successful in stopping the implosion of the system. But soon, the appropriate course of action became more contentious. Should interest rates be raised in response to an uptick of prices that was due to a rise in commodity prices? Should the ECB follow the example of the US central bank and embark on quantitative easing? Should the ECB assume the role of a lender of last resort if a government faced a liquidity crisis? Should fiscal policies quickly return to debt reduction in the face of high public debt? The German answer to all of these questions was to choose the more conservative, more austere option. In some cases, the German opposition to further stimulus got its way; in others, it at least succeeded in delaying or weakening expansionary policies. In the case of the ECB's so-called outright monetary transactions, the promise to support governments threatened by a liquidity squeeze due to speculative pressure on their bonds, a lawsuit filed by German plaintiffs challenged the legality of the promised policy action and thereby damaged ECB credibility.

The strong German opposition against decisive monetary or fiscal stimulus certainly did not help the eurozone recover from its severe recession. However, it would be a gross exaggeration to say that the German stance on these policies was dictated by an ordoliberal mindset of the German government. To be sure, the hawkish views on monetary and fiscal policies perfectly matched the ordoliberal emphasis on sound money and liability. The low regard for the necessity of macroeconomic stabilization was a feature shared with ordoliberalism as well. But clearly, the prosaic motive of national self-interest was more important – "Teutonomik," as Burda (2017) put it. One need not believe in ordoliberalism to resist debt mutualization if the debt in question is someone else's.

National self-interest colored Germany's attitude toward fiscal and monetary policy choices as well. Although the German economy took a heavy hit in the crisis, with GDP down by 5% in 2009 alone, the recovery was swift and employment held up surprisingly well, given the steep fall of production. Soon, Germany was back on a path of solid growth, not much below that of the United States. This resilience was owed in part to good policy, in particular labor market policy, and in part to the robust recovery of the world economy which provided growing markets to the highly competitive German export industries. Against this backdrop, Germany, unlike the rest of the eurozone, had little to gain from further demand stimulus – or worse, it feared suffering adverse effects on its economy from policies designed to lift eurozone production back toward potential and eurozone inflation back toward the target rate of close to 2%.

A number of German opinion leaders go as far as to question the legitimacy of the ECB's 2% inflation target, preferring a number closer to zero as a matter of principle, but also on the grounds that Germany is doing just fine with its inflation rate of under 1% whereas generalized demand stimulus for the eurozone would risk pushing the German inflation rate well above 2% (Stark, 2015). Undeniably, the price level in the periphery needs to fall against German prices if the competitiveness of the periphery is to be restored – as it must once the domestic demand boom is over. This adjustment of relative prices can be brought about either by deflation in the periphery or by inflation in Germany. But why should Germany suffer inflation, many Germans argue, if the point is to undo the effects of past excess inflation in the periphery? Wouldn't prices be ratcheted up every time a eurozone member state has experienced a period of excess inflation if other countries were subsequently asked to engage in catch-up inflation to redress relative prices?

160   *Oliver Landmann*

This line of reasoning is flawed on the grounds of both fact and logic. First of all, the decade of the periphery's domestic demand boom was not a period of generalized excess inflation in the eurozone. Quite to the contrary, the ECB kept the overall inflation rate reasonably close to its 2% target so that above-target inflation in the periphery was roughly matched by below-target inflation in Germany. Second, if the ECB aims at 2% average inflation while the periphery needs a real depreciation, it is a matter of pure arithmetic that the only way both of these aims can be accomplished is by German inflation running above 2% and inflation in the periphery running below 2% for a while. Rejection of this symmetry of adjustment is tantamount to imposing a deflationary bias on the eurozone and outright deflation on the periphery. This would be extremely costly, unfair, and against the inherent logic of a well-run currency union. Germany's refusal to accept symmetric adjustment is reminiscent of the final years of the gold standard, another period when major surplus economies – the United States and France, at the time – imposed the entire burden of adjustment on the deficit countries which were thereby forced into deflation. This violation of the rules of the game ulti-mately hastened the demise of the gold standard.[3]

Reforming the eurozone

As the recovery of the eurozone from the depths of recession has gained strength, attention has increasingly turned to the question of how to reform its institutional architecture. On this question, the two camps of the 'battle of ideas' are once again at cross. Whereas France and Southern Europeans call for more insurance, more solidarity, and more centralized institutions in the quest for monetary and financial stability, Germany is wary of anything that smacks of a 'transfer union' or of weakening market discipline. The task of creating a more resilient institutional framework for the eurozone is compli-cated by the fact that reforms cannot start with a clean sheet, but are bur-dened with the legacy of the past – be it high public debt, non-performing loans in the balance sheets of commercial banks, or macroeconomic imbal-ances. All proposals for risk reduction and risk pooling are burdened with this problem.

In Germany, opposition against any such proposal runs high. Would coun-tries suffering from the continuing costs of past policy errors not attempt to cover these costs out of common pools built to insure against future hazards? Would an insurance company, critics object, offer fire insurance for a build-ing that burned yesterday? In this spirit, a manifesto signed by 154 German professors of economics and business (Manifesto, 2018) warns, among other things:

- against using the European Stability Mechanism (ESM) as a fiscal back-stop in dealing with unsustainable banks, on the grounds that this would ruin the incentive to deal with the problems in the banking sector;

Germany and the euro crisis 161

- against transforming the ESM into a European Monetary Fund (EMF), on the grounds that this would eliminate the veto of the German parliament on certain expenditure decisions;
- against a European deposit insurance system, on the grounds that this would collectivize the costs of mistakes committed by national banks and governments in the past;
- against a European finance minister, on the grounds that this would politicize monetary policy even more than it already is.

The manifesto regards any European solution in the cited areas as a collectivization of liability that destroys good incentives and creates bad ones, leading to outcomes that are inferior to those achieved by keeping the respective decision-making authority on the national level. Things are not quite that simple, of course. To cite just one example, national banking supervision agencies have a dismal record in dealing with the vulnerabilities of national banks. It took the newly created elements of the European Banking Union to set up more meaningful stress tests and to accelerate the resolution of over-indebted financial institutions. By invoking the liability principle as an ordoliberal "cornerstone of the Social Market Economy" in support of its opposition to any sort of a collective European policy toward macroeconomic and financial stability, the manifesto claims to be the voice of ordoliberalism in the debate. On closer inspection, however, the label of ordoliberalism rather appears to cover up for a lack of detailed policy analysis. In particular, there is no assessment whatsoever of the optimal allocation of decision-making authorities to different levels of political organization – European, national, and subnational – along the lines of the subsidiarity principle and of establishing effective democratic control on each level. If ordoliberalism is understood as a doctrine concerned with the effective organization of a market-based economic system, the manifesto has no claim on ordoliberal credentials.

Quite obviously, for progress toward an effective reform of the eurozone to materialize, the task is to find a middle ground between the need for some elements of risk-pooling, coordination, and centralization on the one hand and German fears of a 'transfer union' on the other. Such a middle ground does exist (Zettelmeyer, 2017) and operational ways of defining it have been proposed (e.g. Bénassy-Quéré et al., 2018). In line with ordoliberal thought, any such reform must start from the insight that a system made up of decentralized decision makers requires a set of strong institutions and enforceable rules if they are to act and interact smoothly. Although ordoliberalism may originally have focused on rules for firms and households interacting in competitive markets, the same insight applies to sovereign nations bound together by tightly integrated markets and a common currency. Where the design of a currency union must move beyond ordoliberal thought, however, is in safeguarding macroeconomic and financial stability as much as the stability of the price level.

162   *Oliver Landmann*

This is precisely where the rules and institutions of the eurozone – the debt and deficit rules in particular – have failed. They failed because they missed the relevant trouble spots that were eventually to jeopardize the stability of the EMU. Overt public borrowing was never the core of the problem. Rather, the relevant risks stemmed from the contingent liabilities associated with the invisible fragility of the banking sector. That is why completing the banking union is as urgent a priority for the European Union as is effective fiscal policy.

The way they were designed, the fiscal rules of the EMU acted as a destabilizing force, exacerbating macroeconomic disturbances procyclically. As was well known at the time, fiscal policy must assume a key role in absorbing asymmetric shocks once nominal exchange-rate adjustments are no longer an option. The response to symmetric aggregate shocks can normally be left to monetary policy, provided the central bank has traction. If interest-rate adjustments are ruled out because of a binding zero lower bound, however, fiscal policy becomes even more important for macroeconomic stability. In addition, national fiscal policies create spillovers to other countries, which raises the issue of policy coordination. The case for coordination is particularly strong if monetary policy is constrained by the zero lower bound (Landmann, 2018). Europe was ill-prepared to deal with any of these contingencies.

Several proposals for reforming the fiscal policy framework of the eurozone have been put forward. Since a fiscal capacity strong enough to contain asymmetric cyclical disturbances on its own is not feasible politically at the level of the EMU in the foreseeable future, most proposals aim at nudging national fiscal policies toward a more countercyclical stance. Whatever mechanism is most promising to achieve this, it must recognize the interdependence of the diverse problem areas. Thus, if the resilience of the financial sector is crucial for the state of public finances, fiscal policy cannot be a stabilizing force unless the 'doom loop' linking governments and banks is effectively broken. Moreover, the design of national fiscal policies must take into account that governments lack a national central bank as a backstop in the case of major borrowing needs. Any framework providing for a consistently countercyclical orientation of fiscal policies must ensure that borrowing constraints do not get in the way of the required policy stance. The availability of such a backstop, in turn, requires an effective mechanism disciplining fiscal policy across business cycles so as to keep public debt on a sustainable long-term path. In addition, if market discipline is to play an effective part in restraining governments, a blueprint for an orderly sovereign default must be in place. Obviously, all these elements must be in force simultaneously if a reformed institutional architecture of the EMU is to prove resilient (Bénassy-Quéré et al., 2018). Europe has paid dearly for underappreciating the complexity of this task upon the creation of the EMU.

Setting the technicalities of constructing a workable policy framework aside, the fundamental impediment to progress on this front is the tension between the very need for such a framework and the reluctance of individual eurozone members to give up any national autonomy in favor of supranational European institutions. As pointed out above, what is at stake is not necessarily the creation of a very large European budget, but the willingness to accept guidelines and constraints on those aspects of fiscal policy that are important for the macroeconomic performance of the eurozone. If a fiscal council or a European finance minister had the authority to coordinate the fiscal impulses emanating from national fiscal policy decisions – as measured, say, by the change of structural primary budget balances – this would still leave the lion's share of the tax and spending decisions that are important to national electorates in the hands of domestic authorities.

The ordoliberal emphasis on the congruence of decision-making authority and accountability may suggest that even the delegation of such limited fiscal powers to some European institution requires the establishment of a full European federation with full democratic accountability to its citizens. Which still leaves open the question of sequencing. Feld (2018) forcefully argues that federation must come first before any delegation of fiscal authority can be justified. It is not clear, however, whether this sequencing is viable. If effective macroeconomic stabilization of the eurozone is delayed until citizens feel ready to think of themselves as Europeans as much as they are German, Dutch, or Italian, chances are there will be no Europe left to identify with. Europe may be caught in a vicious circle here. How are citizens to identify with Europe if they see it malfunction so badly?

If Europe is to escape from this bad equilibrium, politicians need to understand what policy areas require Union-wide coordination and collective action and, more importantly, they need the confidence and the conviction to put the pertinent new policies and institutions in place and to demonstrate their effectiveness. Would Germany have written its success story of the *Wirtschaftswunder* if Ludwig Erhard had delayed the liberalization of prices until he had convinced skeptical Germans of the case for free markets?

Conclusion

German ordoliberalism is widely criticized as the theoretical basis of policies that have exacerbated the crisis of the eurozone. Is this criticism justified? As pointed out above, ordoliberalism was designed as a rulebook for running a market economy, not as a blueprint for the architecture of a currency union. Moreover, Germany was far from following a consistently ordoliberal script in the EMU. That said, the agenda of conservative German opinion leaders and policymakers has much in common with the central tenets of ordoliberalism – most importantly, a strong preference for hard money policies and the insistence on the liability principle, both of which are solidly enshrined in the 1992 Treaty of Maastricht.

As argued above, neither the German national interest nor the ordoliberal agenda attach much weight to the prerequisites of macroeconomic stability in

164 *Oliver Landmann*

the eurozone at large. Accordingly, they both favor a narrative of the eurozone crisis which attributes most of the hardship suffered by individual countries to bad policies adopted by those countries themselves, rather than to systemic macroeconomic failures of the overall fiscal and financial architecture of the currency union. Macroeconomic stabilization, it is argued, rewards past bad behavior and weakens the incentive to undertake structural reforms. However, this line of reasoning is flawed. It ignores the political risks of failed macroeconomic stabilization as electorates turn against 'elitist' structural reforms that are perceived as (and often are) regressive in their distributional consequences. It also ignores the need for accommodating demand policies to accompany supply-side reforms if the latter are to succeed.

Resistance against any further deepening of the European currency and banking union runs particularly high in Germany. It may be convenient to phrase objections against any strengthening of European macroeconomic coordination as a defense of fundamental ordoliberal principles, such as liability and responsibility. While concerns about incentive compatibility are legitimate, they are at risk of hardening into a dogmatic resistance against any type of supranational European arrangements even if such arrangements are clearly in the interest of macroeconomic and financial stability in Europe. Ordoliberalism deserves better than being misused as cover for a thinly veiled nationalist conservative agenda. After all, it is a doctrine with a deep understanding of the crucial importance of well-functioning and enforceable rules and institutions for complex systems in which independent entities, driven by self-interest, interact. The eurozone is exactly such a complex system. Unfortunately, the rules and institutions put in place upon the creation of the common currency, some of them at German insistence, have miserably failed.

If Rodrik's (2010) diagnosis of an imbalance between Europe's economic integration and its institutional development is correct, Europe now faces a choice of either allowing its economic and monetary integration to unravel or of completing the institutional integration required to make its common currency sustainable. Continued muddling through is no longer an option. A long-time pioneer of European integration, Germany bears a particular responsibility at this juncture to pave the way for a reform of European institutions and policies, allowing for a well-coordinated, stabilizing management of the eurozone economy.

Notes

1 The author thanks, without implicating them, participants at conferences and workshops at Nagoya University, Meiji University, the German Keynes Society, Harvard University, The University of Freiburg, and the Walter-Eucken-Institut, Freiburg, for valuable comments and suggestions.
2 This assessment appears to be largely shared by Feld et al. (2017).
3 The parallel between the gold standard and the EMU has been highlighted by Eichengreen and Temin (2010).

References

Beck, T., & Kotz, H.-H. (Eds.) (2017). *Ordoliberalism: A German oddity?* VoxEU.org. London, UK: CEPR Press.

Bénassy-Quéré, A. et al. (2018). Reconciling risk sharing with market discipline: A constructive approach to euro area reform, CEPR Policy Insight No. 91. London, UK: CEPR.

Biebricher, T., & Vogelmann, F. (Eds.) (2017). *The birth of austerity: German ordoliberalism and contemporary neoliberalism.* London, UK: Rowman & Littlefield.

Brunnermeier, M., James, H., & Landau, J.-P. (2016). *The euro and the battle of ideas.* Princeton, NJ: Princeton University Press.

Burda, M. (2017). Ordnungsökonomik or Teutonomik? In T. Beck, & H. Kotz (Eds.) *Ordoliberalism: A German oddity?* (pp. 53–60). VoxEU.org. London, UK: CEPR Press.

Cesaratto, S. (2010): Europe, German mercantilism and the current crisis. In B. Emiliano, & F. Guiseppe (Eds.), *The global economic crisis: New perspectives on the critique of economic theory and policy.* London, UK: Routledge.

Dustmann, C., Fitzenberger, B., Schönberg, U., & Spitz-Oener, A. (2014). From sick man of Europe to economic superstar: Germany's resurgent economy. *Journal of Economic Perspectives 28*(1) 167–188.

Eichengreen, B. & Temin, P. (2010). Fetters of gold and paper. *Oxford Review of Economic Policy. 26*(3) 370-384.

Eucken, W. (1952). *Grundsätze der Wirtschaftspolitik.* Tübingen, Germany: Mohr Siebeck.

Eucken, W. (2001). *Wirtschaftsmacht und Wirtschaftsordnung.* Münster, Germany: Lit.

European Commission. (2008). EMU@10: Successes and challenges after 10 years of Economic and Monetary Union, 2.

Feld, L. (2018). The need for a fiscal capacity. In N. Campos & J.-E. Sturm (Eds.), *Bretton Woods, Brussels, and beyond* (pp. 135–140). VoxEU.org. London, UK: CEPR Press.

Feld, L., Köhler, E., & Nientiedt, D. (2017). The "dark ages of German macroeconomics" and other alleged shortfalls in German economic thought. In T. Beck & H. Kotz (Eds.), *Ordoliberalism: A German oddity?* (pp. 41–50). VoxEU.org. London, UK: CEPR Press.

Hien, J., & Joerges, C. (Eds.). (2017). *Ordoliberalism, law and the rule of economics.* Oxford, UK and Portland, OR: Hart.

Landmann, O. (2018). On the logic of fiscal policy coordination in a monetary union. *Open Economies Review 29* 69–87.

Manifesto (2018). "Der Euro darf nicht in die Haftungsunion führen," signed by 154 German professors. *Frankfurter Allgemeine Zeitung*, May 22.

Münchau, W. (2014). The wacky economics of Germany's parallel universe. *Financial Times*, November 17.

Mundell, R. (1961). A theory of optimal currency areas. *American Economic Review 51*(4) 657–665.

Prodi, R. (2000). *Financial Times* interview, December 4.

Rodrik, D. (2010). Thinking the unthinkable in Europe. *Project Syndicate*, December 10.

Samuelson, P. (1955). *Economics.* New York, NY: McGraw-Hill.

Stark, J. (2015). In Europa herrscht Deflations-Paranoia. *Neue Zürcher Zeitung*, January 8.

Wren-Lewis, S. (2015). Who is responsible for the eurozone crisis? The simple answer: Germany. *The Independent*, December 13.

Young, B. (2017). Ordoliberalism as an "irritating German idea." In T. Beck, & H. Kotz (Eds.), *Ordoliberalism: A German oddity?* (pp. 31–40). VoxEU.org. London, UK: CEPR Press.

Zettelmeyer, J. (2017). German ordo and eurozone reform: A view from the trenches. In T. Beck, & H. Kotz (Eds.), *Ordoliberalism: A German oddity?* (pp. 155–163). VoxEU.org. London, UK: CEPR Press.

11 Ten commandments to overcome the eurozone's many crises

If the EMU is to succeed, it must be developed based on rules

Norbert Berthold

If we don't abide by the rules, the Eurozone is going to fall apart around us.
(Wolfgang Schäuble)

Introduction

Things have gone quiet with regard to the euro. At the moment there are no acute crises. Hectic late-night meetings in Brussels, where bleary-eyed politicians scramble to save the EMU, no longer take place. Even Greece is currently neither a source of anxiety nor of dread. Even the impending Italian elections are thus far hardly disturbing financial markets. The Silvio Berlusconis and Beppe Grillos no longer seem so frightening. However, the euro is far from being out of the woods. It is true that unemployment in the EMU is slowly declining, but it is still a concern. In particular, the future of the youth in the South still looks bleak. Government debt still isn't looking good in many places. It is still far too high, with no improvement in sight. Structural reforms are delayed, a policy of austerity is on the blacklist, and redistribution is in fashion. And there is another cause for worry: the share of bad loans from banks is very high, with more in the South than in the North. The next recession could shake banks and mean trouble for their governments. The possibility of a vicious circle still can't be ruled out. A good argument can be made for taking advantage of the currently calmer times to reform the EMU from top to bottom. The following catalogue of ten commandments outlines the major lines along which sustainable, truly rule-bound institutional reform should occur.

First commandment: going forward, the euro should continue to be "money without government"

For some, the denationalization of the EU can't come fast enough. Martin Schulz, the failed chairman of the German Social Democrats (SPD), was hoping for a 'United States of Europe' by 2025. Those unwilling to play along were to leave the EU. Jean-Claude Juncker, President of the European

Commission, wants to force all of the EU member states that meet the criteria for accession to the EMU to adopt the euro. Emmanuel Macron, the French president, is flirting with the ideas of a European finance minister, a eurozone budget and debt pooling. All of these proposals are steeped in the desire to renounce national sovereignty. Their ideological superstructure is a (relatively homogeneous) European community of values. This has always been an illusion. Now it appears grotesque. The cracks in the E(M)U are deepening. Europe is becoming more heterogeneous. It is less and less possible to talk of 'harmony of interests' while conflicts of interest are growing. They increasingly manifest as growing aversion and open hostility. Today, Europe is above all a community of convenience. In some fields it pays for countries to cooperate with one another, while in others they prefer to go their own way. In short, the E(M)U will continue to be an area of heterogeneous nation states. In the future, the euro will continue to be "money without government" (Padoa-Schioppa). And that's a good thing.

Second commandment: the ECB should remain politically independent

Monetary policy is one of the areas where the EMU countries believe(d) that gains are achieved through cooperation. The 'single market project of 1992' is another. In the Maastricht Treaty a common monetary policy was agreed upon. The ECB was installed as a politically independent institution modeled on the German Central Bank. National central banks of the EMU function as its shareholders. Each member country has only one vote, regardless of its economic strength. The ECB was committed to the objective of price stability. The economic policy task is clearly specified. Price stability is the single economic policy goal of the ECB. The participating countries and national collective-bargaining partners are responsible for all other goals. The ECB's independence is in jeopardy for two reasons: It was granted supervision of the banks following the existential euro crisis. And with its policy of 'quantitative easing,' the ECB conducts monetary fiscal policy. In both cases it is dependent upon heavily indebted countries and their distressed banks. The member countries of the EMU need to outsource banking supervision to an independent institution. The ECB will remain independent only if it terminates its contract-breaching monetary fiscal policy as soon as possible.

Third commandment: monetary government financing should continue to be prohibited

The Maastricht Treaty is clear: public debt cannot be financed with the printing press. However, it is not all that easy to determine what monetary government financing is. The ECB is admittedly prohibited from becoming involved in the primary market for government securities. For reasons of 'market maintenance,' however, it is allowed to intervene in the secondary market. The boundary between the two is sometimes hazy. It is undisputed that in times of existential crisis, such as that experienced by the euro in 2010, the ECB is under an obligation to do 'whatever it takes.' This was recently pointed out by the Geneva economist Charles Wyplosz in an interesting interview in "Perspectives of Economic Policy" (2017). However, these times of existential crisis are now long past. It is high time for a change of direction. Meanwhile, another variety of monetary government financing tends to blossom in secret. Highly indebted EMU member states use the 'Target 2 balances' to grant themselves interest-free, unsecured loans at the expense of a few countries, at Germany's expense above all. This is something that Hans-Werner Sinn (2014) has long correctly pointed out. Valuable collateralization of Target 2 loans or their balancing during the year is necessary.

Fourth commandment: national governments should have the say in matters of economic policy

The world doesn't often experience the kind of existential crises, like the finance or euro crises, which could lead to a financial meltdown. In such times, economics functions very differently. However, 'normal' exogenous shocks, which occur frequently, are the rule. National economic policy is able to manage them on its own. Coordinated action by countries does more harm than good. The best defense against supply-side, symmetric, or asymmetric shocks is open goods and factor markets. National economic policy must support them. Constant structural reforms are indispensable. A European single market is helpful. In the case of supply-side shocks, wage and collective-bargaining policy carries the main burden of adjustment in the EMU. Countries are also normally able to deal with demand-side shocks effectively on their own. In spite of fiscal indebtedness rules, with which, admittedly, none in the EMU concern themselves, there is still enough room for maneuver at the national level for countries to close any demand gaps which may arise. This is also necessary, as centralized monetary policy cannot respond to country-specific shocks. Countercyclical national fiscal policy is a great help: surpluses in good times help finance deficits in bad times. There is no reason to coordinate national fiscal policies across Europe – in avoiding doing so, national fiscal sovereignty is also preserved.

Fifth commandment: the architecture of social security should remain nationally organized

The economic policy architecture of the EMU did not come about by accident. Monetary policy is centrally organized, while all other economic policy is decentralized. This institutional arrangement reflects the heterogeneous preferences in Europe. The 'European miracle' is unthinkable without the competition of heterogeneous institutions. This is also true for a central

170   Norbert Berthold

element, namely labor market and social policies. National welfare states reflect heterogeneous preferences. The 'Anglo-Saxon' world is more likely to rely on the market, the 'Nordic' more on the government, the 'continental' more on corporatism, and the 'Mediterranean' more on the family. They all react differently to challenges. It would thus be a big mistake to pin hopes on a unified welfare state in Europe, as has been suggested by Emmanuel Macron. A European social union with uniform legal minimum wages, European collective agreements, uniform regulations for employment protection, a common European unemployment insurance, or harmonized basic social benefits comes into conflict with heterogeneous, national preferences. And there is one more argument against a social union in Europe. Uniform European regulations clog an important valve used by countries (regions) to adapt to exogenous shocks. They would reduce the adaptive capacity of countries. This destabilizes the EMU. Europe should renounce the idea of a social union and continue to rely on heterogeneous, decentralized social security architecture.

Sixth commandment: hands off the four fundamental freedoms in the EU!

The European single market stabilizes the EMU. If (negative) exogenous shocks occur, economic agents (workers and firms) must adapt to the changed circumstances. If they do not manage to do so via relative prices (wages and wage structures), the (internal) adjustment will occur painfully through quantities (unemployment and mobility). The danger of quantitative adjustment increases if economic agents have the power to shift the burden of adjustment to third parties. One such third party may be consumers if the ECB adopts a policy of stronger inflation ('monetary' channel). It would be the government if it increasingly grants financial assistance ('fiscal' channel). In most cases, however, it is the welfare state that must bear the brunt of the adjustment as employment burdens are shifted to pension, health, and unemployment insurance systems ('social' channel). Tougher budget constraints imposed by economic agents clog these channels. Such action is most likely to succeed if competition in goods, services, and factor markets is intensified. The four fundamental freedoms, which also include the free movement of persons in the EU, ensure that this occurs. Competition intensifies, budget constraints become tougher, relative prices are more flexible, and labor and capital become more mobile. All of this contributes to the stability of the EU. Anyone who wants to protect the euro from severe crises in the future must therefore continue to develop the European single market in a competitive manner. Particularly in the services markets, there is still considerable need for (German) action.

Seventh commandment: fiscal free riding should be prevented

If it becomes possible to shift burdens onto others, one's own behavior changes. This does not just apply to individuals. The architects of the EMU recognized this risk ('moral hazard'). They attempted to contain it using fiscal guardrails, but this proved unsuccessful. Nevertheless, the EMU will only be stable if it succeeds in avoiding as many risks as it can and in sharing as few risks as possible. The first is only possible if the EMU countries engage in constant structural reforms and governments ensure that state budgets are sound. Northerners in particular are open to this path. Failure to address the second requirement inevitably leads to a transfer union, destabilizing the EMU and eventually destroying it. Above all it is the southern countries of the EMU who prefer the transfer union model. It's beyond me why 14 German and French economists would bet more strongly on risk sharing, i.e. on a transfer union (Bénassy-Quéré et al., 2018). The EMU will in fact only be stable if it succeeds in installing fiscal guardrails that really work. An effective non-liability clause, the keystone of the EMU (Wyplosz, 2017), is ultimately unavoidable. The 'fall of Greece' must not be repeated. However, Germany, with its outdated 'principle of mutual help,' does not offer a good example of effective exclusion of liability for the EMU. For it to function there, it must be shielded by a 'fiscal cordon sanitaire': a bankruptcy code for countries, no issuance of common bonds (Eurobonds, subordinated bonds, etc.), limited, incentive compatible Target 2 balances, and no European deposit insurance or European unemployment insurance.

Eighth commandment: banks and governments should be separated by a firewall

In the EMU, banks and governments live in a fatal symbiosis. When one catches fire, it also sets the other ablaze. Therefore, the firewall between banks and governments must be strengthened. An initial option is to limit banks' investments in government securities. If countries get into trouble, their negative influence on the soundness of banks is limited. The vicious circle cannot even begin. As a second element, government securities in bank balances must be deprivileged. Government securities are not without risk. They must be backed by equity dependent on the level of risk. If this is done, the incentives of banks to hold risky government securities will be permanently reduced. A third step is to appreciably increase the banks' equity ratios. Proposals allow for shares equivalent to 25–30%. A fourth element should prevent governments from rescuing banks over and over again. Bank collapses must again become possible, regardless of their specious systemic relevance or that claimed by interest groups. The owners and creditors of banks must bear the costs incurred. Bail-ins should replace bailouts. The cornerstone of the

172 *Norbert Berthold*

stronger firewall must be an insolvency code for governments. In the event of bankruptcy they need to restructure their debts instead of resorting to fiscal and monetary bailouts that are funded by other EMU members.

Ninth commandment: the EMU should not implement a permanent EMF

In the euro crisis, the EMU was threatened by the financial meltdown. This was especially frightening for the countries that found themselves looking into the financial abyss. They are calling for a permanent financial fire department to extinguish fires in distressed countries. The European Stability Mechanism (ESM), which rests on intergovernmental agreements, is to follow the example of the IMF and be transformed into an EMF. This proposal is favored by some in the EMU. They want it to be organized according to European Union law, managed by the EU Commission, and jointly financed. This is rash. A European 'professional fire brigade' is superfluous in the EMU. The majority of the fires that countries struggle with are rather small. They can be effectively extinguished by the local (national) fire departments. In spite of the financial and euro crises, large fires are the rare exception to the rule. However, in emergencies, assistance from the larger community may be necessary. Fire departments from the surrounding area (EMU) are then needed to bring such major fires under control. Nevertheless, the creation of a jointly financed 'professional fire brigade' is inadvisable. Constant readiness comes with a hefty price tag. The long 'idle state' between fires will lead such a 'professional fire brigade' to 'foolish' ideas. It will seek out new tasks. In this context the IMF serves as a cautionary tale. The constant presence of a European 'professional fire brigade' and its joint financing contribute to the neglect of local fire prevention measures. An EMF will increase the 'fire risks' in the EMU (Vaubel, 2018).

Tenth commandment: national parliaments should have the last word

It is illusory to believe that the members of the E(M)U will develop into a 'United States of Europe' in the foreseeable future. Countries pursue divergent interests. They find it difficult to relinquish national sovereignty. The most substantial relinquishment has been made by the EMU countries in the area of monetary policy. Not all agree with this course of action. The resistance to the ECB's unconventional monetary policy is growing. However, particularly in financial policy, the member states insist on maintaining their national sovereignty. The proposal of some, such as the French president, to install a European finance minister is neither serious nor expedient. This finance minister would lack political legitimacy. National parliaments should still have the say in matters of financial policy, not the European Parliament. This would only change if genuine joint tasks were created in the E(M)U and supranationally financed. Parliamentary control would then need to take place at the E(M)U level. The European Parliament would then come into play. The influence of national governments would decline. As long as this is not the case, the decision-making rights of the European Parliament ("he who pays the piper calls the tune") and the scope for action of the European Commission are both limited. The E(M)U remains the boarder of the national governments. For the foreseeable future, it will remain an area of heterogeneous nation states that have little desire to relinquish their sovereign rights.

Conclusion

The current mood of calm in the EMU is deceptive. It still rests on shaky foundations. Many 'reforms' of recent years were merely stopgap measures. A consistent plan is still missing. The statics of the EMU continue to be unstable. Glaring structural defects remain unresolved. It will not be possible to patch up the next crisis using the money of others. What the EU needs is institutional reforms. The erratic, discretionary behavior of politics during long nights in Brussels, which only accomplishes hectic, makeshift repairs, is counterproductive. The EMU is never going to get anywhere without clear, credible rules which are also adhered to. Meanwhile, the euro is going to remain 'money without government' for the foreseeable future. This is the reality. The 'United States of Europe' is one of the political smoke grenades of the Jean-Claude Junckers in Europe, providing a smokescreen behind which the EU Commission and the European Parliament can engage in their centralist mischief. In the future as well, it should be national governments that have the primary say in matters of economic policy in the EMU. This is the right response to heterogeneous preferences of citizens in Europe. The E(M)U can only be stabilized if action and liability once more go hand in hand. The EMU cannot get back on its feet economically without real exclusion of liability. A joint liability scheme is politically disastrous as well. The Maastricht Treaty was absolutely right about this. However, it left a systemically important spot blank: the ominous symbiosis of banks and governments. This is a constant source of danger to the stability of the EMU and the two must be separated as soon as possible. If the member states of the EMU orient themselves according to this rule-based Magna Carta, the euro will be successful as well. If they do not, Europeans will see the euro blow up in their faces as soon as another crisis strikes.

References

Bénassy-Quéré, A. et al. (2018). How to reconcile risk sharing and market discipline in the euro area. *VOX* 17. January.
Padoa-Schioppa, T. (2004). *The euro and its Central Bank: Getting united after the Union.* Cambridge, MA: MIT Press.

Sinn, H.-W. (2014). *The euro trap: On bursting bubbles, budgets and beliefs*. Oxford, UK: Oxford University Press.

Vaubel, R. (2018). *Das Ende der Euromantik. Neustart jetzt*. Wiesbaden, Germany: Springer.

Wyplosz, C. (2017). Wir erleben eine historische Transformation Frankreichs. Ein Gespräch mit Charles Wyplosz über die Reformen von Präsident Emmanuel Macron, das notwendige Großreinemachen in der Europäischen Union und das Drama Griechenlands. *Perspektiven der Wirtschaftspolitik 18*(4).

12 Ordoliberalism and the future of European integration

Michael Wohlgemuth

The European project: ordoliberals' early hopes and warnings

The early ordoliberals of the Freiburg School (e.g. Walter Eucken, Franz Böhm) still very much had the nation state as their addressee when they called for an "economic constitution." Their *Ordnungspolitik* remained the task of a "strong (nation) state"; the international dimension was mainly addressed in terms of a strong commitment for free trade and convertible currencies. But others provided notable exceptions.

Hayek's early hopes

Long before he came to Freiburg, Hayek published two important writings on the problems of an international (economic) order: A paper titled "The Economic Conditions of Interstate Federalism" ([1939] 1980) and chapter XV ("Prospects of International Order") in his *Road to Serfdom* (1944).

In his 1939 paper, Hayek makes several points that are relevant for the following discussion:

- Interstate federalism faces the difficulty of subjecting numerous states characterized by diverse social and economic conditions and prospects to common rules. Compared to legislation within a single nation state, an international authority is much less likely to command popular support for rules and regulations that would only benefit specific groups or would determine specific social standards for all to achieve ([1939] 1980, p. 257ff.). Instead, in a regime of voluntary interstate federalism the diversity of social conditions and of citizens' values and interests would only allow agreement on general, abstract, and prohibitive rules of government conduct.
- In order to avoid disintegration of the federation, it would not be sufficient to only prohibit interstate tariffs or quota. To create and preserve a common market, "the federation will have to possess the negative powers of preventing individual states from interfering with economic activity,

176   *Michael Wohlgemuth*

although it may not have the positive power of acting in their stead" ([1939] 1980, p. 267). Such market-creating "negative integration"[1] should also protect interstate competition in its ability to "form a salutary check" on local governments' activities "while leaving the door open for desirable experimentation" ([1939] 1980, p. 268).

- Interstate federalism would thus also frustrate individual (member) states' endeavor to enact interventionist legislation at home ([1939] 1980, p. 258). With free movement, discriminatory burdens placed on particular industries could "drive capital and labour elsewhere" ([1939] 1980, p. 260). Thus, the 'exit' of dissatisfied owners of mobile resources would force governments to resort to more 'exit-resistant' general and abstract rules of '*Ordnungspolitik.*'

  In his *Road to Serfdom* Hayek discusses the "prospects of international order" as "a community of nations of free men" – instead of either "an omnipotent superstate" or just "a loose association of free nations" (1944, p. 236).

- Again, Hayek expects that interventionist planning can find support only within rather small and/or homogeneous nation states. These states "will never submit to the direction which international economic planning involves ... while they may agree on 'negative' rules of the game, they will never agree on the order of preference in which the rank of their own needs and the rate at which they are allowed to advance is fixed by majority vote" (1944, p. 230).

- Not only should the tasks of the international federation be limited to those that can be clearly defined and unanimously adopted; also, its applicability and jurisdiction should be limited to those nations that are willing and capable to cooperate under a common set of rules (1944, p. 237).

As a consequence, Hayek's ideal of a 'community of nations of free men' seems best organized as a 'club': an association of nations that share elementary common values and are thus in a more credible position to commit themselves to adhering to a rule of law enforced by an international third party.[2]

Röpke's and Erhard's early warnings

Among German first-generation neo- or ordoliberal economists, Wilhelm Röpke was one of the few to apply their ideas with almost messianic fervor also to the unfolding project of European integration.[3] According to Röpke (1959a), this integration had to grow 'from the bottom up' and should not be planned 'from above'; it had to focus strongly on subsidiarity and to respect the intrinsic value of European diversity. He consistently warned of the danger of a 'continental supranationalism' that just shifted political power from the nation state to a European authority, destroying freedom and

Ordoliberalism and future European integration   177

diversity in the process. As an alternative to this 'false internationalism,' Röpke called for a liberal, national *Ordnungspolitik* as a prerequisite for international integration. With free market entry and anti-trust, sound convertible currencies, private property and freedom of contract established at home, market actors trading and investing across borders would almost automatically bring about an international spontaneous order in a most depoliticized way.

After the signing of the treaties of Rome, Röpke warned "that Europe could be at grave risk in the name of exaggerated Europeanism" and pointed at the "integration imposed from above" resulting in a centralization of economic policy that would prove to be "an explosive, a tool for disintegration" (Röpke, 1958, [my translations]). One year later, Röpke's two key regulatory requirements for convertible currencies and free trade had largely been met, and he asked himself: "does this mean that the whole cumbersome apparatus of the EEC has become superfluous?" (1959b, p. 77 [my translation]). Röpke was actually hoping for the end of the EEC, as he believed it was an institution with overly interventionist tendencies. On the (mainly French) idea of organizing Europe through "planification" and creating unity through "harmonization," he remarked: "What should be mortar and was sold to us as such, has in fact turned out to be dynamite" (Röpke, 1959b, p. 88 [my translation]) – a phrase that could today provide an apt comment on the eurozone.

Ludwig Erhard was almost as skeptic as Röpke when it came to the early steps toward European integration.[4] If he had had his way, the German government he served would not even have signed the Treaty of Rome. Erhard was horrified by the thought of a European economic community consisting of only six members, and dominated by the French desire to wall off the community from the outside and to promote interventionist social and industrial policies from the inside. Erhard's vision was of a free-trade zone with convertible currencies and freedom of movement for people, goods, services, and capital. His goal was a free market for the free West, including Great Britain and North America. Konrad Adenauer saw this as a snub to reconciliation with France and in 1959 prohibited Erhard from voicing any further criticism of the EEC. But Erhard was not one for avoiding controversy. In 1962 he wholeheartedly dismissed the European Commission's proposal for a far-reaching "fusion of policies" as "primitive planification" (Erhard, [1962] 1988, p. 770). In a praise of Wilhelm Röpke he made clear that "it is exactly the diverse conditions of the environment, of production, of labor and costs that justify the free exchange of goods and services between national economies"; harmonization and equalization would not be prerequisites of successful economic integration but rather the "initiation of disintegration" which is why "the will to organize and harmonize would lead toward the almost certain abyss" (Erhard, 1959, pp. 16, 19 [my translation]).

178 Michael Wohlgemuth

European integration: an interim balance

How could Hayek (in many ways a more radical classical liberal)[5] hold such 'optimistic' prospects for a European integration project whereas Röpke and Erhard were so skeptical? And: who had it right? This is not the place to assess 60 years of European integration from an ordoliberal point of view. But I would argue that all three had it partly wrong: Erhard and Röpke in the 1950s and 1960s would not have imagined that liberal principles such as undistorted competition, forbidden state aid and above all the four basic freedoms (free movement of goods, people, services, and capital) would not just remain declarations of intent in the treaties of Rome but would become a reality for more than 500 million EU citizens. After the Single European Act (1985), these policy declarations became basic principles of European law that were often implemented by the European Commission and the European Court of Justice (ECJ) more consistently in terms of *Ordnungspolitik* than would ever have been the case at national levels, even in Germany.

Above all, citizens of the EU can now assert their basic freedoms against their governments before their national courts or the ECJ – a decisive step toward an (ordo)liberal 'economic constitution' (*Wirtschaftsverfassung*) for Europe.[6] And it was often only by means of the European route that the member states could be persuaded or forced to break up their public or private monopolies in the telecommunications, energy, banking and transport sectors. Erhard's fear that a 'Fortress Europe' would be created as a bastion against free international trade has also been proven to be exaggerated in most sectors (with the notable exception of agriculture).

At the same time, Hayek's optimism that a voluntary association of nation states would grant the federal level only the powers of an "ultra-liberal 'laissez-faire' state" (Hayek, 1944, p. 232) has been proven to be somewhat naïve. Instead, some of Erhard's and Röpke's fears seem to have been justified: 'Interventionism,' 'red tape' and 'economism' have been symptomatic of European integration over recent decades; and dimensions of a European 'colossus' (Röpke, 1958) can certainly be detected in the fact that the EU has amassed over 100,000 pages of legislation, largely standards for EU-wide economic regulation, in its beloved *acquis communautaire*. The EU budget is also largely devoted to distributive purposes with its Common Agricultural Policy and its Regional and Structural Funds. This does not correspond to Röpke's (or, for that matter, Hayek's) idea of 'charity begins at home' (see Sally, 1999).

There are many reasons that might explain the emergence and persistence of such rules as are clearly not universalizable and could even be obviously damaging the interests of large (but latent) groups within the EU.[7] European rules often result from haggling over package deals. Just as on a national level, discriminatory rules that benefit some and harm others can, particularly in combination with privileged access of special interest groups, be brought into a bargaining equilibrium via extensive logrolling. European Union decision-making procedures provide most favorable conditions for non-generalizable rent-seeking deals to be Europeanized as 'law.' European legislation is often not visible to the public (and domestic parliaments) before decisions are taken; and conflicting positions are often 'solved' (mostly in the Council) without identifying who was advocating what. Political deliberation often starts only at the very end of long technocratic drafting process; and political decisions often appear as fait accomplis after some days and nights of haggling behind closed doors. And perhaps worst of all, since there is no European public sphere or Europeanized public opinion that could inform and control European politics, legislation cannot recur to an (informed) consent of a European "demos" (Grimm, 1995).

The more that the EU's jurisdiction leads to centralization and harmonization, the more important it is to pay attention to the more fundamental evil that Röpke mentioned, namely that "'Europe' as the name of a common system of culture, values and feelings includes a very differentiated ... and diverse range of content. Anything monolithic or rigidly cut-and-dried is foreign to it," whereby "it is the nature of Europe to be united in diversity, which is why everything centralized is a betrayal and violation of Europe, including in economic sectors" (Röpke, [1961] 1964, p. 301 [my translation]).

The future of European integration: the EU's five scenarios

In March 2017, just in time for the celebrations of 60 years since the signing of the Rome treaties, the European Commission published a White Paper on the Future of Europe (EU Commission, 2017) offering five alternative scenarios: (1) "Carrying On," (2) "Nothing But the Single Market," (3) "Those Who Want More Do More," (4) "Doing Less More Efficiently," and (5) "Doing Much More Together."

What was meant to be a grand opening of a Europe-wide discourse on the future of the Union, however, only captured the phantasies of a few think tanks and some academics within the 'Brussels bubble.' Unsurprisingly, neither individual governments nor the EU Council endorsed any of the options, which is understandable given the eccentric way some of them were phrased. Option (2), especially, was framed as a regressive neoliberal idea, but actually it reads as rather hostile to open markets, since the scenario assumed zero progress toward free trade in services, no control of state subsidies and no EU trade agreements with external partners.

Thanks to the perverse way it was stated by Mr. Juncker and his team, the market minimalism of scenario (2) was obviously out. Scenario (3) has provoked the most controversy. In Eastern Europe, it was viewed as a clear threat of a 'multi-speed Europe' – with western member states grouped around France and Germany setting the pace, dictating the agenda (generously interpreted by the ECJ) and thus imposing their political and social

180   *Michael Wohlgemuth*

model on Europe. An EU defined by these welfare-state standards would impose rising economic costs on its East European members, who have so far managed to compete and grow in the single market through their lower wages and social standards.

A preferable interpretation of scenario (3) would be a 'variable geometry' in which different countries – 'the willing and capable' – engage in mutual integration and enhanced cooperation in various policy areas.[8] These areas could also be open for non-EU members (e.g. free trade, foreign and defense policies, domestic security, and anti-terrorism). In what follows, I offer an 'ordoliberal' vindication of that model.

'More or less Europe'? Some club-theoretical distinctions

From an ordoliberal point of view, the right question is not: 'more Europe' or 'less Europe.' The task is (a) to identify the common core of a European 'economic constitution' where equal rules should be applicable to all governments and economic agents; (b) to allow cooperation of subclubs of the 'willing and capable' in specific policy areas where overarching consent of all is not (yet) achievable; and (c) to rely on competition among regulatory and social models between these clubs or individual nation states in areas not covered by (a). Once these distinctions are made, it turns out that the EU as a 'multi-purpose club' is both 'too large and deep' in some policy areas and 'too small and shallow' in others.

Economists and political scientists have developed various criteria to help identify policies that should rightly be allocated to a supranational organization. These are largely also in line with the ideas presented by Hayek and Röpke (s.a.):

1   Areas where economies of scale and/or EU-wide externalities are pervasive and differences in political preferences and capabilities among member states are small or reducible (Alesina, Tabellini, & Trebbi, 2017).
2   These policy areas should also be the ones where 'output legitimacy' (due to their problem-solving capacity) can be taken for granted or achieved or the ones where demands on 'input legitimacy' (derived from explicit democratic participatory procedures) are low or could be easily met.
3   In terms of constitutional economics and the 'calculus of consent' (Buchanan & Tullock 1962): these policy areas would be the ones where the unanimity rule (absent strategic voting) could apply in the European Council because both decision-making costs and external costs would be low.[9]

As Hayek (1939, 1944) already argued, these policy areas would mostly create win–win situations by ways of 'negative integration' (dismantling barriers to trade; abrogating rights to intervene); or in terms of Vanberg (2011) these would be areas where 'gains from joint commitment' are obvious. These

Ordoliberalism and future European integration   181

areas largely correspond to the list of Alesina, Angeloni, and Schuknecht (2001).[10]

The basic logic can also be illustrated in terms of the economic theory of clubs (see Ahrens, Hoen, & Ohr, 2005; Wohlgemuth & Brandi, 2006). For the sake of brevity, let me illustrate the basic idea by looking at three main EU policies provided as 'club goods' by the EU for all its members.

The single market club

EU club goods corresponding to the single market include the 'peace dividend' derived from mutual gains from trade and enhanced international division of labor and knowledge. All members are likely to gain from being in the club by benefiting from the 'four freedoms,' which result both in static and dynamic efficiency gains. These mutual gains from trade, investment, and mobility are larger, the larger the internal market already is, i.e. the more members the club has. With respect to the single market, there should thus be no direct rivalry in club good usage; to the contrary, additional members tend to generate economies of scale resulting in even larger efficiency gains.[11]

If the EU were only a free trade area, the determination of the optimal size of the European club would be relatively easy: The optimal size of a free trade agreement is the world. For a pure disarmament club merely focused on the prohibition of protectionism, the corresponding club costs would tend to be low and hardly rising with club size; accordingly, average costs would decrease as new members join.

With respect to positive regulations such as competition rules, consumer protection rules, or production standards within the EU, however, active collective choices are necessary and political views and capacities tend to diverge. As a consequence, corresponding decision-making costs rise. These costs are kept relatively low by delegation to the Commission. However, the natural centralization and harmonization drive of a central bureaucracy can result in increasing external costs as the EU club becomes larger, more heterogeneous, and more actively interventionist. A 'complete' single market with its thousands of regulations directly applicable to all members of the EU (and the European Economic Area), in a 'one-size-fits-all' manner, therefore, can have a finite optimal club size.

The monetary union club

The club good corresponding to the EMU club is the single currency. The politicians' great hopes (ignoring many ordoliberal economists' warnings) were manifold. Some may relate to pure strategic games of power politics (such as the wish to escape the implicit reign of the German Bundesbank over European monetary policies, the 'vision' to use monetary union as a Trojan horse establishing a fiscal union, or the incentive to free ride on the low interest rates justified by the relative robustness of other euro members).

182   Michael Wohlgemuth

Other hopes were based on more economically rational grounds such as reduced transaction costs and currency risks which would lead to more trade, economies of scale, intensified competition, and thus general welfare gains.

However, as now has turned out to be a tragic mistake, the experiment was too daring and too many members were allowed to join the club too early and based on a club constitution that was insufficiently creating credible commitments. Other chapters in this volume will address this issue in detail. The basic club-theoretical takeaway is simple: the EMU club has failed to take account of the different preferences (both tactical and deeply cultural) and capabilities of its members (see Brunnenmeier, James, & Landau, 2016). The 'interdependence costs' in the sense of Buchanan and Tullock (1962) would have indicated a much smaller (initial) number of members.

For the governance of the eurozone, political and economic divergence poses an enormous problem that cannot be accommodated by legal 'flexibility.' There has to be some agreement on rules that are applicable to all members of the currency club. 'Multi-speed' does not work here – there needs to be a much higher degree of economic and political cohesion than one can find today. The problem is that there is no consensus on a European monetary, fiscal, and social model, and the legitimacy and solidarity resources needed for a political or fiscal union are almost exhausted (Wohlgemuth, 2017b).

The Common Agricultural Policy club

The EU still spends around 40% of its budget on agriculture. Although there have been reforms over last decades, one can make the argument that the 'optimal club size' of the CAP even as it is today is around zero. Production and trade of agricultural products could be made part of the general rules of the single market (with due allowance for common food safety regulations if needed or mutual recognition where useful, as happens with specific consumer protection in other sectors); and specific measures of member states to directly support their farming and fishing industries could be allowed as long as the principles of 'undistorted competition' apply.

To summarize this short exercise in applying the Kantian/Hayekian 'test of universalizability' to a basic club theory of European policy: there is both the need for 'more Europe' and 'less Europe.' As a free trade zone, the EU is far too small, the 'optimum club size' would be the WTO or all states willing and capable to open up their markets. As a single market, the EU is still too small, as more countries would benefit from membership and contribute to the benefits of already existing members.[12] As a currency union club, the EU has too soon become too large. And, as an agricultural planned economy, the EU has long overdrawn its credit.

There are many political problems with any attempts to change the given portfolio of EU competences and/or the composition of membership. For some policy areas (e.g. common defense procurement, military cooperation, many aspects of foreign and security policies, asylum, and migration policies) economies of scale and political weight on a global scale would justify 'more Europe' (deeper integration among more nations); but national interests and sovereignty concerns stand in the way. And in those policy areas (e.g. agricultural policy, regional policies, labor market regulations), where preference costs and inefficiencies caused by policy centralization prevail, a return to subsidiarity is effectively averted by the logic of logrolling and package-dealing in the European Council.

Combining universalizability and flexibility: an ordoliberal ideal type

Fully aware of the 'ratchet effect' of European integration creating an almost unchangeable status quo of European competencies and the *acquis communautaire*, and of the enormous difficulties to change the European treaties in any direction (due to the unanimity requirement), one can still try to propose an 'ideal type' for the future of European integration that would be roughly in line with ordoliberal principles such as those outlined above.

The normative zeal and illustrative purpose of this model would be to combine (a) universalizability of common rules in areas where both efficiency and legitimacy could be claimed and (b) flexibility of competing political problem solutions in areas where diversity should be maintained and could serve as an engine for innovation, learning, and progress.

In this ideal-type model of variable geometry, the EU would continue to act as 'guard' of the core *acquis* on the one hand, and on the other hand as 'broker,' 'monitor,' and 'arbiter' of a variable structure of open, flexible, competing integration clubs. All members of the EU would be members of the core; membership in the various subclubs would be optional for the 'willing and capable.' This club-of-clubs approach allows for different intensities of membership in the EU; yet, in contrast to the concentric circles model, the focus is on policies, not on countries.

It is not only the idle product of ideal-type economic reasoning to imagine several different-sized EU subclubs with various members across different policy fields instead of one single overall EU club comprising 28 heterogeneous members. Even though they are still exceptions, there already are a number of different-sized 'subclubs' within the EU. While, for instance, the single market covers not only all EU members, but also three out of four EFTA members (Norway, Iceland, and Liechtenstein), some political integration clubs comprise only a subgroup of EU members, such as the eurozone, or PESCO,[13] or policies based on the EU provisions for 'enhanced cooperation' (the EU patent, EU divorce law, or, still being negotiated: a financial transaction tax or corporate tax base consolidation); and some include not all EU members but add also non-EU members, such as the Schengen Agreement.

184   *Michael Wohlgemuth*

Conceiving the EU as a club of clubs is not only consistent with increasingly relevant parts of EU reality; it is also compatible with the basic 'mutual gains' notion of constitutional economics. In view of the contractarian paradigm, there are good reasons to view flexible instead of one-size-fits-all integration as desirable.

1   *Commitment – flexibility combination.* Defining common core policies and allowing for the formation of optional clubs in the remaining policy realms introduces more flexibility to accommodate the heterogeneous interests and needs in Europe without risking the undisputed gains attained through past integration. This model yields a combination of commitment and flexibility that is preferable both to the status quo and to other proposals for flexible integration like multi-speed or concentric circles.

2   *Reduction of integration costs.* Although administrative costs of handling complexity might increase as a consequence of transforming the EU into a club of clubs, our model may even result in a reduction of overall interdependence costs. With voluntary club formation among the capable and willing, the costs of finding consensus will decrease due to the more homogeneous population within the smaller subclubs. A decentralized, competitive process of club formation with more homogeneous populations would also lower external costs because countries can search for cooperation regarding those functions in which they have a real preference for cooperation, and they are not forced into cooperation with respect to functions for which there is no such demand. This governance structure should in fact rather reduce political transaction costs. Voluntary club formation (entry and exit) reduces the risk of blackmailing by veto players and decreases the necessity for mutual haggling over privileges via logrolling against the common interests of citizens; it also reduces the threat of inefficient package deals and discriminatory rules benefiting some and harming others.

3   *Responsiveness to citizens' preferences.* The ability of citizens to compare institutional arrangements of numerous clubs that involve different costs and benefits corresponding to diverse needs and tastes, alongside the freedom of clubs to modify and differentiate their institutional supply, generates institutional competition among the various integration clubs. Such competition can help to enhance citizen sovereignty, that is, make self-interested politicians and government bureaucrats more responsive to citizens' preferences (Vanberg, 2000). Thereby, competition between integration clubs can cause inefficient clubs to be crowded out and new efficient clubs to be formed.

4   *Flexible integration as an evolutionary 'discovery procedure.'* Compared to its realistic alternatives (centralization and harmonization across policy fields in a one-size-fits-all manner), voluntary club formation and competition appears to be a more promising and less risky procedure to identify and correct political mistakes and to react to a continuously changing variety

Ordoliberalism and future European integration   185

of preferences and problems. Without competition among different forms of integration, inaptly 'harmonized' or centralized 'policy hypotheses' are – for lack of observable and selectable alternatives – hard to identify. Moreover, without competition among nation states or policy clubs, irreversible path dependencies are more likely because – due to complex logrolling agreements – mistakes, even if they are detected, can hardly be revised in 'integrated,' interwoven policy cartels. Hence, as already suggested by Hayek (1939, p. 268), "desirable experimentation" is more likely to happen in a European model of variable geometry that allows competition among national social models and/or among various integration clubs. It can serve as a knowledge-creating 'discovery procedure' of such political preferences and problem solutions "as, without resort to it, would not be known to anyone, or at least would not be utilized" (Hayek, 1968/1978, p. 179; Wohlgemuth, 2008b).

5   *Flexible deepening and widening.* Today, there is an increasing concern about the Union's 'finality,' its 'borders,' or its 'absorption capacity.' These notions owe their dramatic and gloomy clout to the traditional combination of two unnecessarily holistic and constructivist ideologies: 'one size fits all' (for full member states) and 'all or nothing' (for would-be member states). Both fronts seem now slowly to relax. But a more radical relaxation seems to offer a much more adequate solution to many concerns troubling European governments and citizens. Both deepening and widening could be achieved simultaneously, if they were based on integration of the capable and willing in specific policy areas where consent can be found without the traditional resort to power politics, bundling special interests from diverging policy fields.

The model of a union of clubs in addition to a common *acquis* reduced to an undisputed and reasonable core of universalizable policies also has implications for the European Neighbourhood Policy (ENP). Current ENP strategies are aimed at calming and comforting both EU neighbors (potentially want-to-be members) and existing EU members by offering cooperation (and financial support) without full membership – which would indeed pose grave problems of absorption capacity of the EU and adoption capacities of our neighbors (think Turkey or Ukraine). Variable geometry could offer much more immediate and flexible comfort. Full membership would be reduced to such core areas where mutual gains from joint commitment can be offered to both the existing and to many new members. Hence, it would be comparatively easy to turn 'neighbors' into 'members,' e.g. of a core union based on free trade and of additional policies where mutual interests are clearly present, as in the areas of defense and security. It might also offer a way for post-Brexit Britain to stay in the single market (while accepting the rules of the four freedoms and anti-trust) and to join common policies where common interests prevail.

186　*Michael Wohlgemuth*

Summary

The 'ever-closer-one-size-fits-all' project has alienated many citizens from the EU. They see their lives as regulated by a political machine that they cannot democratically hold accountable. The Commission therefore was right to offer alternative scenarios in its outline of the future of EU integration in the White Paper, including the options of 'doing less more efficiently' and 'those who want more do more.' Indeed, there can and should be more flexibility – but mostly in fields outside the 'core' of the European project, that is: outside of the single market, anti-trust, perhaps the common trade policy[14] and – alas! – the common currency.[15]

However, even in these other areas (which include the social union, tax harmonization, and the defense union), a 'two-speed Europe' is not the most convincing form of flexibility. This model takes for granted that there is a common destination agreed by all, which all members states want and will reach at some stage. An 'ever-closer-one-size-fits-all-sooner-or-later' option is not really preferable to genuine 'variable geometry,' where different countries – 'the willing and able' – engage in mutual integration in different policy areas. These forms of cooperation should also be open to non- (or: no-longer) EU members (e.g. single market access, foreign and defense policies, domestic security, anti-terrorism).

Europe would again live up to its motto: United in diversity!

Notes

1　The terms 'negative' and 'positive' integration refer to more recent integration theories, e.g. by Scharpf (1999).
2　The qualification that only states that already domestically subscribe to elementary principles of the rule of law can be members of an international community under the law of peoples is also prominent in Kant's *Perpetual Peace* ([1795] 1991) and Rawls's (2001) *Law of Peoples.*
3　For more details, see Warneke (2013), Petersen and Wohlgemuth (2009), or Sally (1999).
4　See Wohlgemuth (2008a, pp. 386ff.) or Mierzejewski (2005, pp. 229ff.) for details.
5　See Kolev (2017) for an in-depth comparison of Hayek's and Röpke's 'neoliberalism.'
6　On that key concept of ordoliberalism and its implementation in the European treaties, see Streit and Mussler (1994) and Mestmäcker (2012).
7　For a more comprehensive public choice account of European politics, see, e.g. Vaubel (1994) or Wohlgemuth (2017a, pp. 6ff.).
8　In Wohlgemuth and Brandi (2006) we distinguish various models of flexible integration: (a) 'multi-speed' Europe sticks to the 'ever-closer union' and 'one-size-fits-all' mode of integration; it only allows for temporary flexibility; (b) the 'concentric circles' model allows for permanent differences in the grade of integration; but it usually defines integration areas territorially as groups of countries belonging to the 'core' or the 'periphery'; (c) 'variable geometry' or 'enhanced cooperation' is more flexible as it allows all member states (but possibly also non-members) to opt in to particular policies.

Ordoliberalism and future European integration 187

9 'External costs' in the sense of Buchanan and Tullock (1962) occur when a participant in a collective decision has to accept a collective choice that does not reflect her preferred alternative (see Wohlgemuth and Brandi, 2006 for a wider application of this concept to European decision-making).

10 According to Alesina et al. (2001), these areas would include the single market, trade policy, and anti-trust. Moreover, it may contain convertibility of currencies, a Common Foreign and Security Policy (CFSP) as well as police and judicial cooperation of all EU members in criminal matters that show cross-country externalities.

11 It might be debatable whether, from an economic point of view, free movement of people is necessary for allocational efficiency. The pure theory of trade suggests that free movement of labor and of goods are substitutes (following Mundell, 1957). However, the four freedoms can also be seen as complementary (e.g. Schiff, 2006). From a political–economic point of view it can also be debated whether free migration (especially into more generous welfare systems) can command consent from the citizens (as 'club owners') who might see the benefits of their 'club good' diminished by adding new members (e.g. Kolb, 2008).

12 Especially in the realm of services, but also public procurement the single market cannot be said to be 'completed' even among the EU28. The EU Single Market Scorebook http://ec.europa.eu/internal_market/scoreboard/index_en.htm provides a good overview of remaining barriers to trade and provide services in member states. Germany scores very low in compliance with single market norms, especially in the areas of services.

13 Under recently established Permanent Structured Cooperation (PESCO), 25 EU member states (the UK, Denmark, and Malta are not taking part) are allowed to pick freely from a menu of 17 collaborative defense projects (a behavior often termed 'Europe à la carte').

14 The EFTA members of the EEA have proven that it is possible to have their own trade policy and at the same time have full access to the EU single market.

15 Since other contributions to this volume address the monetary union issue at length, I was asked to avoid repeating ordoliberal arguments on the euro in my contribution. My short take in the present framework would be: (a) the current currency union has been a politically oversized and legally underdeveloped club; (b) while it was politically and legally all too easy to join, it is now (politically, legally, and economically) all too brutal to leave (for all involved); (c) since (or: as long as) a break-up of the eurozone into more functional 'subclubs' (e.g. 'North' and 'South') involves unbearable political and economic costs, the eurozone club will have to find a way to commit to common rules that somehow accommodate the capabilities and preferences of both its 'Club Med' and its 'ordo' members.

Bibliography

Ahrens, J., Hoen, H. W., & Ohr, R. (2005). Deepening integration in an enlarged EU: A club-theoretical perspective. *Journal of European Integration* 27 417–439. doi:10.1080/07036330500367366

Alesina, A., Angeloni, I., & Schuknecht, L. (2001). What does the European Union do? *NBER Working Paper 8647*.

Alesina, A., Tabellini, G., & Trebbi, F. (2017). Is Europe an optimal political area? *Brookings Papers on Economic Activity*, Spring 2017.

Brunnermeier, M., James, H., & Landau, J.-P. (2016). *The euro and the battle of ideas*. Princeton, NJ: Princeton University Press.

188 Michael Wohlgemuth

Buchanan, J. M. & G. Tullock (1962). *The calculus of consent: Logical foundations of constitutional democracy.* Ann Arbor, MI: University of Michigan Press.

Erhard, L. (1959). Grußadresse. In A. Hunold (Ed.), *Wilhelm Röpke. Gegen die Brandung* (pp. 12–19). Erlenbach–Zurich, Switzerland: Eugen Rentsch.

Erhard, L. (1962/1988). Planification – kein Modell für Europa. In K. Hohmann (Ed.), *Ludwig Erhard. Gedanken aus fünf Jahrzehnten* (pp. 770–780). Düsseldorf, Germany: Econ.

European Commission (2017). On the future of Europe: Reflections and scenarios for the EU27 by 2025. White Paper, COM (2017) 2025, March 1.

Grimm, D. (1995). Does Europe need a constitution? *European Law Journal 1*(3) 282–302.

Hayek, F. A. v. ([1939] 1980). The economic conditions of interstate federalism. In *Individualism and Economic Order* (pp. 255–272). Chicago, IL: University of Chicago Press.

Hayek, F. A. v. (1944). Hayek, F. (1944). *The road to serfdom.* London, UK: Routledge.

Hayek, F. A. v. (1968/1978). Competition as a discovery procedure. In *New studies in philosophy, politics, economics and the history of ideas* (pp. 179–190). Chicago, IL: University of Chicago Press.

Kant, I. ([1795] 1991). Perpetual peace: A philosophical sketch. In H. Reiss (Ed.), *Kant: Political writings* (pp. 93–130). Cambridge, UK: Cambridge University Press.

Kolb, H. (2008). States as clubs? The political economy of state membership. In H. Kolb & H. Egbert (Eds.), *Migrants and markets* (pp. 120–146). Amsterdam, the Netherlands: Amsterdam University Press.

Kolev, S. (2017). *Neoliberale Staatsverständnisse im Vergleich.* Berlin, Germany: De Gruyter.

Mestmäcker, E.-J. (2012). European economic constitution. In J. Basedow, K. J. Hopt, & R. Zimmermann (Eds.), *The Max Planck encyclopedia of European private law* (pp. 588–592). Oxford, UK: Oxford University Press.

Mierzejewski, A. C. (2006). *Ludwig Erhard: Der Wegbereiter der Sozialen Marktwirtschaft,* Munich, Germany: Pantheon.

Mundell, R. A. (1957). International trade and factor mobility. *American Economic Review 47*(3) 321–335.

Petersen, T. & Wohlgemuth, M. (2009). Wilhelm Röpke und die Europäische Integration. In H. Rieter & J. Zweynert (Eds.), *Wort und Wirkung. Wilhelm Röpkes Bedeutung für die Gegenwart.* Marburg, Germany: Metropolis.

Rawls, J. (2001). *The law of peoples: With "the idea of public reason revisited."* Cambridge, MA: Harvard University Press.

Röpke, W. (1958). Gemeinsamer Markt und Freihandelszone, 28 Thesen als Richtpunkte. *ORDO 10* 31–62.

Röpke, W. (1959a). *International order and economic integration.* Dordrecht, Germany: Springer.

Röpke, W. (1959b). Zwischenbilanz der europäischen Wirtschaftsintegration, Kritische Nachlese. *ORDO 11* 69–94.

Röpke, W. ([1961] 1964). Europa in der Welt von heute. In *Wort und Wirkung* (pp. 292–309). Ludwigsburg, Germany: Hoch.

Sally, R. (1999). Wilhelm Röpke and international economic order. *ORDO 50* 47–51.

Scharpf, F. W. (1999). *Governing in Europe.* Oxford, UK: Oxford University Press.

Schiff, M. (2006). Migration, trade and investment: Complements or substitutes? *CEIS Working Paper No. 89.*

Streit, M. E., & Mussler, W. (1994). The economic constitution of the European Community: From Rome to Maastricht. *Constitutional Political Economy 5* 319–353.

Vanberg, V. J. (2000). Globalization, democracy, and citizens' sovereignty: Can competition among governments enhance democracy? *Constitutional Political Economy 11* 87–112.

Vanberg, V. J. (2011). Liberal constitutionalism, constitutional liberalism and democracy. *Constitutional Political Economy 22* 1–20.

Vaubel, R. (1994). The public choice analysis of European integration: A survey. *European Journal of Political Economy 10* 227–249.

Warneke, S. (2013). *Die europäische Wirtschaftsintegration aus der Perspektive Wilhelm Röpkes.* Stuttgart, Germany: Routledge.

Wohlgemuth, M. (2008a). 50 Jahre Europäische Ordnungspolitik: ordnungs- und konstitutionenökonomische Anmerkungen, *ORDO 59* 381–404.

Wohlgemuth, M. (2008b). Learning through institutional competition. In A. Bergh & R. Höijer (Eds.), *Institutional competition* (pp. 67–89). Cheltenham, UK: Edward Elgar .

Wohlgemuth, M. (2017a). Ein Europa der Zukunft, Schweizer Monat Sonderthema Mai 2017, Zurich, Switzerland.

Wohlgemuth, M. (2017b). Political union and the legitimacy challenge. *European View 16*(1) 57–65.

Wohlgemuth, M., & Brandi, C. (2006). Strategies of flexible integration and enlargement of the European Union: A club-theoretical and constitutional economics perspective. *Freiburg Discussion Papers on Constitutional Economics 06/6.*

13 Ordoliberalism and the eurozone crisis

Toward a more perfect market of jurisdictions?

Thomas Biebricher

Introduction

Supposedly, a crisis is a short and dramatic turn of events. In its original clinical meaning the term denotes the moment in which an illness or condition unveils its truth and conditions either take a turn for the better or for worse. Given this meaning, referral to the developments in the eurozone over the last decade as a crisis borders on conceptual stretching, so drawn out is the 'moment of truth' and so many iterations of it have been witnessed. Even at the time of writing, new clouds conspire on the horizon, with the recently elected government of Italy voicing grievances not only concerning the Dublin regime but also the rules governing the eurozone. But despite the apparent stretching, the notion of a simmering crisis that oscillates between more latent and more virulent phases, still appears to be the most appropriate when it comes to characterizing the trajectory of the eurozone: The financial crisis that was triggered in the US real estate market caused a crisis of banks that were deemed 'too big to fail' and had to be saved by nation states. In Europe, the 'deadly embrace' between banks and sovereign states proved to be fatal not only insofar as states had to take on massive amounts of originally private debt and thus faced increased suspicion by financial markets as to the sustainability of their public finances; the balance sheets of private banks were also full of bonds issued by states and once their creditworthiness was put into question, a second banking crisis loomed, which prompted the need to bail out states so they could continue to pay off their debt. But not only was the rescue mission for states in need, such as Greece, Portugal, and Ireland, based on strict conditionality, i.e. aid was tied to the commitment of recipient countries to adhere to the recommendations, if not to say commands, of the 'Troika' consisting of the European Central Bank (ECB), European Commission, and International Monetary Fund. Simultaneously, a barrage of reforms was passed, new institutions were built and new procedures established in an attempt to make a supposedly deficient regime built on the Maastricht Treaty (1992) as well as the Treaty on Stability and Growth (1997) more waterproof and thus prevent future crises from breaking out in the first place. What remains controversial is not only the effectiveness of this reformed framework of the eurozone, which now includes the provisions of the 'Two-Pack,' the 'Six-Pack,' and the 'Fiscal Compact' as well as the European Stability Mechanism (ESM) and the Banking Union, but also how to assess this regime in its fundamental thrust and what drove European policymakers to their particular interpretation of the crisis which, in turn, resulted in this reformed structure of economic governance.

The thesis I aim to defend in this regard is that we are witnessing a tendency toward what I call the ordoliberalization of the eurozone. Ordoliberalism is a somewhat idiosyncratically German tradition in political economy that was relegated to obscurity outside of expert circles until the onset of the eurozone crisis and, particularly, the response to it (see Biebricher & Vogelmann, 2017). The basic intuition of ordoliberal thought posits that markets are in need of an institutional framework to ensure that they function properly, i.e. a desirable form of competition takes place in them, which provides consumers with the best possible quality of goods and services at the lowest expense possible. The interpretation of the ordoliberalization thesis I would like to defend here extrapolates from this basic ordoliberal intuition that pertained to markets populated by private actors to the eurozone as a market of jurisdictions and argues that the respective framework is to safeguard a desirable form of competition as well, which prohibits certain forms of gaining (short-term) competitiveness and tends to result in the kind of austerity that especially countries in Southern Europe have had to endure over almost a decade now. Ordoliberal thought assumed that enabling markets to function properly required certain extra-economic and, particularly, political conditions. As I will try to show in this chapter, eurozone governance structures have come to bear a significant degree of resemblance to these conditions, although it must be noted at once that it is neither to be expected that there would ever be a complete fit between ordoliberal precepts and political reality, nor do I assume that political actors *consciously* seek to influence such precepts on a regular basis. I simply contend that there is indeed this growing resemblance whether someone is consciously pursuing this project or not.

I begin this chapter with a sketch of my interpretive thesis of an ordoliberalization of the eurozone focusing on the political framework set in place and the kind of competition it is to ensure. This thesis is at odds with two positions. The first one is generally skeptical when it comes to the influence of ideas – be they ordoliberal or whatever else – on political processes and instead points toward the impact of interests and/or institutions. Elsewhere I have developed a detailed critique of such purely interest or institution-based accounts, suggesting that ideas ought to be systematically incorporated in such accounts (Biebricher, 2019); therefore, I focus on a second set of objections. What is in question here is not the general significance of (ordoliberal) ideas. Rather, contemporary representatives of the ordoliberal tradition but also others argue that the governance of the eurozone is not only inadequately characterized as ordoliberal in nature, but represents the very opposite of *Ordnungspolitik*, i.e. the practical implementation of ordoliberal ideas into policy.

192   *Thomas Biebricher*

I will scrutinize the respective arguments and confront them with respective counterarguments leading to the conclusion that the eurozone may not be a perfect ordoliberal market of jurisdictions but that, all countervailing tendencies notwithstanding, the crisis-induced dynamic has moved it closer to this ideal.

The ordoliberalization of Europe

The notion of an ordoliberalization of Europe can be spelled out in different ways (see Biebricher, 2013, 2014; Dullien & Guérot, 2012). The aspects I would like to focus on here are, first and foremost, related to the political framework of the eurozone and a particular type of competition they are supposed to encourage. Ordoliberals had quite distinct views on the tasks of states in creating competition through the setup and enforcement of a 'competitive order' for markets, the problems democracy posed for this undertaking and the role science had to play in it (see Biebricher, 2019). So, let me begin by clarifying the ordoliberal view on these key political conditions for a functioning market and the kind of competition that was supposed to take place on them. Based on this, we can then assess to what extent these requirements are reflected in the current setup of the eurozone.

Just like many other liberals and conservatives, ordoliberals were deeply concerned with the rise of modern mass democracy at the turn of the 20th century that would reach a first climax at the end of World War I with the dissolution of Tsarist Russia, the Austrian-Hungarian Empire and, of course, the German 'Reich,' all giving way to democracies, albeit very different ones. Democracy has always been scorned by its critics for its presumed tendency toward demagoguery and what today might be called populism. But what sets its 20th-century critics apart from the classic tradition of criticism dating back to Plato is the particular focus on the phenomenon of masses and the social psychological problematization of it. Be it Gustave Le Bon, José Ortega y Gasset, or Sigmund Freud in *Group Psychology and the Analysis of the Ego*, the masses elicit a profound anxiety from all of these authors, who depict them as inclined toward irrationality or outright fanaticism. Handing over control of the political process to the whims of wayward and impressable 'mass men' – and women – was not only deemed perilous by ordoliberals, but their concerns were particularly grave. The counterintuitive coordinating mechanisms of market economies were supposedly too difficult to comprehend for the great majority of the population, who instead tended to favor notions of 'planning,' thus jeopardizing the spontaneous order of markets with all of its merits.

However, it was not only the alleged irrationality that a democracy of the masses produced and injected into the political process that gave ordoliberals pause, but also and somewhat paradoxically, the very (instrumental) rationality that they also attributed to the electorate as well as its representatives. Ordoliberals, from the *spiritus rector* of the 'Freiburg School' Walter Eucken to

Wilhelm Röpke, Alexander Rüstow, and others were adamant that 'pluralist' democracy offered an abundance of possibilities to lobby for special treatment under or exemption from certain rules for societal actors, thus undermining the logic of general rules that were to make up economic, political, and legal orders. Given that under democratic conditions they were dependent on the support from groups and individuals, political decision makers were easy prey for the lobbying efforts of (economic) organizations; with political parties often supposedly acting as hardly more than their parliamentary arm. Under these circumstances, the general welfare was inevitably sold out to particularistic interests, be they trade unions and their demands for higher wages or companies striving for monopoly rents. While it would be exaggerated to attribute an outright anti-democratic stance to the ordoliberals, there can be little doubt that they were eagerly searching for ways to at least ameliorate if not neutralize the detrimental effects pluralist mass democracy potentially had on the order of the market and, thus, society more generally.

The solution to the problems the ordoliberals detected in contemporary democracy, which they did not exactly conjure up out of thin air given that the context of their early theorizing was the collapse of a deeply dysfunctional Weimar State into National Socialist dictatorship – seemingly brought about through democratic means – takes us to their view of the state and its functions. Both Eucken and Rüstow are adamant in their demand for what might be called a recentering of state power lest the latter be dissolved under the disintegrating pressures of pluralist democracy (see Biebricher, 2019). For Rüstow it was one of the gravest mistakes of classical liberalism to have missed the point about functioning markets, namely that they require a steadfast umpire capable of enforcing the rules of the game indiscriminately, and that the referee can only be the state. In light of the pressures coming from 'rent-seekers' as well as potentially fanaticized masses, incapacitating the state along the lines of what laissez-faire liberals of the 19th century endeavored, was clearly the wrong recipe to safeguard its proper operation. The independence of the referee presupposes not a weakening of the state but its opposite: "no one [in the classical liberal tradition] noticed … the obvious sociological truth that the strength and independence of a state are interdependent variables, and that only a strong state is powerful enough to preserve its own independence" (Rüstow, 1942, p. 276). And against the tendencies toward a mutual entanglement of state and society in what he called the "economic state" (Eucken, 2017, p. 56), Eucken posited the need for the state to find the "strength to free itself from the influence of the masses and in some way distance itself from the economy" (pp. 68–69). Only by fending off the demands addressed to it could the ideal state of ordoliberalism perform its functions properly; carefully regulating the complexities of the interdependence of various orders making up social totality according to the ordoliberals, and also aggressively keeping economic power in check to ensure the maximum of competition in the interest of consumers – the only truly generalizable interest in a

194　*Thomas Biebricher*

market economy. The state, in short, is to be as unassailable by societal actors and their representatives in the political system as the umpire in a game is off limits for the players. Only such a state would be neither subject to the volatilities of democratic politics nor succumb to the power of (economic) actors but claim its supremacy over them, albeit in strict accordance with the general rules the umpire state stoically monitors and enforces. While none of the ordoliberals was particularly optimistic about the transformation of the state according to their ideals and they had little to offer as far as concrete strategies are concerned, the seemingly detrimental trajectory of the state's development only added to the urgency of their pleas. Even beyond the admittedly dire context of the Weimar State, Eucken would not change the tune of his critique of the state; in the posthumously published *Principles of Economic Policy* he notes with alarm: "Everywhere there is the undermining of state authority through particularistic forces that represent particularistic interests … a state with a unified and consequent will formation … is indispensable today. All economic policy is seemingly placed in jeopardy, because the state fails as an ordering power" (1960, pp. 329–330).[1]

The final element that is of major importance in order to capture the non-economic preconditions for functioning markets is science. The ordoliberals, and among them Eucken and Rüstow in particular, showed a remarkable faith in what the social sciences, including economics, could achieve, if only their practice adhered to the correct methodology. Eucken devoted significant intellectual energies to the question of a truly scientific economics, or, what was then called *Nationalökonomie*. In his *Nationalökonomie wozu?*, originally published in 1934, he already formulates a rather bold assessment of the powers of political economy:

> By reaching truths on the basis of the method described that are necessary, general and simultaneously close to reality [*wirklichkeitsnah*] by expressing these in theory, political economy has found the Archimedean point, from which objective and exact knowledge of certain relationships in individual, concrete reality can be generated.
>
> (Eucken, 1954, p. 29)

The 'correct methodology' would be spelled out as the 'morphological analysis' Eucken put forward in his seminal *Foundations of Economics* published in 1940, which claims to distill a number of 'pure types' of economic orders out of economic reality and thus contributes to the kind of knowledge Eucken already envisaged in the quote from 1934: Knowledge that is robust and reliable ('objective' and 'necessary') but not as inconsequential as the formal modeling of ivory tower economists. For Eucken this kind of knowledge was not only to be sought after for purely scientific reasons but also because it offered scientists a unique and important role to play in the political process. Two years before the *Foundations* Eucken had already coauthored an editorial with two other leading members of the Freiburg School Franz Böhm and Hans Großmann-Doerth, in which the ambitions of these 'men of science' were clearly on display:

> Men of science, by virtue of their profession and position being independent of economic interests, are the only objective, independent advisers capable of providing true insight into the intricate relationships of economic activity and therefore also providing the basis upon which economic judgements can be made.
>
> (Böhm, Eucken, & Großmann-Doerth, 2017, p. 27)

Based on their privileged access to the truth granted by the right methodology, it is scientists such as the ordoliberals themselves who should provide expertise for political decision makers: "Accordingly, the authors consider the most urgent task for the representatives of law and political economy is to work together in an effort to ensure that both disciplines regain their proper place in the life of the nation" (Böhm, Eucken, & Großmann-Doerth, 2017, p. 28). This plea for a consultative role for the sciences is clearly consistent with what we already know about ordoliberal views of state and democracy, complementing the skepticism with regard to pluralist mass democracy with a healthy dosage of technocracy. In other words, the antidote to the interest-mongering of particularistic groups and the demagoguery of the ideologues is the detached and measured judgment of the experts, which is to inform state will formation rather than the official and unofficial channels that connect it to society in a democracy. Conversely, "if men of science relinquish this role or are deprived of it, then other less competent advisers take over – the interested parties" (Böhm, Eucken, & Großmann-Doerth, 2017).

In sum, the elements of what in Foucaultian terminology might be referred to as an 'ordoliberal governmentality' add up to a kind of technocratic government, in which the truths of experts guide political practice with a 'strong' state as its prime instrument, which must be as resourceful and capacious in the implementation, as it must be shielded against the (democratic) influence of society and economy.

To what extent are these extra-economic conditions of functioning markets reflected in the current governance setup of the eurozone? If one of the main concerns of ordoliberals was that unruly electorates roused by ideologues as much as the sheer self-interest of particular groups could gain control over political decision-making through the channels of democracy, they could breathe a little easier when assessing the eurozone in this regard. After all, the Troika that was put in charge of enforcing the memoranda of understanding, which states in need had to sign, is hardly legitimized democratically and still capable of de facto dictating economic policy decisions to the recipient countries of aid money. Furthermore, the ECB has emerged as one of the key political actors in its own right over the course of the eurozone crisis, and while it may be slightly overstated that it is the one true

196   *Thomas Biebricher*

sovereign of the eurozone, as some commentators have alleged (see Streeck, 2015), there can be no doubt that Mario Draghi and his future successor wield extraordinary influence over political decisions. And while there are provisions for holding the ECB democratically accountable, e.g. through hearings before the European Parliament, it is a very optimistic assessment to assume that parliamentarians have any recognizable leverage in arguing with the ECB over its course of action.

If the eurozone crisis has added to the influence of the ECB, the same is true for the other European member of the former Troika, the European Commission. It is in charge of monitoring the regime of rules governing the eurozone which has been amended and tightened through the various reforms passed since 2011. Now, national parliaments have to comply with the schedule of the 'European Semester' and they have to submit their draft budget to the Commission before they actually introduce it to the respective national parliament. The Commission then evaluates the draft budget to assess whether it is in accordance with the economic prospects of the country as well as the rules regarding deficits, debts, and macroeconomic imbalances, and issues recommendations in case the budget is deemed unsustainable in light of these rules. However, the Commission not only monitors and recommends, but in principle it is also empowered to enforce the rules regarding deficits, debts, and imbalances, using the 'corrective arms' of the so-called (and tightened) excessive deficit procedure and the newly created macroeconomic imbalance procedure. If a country continuously disregards the recommendations of the Commission while in violation of the rules, it can issue considerable fines to the countries in question. In the past, the effectiveness of this 'corrective arm' had been significantly hampered by the fact that a majority in the Council had to agree to initiate a procedure and issue fines. Delinquent countries could easily form alliances with others to strike down potential sanctions, even when they were recommended by the Commission. The 'Six-Pack' not only introduced stricter rules for the excessive deficit procedure and a novel macroeconomic imbalance procedure, but also the reverse majority principle, which states that recommendations by the Commission with regard to the initiation of procedures or the issuing of fines are adopted unless there is a majority against it, making the recommendations by the Commission 'quasi-automatic.' In sum, all intergovernmentalist skepticism notwithstanding, it seems that the Commission is indeed the "unexpected winner of the crisis" (Bauer & Becker, 2014). Now, the Commission is obviously not (yet) the equivalent of a strong state on the European level, but at least it comes closer to the ordoliberal idea than the average government exposed to direct democratic pressures. When it comes to insulation from such pressures, the Commission proves to be fairly unassailable – at least with regard to official democratic channels. In sum, what is in place in the eurozone after the reforms of the last seven years is a governance structure where a host of rules concerning economic matters are monitored and enforced by the European Commission (and other non-majoritarian institutions), which

Ordoliberalism and the eurozone crisis 197

may yet lack the *capacity* to do so even against powerful countries, but at least exhibit the kind of insulation from democratic pressures and the ensuing *autonomy* that was considered essential by ordoliberal thinkers.

Finally, there is the role of science in the current eurozone regime and, as it turns out, the technocratic visions of ordoliberal thinkers have also been realized here in a certain sense. The charge of technocratic micromanagement by the European Union regarding light bulbs or vacuum cleaners is a cliché often mobilized by Euroskeptics, but this is not what I have in mind. Rather it is technocratic rule in the specific sense of the term, i.e. dealing with political matters as if they were technical matters to be decided upon solely based on the respective expertise. The lengthy 'in-depth country reports' the Commission compiles as part of its monitoring duties are full of recommendations as to how to address certain economic problems and developments in need of adjustment. And the way they are approached in the reports is precisely the way one would deal with a technical issue that yields one optimal solution. Now, to be sure, expertise is a valuable resource for policymaking and there is no general reason why it should not figure in the respective processes. Furthermore, there may even, in principle, be something like a politics of regulation pertaining to certain issues, where solutions are pareto-optimal, i.e. whatever the particular solution suggested by experts, they do not put anyone affected by the respective decision at a disadvantage. In such cases, it may be not only unproblematic from a democratic point of view to delegate decision-making powers to non-majoritarian institutions, as Giandomenico Majone has famously argued, but actually desirable to remove the respective issues from the genuinely political agenda and treat them as technical matters: After all, they are neutral in their distributive effects and science may offer uncontroversial solutions that may lead to an overall 'de-contestation' of the issue in question (see Majone, 1994). However, the majority of the recommendations by the Commission pertain to matters where decisions are neither neutral as to their distributive effects nor is there any consensus among scientists regarding the proper solutions to a given problem. Accordingly, these are then decisions of an inherently political nature in a twofold sense: Not only are they contested vehemently within the realm of science but they excise a toll from particular groups of the population and therefore require a much stronger democratic legitimation than a presumably pareto-optimal politics of regulation would. Therefore, it seems apt to refer to the eurozone framework as a form of technocratic government, which, in principle, conforms to the kind of depoliticized expert rule the ordoliberals advocated.

As has been already noted, in the ordoliberal vision the framework of markets was designed in such a way to ensure not only a maximum of competition but also competition that was deemed desirable. After all, competitive pressures can also be responded to by burning down your competitor's factory or by colluding with others to price this particular competitor out of the market. However, the ordoliberals wanted to ensure that markets produced only a desirable form of competition, namely "*Leistungswettbewerb*"

198   *Thomas Biebricher*

or 'performance competition' (Eucken, 1960, p. 247). This meant that competitiveness could only be gained by offering better products and/or cheaper prices, thus benefiting consumers. Analogously, the framework for the market of jurisdictions that is the eurozone is also to ensure certain forms of competition and preclude others: For example, devaluing one's currency is obviously no longer an option to gain (short-term) competitiveness, as it used to be for countries such as Italy or France before the advent of the Economic and Monetary Union (EMU). Instead, the only way to regain competitiveness is supposedly the internal devaluation achieved through politics of austerity and what is euphemistically referred to as 'structural adjustments.' Some would suggest that this is an unintended *defect* of an 'incomplete' EMU, in which a common monetary policy remains unmatched by fiscal political instruments on the European level to fight 'asymmetrical shocks,' i.e. local and regional crises, as an alternative to the erstwhile possibility of devaluation. However, the honorary president of the Walter Eucken Institute in Freiburg, American public choice and neoliberal theorist James Buchanan once pointed out that this may not have to be considered a defect but rather a desirable effect:

> The EMU has been criticized because it is alleged to take away one dimension of adjustment to shifting economic circumstances in particular countries and to force internal institutional adjustments in place of exchange rate shifts. It may be argued, however, that because exchange rate adjustments cannot take place that serve to cover up the requirement for internal reforms ... the institutional structure will be moved to further reforms.
>
> (2004, p. 16)

So Greece, Portugal, and others have to cut public expenditure, privatize public assets, and liberalize labor markets, which will lower unit labor costs and thus make their economies more competitive. However, the problem with this quintessential ordoliberal interpretation and solution to the eurozone crisis is that someone will have to consume all these more competitively produced goods, and therefore not everyone can be austere at the same time – but countries such as Germany show no inclination of moving away from the *Schwarze Null*, i.e. a balanced budget. Moreover, the rules of Europe's economic constitution make it simply mandatory to at least pursue this goal, so it is unclear how the recipes of austerity are to play out favorably in the European context. And while commentators now proclaim the Greek patient to be past the moment of crisis, implicitly affirming the effectiveness of the bitter medicine of austerity, this has a slightly hollow ring to it after almost a decade-long economic downturn with a devastating social impact on anyone but the rich in Greece.

This, then, is a sketch of the thesis of an ordoliberalization of Europe, which, in my reading, pertains in particular to the extra-economic conditions of a market of jurisdictions, which is to ensure only desirable forms of competition and thus, implicitly, suggests to all the countries of the eurozone with their range of cultural economies of capitalism that they should be a little more like Germany and its export-oriented neo-Rhenish capitalism based on wage moderation and low domestic demand. Let me now turn to the set of objections mentioned at the beginning that ask whether the eurozone really looks anything like an ordoliberal dream come true or rather an ordoliberal nightmare.

The eurozone: ordoliberal dream or nightmare?

A number of accounts that deny any ordoliberal imprint on the German-led crisis management of the eurozone and the ensuing reform efforts do so on the basis of a solely interest-based explanation (see for example Young, 2017) but restrictions of space do not permit me to engage with these more fundamental arguments concerning the explanatory significance of ideas and interests respectively, which I have discussed extensively elsewhere (see Biebricher, 2019). The remaining positions base their skepticism with regard to the ordoliberal impact not on general objections to ideas as explanatory factors, but rather point to aspects of the current EMU that seem difficult to reconcile with ordoliberal ideas. As far as I can see, these aspects are the 'unorthodox' policies of the ECB, the ESM, and its alleged undermining of the no-bailout clause contained in the European treaties, the legally questionable architecture of the reformed euro regime, and the room for discretion opened up by the new instruments for the Commission, which is at odds with the ordoliberal postulate of a strictly rule-based politics (see, e.g. Feld, Köhler, & Nientiedt, 2015; Joerges, 2015, 2017).

While it lies beyond the scope of this chapter to engage with all of these points in a detailed manner, let me at least provide some duly succinct responses to each: With regard to the ECB policies, there is little doubt that from an ordoliberal view quantitative easing and Draghi's vow to do 'whatever it takes' to save the euro are rather problematic, given the centrality of a stable monetary order in Eucken's and other ordoliberal accounts. Still, let us not forget that the ECB's policies did not lead to any inflation; if anything, they were its last resort to battle deflationary tendencies. Thus, the postulate of (upward) price stability was hardly in jeopardy and, on the other hand, the ECB's announcements and actual policies probably did more to save the EMU from breaking up than any number of other reforms. Furthermore, while the ECB did back countries faced with bankruptcy as well as others by buying their bonds off secondary markets and thus reducing the yields on them, this was hardly a matter of charity, given that the ECB made it abundantly clear in actual letters to certain governments that their liquidity would be cut off, were they to refuse to enact the structural reforms demanded of them. Similarly, the ESM was designed to support struggling countries and offer emergency help, which prompted a number of observers to question its compatibility with the no-bailout principle. But this help also came with

200   *Thomas Biebricher*

strings attached because, as noted above, the former Troika oversaw the progress made in passing the structural reforms, and the next tranche of aid money could in principle be withheld whenever the reports showed insufficient progress in implementing the demands formulated in the 'memoranda of understanding.' In other words, while these policies may not have been ordoliberal in nature they still served an ordoliberal goal, namely to make countries strive for competitiveness in the desirable fashion described above, i.e. through structural reforms and internal devaluation. ESM and ECB policies were a price to be paid for a European market of jurisdictions that was to function more perfectly in the future.

Some commentators point to the questionable legal quality of the reformed euro regime as evidence of its non-ordoliberal nature. Indeed, ordoliberal thought always insisted on the proper juridification of frameworks for market orders and others. After all, they spoke of the legal dimension of the competitive order that would ensure market competition as an 'economic constitution.' The politics of crisis management, including a number of reforms, have been problematized from a legal point of view, be it that they allegedly violate the no-bailout clause in the case of the ESM, overstep the boundaries of the ECB mandate in the case of the Bank's policies, or are in conflict with European law in the case of some provision both of the Fiscal Pact as well as the Six-Pack. The conclusion drawn from this by many is that the eurozone is the very opposite of what ordoliberalism strove for, namely a regime of emergency measures that borders on the extralegal and is a far cry from the simple elegance of an economic constitution. However, without being too legalistic, it is worth pointing out that despite all the talk of extralegality, the debatable aspects have so far all been upheld when they were challenged before national or European courts. Furthermore, while the legal situation is certainly messier than what an ideal ordoliberal arrangement might look like, the fact remains that the overall goal of a juridification of economic policy has so far hardly been undermined by it. And there is no reason to rule out the possibility of transposing the various rules formulated in differing systems of law into a single, more homogeneous medium of law, thus moving closer to the ordoliberal idea. The import of some of the provisions of the Fiscal Compact, which is a treaty according to international law, into EU law already points in this direction.

This leaves us with a last reason to object to the characterization of the trend in eurozone governance restructuring as one of ordoliberalization: The rationale behind the juridification of economic policy that ordoliberals espoused was that it would reduce the possibility of discretionary decision-making and thus immunize governmental policy against volatile demands from society, be it through official democratic channels or other forms of influence. The ideal envisaged were rules that would practically apply themselves and bind the sovereign and its representatives in their own interest, just as Odysseus had himself tied to the mast of his ship for his own good, leaving him no further room for discretion. But despite all the juridification that has undoubtedly taken place over the years, building on an already extensive legal architecture in the form of the Maastricht Treaty and the Stability and Growth Pact, it cannot be denied that there remains significant scope for discretionary decision-making even, and maybe particularly, under the reformed eurozone regime. What has been described above as part of the technocratic element of the governance structure, namely the detailed country reports, is not easily reconcilable with the notion of a regime of uniform and self-applicatory rules: The highly individualized recommendations that are part of the reports seem to fly in the face of abstract and general rules as the preferred instrument of ordoliberal policymaking. Furthermore, while the reverse majority principle has automatized certain aspects of the rule-application procedure, there obviously remains room for discretion with regard to the European Commission, since it is still up to them to decide whether a certain procedure should be initiated or fines be issued. It is no secret that the Commission under the presidency of Juncker has not made use of its new instruments as rigorously as any proponent of ordoliberal ideas would have hoped, giving countries such as France and Italy a considerable degree of leeway in dealing with debts and deficits. Now, this issue deserves a more extensive discussion than I can offer here but despite objections that could be raised against the reading presented here, at the end of the day, the overall point is valid: The European market of jurisdictions remains imperfect from an ordoliberal perspective because its rules are still not enforced with sufficient stringency and, more generally, the "lash of competition," as Eucken once called it, is still not felt by all in the same manner. But this does not imply that the ordoliberalization thesis is principally mistaken. Rather, it suggests that political reality is the resultant of political forces pursuing often contravening projects, and if the reforms so far fail to satisfy proponents of an ordoliberal ordering of the European market of jurisdictions, they are likely to push for more reforms that will ameliorate the defects that continue to plague the market framework. In my view, there are two issues, in particular, that are high up on the list of further reforms from an ordoliberal perspective. First of all, the Commission may be well insulated from democratic pressures, but since it is apparently still hesitant to make full use of its sanctioning instruments in order to enforce the tightened regime of rules and regulations governing the eurozone, the solution might be to move the respective competences to other institutions. The Juncker Commission is a self-described 'political' Commission, so in order to truly depoliticize the rule-application process and let only 'the facts' and scientific expertise decide, the enforcement of the market framework might have to be even further removed from political influence: For example, the respective powers could be delegated to officials in an ESM, which is turned into a European Monetary Fund. Here, the political motives that still underlie the actions of the Commission may no longer hold any influence, and the rules might be applied and enforced as stoically by the experts as the metaphor of the umpire always suggested.

202 *Thomas Biebricher*

The other major defect of the eurozone as a market is a missing insolvency order. If competition is to function properly, it is not only necessary that market rules are applied rigorously, but also that market actors who are outcompeted actually have to leave the market. While the no-bailout clause suggested this possibility, it was arguably never taken seriously by investors until the Germans signaled in the early days of the eurozone crisis that they were not inclined to save Greece – and thus actually triggered the systemic crisis. From there on, actors were fundamentally uncertain to a Knightian degree whether a Greek bankruptcy and/or exit from the eurozone would be the best among many bad options or rather lead to a meltdown of the entire eurozone with unforeseeable consequences. In any case, it became clear that one of the most fundamental elements of market competition in its ordoliberal interpretation, i.e. the link between risk, liability, and market exit, was de facto missing in the eurozone market framework. Therefore, the other major reform that would conform to ordoliberal designs would be the introduction of a sovereign insolvency procedure along the lines of private insolvency orders that would ensure that the mechanisms of truly competitive markets could be brought to bear on market actors with all potential consequences. After all, "if the market is to rule one must not refuse to adjust to its requirements," as Eucken notes in his *Principles of Economic Policy* (1960, p. 371). Now, it may appear to be speculative to characterize these reforms as quintessential ordoliberal desiderata, but they are not conjured up out of thin air; rather, they are demands raised by the contemporary banner bearers of the ordoliberal tradition, be it the former ECB chief economist Jürgen Stark, Bundesbank president Jens Weidmann or former Finance Minister Wolfgang Schäuble: "A more rigorous interpretation of the rules could be achieved by giving responsibility for fiscal surveillance to an independent authority instead of the Commission," said Weidmann in a speech in early 2017 (Weidmann, 2017), and in his last 'non-paper' for the Eurogroup, Schäuble floated a very similar idea of moving the responsibilities for fiscal surveillance to the ESM. Weidmann (2013) also repeatedly pointed to the need to introduce an insolvency order for states, which has recently been affirmed by Stark (see Buchter & Schieritz, 2018, p. 25), and it is well known that during the showdown with Greece in 2015, Schäuble was floating a plan for a temporary Grexit, pointing in the same direction.

I have no intention to suggest that there is anything inevitable about these reforms coming to pass, nor is there anything inevitable about the ordoliberalization of Europe more generally. However, as I have tried to show in this chapter, the tendencies toward it are clearly detectable and while it continues to be a 'work in process,' there is no reason to assume that the forces that do this work – in alliances as well as conflict with others – will rest anytime soon.

Note

1 All translations from German are mine.

References

Bauer, M., & Becker, S. (2014). The unexpected winner of the crisis: The European Commission's strengthened role in economic governance. *Journal of European Integration 36*(3) 213–229.

Biebricher, T. (2013). Europe and the political philosophy of neoliberalism. *Contemporary Political Theory 12*(4) 338–375.

Biebricher, T. (2014). The return of ordoliberalism in Europe: Notes on a research agenda. *i-Lex 9* 1–24.

Biebricher, T. (2019). *The political theory of neoliberalism.* Stanford: Stanford University Press.

Böhm, F., Eucken W., & Großmann-Doerth, H. (2017). The Ordo-Manifesto of 1936. In T. Biebricher & F. Vogelmann (Eds.), *The birth of austerity: German ordoliberalism and contemporary neoliberalism* (pp. 27–39). London, UK: Rowman & Littlefield.

Buchanan, J. (2004). Constitutional efficiency and the European Central Bank. *Cato Journal 24*(1/2) 13–17.

Buchter, H., & Schieritz, M. (2018). 'Wir waren doch keine Idioten.' Gespräch mit Jürgen Stark, Theo Weigel und Jürgen Regling. In *Die Zeit* 27 vom 28. Juni 2018, pp. 24–25.

Dullien, S., & Guérot, U. (2012). *The long shadow of ordoliberalism: Germany's approach to the euro crisis.* European Council of Foreign Relations Policy Brief 49.

Eucken, W. (1954). *Kapitaltheoretische Untersuchungen.* Tübingen, Germany: Mohr Siebeck.

Eucken, W. (1960). *Grundsätze der Wirtschaftspolitik.* Tübingen, Germany: Mohr Siebeck.

Eucken, W. (2017). Structural transformations of the state and the crisis of capitalism. In T. Biebricher & F. Vogelmann (Eds.), *The birth of austerity: German ordoliberalism and contemporary neoliberalism* (pp. 51–72). London, UK: Rowman & Littlefield.

Feld, L. P., Köhler, E. A., Nientiedt, D. (2015). Ordoliberalism, pragmatism and the eurozone crisis: How the German tradition shaped economic policy in Europe. *CESIFO Working Paper 5368.* Munich, Germany.

Joerges, C. (2015). The legitimacy *problématique* of economic governance in the EU. In M. Dawson, H. Enderlein, & C. Joerges (Eds.), *The governance report 2015* (pp. 69–95). Oxford, UK: Oxford University Press.

Joerges, C. (2017). Europe after ordoliberalism: A Philippic. In T. Biebricher & F. Vogelmann (Eds.), *The birth of austerity: German ordoliberalism and contemporary neoliberalism* (pp. 197–220). London. UK: Rowman & Littlefield.

Majone, G. (1994). The rise of the regulatory state in Europe. *West European Politics 17*(3) 77–101.

Röpke, W. (1960). *A humane economy: The social framework of the free market.* Chicago, IL: Henry Regenery [1958].

Rüstow, A. (1942). Appendix. General sociological causes of the Economic disintegration and possibilities of reconstruction. In W. Röpke, *International economic disintegration,* (pp. 267–283). London, UK: W. Hodge.

Schimmelfennig, F. (2015). Liberal intergovernmentalism and the euro area crisis. *Journal of European Public Policy 22*(2) 177–195.

Streeck, W. (2015). Heller, Schmitt and the euro. *European Law Journal 21*(3) 361–370.

Weidmann, J. (2013). Crisis management and regulatory policy. Walter Eucken lecture from 11.02.2013. Available at www.bundesbank.de/Redaktion/EN/Reden/2013/2013_02_11_weidmann_eucken.html

Weidmann, J. (2017). Prospects for the economy. Speech delivered at the Jahresempfang der Wirtschaft, 07.02.2017. Available at www.bundesbank.de/Redaktion/EN/Reden/2017/2017_02_07_weidmann.html

Young, B. (2017). Is Germany's and Europe's crisis politics ordoliberal and/or neoliberal? In T. Biebricher & F. Vogelmann (Eds.), *The birth of austerity: German ordoliberalism and contemporary neoliberalism* (pp. 221–237). London, UK: Rowman & Littlefield.

Part III

Advancements of the ordoliberal framework after the crisis

14 Toward a European social market economy?

The normative legacy of Walter Eucken, Alexander Rüstow, and beyond

Julian Dörr, Nils Goldschmidt, and Alexander Lenger

Introduction

Worldwide, GDP per capita has increased significantly since the 1980s (Deaton, 2013; World Bank, 2018). Over the same period, however, and while economic welfare in general has increased, inequality in income and wealth has also increased significantly (OECD, 2011, 2015). There is a substantial amount of literature showing that we are currently facing a period of new polarization (Giesecke, Heisig, & Solga, 2015; Milanovic, 2005; OECD, 2015; Piketty, 2014; for a critique of these interpretations, see Sutch, 2017; van Zanden, Baten, Foldvari, & van Leeuwen, 2014) and a concentration of market success (Frank & Cook, 1996; Hacker & Pierson, 2010). In a nutshell: social inequality is on the rise again (Lenger & Schumacher, 2015; Piketty, 2014; Stiglitz, 2012).

Even for Europe, a growing socioeconomic divide can be observed, both between nations and within the nations themselves. Overall inequality in Europe has been rising over the past decades, and has intensified since the onset of the global financial crisis. Today, the average income of the richest 10% is around 9.5 times higher than that of the poorest 10%. Furthermore, wealth is shared unequally: The wealthiest 10% of households hold 50% of total wealth, whereas the poorest 40% own little over 3%. The levels of debt are high: In the OECD, half of households hold debt, and one-tenth is over-indebted. In terms of overall employment, major inequalities persist in Europe. For example, while unemployment rates in Iceland are 4%, in Greece they are close to 24%. Low-skilled young people who are disconnected from both employment and learning represent 17% of 15- to 29-year-olds in the EU (OECD, 2017). Inequality unquestionably has negative effects for Europe:

> Inequality can ... lower social trust in institutions and fuel political and social instability, in a number of ways. First, the higher the level of

208　*Julian Dörr et al.*

economic inequality, the higher will be the "social barriers" between groups and the less individuals will feel familiar with and connect to other people. Second, inequality may generate a perception of injustice: it is difficult to develop trust in others if they are seen as having unfair advantages. Finally, unequal communities may disagree over how to share (and finance) public goods, and those disagreements can in turn break social ties and lessen social cohesion.

(OECD, 2017, p. 5)

In light of this data, and of Europe's heterogeneous economic cultures (Brunnermeier, James, & Landau, 2016; Hall, 2014), the question must be asked as to whether – and, if so, how – a European *Ordnungspolitik* can be constructed. Our main argument is as follows: Ordoliberalism supplies a normative framework for a modern Europe, one that legitimizes the relevance of a genuinely European social market economy, i.e. to "find an effective and lasting system, which does justice to the dignity of man, for this new industrialized economy with its far-reaching division of labour" (Eucken, [1940] 1950, p. 314). This goal is key to European development.

This chapter is structured as follows: First, we shortly sketch out Walter Eucken's main idea on implementing social policy. Second, the subsequent improvement of Eucken's normative approach by constitutional political economy will be discussed (third section). Consequently, the rules of a society in general, their actual normative legitimation, and the resulting distribution patterns must be the object of economic analysis, something that Alexander Rüstow has already advocated in his calls for *Vitalpolitik* (fourth section). A modern concept meeting these demands is Amartya Sen's capability approach (fifth section). Finally and at length, we discuss the observations sketched out here in the context of the actual European economic framework, demonstrating that a reformed EU Cohesion Policy could be considered a kind of *Vitalpolitik of nations* realizing a European social market economy (sixth section). The chapter closes with a brief summary.

Walter Eucken and the concept of the privilege-free order of competition

The social market economy in postwar Germany is an explicit attempt to combine an efficient market economy with the demands of social security and the corresponding sense of justice in the population (Mureşan, 2014). According to the Freiburg School, the answer to this sociopolitical issue can be found in the establishment of the *privilege-free* order of competition. With hindsight, Franz Böhm gives the following account of the Freiburg School's goals:

The question that concerned us all … was the question of private power in a free society. It necessarily leads to the question of how a free economy is structured. From there one comes to the question of what types and possibilities there are, what role power plays in them, both the power of government and the power of private individuals and private groups, and which currents of order occur when a different distribution of power develops within the state and the society than that which is in conformity with the respective economic system.

(1957, p. 99; our translation)

In short, competition functions as the "greatest and most ingenious instrument of disempowerment in history" (Böhm, 1961, p. 22, our translation). Any position of (market) power that one might have achieved can always be threatened by other competitors, whereas the absence of competition results in reliance on those who possess the rights to scarce goods (see also Eucken, [1940] 1950, pp. 263–274, [1952] 2004, pp. 175–179, 291–301). The ordoliberal argument is thus two-tiered: Without a proper sociopolitical framework, competition creates a group of systematic losers, given that one's position in the market ultimately determines one's position of power. Consequently, economic competition must be configured in such a way as to ensure the virtual disempowerment of economic actors.

In this context, it is one of Eucken's most outstanding accomplishments to have centered the focus on the *integration* of economic and social policy. Eucken writes:

There is no economic political action that does not at the same time have, directly or indirectly, a social impact and social meaning. Therefore, anyone who wants to represent social interests should turn his attention primarily to the arrangement of the comprehensive order. By applying a general *Ordnungspolitik* the emergence of social issues must be prevented.

([1952] 2004, p. 313; our translation, our emphasis)

From an ordoliberal perspective, the most desirable economic and societal order is consequently one that always fulfills two criteria simultaneously: First, it must meet the criterion of economic efficiency, coordinating the actions of the individual economic actors in such a way that an economically valid and scarcity-limiting competitive process emerges. Second, it must also meet the criterion of social equity, that is, realizing an acceptable level of embeddedness in the social structure of a market society.

Economic efficiency and social equity: a consensus on constitutional interests

To legitimize such a challenge, constitutional political economy goes one step further than the ordoliberal concept: By distinguishing between actions and outcomes that occur within the scope of certain rules and that system of rules

210   *Julian Dörr et al.*

itself, it is able to balance efficiency and equity endogenously (see Buchanan, 1975, 1987; Congleton, 2014; Vanberg, 1994, 2005). The criterion of assessment for the equity of a system of rules, and therefore a specific social arrangement, is the fairness of the decision process. Whereas in traditional welfare economics, rules are assessed according to the extent to which the outcomes correspond to an 'equitable' distribution, in constitutional political economy, equity is measured by the extent to which the system of rules from which various outcomes may emerge is the result of an 'equitable' decision process.

From the procedural perspective of James Buchanan's constitutional economics (1975), rules are considered equitable when they are based on the *voluntary consent* of the individuals involved. Buchanan argues that the legitimizing function of voluntary consent, assumed to be present in market economy exchange processes, must also hold at the *constitutional level*, i.e. the level at which a community's members collectively decide upon the rules which are to determine their social coexistence (Vanberg, 1994, pp. 208–234). These rules represent the *constitutional interests* on which a consensus can be achieved; unlike the *privileged interests* of individual members of the community, these interests correspond to all members' shared interest in the validity of the decisive rules. Rules are thus not evaluated according to principles of equity that are held a priori to be valid; a positive assessment is the result of the effective consent of all participants to a specific constitutional arrangement (Brennan & Buchanan, 1985, ch. 7).

When it comes to the issue of identifying the normative and positive conditions for constitutional rules which are mutually beneficial for all participants, a thought experiment is employed in which constitutional questions are dealt with *as if* informed decisions regarding the institutional rules of the subsequent coexistence were to be made from a *fictional* 'original position' (see Rawls, 1971). Which principles would informed and rational humans in the same starting position agree upon in order to establish constitutionally equitable – and at the same time efficient – rules? The key characteristic of this kind of decision-making situation has to be, above all, the assumption of ignorance regarding both one's own abilities and opportunities and the future economic positions of the members of society in question (albeit, at the same time, with knowledge of economically efficient rules and their alternatives). Such a 'veil of uncertainty' (Müller, 1998) reduces strategic interest in the implementation of individual persons' or groups' privileged interests.

Thus, constitutional economics has theoretically resolved the classic conflict between efficiency and equity that influences everyday politics to a considerable degree in matters of, for example, economic growth, alternative sociopolitical initiatives, or income distribution. The constitutional consensus serves to achieve equity, as the assumptions can be made that – on the one hand – in democratic market economies with legally binding constitutions individuals will have the greatest possible opportunities to realize their own personal goals (Hayek, 1973), and – on the other – the individuals in question

Toward a European social market economy? 211

will consent voluntarily only to an economically efficient framework of rules (Buchanan, 1975, p. 51).

Back to reality: inequality and political acceptance

Nevertheless, sociopolitical arrangements cannot be legitimized solely by hypothetical positive functional characteristics such as efficient competition. Rather, their legitimacy arises from the actual consent of the individuals involved, for in principle both the existing *rules for* and the resulting *outcome patterns in* the distribution of goods and chances must be the object of consideration. This is the key European problem; whereas, from a political perspective, an appropriate democratic framework of regulations has been achieved, the resulting outcome patterns with regard to disparity in Europe have not sufficiently been taken into consideration. Consequently, if the actual patterns of distribution *systematically* and *persistently* fail to correspond to the justice expectations of a large number of people, it might reasonably be assumed that these people will factually not consent to an order of this kind. Rather, a reform of rules or the correction of outcomes become necessary (Vanberg, 2004, p. 157). Even if well-informed participants have collectively agreed upon an ostensibly equitable regulatory framework, this order will lose its effective legitimacy if it becomes clear that it systematically generates *one* specific group of 'losers.'

Consequently, for agreements on social arrangements like a social market economy, the legitimation criterion is not limited to voluntary consent at the point in time when the original agreement was made; rather, *lasting* voluntary consent of the actors involved *over time* is the decisive criterion of assessment (Vanberg, 2003).

> In any real-world setting, of course, the discussion of institutional rules affecting income-wealth distribution must take place in recognition of existing legal definitions of property rights, of existing political decision-making mechanisms, and of predicted patterns of income distribution as well as predicted positions of persons within these predicted distributions.
> (Buchanan & Bush, 1974, pp. 156–157)

In this sense, the key task is to configure the political process in such a way that a pattern of outcomes emerges which all affected individuals will factually accept as equitable (see Yanovskiy & Ginker, 2017).

Alexander Rüstow, another proponent of ordoliberalism, developed the concept of *Vitalpolitik* to demonstrate the necessity of concrete politics to achieve this goal. His approach is characterized by the notion that the 'freedom to do something' demands certain prerequisites: Individuals require both the material and immaterial capability to make use of freedoms and rights. Accordingly, *Vitalpolitik* makes the enhancement of life perspectives (or life circumstances) its key guiding principle. The goal of this policy is to

212 *Julian Dörr et al.*

create 'vital' conditions for a humane life (*Lebenslage*), which means the framework for a meaningful, dignified, and humane predisposition to a fair life (Dörr, 2017, pp. 9–63). Consequently, his twofold approach calls for an improvement of living conditions on the one hand, and highlights the path to realize such arrangements by focusing on de facto chances of individuals on the other hand. For Rüstow, the main restriction for realizing humane living conditions is the unequal distribution of starting conditions. Consequently, Rüstow considered *Vitalpolitik* an:

> economic and social policy which deliberately does not seek peak per-formances or record-breaking results involving the development of wages or other economic curves. After all, one can neither live from upward-sloping curves, nor does it make one happy. It rather asks what can be done to make individual persons happy and content.
>
> (Rüstow, 1963 [1957], p. 182f.)

A policy of compensating for social inequalities is therefore an essential element of, and indeed guarantee for, the actualization of individual life goals.

Participation and capability as key elements of modern economic and social policy

Amartya Sen's concept of participation represents, to some extent, a new variant of the perspectives we have described up to this point. Taking up the ideas of the Freiburg School and of constitutional political economy, Sen's capability approach is an explicit attempt to reconcile an efficient, privilege-free economic order with the desire for genuine social self-actualization, and to realize, in principle, an order that is free of discrimination. Whereas the goal of a privilege-free order is merely to ensure that all market participants have the same (starting) opportunities, i.e. not to favor any competitor, a discrimination-free order allows all citizens to participate in the market, which means in particular ensuring identical starting positions or at least com-parable circumstances and guaranteeing persistent equity of opportunities.

It is in this sense that negative freedom ('the freedom to act') must be sup-plemented with positive freedom ('the freedom to achieve'), which can only be ensured by the actual presence of certain "capabilities" for the fulfillment of fundamental needs (Sen, [1992] 2003, p. 102, 1994, p. 125).[1] Opportun-ities for self-realization are defined by Sen as the full ability to "prefer the scenario of free choice over that of submission to order" (1999, p. 27), and as such represent the freedom of an individual to realize different plans in life (p. 93). In his analysis of famines, Sen illustratively demonstrates that the scar-city of available foodstuffs is not just the result of a lack of economic resources, but equally the outcome of a significant lack of political participa-tion. From his diagnosis that underdevelopment and hardship are a con-sequence of the inequitable distribution of economic and political rights, Sen

Toward a European social market economy? 213

infers a normative ideal of freedom that draws on the individual capability for self-actualization in the sense of "qualitative freedom" (Dierksmeier, 2018). Sen includes, among other things, the potential to live free of avoidable illnesses and hunger, to be able to follow one's own occupational goals, to participate in societal life, and to be allowed to practice one's religion, as well as to have political freedoms and essential civil rights (Sen, 1999, pp. 24–25). The freedom to be able to realize one's own welfare by way of these opportunities is of central importance to the capability approach; poverty, on the other hand, means a lack of opportunities for self-actualization and a lack of freedoms.

The notions of participation and capability exhibit, in three ways, a remarkable similarity to the ordoliberal concept. First, both approaches emphasize the necessity of aligning economic resources with social functions:

> In fact we have excellent reasons to want more income and wealth. But not because income and wealth are desirable for their own sake, but because they are usually wonderful all-purpose means to gain greater freedom in choosing the lifestyle we consider reasonable.
>
> (Sen, 1999, p. 25)

Second, Sen stresses – very much in line with constitutional political economy – the analytical division between the level of rules and the level of outcomes (see Sen, 1994, 1999). By placing the focus of his observations firmly on the substantial freedoms which individuals value for subjective reasons (for example Sen, 1999, pp. 30–31), Sen's reflections on ethical considerations similarly take the ability of the individuals involved to reach a consensus to be a normative referential criterion. Third, and lastly, Sen (1999, pp. 33–36) assumes, here in line with Eucken, that non-ordered market processes will systematically disadvantage specific groups in society. Thus, by defining the normative setting of goals as a positive, qualitative process, Sen successfully expands upon the traditional ordoliberal perspective.

Accordingly, social policy is to be understood as enabling social participation in general by way of participation in the market, where of course a central element of instrumental freedom is economic opportunity, especially an individual's potential to accumulate their own resources for consumption, production, or exchange (Sen, 1999, p. 53). This also includes the ability, using one's own labor, to participate in the productive process and to earn an income that guarantees sufficient consumption.

Summing up, we should keep in mind that constitutional political economy has delivered a formal argument according to which an order is desirable when all individuals involved are able to act under the same conditions (see Buchanan, 1975; Hayek, 1973). Sen (1999) expands this argument significantly by taking into account that in reality not all participants are equitably involved in societal processes, as social inequalities are characteristic of modern societies, and as such the setting of goals in modern economic and

214 *Julian Dörr et al.*

social policy must be oriented toward the realization of participation through capability.

EU Cohesion Policy: a *Vitalpolitik for Nations*?

In line with the arguments made above a modern Europe should be judged according to the extent to which it is able to offer all members of a society the chance to be a full member of society and to enjoy an appropriate standard of living. As such, these ideas correspond directly to the call for *equity of participation* or *involvement*.

The notional concept of a *Vitalpolitik for Nations*, derived from Alexander Rüstow's *Vitalpolitik*, has proven useful in successfully transferring the concept of participation to the European level (Dörr, 2016a, 2017). Analogous to Rüstow's approach, the goal here is to enable all EU citizens to participate in market processes and thus in societal life in general. It is not enough to create a common and discrimination-free single market with formal rights of participation. Additionally, active policies intended to create equitable European structures are necessary. The integration of European economies into a common market thus requires an analysis of the opportunities they actually offer for access to and participation in market activity. Central obstacles here might include the categories mobility and education. Although de jure the EU largely guarantees freedom of movement and establishment, the extent to which EU citizens actually have the opportunity to emigrate for work, or to leave their native regional authorities at all, is open to question (OECD, 2014). Factors that determine mobility include, for instance, a well-developed transportation infrastructure, practical regulations for entitlement to social security, or the mutual acknowledgment of national qualifications. Barriers to mobility exist equally for individuals, corporations, and factors of production. Education is an important tool for expanding individuals' perspectives by means of participation in the labor market, and thus ensures their mobility. It has already been noted here that participation can only be realized if individuals are truly able to utilize their options for organizing their own paths through life. Participation in competitive market societies in collaborative economic orders necessitates, above all, relevant qualifications – acquired both at home and in the educational system – which provide the individuals in question, as *producers* of their own labor, with the necessary competitiveness on the supply side of the market process.

Particularly in rural regions, there may be a number of these obstacles to participation in the single market, as the administrative authorities here have fewer financial resources at their disposal for the provision of the relevant capabilities. If we accept the view that genuine barriers clearly do exist, then it seems reasonable to call for greater efforts in enabling participation in the single market. Consequently, a reduction in conflicting, geographically salient combinations of factors, in the distribution of international inequality, and in the degree of national inequality between rural and urban regions is needed

(Wibbels, 2005). For this reason, a *Vitalpolitik for Nations* must comprise a combination of negative and positive civil liberties, a technique which seems particularly appropriate with regard to the development needed to bring the 'poorer' nations of Central and Eastern Europe in line with the 'older' members of the EU; the integrative approach aims for the far-reaching advancement of the living conditions in a society, which – particularly in transitional states with severe social inequality – seems more important than a mere focus on macroeconomic indicators as criteria for investment (Dörr, 2016b).

This policy of enabling states, via European assistance, to allow their populations to participate in a market free of privilege and discrimination, can be linked to the theoretical reflections on constitutional political economy and the criterion of consent (as discussed in the third section): A *Vitalpolitik for Nations* would be in the interest of, and thus likely to achieve a consensus among, all EU citizens, as it cannot be in the interest of all individuals to leave certain nations, in the medium term, in a condition of socioeconomic underdevelopment, thus impeding their populations' participation in the single market. Instead, an EU with funding policies for underdeveloped nations would be in the constitutional interest of its citizens, who would consent to this format because it offers all participants the chance of a better life compared to an EU which, for example, ignores the fact that the post-socialist and, to a lesser extent, the Mediterranean members have a historically justifiable gap to close, and would thus be in danger of not utilizing the single market to its full potential. This kind of negligence can have tangible consequences for pan-European integration; the European project is sustained by the approval of its citizens, and if they lose confidence in the EU's ability to solve economic and social problems, an increase in dissatisfaction with Europe is likely to follow (EU Commission, 2013).

The European Union, with its European regional and structural policies, already has access to a toolbox that could help address its goal of improving socioeconomic conditions. The EU's Cohesion Policy has, for almost 30 years, followed the goal of eliminating or at least alleviating regional disparities, and in this way increasing the quality of life throughout the Union (Bache, 2008; Leonardi, 2005). With the five European Structural and Investment Funds, of which the European Social Fund and the European Regional Development Fund are surely the most well known, the EU supports numerous projects, which can be proposed both by governmental offices and by corporations. This policy field is, from a financial perspective, the EU's best-equipped portfolio: In the period 2014–2020, it will have distributed a total of approximately €350 billion, which is about one-third of the EU's entire budget of approximately €1 trillion (EU Commission, 2015). The EU Commission itself has an expressly positive estimation of the effect of the Cohesion Policy, and thus defends its continued existence. The Commission's most recent cohesion report on the progress brought about by structural funding makes reference to the policy of subsidizing a total of 1.1 million small and

216 Julian Dörr et al.

mid-sized businesses, supporting 7.4 million unemployed in their search for a job, and helping 8.9 million people acquire new qualifications. Furthermore, €16 billion were invested in the digital economy, the expansion of electronic government services was continued, and 15 million households were provided with access to broadband internet. Moreover, the funds invested in energy efficiency, environmental protection, the reduction of social exclusion, and the improvement of public transportation and the trans-European road and rail network. In this way, the Cohesion Policy contributes, in the context of the continuing economic disparities between and the high levels of unemployment in many regions, to a more equitable and social EU (EU Commission, 2017). The media response to this thoroughly positive depiction, however, is largely dismissive, often concentrating on infrastructure projects which do not fulfill their remit, or even on the misuse of funding. Of course, even the successes should be examined critically, especially considering the great levels of expenditure (e.g. ; Bachtler & Wishlade, 2004; Swidlicki, Ruparel, Persson, & Howarth, 2012). Although some recipient regions, such as Ireland, have exhibited positive development, in other regions like southern Italy, quality of life, and economic prosperity have scarcely improved in the past decades. If we analyze the Cohesion Policy from the perspective of a *Vitalpolitik for Nations*, we can establish the existence of four structural deficits, which also explain the stagnation of some regions (Dörr, 2017):

First, its structural policy systematically contravenes one of the EU's fundamental building blocks, the principle of subsidiarity, according to which the intervention of European institutions is only justifiable if the preceding levels in the hierarchy are not able to reach a satisfactory solution, or cannot be made to do so. The EU is only supposed to act when regions and their superordinate national structures lack the necessary funding to pursue economic development themselves. From this perspective, structural support is a reasonable solution for economically weak countries like Romania, or for supranational problems that demand the coordination of the countries involved. If we look at the prevailing practices, however, it seems right to ask if the support being given is genuinely needs based: First, even the wealthy and transitional regions will receive considerable structural funding, around €90 billion, between now and 2020 (this is approximately one-third of all capital aid). Second, there are a number of regions which are in need of assistance, counting as they do as poor, but which are also part of relatively wealthy nations, themselves quite able to generate suitable development policies for their weaker regions. Here is an illustrative example for the assistance of economically weaker regions from the period 2007–2013: Greece, which has a per capita GDP of 92% of the EU average, received funding to the value of approximately €1,757 per inhabitant, while Poland received almost the same amount of assistance, but only has 54% of the wealth. Finally, yet importantly, the transfers also represent a repayment of a nation's own contributions to the EU (for Germany between 2014 and

Toward a European social market economy? 217

2020, this will be around 10%), and thus favor net contributors as well as net recipients (Dörr, 2016c).

Second, a transformation can be observed in the distribution of assistance, one which has gone widely unnoticed, taking place behind the scenes and without any express ruling from the member states or indeed the EU's citizens themselves: Since 2007, the Cohesion Policy has promoted investment in all regions of the EU in order to create jobs and support research, instead of concentrating on the ostensibly underdeveloped regions. This paradigmatic change has been accompanied by the Lisbon Agenda, which has given itself the ambitious goal of making Europe the "most competitive and dynamic knowledge-based economy in the world" (EU Council, 2000), and also by the strategy that succeeded it, Europe 2020 (Nugent, 2010). Structural policy, too, is subordinate to the overarching motive to increase competitiveness, thus giving it new significance. The discourse now is not merely one of reducing the wealth divide, but focuses on new goals like the ability to innovate, and environmental and climate protection. This paradigmatic change in structural aid can, to an extent, be interpreted as an attempt to establish a "Ersatzwirtschaftspolitik," a 'replacement' economic policy (Dörr, 2017, p. 214), one already able to take on, albeit informally, the responsibilities of economic governance, working on a factual basis and compensating for the missing contractual regulations. Of course, it is in its early stages: Regional and structural policy does not have all the necessary economic competencies, nor does the EU Commission have the monopoly on decision-making here. However, it is crucial to emphasize the fact that this reconfiguration of the Cohesion Policy has paved the way for further delimitation, one that supplants plans to assist the neediest regions in catching up with the more developed ones.

Third, the orientation toward informal economic policy can at times lead to extreme effects of distribution. For example, Upper Bavaria, and thus the city of Munich, received around €886 million in structural funding between 2007 and 2013, despite Bavaria as a whole having a per capita GDP of 137.9% of the EU average, which certainly means its level of wealth is above average, and despite Bavaria also being, indirectly, an important financial contributor to the EU budget. This approach not only commits funding to wealthier areas when it could otherwise be employed in truly weak regions, but it also necessitates a cost-intensive policy of distribution. There are no convincing reasons as to why the involvement of the EU would increase efficiency compared to national structural assistance.

Finally, not enough attention is paid to circumstances in recipient nations. All EU nations exhibit differing institutions, administrative traditions, and cultural characteristics – in short, there exist very different economic cultures, so there can be no universal blueprints for economic development, an insight that other institutions such as the World Bank and the IMF have begun to take seriously. As such, different problems and situations demand different approaches; the new member states in Central and Eastern Europe, for

218 *Julian Dörr et al.*

example, need more help than older members in the expansion of their administrative capacities and in securing democratic and constitutional structures. Assistance of this kind would be more appropriate than the payment of grants to corporations, which distort competition, and which often result in deadweight losses.

Even this brief analysis has yielded an ambivalent portrayal of the Cohesion Policy; although it is an essential instrument in the economic policy of the EU's provision of funding for its member states, it is neither the result of a coherent theoretical framework – it is more a political field which has emerged over the history of integration by way of political horse-trading (see Dinan, 2010) – nor can it be said to have had a clear, positive effect. If we adhere, however, to the notion that the European Union does need a functioning *Vitalpolitik for Nations* in order to improve the actual circumstances of its citizens and provide them a framework for a good and successful life, then the need for a reform of structural aid policy is clear. The point of orientation for this ordoliberal-motivated renewal of the Cohesion Policy has to be the question as to the configuration of intelligent measures for the enablement of underdeveloped economies, measures which all EU citizens would agree are in their own interests and which simultaneously would help those affected to help themselves contribute to a form of 'regional participatory equity.'

Conclusion: European social market economy

Using the observations expressed in this chapter, we can now more accurately describe a *European* social market economy (Velo & Velo, 2013). If we consider freedom not just to be the greatest goal of, but also the most important means of, achieving societal development, then competition and efficiency are not ends in themselves, but a useful tool in the construction of society. Whereas it might once have been true that a market economy could be considered social if it was well ordered ('the best social policy is a good economic policy'), the task faced by today's European social and economic politics is to include individuals in the European single market.

On the European level, however, this will require measures of social and economic policy in order to overcome unequal infrastructural circumstances (Velo & Velo, 2013). Accordingly, we argue for the continuation and intensification of the European Cohesion Policy as the basis of a truly European *social* market economy. This policy can, following Alexander Rüstow, be thought of as a *Vitalpolitik* for the EU's member states, and aims to bring about equity of initial prospects through funding for underdeveloped regions and population groups.

Note

1 The capability approach was first developed by Amartya Sen (1980, 1984, 1999), and consolidated by Martha Nussbaum (1992, 2003, 2006). For an overview of the capability approach, see Robeyns (2005).

Bibliography

Bache, I. (2008). *Europeanization and multilevel governance: Cohesion policy in the European Union and Britain*. Lanham, MD: Rowman & Littlefield.

Bachtler, J., & Wishlade, F. (2004). Searching for consensus: The debate on reforming EU. *EoRPA Paper 04/4*.

Biebricher, T., & Vogelmann, F. (Eds.) (2017). *The birth of austerity: German ordoliberalism and contemporary neoliberalism*. London, UK: Rowman & Littlefield.

Böhm, F. (1957). Die Forschungs- und Lehrgemeinschaft zwischen Juristen und Volkswirten an der Universität Freiburg in den dreißiger und vierziger Jahren des 20. Jahrhunderts. (Das Recht der Ordnung der Wirtschaft). In Wolff, H. J. (Ed.), *Aus der Geschichte der Rechts- und Staatswissenschaften zu Freiburg i. Br.* (pp. 95–113). Freiburg, Germany: Albert.

Böhm, F. (1961). Demokratie und ökonomische Macht. In Institut für ausländisches und internationales Wirtschaftsrecht an der Johann Wolfgang Goethe Universität Frankfurt (Ed.), *Kartelle und Monopole im modernen Recht* (pp. 3–24). Karlsruhe, Germany: C.F. Müller.

Brennan, G., & Buchanan, J. M. (1985). *The reason of rules: Constitutional political economy*. Cambridge, UK: Cambridge University Press.

Brunnermeier, M., James, H., & Landau, J.-P. (2016). *The euro and the battle of ideas*. Princeton, NJ: Princeton University Press.

Buchanan, J. M. (1975). *The limits of liberty: Between anarchy and Leviathan*. Indianapolis, IN: Liberty Fund.

Buchanan, J. M. (1987). The constitution of economic policy. *American Economic Review* 77(3) 234–250.

Buchanan, J. M., & Bush, W. C. (1974). Political Constraints on Contractual Redistribution. *American Economic Review* 64(3) 153–157.

Cohesion Policy, European Policy Research Paper Nr. 55.

Congleton, R. D. (2014). The contractarian constitutional political economy of James Buchanan. *Constitutional Political Economy* 25(1) 39–67.

Deaton, A. (2013). *The great escape: Health, wealth, and the origins of inequality*. Princeton, NJ: Princeton University Press.

Dierksmeier, C. (2018). Qualitative freedom and cosmopolitan responsibility. *Humanistic Management Journal* 2(2) 109–123.

Dinan, D. (2010). *Ever closer union: An introduction to European integration* (4th ed.). London, UK: Palgrave Macmillan.

Dörr, J. (2016a). "Vitalpolitik für Staaten"? Eine alternative Sicht auf die europäische Kohäsionspolitik. In Dörr, J., Goldschmidt, N., Kubon-Gilke, G., Sesselmeier, W. (Eds.), *Vitalpolitik, Inklusion und der sozialpolitische Diskurs. Theoretische Reflexionen und sozialpolitische Implikationen* (pp. 145–153). Münster, Germany: LIT.

Dörr, J. (2016b). Die Bedeutung der Kohäsionspolitik für die europäische Integration: Aktuelle Bestandsaufnahme eines unbekannten Politikfeldes. *ZFAS Zeitschrift für Außen- und Sicherheitspolitik* 9(1) 27–37.

220 *Julian Dörr et al.*

Dörr, J. (2016c). Die europäische Kohäsionspolitik auf dem Weg zu einer "informellen Wirtschaftspolitik"? *ORDO Jahrbuch für die Ordnung von Wirtschaft und Gesellschaft 67* 193–221.

Dörr, J. (2017). *Die europäische Kohäsionspolitik. Eine ordnungsökonomische Perspektive.* Berlin, Germany: De Gruyter.

Eucken, W. ([1940] 1950). *The Foundations of Economics. History and Theory in the Analysis of Economic Reality.* London, UK: W. Hodge.

Eucken, W. ([1948] 1982). The social question. In Ludwig-Erhard-Stiftung (Ed.), *Standard texts on the social market economy: Two centuries of discussion* (pp. 267–275). Stuttgart, Germany: Gustav Fischer.

Eucken, W. ([1952] 2004). *Grundsätze der Wirtschaftspolitik* (7th ed.). Tübingen, Germany: Mohr Siebeck.

EU Commission. (1990). One market, one money: An evaluation of the potential benefits and costs of forming an economic and monetary union. Brussels, Belgium.

EU Commission. (2013). Flash Eurobarometer 384. Citizens' awareness and perceptions of EU regional policy.

EU Commission. (2015). Europäische Struktur- und Investitionsfonds 2014–2020. Offizielle Texte und Kommentare. Brussels, Belgium.

EU Commission. (2017). Siebter Bericht über den wirtschaftlichen, sozialen und territorialen Zusammenhalt. Meine Region, mein Europa, unsere Zukunft, Brüssel.

EU Council. (2000). Schlussfolgerungen Europäischen Rates Lissabon 23–24.03.2000.

Frank, R. H., & Cook, P. J. (1996). *The winner-take-all society: Why the few at the top get so much more than the rest of us.* New York, NY: Penguin.

Giesecke, J., Heisig, J. P., & Solga, H. (2015). Getting more unequal: Rising labor market inequalities among low-skilled men in West Germany. *Research in Social Stratification and Mobility 39* 1–17.

Hacker, J. S., & Pierson, P. (2010). *Winner-take-all politics: How Washington made the rich richer – And turned its back on the middle class.* New York, NY: Simon & Schuster.

Hall, P. A. (2014). Varieties of capitalism and the euro crisis. *West European Politics 37* 1223–1243.

Hayek, F. A. v. (1973). *Law, legislation and liberty. Volume 1: Rules and order.* Chicago, IL: University of Chicago Press.

Hien, J., & Joerges, C. (Eds.) (2017). *Ordoliberalism, law and the rule of economics.* Oxford, UK: Hart.

Lenger, A., & Schumacher, F. (Eds.) (2015). *Understanding the dynamics of global inequality: Social exclusion, power shift, and structural changes.* Heidelberg, Germany: Springer.

Leonardi, R. (2005). *Cohesion policy in the European Union: The building of Europe.* Houndmills, UK: Palgrave Macmillan.

Milanovic, B. (2005): *Worlds apart: Measuring international and global inequality.* Princeton, NJ: Princeton University Press.

Müller, C. (1998). The veil of uncertainty unveiled. *Constitutional Political Economy 9*(1) 5–17.

Mureşan, S. S. (2014). *Social market economy: The case of Germany.* Cham, Switzerland: Springer.

Nugent, N. (2010). *The government and politics of the European Union* (7th ed.). Houndmills, UK: Palgrave Macmillan.

Nussbaum, M. C. (1992). Human functioning and social justice: In defense of Aristotelian essentialism. *Political Theory 20*(2) 202–246.

Nussbaum, M. C. (2003). Capabilities as fundamental entitlements: Sen and social justice. *Feminist Economics 9*(2/3) 33–59.

Nussbaum, M. C. (2006). *Frontiers of justice: Disability, nationality, species membership.* Cambridge, MA: Belknap Press.

OECD. (2011). *Divided we stand: Why inequality keeps rising.* Paris, France: OECD.

OECD. (2014). *Matching economic migration with labour market needs.* Paris, France: OECD.

OECD. (2015). *In it together: Why less inequality benefits all.* Paris, France: OECD.

OECD. (2017). *Understanding the socio-economic divide in Europe.* Paris, France: OECD.

Piketty, T. (2014). *Capital in the twenty-first century.* Cambridge, MA: Harvard University Press.

Rawls, J. (1971). *A theory of justice.* Cambridge, MA: Belknap Press.

Robeyns, I. (2005). The capability approach: A theoretical survey, *Journal of Human Development 6*(1) 93–114.

Rüstow, A. ([1957] 1963). Hat der Westen eine Idee? In S. Hoch & A. Rüstow (Eds.), *Rede und Antwort. 21 Reden und viele Diskussionsbeiträge aus den Jahren 1932 bis 1962* (pp. 165–189). Ludwigsburg, Germany: Hoch.

Sen, A. K. (1980). Equality of What? In S. M. MacMurrin (Ed.), *The Tanner lectures on human values* (pp. 195–220). Utah: University of Utah Press.

Sen, A. K. (1984). Rights and capabilities. In A. K. Sen, *Resources, values and development* (pp. 307–324). Cambridge, MA: Harvard University Press.

Sen, A. K. (1994). Markets and the freedom to choose. In H. Siebert (Ed.), *The ethical foundations of the market economy: International workshop* (pp. 123–138). Tübingen, Germany: Mohr Siebeck.

Sen, A. K. (1999). *Development as freedom.* New Delhi, India and Oxford, UK: Oxford University Press.

Sen, A. K. ([1992] 2003). *Inequality re-examined* (reprint). Oxford, UK: Oxford University Press.

Stiglitz, J. E. (2012). *The price of inequality: How today's divided society endangers our future.* New York, NY: Norton.

Sutch, R. (2017). The one percent across two centuries: A replication of Thomas Piketty's data on the concentration of wealth in the United States. *Social Science History 41*(4) 587–613.

Swidlicki, P., Ruparel, R., Persson, M., & Howarth, C. (2012). *Off target: The case for bringing regional policy back home.* Open Europe.

Trantidis, A. (2017). The problem of constitutional legitimation: What the debate on electoral quotas tells us about the legitimacy of decision-making rules in constitutional choice. *Constitutional Political Economy 28*(2) 195–208.

van Zanden, J. L., Baten, J., Foldvari, P., & van Leeuwen, B. (2014). The Changing shape of global inequality 1820–2000: Exploring a new dataset. *Review of Income and Wealth 60*(2) 279–297.

Vanberg, V. J. (1994). *Rules and choice in economics.* London, UK and New York, NY: Routledge.

Vanberg, V. J. (2003). Citizens' sovereignty, constitutional commitments, and renegotiation: Original versus continuing agreement. In A. Breton, G. Galeotti, P. Salmon, & R. Wintrobe, (Eds.), *Rational foundations of democratic politics* (pp. 198–221). Cambridge, UK: Cambridge University Press.

222 *Julian Dörr et al.*

Vanberg, V. J. (2004). The status quo in contractarian–constitutionalist perspective. *Constitutional Political Economy 15*(2) 153–170.

Vanberg, V. J. (2005). Market and state: The perspective of constitutional political economy. *Journal of Institutional Economics 1*(1) 23–49.

Velo, D., & Velo, F. (2013). *A social market economy and European Economic Monetary Union.* Bern, Switzerland: Peter Lang.

Wibbels, E. (2005). Decentralized governance, constitution formation, and redistribution. *Constitutional Political Economy 16*(2) 161–188.

World Bank. (2018). World Bank Indicators, Washington, DC.

Yanovskiy, M., & Ginker, T. (2017). A proposal for a more objective measure of de facto constitutional constraints. *Constitutional Political Economy 28*(4) 311–320.

15 The enigma of German ordoliberalism

Is there a future for a European social market economy?

Brigitte Young

Introductory comments

The sovereign debt crisis starting in 2010 has split the eurozone not only along geographical lines among northern current account surplus and southern deficit countries, the fissure also reflects a deep ideological "battle of ideas" (Brunnermeier, James, & Landau, 2016; Young, 2015b) in how to resolve the embattled eurozone. Particularly, Anglo-Saxon academics and the media criticized the German government for its focus on a rule-based stability culture and its emphasis on a fiscal straitjacket for indebted peripheral eurozone countries. The pressure for strict fiscal consolidation has only limited support among the "Anglo-Saxon–Latin pragmatism" of economic policymaking (Beck & Kotz, 2018, p. 1). Many of these narratives are highly negative and blame the rule-based ordoliberal tradition, also known as the Freiburg School, for its influence on German policymaking.

Mark Blyth (2013) was one of the first academics to make a connection between the German austerity culture and ordoliberalism. His main argument was that by insisting on austerity, the demand-side macro-stabilization management was ignored, worsening the economic growth gap in the peripheries. Others criticized Germany's insistence on strengthening competitiveness in the peripheral countries, meaning as Biebricher (2014) suggested, cutting wages and costs in countries suffering from economic recession. In other words, the discourse of competitiveness is part of an ordoliberal mantra to force peripheral countries to embark on supply-side structural reforms. Others point to the danger of an inherent authoritarianism in ordoliberal thinking, thus creating the basis for an undemocratic and technocratic eurozone governance regime (Bonefeld, 2012, 2015; Oberndorfer, 2015).

That a linkage is made between German fiscal rule-based orthodoxy in managing the eurozone crisis and ordoliberal principles is in no small part due to the frequent reference of German policymakers to ordoliberalism. Jens Weidmann, president of the German Bundesbank, has mentioned Walter Eucken, one of the original founders of the Freiburg School, in 33 of the 106 speeches he has given since becoming president of the Bundesbank in 2011. The most frequent support came from the former Finance Minister, Wolfgang

224   *Brigitte Young*

Schäuble. Not only did he mention in his talks that he hails from Freiburg, but more importantly he invoked the ordoliberal concepts associated with *Ordnungspolitik* in 36 of his 80 speeches and interviews on the eurozone crisis between January 2010 and December 2015 (Hien & Joerges, 2018).

Not even the German political parties stray much in their rhetoric from the supposed ordoliberal ideas of fiscal prudence and the importance of competition for peripheral countries to achieve the much-needed economic growth, as the 2013 Coalition Agreement between the Christian Democratic Union/Christian Social Union (CDU/CSU) and the Social Democratic Party (SPD) demonstrates. The SPD fully endorsed the notion of price stability (perhaps in a more palatable form of *austerity lite*) and the emphasis on competition as the way out of the crisis for the indebted countries. In fact, the Coalition Agreement of 2013 mentions *competition* (*Wettbewerb*) and acquiring the skills or ability to become competitive (*Wettbewerbsfähigkeit*) 54 times in a 185-page document (Koalitionsvertag, 2013; Young, 2014). Even in the new 2018 Coalition government, the designated SPD Finance Minister, Olaf Scholz, declared that the SPD stands for solid finance, and that it will retain the *Schwarze Null* of his CDU predecessor, Wolfgang Schäuble. He further emphasized that "a finance minister in Germany is foremost a *German finance minister*" (*Spiegel Online*, 2018).

The discussion on whether German policymakers and some economists live in a 'parallel universe' in comparison to US economic pragmatism including the southern eurozone countries (including France), which Beck and Kotz refer to as "Anglo-Saxon–Latin pragmatism of economic policy making' (2018, p. 1), has gained fresh ammunition with the election of Emmanuel Macron as French president in 2017. In his near two-hour speech in September 2017 at the Sorbonne in Paris, Macron laid out a radical vision for a more "sovereign, united and democratic" European Union spanning issues such as the eurozone, security and defense, and migration (*Financial Times*, 2017a, p. 2). In regard to eurozone economic policy, Macron called for a euro-area budget, funded by corporate tax receipts (which includes a proposal for harmonizing corporate tax regimes across the EU member states), a euro finance minister with fiscal policy competence, complemented with a separate euro parliament, and revived attempts for a common financial transaction tax.

However, Macron's vision of risk-sharing goes against the ideas of Germany's stability culture. In fact, Brunnermeier et al. (2016) have referred to an impasse in their book, titled, *The Euro and the Battle of Ideas*. They argue that the problem with the euro is not so much a design flaw, but more fundamentally a difference among economic traditions which lead to national stereotypes of what represents typical *French and German* ideas. These different economic thoughts were played out during the European sovereign debt crises and Germany's insistence on fiscal prudency following a rule-based system versus France's notion of discretionary politics and risk-sharing to overcome the eurozone crisis.

Is there a future for a European social market economy? 225

Similarly, the macroeconomists Beck and Kotz (2018) have taken up this argument of a fault line between German economists and policymakers and those advocating a more pragmatic approach found among US economic policymakers and academics (as well as French and southern eurozone peripheral eurozone countries). As such, the chapters in the e-book *Ordoliberalism: A German Oddity?* (2018), written mostly by economists from both sides of the Atlantic, focus on the historical origin of the ordoliberal tradition of economics, ordoliberalism and macro-management, ordoliberalism and global imbalances, and ordoliberalism and its influence on German crisis policymaking. While many of the articles refer to the insistence on a public narrative of the German stability culture, in response to the crisis many economists nevertheless cite pragmatism, flexibility, and a less rule-based approach of the German policymakers, an argument largely ignored by ordoliberal critics.

The chapter is structured as follows. The next section introduces the main ideas of the Freiburg ordoliberals as mentioned in the *Ordo Manifesto* of 1936. Subsequently I will focus on some chapters of Eucken's *Grundsätze der Wirtschaftspolitik* ([1952] 2017 translated texts)[1] and show that Eucken was cognizant of the need to adapt rules according to different national circumstances and time horizons. More importantly, he realized that perfect competition may be incoherent and detrimental, and thus political intervention may be necessary to correct the outcomes.

The third section will return to the question of whether a German rule-based system with its emphasis on fiscal prudency and the French insistence on risk sharing prevents the creation of a social Europe as suggested by Jean-Claude Juncker on assuming the EU Commission presidency in 2015. At the 2017 Gothenburg summit, the EU member states committed themselves to a new social agenda as envisioned in the European Pillar of Social Rights. While the Freiburg Scholars may be skeptical about a social Europe, the ideas of Alfred Müller-Armack, who coined the term *Soziale Marktwirtschaft* and which functioned as the basis for the German model after World War II (WWII), may offer some insights for macroeconomic stabilization measures. His intent was to reconcile ordoliberalism with social politics in his conception for a *German social market economy* to institutionalize a fairer compromise between competitive markets and social solidarity (Müller-Armack, 1976a; Vanberg, 2002). The debate on the social politics of Müller-Armack may provide some substance to the rather abstract debate of a European Pillar of Social Rights.

A competitive market order depends on the economic and legal context

Ordoliberalism is not reducible to one *Weltanschauung* (Berghahn, 2015; Dyson, 2017; Feld, Köhler, & Nientiedt, 2015; Hien & Joerges, 2017; 2018; Vanberg, 2015; Young, 2015a, 2015b, 2017a, 2017b, 2017c). It is useful to distinguish between the ordoliberal economists and jurists of the

226 *Brigitte Young*

Freiburg School, centered around Walter Eucken, Franz Böhm, and Hans Großmann-Doerth, and the more sociological branch around Wilhelm Röpke, Alexander Rüstow, and Alfred Müller-Armack (Sally 1996; Young 2015a, 2017c). Nevertheless, they all shared their antipathy to the classical liberalism or laissez-faire. Röpke and Rüstow differ from the Freiburgers in that they believed that the socioeconomic and political crisis of the first half of the 20th century was due to a cultural crisis of modernization rather than reducing it to economic issues alone. Particularly Rüstow calls for a *Vitalpolitik* (organic policy) that would organize the living space of workers in rural, or semi-agrarian settlements to avoid the negative influence of modern living for the lower strata of society (Biebricher & Vogelmann, 2017, p. 140).

In contrast to these ideas of social engineering for the working class, the Faculty of Law and Economics at the University of Freiburg developed the legal and economic perspectives of what later became known as the Freiburg School tradition, which today is the best-known branch of ordoliberalism (Vanberg, 2015).

The exponents of what was initially called the *neoliberal* circle came together in Paris 1938 to celebrate Walter Lippmann's book, *The Good Society* ([1937] 2017), in which he called for a revival of liberalism to counter what he perceived as the choices propagated by American leaders between liberty and security. The participants of the *Colloque Lippmann* united in rejecting the economic reductionism which understood the market only in terms of a utilitarian efficiency device (Böhm, Eucken, & Großmann-Doerth, [1936] 2017; Sally, 1996). Instead they emphasized a normative–ethical foundation of economics, delineating an important role for the state to set the constitutional framework for economic competition in order to ensure liberal outcomes to serve the larger interests of society. In conceptualizing a new (neo)liberalism, the proponents of a *third way* combined economic efficiency with human decency to achieve a just and stable social order, one that contrasted with the key concepts of laissez-faire, which believed in the naturalness of the market and the self-regulating power of market forces. Laissez-faire economists such as David Ricardo, Thomas Malthus, Edmund Burke, and the adherents of the Austrian school such as Ludwig von Mises, and later Milton Friedman, argued that unfettered economic competition was superior to any form of state guidance in economics.

Neoliberal thinkers of that period held the discredited economic orthodoxy of the 1920s responsible for the world turbulences in the 1920s. On both sides of the Atlantic, American presidents Calvin Coolidge and Herbert Hoover as well as the German Chancellor Heinrich Brüning disregarded the economic freefall accompanied by huge unemployment numbers and tried to rescue the dismal state of affairs via budgetary austerity and restrictive monetary policies. The results are well known. These dire circumstances threw open the gates to either totalitarian fascism or Soviet communism. In contrast, the participants in Paris saw their mission to present a reformulated

Is there a future for a European social market economy? 227

new liberalism as an alternative between totalitarianism and a defunct laissez-faire doctrine (Sally, 1996).

In their jointly written *Ordo Manifesto* of 1936 (originally titled *Unsere Aufgabe*), the Freiburg economists and jurists Franz Böhm, Walter Eucken, and Hans Großmann-Doerth, set out their ordoliberal ideas of the interdependence of economic, legal, political, and social order. The text not only exemplifies the basic ideas of ordoliberalism. At the same time, the authors wanted to demonstrate the practical implications of ordoliberalism beyond academics. The text starts out with a critique of the marginalization of both political economy and the law in the decision-making processes of economic policies. This marginalization, or dethronement, they saw as a result of the rise of the historical school and the increasing fatalism inherent in the Marxist notion of historical determinism. Particularly, they deride historicism for its inability to generate robust and abstract knowledge about economic processes, which according to the authors, has led to arbitrariness and a kind of relativism. In contrast, the ordoliberals developed the idea of an 'economic constitution' (*Wirtschaftsverfassung*), a kind of normative roadmap to focus on the interdependence of political, legal, and moral orders independent of their own immediate economic interests. The ordoliberals believed that 'the economic constitution must be understood as a general political decision as to how the economic life of the nation is to be structured' (Böhm et al., [1936] 2017, p. 36).

Walter Eucken and his cohorts were most concerned with developing a conceptual foundation for a consciously formed and instituted *ordo*, which Eucken called *Ordnung der Wirtschaft* (order of the economy), instead of a historically given order, a *Wirtschaftsordnung* (economic order). In this context the resulting market order was a synthesis of legal and economic ordering (Eucken, [1952] 1990). Their target was the rise of massive economic private power groups which were able to shape the law in their own interest. Private monopolies had been growing since the closing decades in the 19th century and both the principles of the commercial code and constitutional law were ignored to the detriment of economic development. Private power in laissez-faire leads to distortions in the market mechanism by crippling the price mechanism, but these authors also warned of the increasing state power in Soviet centralized socialism and European fascism. The answer was not to delegate power to interest groups so they could balance the various economic interests. Instead, the authors of the *Manifesto* saw the answer in decentralizing power through a competitive market. An *Ordo* is thus seen as consisting of a competitive order (*Wettbewerbsordnung*) regulated by a constitutional order (*Ordnungspolitik*) intimately linked and regulated by the rule of law (*Rechtsstaat*) (Böhm et al., [1936] 2017; Eucken, [1952] 1990; Sally, 1996; Vanberg, 1998, 2014, 2015).

These ideas of a *Wirtschaftsverfassung* were not fully fleshed out due to the untimely death of Walter Eucken in 1950. It was Victor Vanberg in cooperation with James Buchanan who advanced the concept of

228   *Brigitte Young*

constitutional economics and in the process modernized and transformed many of the original ideas of ordoliberals. The new perspective drew on public choice theory and constitutional economics. Accordingly, the constitutional dimension of the liberal paradigm not only has to encompass an economic constitution (*Ordnungspolitik*), but also to establish and maintain an appropriate political constitution (*Ordnungstheorie*). Politics should be constrained by rules rather than follow discretionary authority to respond to particular governance problems, since the latter rests on expediency at the expense of long-term considerations (Vanberg, 1998, 2015).

In explaining why rules are preferable to discretionary authority, Vanberg cites three reasons. The first reason is the existing *knowledge problem*, which Hayek had problematized as "incurable limits of our knowledge and powers of reason," making rules essential in a world of complex reality (Vanberg, 2015, p. 14). Two additional rules are subsumed under the incentive and reputational categories. Incentive problems refer to psychological concerns, in that humans are tempted to over-weight current needs and short-term effects. In such circumstances, rules force or guide individuals to consider long-term consequences. The advantage of rules is equally demonstrated in cases where personal reputation and predictability in social interactions are of primary concern. Rules in such circumstances would constrain opportunistic behavior which is more apt to occur where discretionary choices prevail (Vanberg, 2015; Young, 2017a, 2017b).

Mostly ignored by critics of a rule-based economic system is Eucken's warning about the need for flexibility and adaptability to provide incentives for innovation. "Rigid rule-following and bureaucratization lead to failure or collapse, whether this involves private firms or companies" (Eucken, [1952] 2017, p. 51). Further in chapters 5 and 6 of the *Grundsätze der Wirtschaftsordnung*, Eucken specifically points out that any economic constitution that is capable of resolving future problems has to take into account different kinds of market forms. He cites the different national conditions in France and Germany and thus concludes that since "each nation starts from a different baseline, presents its own particular constellation of power, possesses its own economic policy potential and faces distinct challenges … No common economic policy code, valid for all nations, is conceivable" (Eucken, [1952] 2017, p. 104). Not only will national conditions prevail in different parts of the world, they will also differ depending on the time period. Economic policymaking thus depends on focusing on the ordering problem of identifying specific principles, consisting of constitutive principles to create or constitute an economic order, and as a second step regulative principles for the maintenance and functioning of the competitive order.

Irrespective of setting out these ordering principles for a competitive order, Eucken warns that "despite its great utility, perfect competition can still be damaging and incoherent. From this it also follows that the need for economic policy intervention will endure once a competitive order has been achieved" ([1952] 2017, p. 106). Given these caveats, it seems rather strange that critics only focus on fixed rules in ordoliberalism, but fail to read the nuanced perspective in terms of national differences, differences in time frames, and above all to mention that these rules will remain incomplete due to unintended consequences.

Are the battles between France and Germany immutable?

Is the battle of ideas between France and Germany so immutable as to preclude a consensus on more solidarity and not just solidity in advancing EU integration? There are three possible reasons why this immutability may be more an artifact of political and media narratives than reality. First, as Eucken reminded us, rules of the game are not written for all times, they have to be acceptable in terms of distributional outcomes. As Vanberg notes there is a priori no reason why these rules should not be chosen or changed, where feasible, with the intention of bringing the expected pattern of outcomes closer to the normative standards that are important to the participants in the game, or setting certain limits to the acceptable range of variation for certain market outcomes, such as income and wealth distribution (Vanberg, 1988; Young, 2015a).

There is a second reason. In answering whether there is a fault line between German economists and policymakers and more practical American (including France and others) economists, the majority of the authors of the various chapters in the e-book *Ordoliberalism: A German Oddity?* (Beck & Kotz, 2018), conclude that German policymaking had more to do with pursuing national interest, seeking national advantage, and national egotism than with ordoliberal ideas shaping the eurozone crisis management. In fact, some ordoliberals took their disagreements with the German government to the German constitutional courts in Karlsruhe to argue against the European Central Bank overstepping its mandate of price stability (Hien & Joerges, 2018). Hence, German ordoliberals are of the opinion that the principle of price stability was in reality never applied. Others suggest that German government leaders applied ordoliberal ideas only as long as it was in line with their interests (Beck & Kotz, 2018, p. 14). Similarly, Hien and Joerges (2018) speak of the 'failure of the ordoliberal project' and in fact argue that Schäuble's call for self-reliance, discipline, austerity, and modesty, are to be found not only in first-generation ordoliberalism, but also in the ethos of pietistic Protestantism. "This is, however, a highly superficial adaptation of ordoliberalism lacking greater theoretical potency, but with considerable acceptance in the German electorate" (Hien & Joerges, 2018, p. 21).

Last but not least, we should 'dare' to provide a vision to the present private power distorting finance capitalism that has captured state ministries and international organizations and ushered in the worst recession in 2007/2008. This is all the more important considering that the Anglo-American laissez-faire economics based on the self-regulating market and

230   Brigitte Young

anti-state rhetoric, which has dominated global economics since the time of Margaret Thatcher and Ronald Reagan, has no answers to the present financialization. Even die-hard free marketeers have come to realize that free markets are not natural and self-regulating, as Polanyi has so persuasively argued against the laissez-faire regime of the 20th century. Thinking about alternatives is crucially important given the call for deeper European integration. As the present discussion of the democratic deficit and the anti- or skeptical European voices demonstrate, the European project is seen by many as unfair as the gap between rich and poor has widened since the 1980s. This has encouraged right-wing parties and nationalist tendencies to question the entire European project. As a possible answer to such centrifugal tendencies, it may behoove us to build on some ordoliberal ideas to generate a vision for an inclusive European social market economy based on democratic procedures and citizens' interests. Undoubtedly, we need rules for the economy to function, but also discretion to intervene when "perfect competition is incoherent and damaging" (Eucken, 1952/2017, p. 106).

Social Europe embedded within a European social market economy

A socially fair European Union requires a comprehensive framework in the form of a European social market economy. This is not a new idea. Article 3 of the Lisbon Treaty has already spelled out the goal of a social market economy, meaning that social concerns should be considered throughout the decision-making process. However, it did not provide details about the institutional structures required for a social market economy. Building such structures at the EU level is all the more difficult, since the social partners are not key players in this process. The Single European Act of 1986 and the Maastricht Treaty of 1992 were concerned with economic and monetary matters and left the social dimension to be dealt with at member state level. The major obstacle in EU social integration is the multilayered institutional mismatch between EU market structures and nationally fragmented institutional arrangements. An added difficulty is the rise of virulent nationalism as witnessed in the form of Brexit and populism in many member states. As a result, national governments continue to insist that social and labor policies are 'their' competences, demanding national priority over common EU solutions (Semmler & Young, 2017).

Given these national preferences, social policy has been a stepchild in European integration, creating a constitutional asymmetry between policies promoting market efficiencies and policies promoting social protection and equality (Scharpf, 2002). The European Court of Justice has often strengthened the freedom of competition over fundamental social rights. Its judgment meant that national social rights, such as the right to strike, collective agreements, or pursuing wage policies were not allowed to interfere 'excessively' with the freedom of competition. In response, Mario Monti warned in 2010

Is there a future for a European social market economy?   231

that the subordination of social rights had the potential to alienate large portions of the workers' movement and trade unions from the European project (Bosch, 2017).

This alienation has become reality among the European populace, including many citizens bearing the brunt of austerity measures in the southern periphery, and among members of the populist right-wing movements on the European continent. Yet a reform program that would make the monetary union sustainable and acceptable to ordinary people must be premised on the idea that the stability and integrity of financial markets, free trade, and free movement of labor depend upon a fairer balance between markets and social cohesion. Money and banking, trade, capital flows, and movement of labor are not just technical issues reserved for experts, they also have important social, cultural, and political dimensions and may have negative externalities across member state territorial boundaries.

Can the ideas of the social market economy offer some guidance on how to institutionalize a fairer compromise between competitive markets and social solidarity? The origin of the social market economy goes back to the German economist Alfred Müller-Armack, who coined the term *Soziale Marktwirtschaft* after WWII to rebuild, with Ludwig Erhard (first as economics minister, and then as chancellor), a warn-torn German economy. Müller-Armack belonged to the initial group of neoliberal economists and lawyers in the 1930s who opposed Anglo-Saxon laissez-faire liberalism. Rejecting the idea of self-regulating markets, postwar German policymakers faced the challenge of setting up a constitutional framework to establish both political and economic democracy within a federal system that did not rely on a strong centralized state. Business had to be free to operate within a market economy that was explicitly competitive. The social market economy also contained a major social element, since there were millions of refugees, war widows, orphans, war veterans, and poor pensioners who could not be left exposed to market forces and had to be integrated into the new market economy. What matters most for our argument is that the social market economy was not the outcome of a strict technocratic, ordoliberal rule-based system but rather political leaders had to make concessions and compromises with existing sociopolitical forces (Berghahn, 2015).

Ludwig Erhard had to take into account the interests of the American occupation forces, demands of the Social Democrats and the impoverished working class, destitute war veterans, West German big business, especially in the Ruhr region as well as the *mittelständische* firms of southern Germany (Berghahn, 2015). This pragmatism in creating a new federal economic system with weak centralization but a strong federal component institutionalized in the second chamber of the German parliament (Bundesrat) may hold out some promise for building a European social market economy despite the fragmented and centrifugal tendencies among EU member states.

Of course, the ideas of Müller-Armack must be updated, as they are overly normative and a top-down paternalistic approach to achieve a

232 Brigitte Young

balance between market freedom and social security. They must also be adopted to a post–Westfalian (non–nation–state–centered) European political environment. This is in line with Müller-Armack's ideas of continued development of the social market economy. In 1962, he already proposed a second phase of the social market economy to adapt to the fast technological changes that were taking place (Müller-Armack, 1976b, p. 156). However, his core concepts still hold today. Thus, the overriding essence of the social market economy for Müller-Armack is a "peace order" (1972/1981). This meant that the social market economy is a historic attempt to include all social groups in the results and successes of the expanding markets. This, according to Müller-Armack, would lead to a domestic easing of tensions, which is a requirement for designing a free and democratic state. A social market economy was thus a contribution to domestic and international peace.

Müller-Armack goes beyond suggesting interventions in the economic order. For him, the social praxis implies shaping the entire scope of social life (*Gesellschaftspolitik*). Politics is thus not the result of a rule-oriented constitutional order, but is outcome-oriented and requires discretionary intervention. Interpreting market failures as integral to free markets, Müller-Armack stipulated that since the constant adaptation of the market economy imposes high social hardships, which individuals are forced to bear in their helpless and anonymous role, it is important to reduce justified and unjustified fears arising from the (otherwise unfettered) mechanism of free markets (Lange-von Kulessa & Renner, 1998; Müller-Armack, 1976b, pp. 156–159; Vanberg, 2002). Thus, there is "a need to build social institutions designed to provide the increasingly isolated present-day human being with the awareness and also the objective safeguard of a comprehensive social concept." Poetically he concludes that "[T]he current of its expansion, its technology and its sociological restratifications is so strong and carries us so fast that the vanishing view of the old shore is no great aid to safe navigation unless we come to terms openly with the conditions of the currents" (Müller-Armack, 1976b, p. 158).

Understandably, given the compliance failure of the Stability and Growth Pact, the Maastricht Treaty, Two- and Six-Packs as well as the Fiscal Compact and the fear of moral hazard, some macroeconomists argue that social and fiscal capacities for countercyclical policies as advocated in the Five Presidents' Report are illusory at the EMU level. Thus, social and fiscal policies are best left to the nation state. However, it is not clear why social policies underpinned by unemployment insurance fail as a regional public good benefiting the citizens of the member states. That social policies are prone to higher implementation problems, are more vulnerable to distributional conflicts and to moral hazard makes these policies no different from agricultural, nuclear, climate and energy policies, a banking union with a European Stability Mechanism as a redemption fund for banking liquidity crises, or fighting terrorism.

Is there a future for a European social market economy? 233

In all these examples, collective tasks are resolved at the European level when they can no longer be resolved at the individual member state level. In other words, there is cooperation at the EU level to ensure that public goods are provided to all the citizenry. That in the process some national sovereignty is transferred to the EU level has been accepted as long as people feel it is in their common interest.

Conclusion

Doomsday scenarios about the survival of the euro, and the EU itself have gained prominence since Brexit. The uncertainty has further increased since President Trump applauded the decision of the British people to leave the EU and expressed his open hostility to it. While we cannot deny the endogenous and exogenous challenges facing the European Union, and especially to the European Monetary Union, these challenges can also function as an opportunity and incentive to think about how we can achieve a European social market economy that does not subordinate issues of fairness and equality to market competition.

The ideas of ordoliberalism may not have to be discarded on the heap of history, but may provide new ideas for a time when human beings feel insecurity which they cannot assess, and are gripped by vague anxiety about life and future, "and that he seeks refuge in groups and associations which carry his own inner unease, magnified out into the public" (Müller-Armack, 1976b, p. 157). Though Müller-Armack wrote this in 1976, it is just as applicable to the present situation to cope with their insecurities and anxieties.

There are many proposals to reshape the institutional structure of the EU and EMU starting with Emmanuel Macron's suggestion for a eurozone finance minister with fiscal policy competence, and a separate euro parliament. In contrast, Jean-Claude Juncker is calling for reshaping the European Stability Mechanism into a European Monetary Fund as a last backstop for the euro-area's system of handling banking crises. In addition, he is calling for an economy and finance minister, combining the existing posts of EU economy commissioner and Eurogroup president. Lastly, he is pushing to create a stabilization function to help out any member state hit be economic shocks (*Financial Times*, 2017b).

While these proposals are an important step forward, the social issues are left rather vague. The intent of the chapter was to fill this deficit by rediscovering some older ideas of the German social market economy to realize that a market economy has to be supplemented by a social policy "which views men not only functionally as a producer and consumer but also in his personal existence" (Müller-Armack, 1976b, p. 152).

234   *Brigitte Young*

Note

1 I use the translated text of the *Ordo Manifesto* of 1936 as well as some of the chapters of Eucken's *Grundsätze der Wirtschaftspolitik* (1950), so that non-German speaking scholars can refer to the texts. Biebricher and Vogelmann (2017) have for the first time made translations of some of the German texts by Walter Eucken, Franz Böhm, and Alexander Rüstow available in English.

Bibliography

Beck, T., & Kotz, H. H. (2018). *Ordoliberalism: A German oddity?* VoxEU.org. London, UK: CEPR Press.

Bénassy-Quéré, A., Ragot, X., & Wolff, G. B. (2016). Which fiscal union for the euro area? Bruegel Policy Contribution, issue 2016/05.

Berghahn, V. (2015). Ordoliberalism, Ludwig Erhard, and West Germany's "Economic Basic Law." Special issue German ordoliberalism, *European Review of International Studies*, 2/2015, 37–47. https://doi.org/10.3224/eris.v2i3.23447

Biebricher, T. (2014). The return of ordoliberalism in Europe – Notes on a research agenda. *i-lex*. Scienze Giurdiche, Scienze Cognitive e Intelligenza artifiale. Rivista quadrimestrale online. May 21, www.i-lex.it

Biebricher, T., & Vogelmann, V. (2017). *The birth of austerity: German ordoliberalism and contemporary neoliberalism*. London, UK and New York, NY: Rowman & Littlefield.

Blyth, M. (2013). *Austerity: The history of a dangerous idea*. Oxford, UK: Oxford University Press.

Böhm, F., Eucken, W., & Großmann-Doerth, H. (1936/2017). *The Ordo Manifesto of 1936* (English translation). In T. Biebricher & F. Vogelmann (Eds.), *The birth of austerity* (pp. 27–39) London, UK and New York, NY: Rowman & Littlefield.

Bonefeld, W. (2012). Freedom and the strong state: On German ordoliberalism. *New Political Economy* 17(3) 633–656.

Bonefeld, W. (2015). Crisis, free economy and strong state: On ordoliberalism. *ERIS* 2(3) 16–26.

Bosch, G. (2017). After Brexit: Prioritising a social Europe. *Social Europe*, 24. January 2017, www.socialeurope.eu/2017/01/brexit-prioritising-social-europe

Brunnermeier, M. K., James, H., & Landau, J. P. (2016). *The euro and the battle of ideas*. Princeton, NJ: Princeton University Press.

Dyson, K. (2017). Ordoliberalism as tradition and as ideology. In *Ordoliberalism, law and the rule of economic* (pp. 87–99). Oxford, UK and Portland, OR: Hart.

Eucken, W. (1952/1990). *Grundsätze der Wirtschaftspolitik*, 6. Auflage, Tübingen, Germany: Mohr Siebeck.

Feld, L., Köhler, E., & Nientiedt, D. (2015). Ordoliberalism, pragmatism and the eurozone crisis: How the German tradition shaped economic policy in Europe. *ERIS* 2(3) 48–61.

Financial Times. (2017a). Future of Europe: Macron vision tackles sensitive topics head-on, 28.09.2017, p. 2.

Financial Times. (2017b). Brussels backs crisis fighting fund. 07.12.2017, p. 3.

Hien, J., & Joerges, C. (2017). *Ordoliberalism, law and the rule of economics*. Oxford, UK and Portland, OR: Hart.

Hien, J., & Joerges, C. (2018). Dead man walking: Current European interest in the ordoliberal tradition, *EUI Working Papers*, Department of Law, 2018/03, European University Institute, Badia Fiesole.

Is there a future for a European social market economy? 235

Koalitionsvertrag. (2013). CDU/CSU, SPD, Deutschlands Zukunft Gestalten (Shaping Germany's Future), November 27, www.tagesschau.de/inland/koalitions vertrag136.pdf

Lange-von Kulessa, J., & Renner, A. (1998). Die Soziale Marktwirtschaft Alfred Müller-Armacks und der Ordoliberalismus der Freiburger Schule – Zur Unvereinbarkeit zweier Staatsauffassungen. *ORDO*, issue 49, Stuttgart, Germany: Lucius & Lucius, 79–104.

Lippmann, W. ([1937] 2017). *The good society*. New York, NY: Routledge.

Müller-Armack, A. (1972/1981). Die Soziale Marktwirtschaft als Friedensordnung. Republished in *Genealogie der Sozialen Marktwirtschaft. Frühschriften und weiterführende Konzepte (Beiträge zur Wirtschaftspolitik)*, *34*(2) Bern, Switzerland and Stuttgart, Germany: Haupt, 239–243.

Müller-Armack, A. (1976a). Die zweite Phase der Sozialen Marktwirtschaft. Ihre Ergänzung durch das Leitbild einer neuen Gesellschaftspolitik, in *Wirtschaftsordnung und Wirtschaftspolitik*, Bern, Switzerland and Stuttgart, Germany: Haupt, 129–145.

Müller-Armack, A. (1976b). Thirty years of social market economy. In Josef Thesing (Ed.), *Economy and development* (pp. 146–162). Mainz, Germany: Hase & Köhler.

Oberndorfer, L. (2015). From new constitutionalism to authoritarian constitutionalism: New economic governance and the state of European democracy. In J. Jäger & E. Springler (Eds.), *Asymmetric crisis in Europe and possible futures*. London, UK and New York, NY: Routledge.

Sally, R. (1996). Ordoliberalism and the social market: Classical political economy from Germany. *New Political Economy* *1*(2) 233–257.

Scharpf, F. (2002). The European social model. *Journal of Common Market Studies* *40*(4) 645–670.

Semmler, W., & Young, B. (2017). Rebooting Europe: What kind of fiscal union – What kind of social union? *Working Paper 13/2017*. Department of Economics, the New School for Social Research.

Spiegel Online. (2018). Scholz will die Schwarze Null. 10.02.2018, www.spiegel.de/ politik/deutschland/grosse-Koalition-Olof-Scholz-will-die-schwarze-Null-a-1192666.html

Vanberg, V. (1988). "Ordnungstheorie" as constitutional economics – The German conception of a "social market economy." *ORDO* (39) 17–31.

Vanberg, V. (1998). The Freiburg School of Law and Economics: Predecessor of constitutional economics. In Peter Newman (Ed.), *The new Palgrave dictionary of economics and the law* (vol. 2, pp. 171–179). London, UK: Macmillan.

Vanberg, V. (2002). Soziale Sicherheit, Müller-Armacks "Soziale Irenik" und die ordoliberale Perspektive. In R. H. Hasse & F. Quaas (Eds.), *Wirtschaftsordnung und Gesellschaftskonzept* (227–260). Bern, Switzerland and Stuttgart, Germany: Haupt.

Vanberg, V. (2014). *Ordnungspolitik*, the Freiburg School and the reason of rules, *i-lex* 9, 205–220.

Vanberg, V. (2015). Ordoliberalism, *Ordnungspolitik*, and the reason of rules. *ERIS* *2*(3) 27–36.

Young, B. (2014). German ordoliberalism as agenda setter for the euro crisis: Myth trumps reality. *Journal of Contemporary European Studies* *22*(3) 276–287.

Young, B. (2015a). Introduction: The hijacking of ordoliberalism, Special issue on German ordoliberalism, *European Review of International Studies* *2*(3) 7–61.

Young, B. (2015b). The battle of ideas in the eurozone crisis management: German ordoliberalism versus post-Keynesianism. In S. Fadda and P. Tridico (Eds.), *The*

236 *Brigitte Young*

economic crisis in social and institutional context (pp. 78–90). London, UK and New York, NY: Routledge.

Young, B. (2017a). What is neo-liberal in Germany's and Europe's crisis politics? In J. Hien & C. Joerges (Eds.), *Ordoliberalism, law and the rule of economics* (pp. 129–141). Oxford, UK and Portland, OR: Hart.

Young, B. (2017b). Is Germany's and Europe's crisis politics ordoliberal and/or neoliberal? In T. Biebricher & F. Vogelmann (Eds.), *The birth of austerity: German ordoliberalism and contemporary neoliberalism* (pp. 221–237). London, UK and New York, NY: Rowman & Littlefield.

Young, B. (2017c). Ordoliberalism as an "irritating German idea." In T. Beck & H. H. Kotz (Eds.), *Ordoliberalism: A German oddity?* (pp. 31–40). VoxEU.org. London, UK: CEPR Press.

16 The future of German ordoliberalism

Lars P. Feld and Ekkehard A. Köhler

Introduction

As Paul Romer (2015) recently reminded us, the ability of economists to form a consensus is undermined by those who disguise normative convictions as science. His paper on 'mathiness' is concerned with the conflation of politics and science into 'academic politics,' i.e., the abuse of scientific methods to further a political agenda. Similarly, in a wide-ranging discussion of economic methodology, Dani Rodrik (2015) cautions that economists' statements often contain hidden value judgments. The problem of ideological bias is particularly relevant when economists are called upon to evaluate public policies (Rodrik, 2015, pp. 186–196).

The difficulty of using positive economic analysis for practical purposes while maintaining its scientific rigor will, in the following, be illustrated by the example of German ordoliberalism. Adherents to this school of thought have sometimes been criticized for lacking a clear commitment to the fact that the goals of economic policy are decided upon by the political process rather than the enlightened members of the economic profession. Our chapter recounts this debate from the late 1980s to the present day and adds comments on the future viability of the ordoliberal research program.

Ordoliberalism originates from the so-called Freiburg School of the 1930s, a group of scholars at the University of Freiburg led by economist Walter Eucken and lawyer Franz Böhm. Their aim was to investigate the interdependency of legal–institutional structures and economics. The Freiburg School's field of study encompasses both a theoretical research agenda (*Ordnungstheorie*) and a rule-based approach to economic policy (*Ordnungspolitik*).[1] Ordoliberal ideas have shaped Germany's postwar economic order – the social market economy – and remain an important, if sometimes controversial, influence on German economic policy in the 21st century (Feld, Köhler, & Nientiedt, 2015).

The discussion on the normative element in German ordoliberalism may contain some important lessons for the English-speaking world as well. All too often, the question of the origin of normative assessments is cast aside in order to provide practical advice. Such an approach ignores the vast

238 *Lars P. Feld and Ekkehard A. Köhler*

differences in opinion among economists on pressing issues of economic policy as well as the assumptions implicit in our methods. As the following sections will attest, economists are well advised to critically examine the influence of their politics on their scientific endeavors.

The critique of ordoliberalism in the 1980s and the relationship with constitutional economics

A methodological debate in German ordoliberalism had long been overdue. During the Cold War era, it was generally accepted among economists to make policy recommendations based on external value judgments. Private property, freedom of contract, and the need for an institutional framework provided by the state were often taken for granted. In Germany, Eucken's "constitutive principles" of a free market economy (Eucken, 1952/2004, pp. 254–291) lent themselves to becoming the standard norm, not least because every economist knew them from his or her undergraduate studies. This way, critical reflections on the importance of a value-free economic science were delayed.

Gebhard Kirchgässner's critique of ordoliberalism

Gebhard Kirchgässner (1988) criticizes ordoliberalism from the perspective of public choice theory.[2] He maintains that, while many contributions of ordo-liberal economists are seemingly objective, they contain hidden value judgments. The argument is this: Ordoliberals often evaluate measures of economic policy by asking whether they conform to Eucken's principles. At the same time, the question of whether these principles correspond to the political will of the members of society is neglected (Kirchgässner, 1988, pp. 55–58, 62–65). This seems to indicate that ordoliberals base their policy recommendations on some type of superior knowledge (Kirchgässner, 1988, p. 53). Kirchgässner argues that ultimately, this approach bears resemblance to the concept of a "benevolent dictator" employed by welfare economics (1988, pp. 58–62). Indeed, Eucken assumed that the outcome of the political process has to be taken as given by the economist (1940/1950, pp. 213–216). Similarly, Böhm (1973, p. 20) was critical of an economic analysis of political decision-making. From this point of view, traditional ordoliberalism clearly falls short of public choice theory.

During the ordoliberal renaissance of the 1980s and 1990s, supporters of ordoliberalism attempted to canonize Eucken's policy recommendations in order to gain support for their anti-interventionist position. Kirchgässner remarks: "That discussions about the theory of ordoliberalism at times take such a dogmatic turn possibly speaks in favor of its founder, *Eucken*, but not necessarily his descendants. Rather, it could be an indication that this theory has not been developed further since his death" (1988, p. 65).[3] According to Kirchgässner, the "dogmatic" adherence to Eucken's principles leads

The future of German ordoliberalism 239

ordoliberal scholars to agree with the call for strong, independent politicians who have the "courage" to pursue long term political objectives and implement Eucken's economic program (1988, p. 59). While Eucken and Böhm – who were part of the German resistance movement against Hitler – certainly did not subscribe to a totalitarian conception of the state (Dathe, 2010), Kirchgässner's critique reveals a serious methodological problem that did not receive enough attention by traditional ordoliberalism.

Viktor Vanberg's development of the Freiburg approach

In a number of articles, Viktor Vanberg (1988, 1997) links the research program of the Freiburg School to constitutional economics, the approach initiated by James Buchanan. At the heart of constitutional economics lies the idea that the outcome of human interactions – e.g. in the marketplace – depends on the institutional framework in which these interactions take place, and that this framework itself is the subject of deliberate choice. Constitutional economics, then, investigates the working properties of rules and institutions within which individuals interact, rather than interactions within rules (Buchanan, 1990).

Constitutional economics is based on two core assumptions. First, it is committed to *methodological individualism* in that it assumes that social phenomena can only be explained in terms of the actions of individual human beings. This denies any 'organic' understanding of collectives such as the state. Second, as an applied science, constitutional economics maintains that the legitimacy of social arrangements can only be derived from the voluntary consent of the individuals involved – a concept referred to as *normative individualism* (Vanberg, 2005, p. 24).

Because individuals are seen as the only carrier of values, to 'improve' the legal–institutional framework means to improve its responsiveness to the wishes of the individual members of society. In the case of markets, the term *consumer sovereignty* is used to denote the ideal that the interests of consumers (rather than producers) should be the driving force of the economic process. Vanberg argues that such a procedural (i.e. process-oriented) criterion can be identified for the political process as well:

> *Citizen sovereignty* means that the individuals who constitute the citizenry of a democratic polity are the ultimate sovereigns in whose common interests the polity should be operated ... In other words, citizen sovereignty requires that the "producers of politics," politicians and government bureaucrats, are made most responsive to citizens' common interests.
>
> (Vanberg, 2005, p. 42)

Similar to constitutional economics, the members of the Freiburg School maintained that the best way of improving the outcome of markets is to

240   Lars P. Feld and Ekkehard A. Köhler

improve their legal–institutional framework. In assessing the desirability of economic constitutions, they employed a procedural criterion almost identical to consumer sovereignty, referred to as 'performance competition' (*Leistungs-wettbewerb*). Vanberg argues, that, since the concept of citizen sovereignty must be understood as the logical equivalent of consumer sovereignty in the field of politics, representatives of the Freiburg School such as Eucken and Böhm could – in principle – have agreed to citizen sovereignty as the normative criterion against which different political arrangements are evaluated (1997, p. 724). The similarity between the Freiburg School and Buchanan's constitutional economics suggests a convergence of these research programs: "There are certainly sufficient affinities to allow for a fruitful dialogue between the tradition of *Ordnungstheorie* and the yet emerging paradigm of *Constitutional Economics*" (Vanberg, 1988, p. 28).

The new German *Methodenstreit*

The "new German *Methodenstreit*" (Caspari & Schefold, 2011, p. 11) began when the University of Cologne replaced several chairs for economic policy with a macroeconomics research group. The decision was followed by an appeal published in May 2009 under the title "Save Economic Policy in the Universities." It was signed by 83 professors of economics. Shortly thereafter, no fewer than 188 of their colleagues answered with a text titled "Rebuild German Economics According to International Standards." The ensuing discussion revolved around the role of mathematics in economics and the question of whether the restructuring of departments would lead to a neglect of the institutional aspects of economics.[4] It also touched on the future viability of ordoliberalism because many – but certainly not all – advocates of economic policy as an independent branch of study were associated with the ordoliberal tradition. In the following, we will summarize some of the contributions to this discussion.

Goldschmidt et al. (2009) emphasize the embeddedness of economic questions in a larger societal context. According to them, economists have been occupied with two kinds of problems since the work of Adam Smith: First, with the regularity of economic processes and second, with the interaction of these processes with their social environment. With reference to Eucken's concept of the "interdependence of orders" (such as the economic, political, or legal order – see Eucken, 1952/2004, pp. 180–184), Goldschmidt et al. argue that a "contextual analysis of economic activity" is needed in order for economics to continue to be relevant. They acknowledge that this type of analysis is not exclusive to German ordoliberalism, but has been undertaken by many different scholars, among them Douglass North and Amartya Sen.

Schmidt and aus dem Moore (2009) defend the formalization of economics as well as the emphasis on microeconomics, macroeconomics, and econometrics as core areas of study. In their opinion, the question of an appropriate legal–institutional framework cannot be satisfactorily answered if one ignores

The future of German ordoliberalism   241

the advances made in economics during the last decades, many of which were related to the use of mathematics in the field. The two authors maintain that mathematical methods lead to consistent argumentation as well as 'scientific modesty,' particularly in quantitative research. Econometrics is important because empirical evidence is needed to support or contradict theoretical hypotheses: If society does not want to make decisions based on religious dogmas or ideology, economic problems will have to be approached by using evidence-based policy.

In the opinion of Sinn (2009), modern economics needs more researchers willing to obtain knowledge about political institutions. He explains this by saying that in the western world, many governments control more than half of national income, thus interfering severely with the freedom of choice of individual citizens. In addition, economists should be able to take into account the many laws and regulations that affect economic decision-making. According to Sinn, what is required to provide policymakers with well-founded arguments are economic theory and econometrics as well as institutional economics in the style of German public finance (*Finanzwissenschaft*) and economic policy (*Wirtschaftspolitik*).

Kirchgässner (2009) views the appeal of the 83 professors as the demand for a German *Sonderweg* – which he rejects categorically. He argues that institutions have played a large role in international discussions and points to the field of new institutional economics in particular. Kirchgässner adds that the influence of institutions on economic variables such as growth must be analyzed at least partly by relying on statistical–mathematical methods. That such investigations will abstract from important features of reality is true for any kind of mathematical modeling and does not by itself diminish their results.

The discussion on the future development of ordoliberalism

After the battle over methods of 2009, the discussion on the future of ordoliberalism continued. Two types of proposals can be distinguished: First, the accentuation of the normative aspects of ordoliberalism with certain ethical principles in mind; and, second, the pursuit of a strictly positive research agenda.

Goldschmidt (2011) aims to modernize ordoliberalism by stressing the normative convictions that, according to him, the work of the Freiburg School is based on. He argues that these convictions support a social policy agenda in the style of Alexander Rüstow's 'organic policy' (*Vitalpolitik*; see Rüstow, 1961). Based on external value judgments – Sen's capability approach – such an agenda could be directed at "the conscious political ... promotion of living conditions that provide opportunity for the individual" (Goldschmidt, 2011, p. 151). From the perspective of constitutional economics, there may be good reasons to recommend such an aim for social policy. What is missing from the analysis, however, is a discussion of

242 *Lars P. Feld and Ekkehard A. Köhler*

arguments of prudence that could be invoked in favor (or against) such a position. At this point, Goldschmidt (2011) resorts to a statement that is reminiscent of Kirchgässner's charge of ideology: "Hence, the [above] concept is clearly ordoliberal in the sense of the Freiburg tradition." However, arguments in favor of a particular social order should be convincing without recourse to a tradition.

Goldschmidt and Lenger (2011) try to solve this problem by stating that the legitimation principle of voluntary consent – as employed by constitutional economics – requires people to agree with both the general rules of a market economy and the outcome of the economic process. Thus, the "non-discriminatory" nature of an ordoliberal economic constitution should manifest itself in fair rules as well as the "fair" distribution of economic benefits (Goldschmidt & Lenger, 2011, p. 301). While the choice of rules always reflects considerations about possible outcomes associated with them, elevating distributive justice to a procedural criterion is a difficult task. This is due to the fact that the implementation of distributive principles will, at least to some extent, interfere with both consumer and citizen sovereignty. From our point of view, distributive ideas should be subjected to a test of approval instead of replacing it.

A possible alternative is the positive approach to constitutional economics advanced by Voigt (1997, 2011). He distinguishes between two types of research concerned with the economic importance of constitutions: First, a *normative* type that asks how constitutional rules can be legitimized. Buchanan's work provides an example for this type. Second, a *positive* type that analyses the economic effects of different rule regimes and the emergence or modification of constitutional rules. Positive constitutional economics, then, is concerned with the economic results produced by different political systems – e.g. direct vs representative democracy, majoritarian vs proportional elections, presidential vs parliamentary systems – as well as the determinants for the emergence of particular rule regimes. Voigt notes that further research is needed with regard to the second aspect, i.e., the task of "endogenizing constitutions" (Voigt, 2011, p. 206).

Voigt (1997, 2011) remains relatively vague as to the implications of his analysis for ordoliberalism. Still, his surveys suggest that he views positive constitutional economics as having unequivocal advantages over the normative variant. In defense of the latter, it should be emphasized that the term 'normative' as used by Voigt denotes a certain field of study and not an attempt to derive *actual* normative statements ('what ought to be'). Normative constitutional economics in the sense of Buchanan is not less scientific than its positive counterpart: After all, the principle of normative individualism places value decisions firmly in the hand of sovereign citizens.

Conclusion: the future viability of German ordoliberalism

The future viability of ordoliberalism derives from its proximity to constitutional economics. Admittedly, traditional ordoliberalism incorporates many different strands (Eucken, Müller–Armack, Röpke, Rüstow, etc.). It must be admitted, too, that Eucken and Böhm opposed the extension of economic analysis to the political process to varying degrees. Still, because of the closeness of their arguments to constitutional economics (see above, section on Vanberg), the members of the ordoliberal Freiburg School would, in all likelihood, not have objected to the use of voluntary agreement as the ultimate legitimizing principle for political action.

A modern ordoliberal research agenda can analyze theoretically and empirically, while taking into account the institutional environment, how an economic and political order may be constructed that is responsive to the citizens' common interests. As a starting point, such an approach should embrace John Rawls's notion of society as "a cooperative venture for mutual advantage" (Rawls, 1999, p. 4). From this perspective, democratic societies must be understood primarily as collective arrangements that are supposed to advance the common interests of their members, or, in a word, "citizen cooperative[s]" (Vanberg, 2015, p. 3). Note that this definition does not presuppose institutional characteristics of the political system, such as voting rules. Rather, it is based on the conviction that, as a matter of principle, political legitimacy can only be derived from the consent of the individuals involved.

Following the Rawlsian definition, the question of which framework of rules is most beneficial to the members of the citizen cooperative is open to discussion. Citizen sovereignty, then, can serve as a procedural criterion against which different rules are evaluated. What is more, it must be understood as an appeal to search for new institutions that strengthen the position of sovereign citizens. Such institutional arrangements have to be identified as part of a positive research program. Only in a second step can they be proposed to the citizens as a way to realize mutual gains from joint commitment. Within the positive research program, theoretical insights need to be rigorously evaluated against empirical evidence; for this process of examination, mathematical and econometric methods are needed. Despite the complexity of economic phenomena, this approach, if pursued in all modesty, has a good chance of advancing the ordoliberal contribution to economics.

Notes

1 For an introduction to the research program of the Freiburg School and the different strands of ordoliberal thinking, see Sally (1996).
2 To be more precise, Kirchgässner's critique is directed against Eucken (1940/1950, 1952/2004) as well as the different authors who publish in the journal *ORDO* (Kirchgässner 1988: 54). The journal was originally founded by Eucken and Böhm in 1948.

244 Lars P. Feld and Ekkehard A. Köhler

3 All translations by the authors, unless indicated otherwise.
4 Both appeals are published in the volume by Caspari and Schefold (2011). Lars P. Feld has signed neither document.

References

Böhm, F. (1973). Eine Kampfansage an Ordnungstheorie und Ordnungspolitik. Zu einem Aufsatz in Kyklos. *ORDO 24* 11–48.

Buchanan, J. (1990). The domain of constitutional economics. *Constitutional Political Economy 1*(1) 1–18.

Caspari, V., & Schefold, B. (Eds.). (2011). *Wohin steuert die ökonomische Wissenschaft? – Ein Methodenstreit in der Volkswirtschaftslehre.* Frankfurt, Germany: Campus.

Dathe, U. (2010). Walter Euckens Weg zum Liberalismus (1918–1934). *Freiburg Discussion Papers on Constitutional Economics 09/10.*

Eucken, W. (1940/1950). *The foundations of economics: History and theory in the analysis of economic reality.* London, UK: W. Hodge.

Eucken, W. ([1952] 2004). *Grundsätze der Wirtschaftspolitik.* Tübingen, Germany: Mohr Siebeck.

Feld, L., Köhler. E., & Nientiedt, D. (2015). Ordoliberalism, pragmatism and the eurozone crisis: How the German tradition shaped economic policy in Europe. *European Review of International Studies 2*(3) 48–61.

Goldschmidt, N. (2011). Vom Glück und von Gärten – Moderne Ordnungs-ökonomik und die normativen Grundlagen der Gesellschaft. In V. Caspari & B. Schefold (Eds.), *Wohin steuert die ökonomische Wissenschaft? – Ein Methodenstreit in der Volkswirtschaftslehre* (pp. 145–166). Frankfurt, Germany: Campus.

Goldschmidt, N., & Lenger, A. (2011). Teilhabe und Befähigung als Schlüsselelemente einer modernen Ordnungsethik. *Zeitschrift für Wirtschafts- und Unternehmensethik 12*(2) 295–313.

Goldschmidt, N., Wegner, G., Wohlgemuth, M., & Zweynert, J. (2009). Was ist und was kann Ordnungsökonomik? *Frankfurter Allgemeine Zeitung,* June 19.

Kirchgässner, G. (1988). Wirtschaftspolitik und Politiksystem: Zur Kritik der traditionellen Ordnungstheorie aus der Sicht der Neuen Politischen Ökonomie. In D. Cassel, B.-T. Ramb, & H.J. Thieme (Eds.), *Ordnungspolitik* (pp. 53–75). Munich, Germany: Vahlen.

Kirchgässner, G. (2009). Der Rückzug ins nationale Schneckenhaus. *Frankfurter Allgemeine Sonntagszeitung,* June 15.

Rawls, J. (1999). *A theory of justice* (rev. ed.). Cambridge, MA: Harvard University Press.

Rodrik, D. (2015). *Economics rules: The rights and wrongs of the dismal science.* New York, NY: Norton.

Romer, P. (2015). Mathiness in the theory of economic growth. *American Economic Review 105*(5) 89–93.

Rüstow, A. (1961). Organic policy (Vitalpolitik) versus mass regimentation. In A. Hunold (Ed.), *Freedom and serfdom: An anthology of western thought* (pp. 171–190). Dordrecht, Germany: Reidel.

Sally, R. (1996). Ordoliberalism and the social market: Classical political economy from Germany. *New Political Economy 1*(2) 233–257.

Schmidt, C., & aus dem Moore, N. (2009). Quo vadis, Ökonomik? *Frankfurter Allgemeine Zeitung,* May 22.

Sinn, H.-W. (2009). Der richtige Dreiklang der VWL. *Frankfurter Allgemeine Zeitung*, June 22.

Vanberg, V. (1988). "Ordnungstheorie" as constitutional economics – The German conception of a "social market economy." *ORDO 39* 17–31.

Vanberg, V. (1997). Die normativen Grundlagen von Ordnungspolitik, *ORDO 48* 707–726

Vanberg, V. (2005). Market and state: The perspective of constitutional political economy. *Journal of Institutional Economics 1*(1) 23–49

Vanberg, V. (2015). Competitive federalism, government's dual role, and the power to tax. *Freiburg Discussion Papers on Constitutional Economics 15/05.*

Voigt, S. (1997). Positive constitutional economics – A survey. *Public Choice 90*(1–4) 11–53.

Voigt, S. (2011). Positive constitutional economics II – A survey of recent developments. *Public Choice 146*(1–2) 205–256.

17 Ordoliberalism and beyond

Economic liberalism for the 21st century

Malte Dold and Tim Krieger

Introduction

Taken together, the chapters of this book exemplify a diversity of viewpoints within contemporary scholarship on ordoliberalism. In light of the ongoing institutional crisis in Europe, they provide explanations and historical contextualization and raise important challenges for the modernization of the ordoliberal research agenda. The final chapter cannot do justice to the richness of the various perspectives developed in each chapter. Hence, it does not attempt to summarize them. Rather, this chapter ties together some key thoughts of the book and provides an outlook on ordoliberalism's prospects as a 'living tradition.'

This chapter's thesis is the following: If ordoliberals want to be relevant in the 21st century, they need to escape pure exegesis of their past heroes, rediscover the reforming spirit of their liberal ideals, and apply them anew to the existing socioeconomic challenges in Europe. The attractiveness of ordoliberalism has always been a scholarly reaction to existing societal conflicts and its attempt to overcome them by systematically studying incentives, rules and institutions in concrete historical circumstances.[1] We think that successful ordoliberal scholarship is driven by the positive insight that well-functioning markets are embedded in a complex system of social, political, and legal orders and that power concentrations in business and politics are the main impediments for societies to thrive and prosper. In doing so, ordoliberalism should embrace a positive–empirical understanding of science on the level of comparative institutional analysis. In order to find the desirable alternative among many possible institutional arrangements, ordoliberalism should explicate its normative commitment to liberal values (such as individual opportunities for economic and political participation) and clarify its moral defense of free, open, and competitive markets.

This chapter comprises three sections. First, it carves out four core ideas of a contemporary ordoliberalism without getting into the weeds of concrete policies or philosophical subtleties. Second, it identifies some pressing socioeconomic issues in Europe that are endogenous to our current liberal economic order and which demand ordoliberal responses. And, finally, it argues

Ordoliberalism and beyond   247

that future successful ordoliberal research will not be in technical economics, but rather in the growing field of philosophy, politics, and economics (PPE), which respects ordoliberalism's traditional roots in legal–institutional analysis. The nature of this chapter is deliberately explorative and provocative. It sketches the contours of – what we would call – a *contemporary ordoliberalism*.

Four core ideas

As many scholars have rightly noted (see, e.g., Kolev's opening chapter to this volume), ordoliberalism started as part of a larger liberal movement in the interwar and postwar periods. Ordoliberal thinkers developed their ideas as a reaction to political and economic ills of their times (e.g. crony capitalism in the Weimar State, authoritarianism in Nazi Germany, collectivism in the Soviet Union). In post-World War II Germany, their ideas helped create the model of 'social market economy' that fostered Germany's economic success story of the 1950s and 1960s. During all this time, ordoliberalism was not a monolithic tradition. As early as in the 1940s, Röpke and Rüstow developed their sociological form of ordoliberalism (primarily concerned with social stability and cohesion) that was quite distinct from Böhm's and Eucken's more legal–economic agenda (primarily concerned with welfare-improving properties of competitive markets).

However, there are certain unifying features of ordoliberal thinking that this section will try to distill. Like classical liberals, ordoliberals envision a society in which market exchange and political cooperation allows individuals to flourish. However, ordoliberals emphasize the need to protect individuals not only from state power but also from power concentration in the business world, where non-ordered market processes may produce systematic disadvantages for certain social groups. Therefore, one of the main differences between classical liberals in the Anglo-American world and ordoliberals in Europe is the latter's belief in the necessity of a strong state to order market processes.[2] In this sense, ordoliberalism has a rational constructive core that is more optimistic than classical liberalism's mistrust of political action. As we will argue in the following, in a contemporary conception of ordoliberalism, the state is a central player that (a) cocreates a framework of rules which provide the order for free, open, and competitive markets, (b) is strong enough to resist the influences of special interest groups, (c) provides protection against socioeconomic hazards in the form of an activating welfare system, and (d) is constrained by the two regulatory ideals of consumer and citizen sovereignty.

Rules of the game

The most fundamental idea of ordoliberalism is the conviction that markets must be embedded in non-market institutions (such as the judiciary, educational and religious institutions, the media, 'civil society').[3] Put differently,

248   *Malte Dold and Tim Krieger*

the properties of markets depend on well-designed and well-enforced legal and social rules. Ideally, these rules are *general* (they do not grant individual privileges) and *stable* (they are predictable and reliable) in order to facilitate private arrangements of market participants. Without these rules, fraud, theft, and breaches of contract would prevail and the physically strongest market actor would define the outcome of the market game. In contrast, ordoliberal rules aim at securing inclusive, i.e., free, open, and competitive markets.[4] Absent externalities, 'freedom' means that market actors should be able to freely enter contracts and exchange goods on their own terms. 'Openness' means that all people, regardless of their economic or political power, are given a chance to participate at equal terms in market exchanges. And 'competition' means that (a) market success is to be decided based on the superior performance of the market actors and (b) it is the market (i.e. the interplay between demand and supply) and not any single market actor that defines prices for goods and services. In addition to the rules of the market, ordoliberals favor predefined rules of the political game that prevent discretionary and arbitrary policy interventions with the aim of directing economic processes. In other words, a sustainable liberal order requires a disciplinary framework of binding precommitments (e.g. for fiscal and monetary policies). 'Thinking in rules' can also be regarded as a response to the standard critique against economics that human beings are not fully rational. Ordoliberalism does not need this assumption since the 'rationality' of markets is embodied in the right rules, not in discrete actions of individuals.

Dispersion of power

A second and related idea is ordoliberalism's conviction that power concentration – stemming from the state, from the market, and from other social orders – can become problematic for the broadly shared realization of social welfare (Eucken, 1952, pp. 175–179). In doing so, ordoliberalism differs from conservatism since it believes that hierarchy and aristocracy tend to become sources of oppression. When groups become so powerful that they are able to shape the rules of the game in their favor, market processes lose most of their welfare-generating potential. The reason is that market participants might find it more profitable to invest in rent-seeking and lobbying (e.g. for protection from competition, lower taxes, or higher subsidies) rather than selling consumers better and cheaper products. In addition, the system might be perceived as unfair if people get the impression that the market only benefits the already powerful and mighty. Then, the economy might not only be less economically dynamic, but also lose its socially integrative function. Ordoliberalism understands that economic privilege and political privilege are two sides of the same coin. Concentration of power reduces the efficiency of markets and at the same time fosters rent-seeking in politics.[5] Ordoliberalism aims to disperse power through the implementation of general rules and competition in the economic and the political realm. In markets, it is typically anti-trust

Ordoliberalism and beyond 249

legislation that ensures that competition works as "the most magnificent and most ingenious instrument of deprivation of power in history" (Böhm, 1960, p. 22). The best way to disperse political power is seen in effective participation of the public in political decision-making processes (Vanberg, 1997a, p. 724). In order to foster political participation, ordoliberalism embraces the ideas of decentralization and federalism on the national level and the principle of subsidiarity on the level of international governance, i.e., political authority should be allocated to the lowest competent institutional unit (Vanberg, 1997b, p. 190).

Protection against socioeconomic hazards

Ordoliberals are explicit about the necessity of a legal–political order to address questions of social justice. Grounded in Eucken's (1952, p. 1) conviction that "social security and social justice are the greatest concern of our time," most contemporary ordoliberals agree with Böhm (1937, p. 185) that a liberal economic agenda will lose its support if it does not take the 'social needs' of its constituents seriously. Although he never specified the technical details, Eucken (1952, pp. 300–304) also conceded that a moderately progressive taxation, redistribution of income, and minimum wages are justified in order to reduce particular cases of socioeconomic hardships. From an ordoliberal perspective (Eucken 1950, pp. 239–241), it is not enough that an economic system be *efficient* (i.e. it helps to overcome scarcity problems), but it is essential that it also be *humane* (i.e. it enables a self-determined life for individuals). This means that a well-functioning economy is the primary means for social integration, but the state has a (partial) responsibility to implement social policies and an activating safety net that ensures equal opportunity for economic and political participation (see Dörr, Goldschmidt, and Lenger in this volume).

Consumer and citizen sovereignty

The normative core of ordoliberalism is the idea that the legitimacy of collective action derives from the consent of the individuals involved (see Feld and Köhler in this volume). This starting point leads to the ideals of *consumer sovereignty* in market settings and *citizen sovereignty* in political processes: markets are regarded as well functioning when the supply of goods reacts swiftly to changing consumer demands; the political realm is considered to be well functioning when politicians and government bureaucrats are responsive to citizens' common interests (Vanberg, 2005, pp. 41–44). Consequently, a contemporary ordoliberalism cannot simply rely on Eucken's constitutive principles for an economic order. Such an approach would not take citizens seriously in their normative status as the ultimate sovereign, but derive economic policy measures from a technocratic top-down approach. It is essential to ordoliberal reasoning that societies' mores and values predate the reasoning

250 *Malte Dold and Tim Krieger*

of the political economist. Therefore, contemporary ordoliberals have to abstain from imposing a liberal economic agenda upon unwilling citizens, and must instead enter a public debate where, by means of moral and economic arguments, they can convince citizens of the superiority of economic liberalism. This will help prevent backlashes in the form of populism or disenchantment with politics since citizens are given an active role in the political and economic debates of our times.

In all four ideas, positive–economic arguments coincide with normative–philosophical reasoning, and theoretical idealization concurs with applied policy recommendations. This combination of the pragmatic ('realpolitik') and the visionary ('economic utopia') is deliberate: ordoliberal thinking embraces the analysis of social systems as 'interdependent orders.' Even though the economic subsystem might have a different logic from the legal–political one, ordoliberals think about their diverse interrelations, in theory and in practice. In doing so, ordoliberal scholarship transcends the logic of efficiency and balances economic values with democratic concerns for an egalitarian relationship among citizens (market and political exchanges are seen as 'cooperation among equals'). Dyson (see chapter in this volume) rightly observes that the novelty of ordoliberalism does not lie in its contribution to economic theory, but its particular way of thinking about the organization of economics and its relation to the social and political order. In a nutshell, ordoliberalism provides a framework with a deep understanding of the essential role of formal and informal institutions in a productive and humane market economy.

A crisis of the European liberal order

In recent years, commentators have noticed that the European liberal order is 'under attack' (*Der Spiegel*, 2018; *The Economist*, 2018). Traditional parties of the center are in decline. In the first German election after the fall of the Berlin Wall, the traditional parties of the political center won over 80% of the vote. In 2018, this number fell to 45%, compared with a total of 41.5% for the far right, the far left, and the Greens.[6] Populist movements of the right and the left have won elections, or significant shares in parliaments, in many European countries (Poland, Hungary, Italy, Greece, to name but a few). While 'populism' is a loose label, most of these movements share an anti-establishment orientation, an opposition to supranational institutions and open economies, and an appetite for authoritarian governance (Rodrik, 2018). In doing so, these movements have been successful by defining themselves in opposition to a liberal political and economic agenda. After the collapse of the Soviet Union, most public intellectuals in Europe believed that the combination of a competitive market economy, a liberal and open democracy, and the rule of law was more attractive than any other form of social order (Fuest, 2018). This belief has been seriously shaken by the success of the rising populist powers in recent years. The taken-for-granted connection between economic openness and liberal democracy is being severely tested.

A fundamental asymmetry

There is an ongoing debate in economics and other social sciences over the causes of the current rise of populist movements (see, e.g., Gidron & Hall, 2017; Guiso, Herrera, Morelli, & Sonno, 2017; Inglehart & Norris, 2017; Mudde & Kaltwasser, 2017). While there are a number of potential explanations (e.g. globalization, immigration, digitization), most scholars agree that *individual economic anxiety* and *distributional struggles among social groups* play a pivotal role (Rodrik, 2018). Interestingly, both of these drivers are endogenous to our current liberal economic order in Europe, which is built on a fundamental asymmetry: the benefits of open borders and economic integration are distributed unevenly, favoring a well-educated and mobile urban elite while neglecting less-educated workers, often in rural areas. Not surprisingly, a new political divide has emerged along these lines, with metropolitan voters backing the liberal economic agenda and rural citizens increasingly backing populist campaigns (Collier, 2018, p. 125). In the following, we will discuss some of the possible causes of this new divergence.

First, property in the form of urban land has become a driving factor of inequality in OECD countries. In recent years, most of the productivity growth and wealth creation has taken place in big cities. The OECD (2017) estimates that the productivity gap between big cities and rural areas has widened by 60% in the last 20 years. Thirty years ago, in big European cities (like Paris or London) the median household spent around 28% of its income on rent. Today this number is 40% (*The Economist*, 2018). While this trend is a 'windfall gain' for the small group of urban property owners, it reduces the chances of economic participation for a large number of city dwellers in rented apartments. Of course, the latter group also benefits from the economic boom through wage growth. However, in many cases, their higher wages cannot compensate for the disproportionally high rents and they end up with a net income loss. Similarly, people in rural areas who cannot afford city rent stand no chance to benefit from high productivity cities with better economic perspectives. The urban elite lives increasingly in 'social echo chambers': they go to the same universities, marry each other, live in the same neighborhoods and share the same social networks. The influence of these 'social echo chambers' is enhanced through different parenting styles that transmit economic advantages in subtle ways by shaping future preferences of children, e.g., through family culture and shared beliefs (Doepke & Zilibotti, 2019). There is an increasing 'parenting gap' between richer (well-educated) and poorer (lower-educated) households that contributes to diminished social mobility due to lower human and social capital investments in children from disadvantaged socioeconomic backgrounds (Corak, 2013; Jerrim & Macmillan, 2015).

Second, many important economic regulations in the last few decades (e.g. in the financial sector, in trade agreements, or in industrial policymaking) have been driven by a business-led agenda (*The Economist*, 2018). The underlying logic is trickle-down economics: by satisfying the interests of big corporations, the benefits will eventually percolate to the rest of society.[7] However, the result is that big companies exert significant market power, overcharge their customers, and are not particularly innovative (e.g. Weiss & Wittkopp, 2005). This increase in market power is often accompanied by a change in strategy. Big corporations, who initially gain high market shares by product innovation and superior efficiency, often use their market power to buy startups or lobby for various barriers to entry to protect their positions (Munger & Vilarreal-Diaz, 2019). This makes it harder for new firms to enter the market or smaller firms to grow.[8]

Third, in many European economies, workers have not gained a bigger share of the increased economic pie (Guiso et al., 2017). In fact, an institutional neglect of labor (e.g. in terms of stagnant real wages and reduced bargaining rights) might have contributed to an increase in economic insecurity for low- and medium-skilled workers (Rodrik, 2018). There is no clear consensus in the literature as to the causes of the recent decline in the labor share of income. In advanced economies, import competition and offshoring have contributed to long-term losses in middle-skill occupations and displacement of middle-skilled workers to lower-wage occupations (Dao, Das, Koczan, & Lian, 2017).

Fourth, technological progress and the rise of 'superstar firms' help to explain a substantial part of the overall decline in the labor share of income in advanced economies, with a larger negative impact on middle- and low-skilled workers (Autor, Dorn, Katz, Patterson, & Van Reenen, 2017). Superstar firms are companies that increasingly dominate their industries through high productivity; they yield high profits with a relatively low share of labor in firm value-added and sales. Autor et al. (2017) find that these superstar firms reap much larger rewards compared to prior eras and that they disproportionately inhabit industries experiencing faster technological change (such as the high-tech, retail, and transportation industries). As the importance of superstar firms increases with globalization and digitization, the aggregate labor share will tend to fall further in the future with some industries having an increasingly 'winner takes all' aspect.

Fifth, this trend can be seen most clearly in the digital economy. Data on consumer behavior is one of the most valuable commodities in the digital economy. Due to a lack of regulatory protection of consumers' rights over their data and privacy, big tech companies have collected and monetized consumer data, but the users who have created these data have received no direct compensation (Dold & Krieger, 2017a, 2017b). In addition to this distributive aspect, there is a growing concern about a self-enforcing power mechanism in the digital economy. Tech companies enjoy network effects (the more users a platform has, the more attractive it becomes for the next user to join the platform) which means that they are bundling even more goods and services together on their platforms (Haucap & Heimeshoff, 2014). In addition, these platforms serve as crucial intermediaries that integrate across business lines, granting them control over the logistical infrastructure on which their rivals depend (Khan, 2016). The rise of learning algorithms further increases the power of companies with access to consumer data. By pairing the collection of user data with better algorithms, incumbent firms tie consumers to their platforms. Hence, there is an inherent risk in the digital economy that an increasing amount of industries will be dominated by a few companies at the expense of consumer welfare.

Finally, in unequal societies richer and better-educated workers might lack the self-interested motivation to vote for redistributive efforts (e.g. in the form of fiscal redistribution and education finance) even if they help increase overall economic output and welfare. This is because rich and high-skilled workers reap higher net benefits from an unequal system in the short run. Reflecting the fact that rich voters exert more influence in the political process,[9] redistributive policies might then command less political support in an unequal society compared to a more homogeneous one (Bénabou, 2000). Over time, the quality of public services can deteriorate in unequal societies if permanent (and unconstrained) winning coalitions promote the interests of their own members at the expense of others (Buchanan & Congleton, 1998).[10] In principle, a country could decide to tax high-skilled labor and finance these services. In fact, more globalized economies require larger governments to better accommodate the risk of external shocks (Rodrik, 1998a). However, that is often not in the self-interest of the winning coalition within a country since internationally mobile firms and capital could migrate to lower tax regimes. Hence, taxation at the national level shifts away from capital and high-skilled labor in a globalized world (Rodrik, 1998b).

Taken together, it is fair to assume that these economic and political dynamics systematically benefit high-skilled workers (especially in urban areas) but lose sight of low-skilled ones (especially in rural areas). This form of inequality may be good for the future incomes of high-skilled workers (i.e. they become richer), however, it may be bad for the future incomes of low-skilled ones (i.e. they fall even further behind).[11] Admittedly, some of the economic benefits to better-skilled workers will trickle down to lower incomes. However, the aforementioned dynamic may lead to new forms of socioeconomic fragmentation and the long-term consequence that low-skilled workers may find it increasingly difficult to climb the socioeconomic ladder. In countries that were traditionally built on a collective belief in upward social mobility ('from rags to riches'), this new societal stratification bears the risk of severe social frictions (Eggert & Krieger, 2009).

Contemporary ordoliberal responses

The responsiveness of politics to the common interests of its citizens is one of the central normative ideas of ordoliberalism (see core ideas above). Taking the advocacy for citizen sovereignty seriously, a contemporary ordoliberalism

254 *Malte Dold and Tim Krieger*

has to think creatively about democratic norms of representation, participation, and deliberation when it comes to European economic policymaking. Contrary to the epistocratic nature of some of the original ordoliberal policy proposals (think of the top-down character of Eucken's constitutive principles), a contemporary ordoliberalism should give power to communities as a 'third pillar' between national/supranational institutions and the market. We will only end up with a truly European community if policies are responsive to the concerns of the citizens whose lives are structured around overlapping local communities (Rajan, 2019). A consequent implementation of the *principle of subsidiarity* (i.e. political authority should be located at the lowest institutional unit with competence for the issue at hand) may help give local communities the ability to 'voice' their concerns and get them heard in the political process, but also give the members of the communities the possibility to 'exit' to other communities if local policies in their communities adversely affect their interests (Vanberg, 1997b). This does not mean that citizen sovereignty demands scaling back substantially our current form of supranational political organization. Having only a decentralized system of small political units leads to inefficient solutions due to 'barriers of entry and exit' (think of mobility costs between jurisdictions arising from a plethora of educational standards) and 'external effects' (think of transnational terrorism[12] or climate change). Complex and overlapping social orders that involve European standards, national policies and local initiatives will be an essential part of a system of European economic governance that is responsive to the interests of its constituents-citizens (Ostrom, 2000).

The EU project has been rather successful in promoting growth, but it has not done enough to ensure that the welfare gains are shared broadly. We think that this carries two main implications. First, at the bottom of the income distribution, ordoliberal reasoning invites the implementation of policies that enable individuals' competent participation in market transactions and political discourse. At the top of the income distribution, ordoliberalism fosters the implementation of institutions that secure 'performance-based competition,' which hampers political capitalism, i.e., the detrimental concentration of economic and political power. The guiding idea is that 'working from both ends' will increase citizen sovereignty and instantiate a broader distribution of prosperity.

The systematic and persistent disadvantage of certain social groups (e.g. low-skilled workers, the rural population, the long-term unemployed) produces market outcomes that are not conducive to long-term, inclusive growth. Cleavages between different social groups can lead to conflictual forms of competition, such as 'prevention competition' (where producers invest in conflict activities that prevent competition from other market participants, rather than improving one's own performance) or even more severe forms of 'struggle-type competition' (where market participants invest in conflict activities aimed directly at damaging more powerful social groups).[13] Conflict activities comprise indirect measures such as protest voting for

Ordoliberalism and beyond 255

'anti-system parties.' They also comprise more overt measures, such as investment in the implementation of market entry barriers, obstruction, or corruption. These are all wasteful investments aimed at a non-market driven reallocation of existing property rights that improve a market actor's relative bargaining power to win a conflict in the next round. Often, the simple threat of a potentially destructive activity suffices to reduce market efficiency since market participants invest inefficiently high sums in protective measures against conflict (e.g. in the form of legal advice).

In addition to the efficiency loss from socioeconomic cleavages, the current imbalance is inconsistent with the normative core of ordoliberalism, particularly with its inclusive definition of markets, its mistrust of power imbalances and its advocacy of economic and political participation. While it is true that most of Europe has achieved a decent formal framework for democracy, the resulting 'distributive struggle' between low- and high-skilled workers has not gotten sufficient attention in debates among economists. This is problematic as the current rise in populism makes unequivocally clear. It is fair to assume that the support for the European economic order will further erode if it continues to produce the same group of 'losers.' In order to counter the process of social fragmentation, economists have to think creatively about how to increase citizens' opportunity to participate in political and economic processes (see Dörr et al.'s chapter in this volume).

A contemporary ordoliberalism can help find solutions to the aforementioned challenges within the existing institutional structure of the EU (which, we think, is a historical achievement that has helped secure peace between the European nations). From an ordoliberal perspective, the idea of the European Single Market with its goal to implement the 'four freedoms' (free movement of goods, capital, services, and labor) is a sensible way to foster competition, regional specialization, and overall growth. However, it is true that these necessary preconditions for well-functioning markets are not sufficient to secure balanced growth that is distributed more equally across the European regions. A more inclusive form of growth requires a consequent application of the principle of subsidiarity and a better form of labor mobility within and between countries.

Following the principle of subsidiarity, workers who are negatively affected by structural changes in the economy should be first and foremost supported on the national level. If these workers are not satisfied with the perspectives in their home countries, they should have the possibility to migrate to other parts of the EU. This will incentivize their home countries to find local solutions in order to avoid losing a substantial share of their labor force. On the national level, a neglect of long-term investment in education has contributed to the current socioeconomic imbalance within and between European countries. Here, the facilitation of activating labor market programs (e.g. access to programs of life-long learning and skill upgrading throughout workers' careers) can help workers cope better with disruptions caused by technological progress and global integration. In times

256 Malte Dold and Tim Krieger

of digitization and globalization, public programs aimed at increasing the human capital of workers are likely to be more effective than industrial or agricultural policies trying to preserve an inefficient status quo. Investments in education are key for fighting unemployment among low-skilled workers, but they take time to become effective. Some low-skilled workers might be more permanently affected by structural changes in the economy so that redistributive measures might be required as well. Following the subsidiarity principle, redistributive policies have to be legitimized by each country's social contract, respecting its 'citizens' sovereignty' and tailored to specific circumstances on the national or local level.

The subsidiarity principle also demands solutions at the supranational level that go beyond support for principles of a common and discrimination-free single market with formal rights of participation. Europe-wide programs that increase worker mobility through educational and professional standardization, predistributional policies aimed at decreasing disparities in access to infrastructure, and repealing market-entry barriers can help realize positive cross-border externalities. Ultimately, the subsidiarity principle will decide which of these programs should be located at the communal, national, or supranational level. Yet, it seems necessary to coordinate these measures at the European level in order to secure worker mobility and an incentive-compatible harmonization of the regulatory framework.

An example of an incentive-compatible harmonization is the principle of delayed integration as a rule for taxing migrants (Richter, 2004; Weichenrieder & Busch, 2007). The mobility of high-skilled workers poses a threat to the viability of redistributive policies, since each region has an incentive to undercut other regions' tax rates in order to attract high-skilled labor. Delayed integration can be seen as an answer to this problem. It requires that workers who emigrate have to continue paying taxes in their home countries for a certain period and immigrants be taxed in the host country only after a period of transition. In doing so, it changes governments' incentives regarding their tax plans in a way that may limit tax competition and curb a 'race-to-the-bottom' dynamic. Given the implementation of delayed integration, a current reduction in the tax rate by a single country does not suffice to attract workers who want to pay less taxes. A potential emigrant would still have to pay taxes in her home country during the grace period. The promise of host countries (who want to attract high-skilled taxpayers) to offer lower taxes in the future might also not be credible, since each country has an incentive to tax workers heavily after the grace period as they know that these taxpayers cannot evade this tax increase by emigrating (at least in the short term). Regulatory reforms such as delayed integration work well in a coordinated federation, but not necessarily in a system of completely independent nation states (Weichenrieder & Busch, 2007). Thus, the EU has to work together with national governments on mechanisms that carefully weigh the costs of reduced labor mobility on the individual level and the benefits of less harmful tax competition on the systems level, while retaining incentive compatibility as much as possible.

In addition to labor market-oriented policies and setting proper incentives for redistributive taxation, the existing competition policy framework has to be updated to deal with the nature of market concentration in the 21st century (Khan, 2016). Here, the European Commission needs to continue its tough stance on policing mega deals between industrial conglomerates (for instance, between Alstom and Siemens). When it comes to big tech companies, the General Data Protection Regulation (EU, 2016/679) is a step in the right direction since it harmonizes the regulatory framework for individual privacy and data protection. However, ordoliberal thinking requires us to go one step further and ask how we can strengthen the underlying market mechanisms (Dold & Krieger, 2017a, 2017b). The main idea is to consider the user-generated data as a good for which, theoretically, both market sides can hold property rights. Currently, there is no regulatory framework and the acquisition of property rights happens unilaterally on behalf of the tech companies, while the users who create these data receive no direct compensation. Users are usually not aware of the degree to which companies collect their data and they do not know how valuable their data are. This means that users have no incentive to provide the optimal level of data, which might cause allocative inefficiencies. Based on their ideal of an inclusive market economy, contemporary ordoliberals might want to argue for regulating this important area of modern economies, particularly considering the one-sided distributional effects in favor of big tech. Given the right market infrastructure and technological approach,[14] a property rights perspective would allow the user to charge fees and redistribute some of the current surplus of the tech companies back to the original data producers, i.e., the private users. In addition, this would increase the efficiency of the digital economy, give 'data labor' an active stake in the creation of social value, and thus increase overall welfare.

The aforementioned proposals are mostly a reaction to policy failures of the last decade. In the years since the last financial crisis, societies in Europe have undergone fundamental socioeconomic changes. The economic downturn in 2008 was the worst since the depression in the late 1920s. Southern European economies have especially suffered in the aftermath of the crisis in the form of high youth unemployment and stagnating living standards. The European Commission (together with the International Monetary Fund and the European Central Bank) reacted with several bailout packages. At the time, this seemed the sensible and necessary strategy in the eyes of many experts. Yet, the fact that these economic programs felt externally imposed to the affected citizens (in combination with the lingering crisis) has led to a fundamental erosion of trust in European political institutions − both on behalf of citizens in the crisis-affected countries as well as in the richer countries of the European North (Algan, Guriev, Papaioannou, & Passari, 2017).[15] The promise that Europe would become the "most competitive and dynamic knowledge-based economy in the world" (EU Council, 2000) seems like an empty cliché to many people. In addition, the current form of economic order has increased the 'rational ignorance' of many citizens who see little

258 *Malte Dold and Tim Krieger*

chance of affecting the outcome of the economic policymaking process with their votes. The consequence has been a crowding-out of European citizenship (i.e. the identification with and participation in EU rule-making) and a widespread embrace of nationalism and populism as possible alternatives.

Against this backdrop, it is therefore time to reconsider which actors and institutions dominate the policy agenda in Europe. Currently, rent-seeking groups in the private sector hold disproportionate political influence (think of the role of big banks or pharmaceutical companies in setting their own standards). This comes with a systematic weakening of consumer interests in the negotiating process (Rodrik, 2018). One of the consequences is that many Europeans do not see the economic elite as part of the solution, but as the cause of the current crisis. In the view of the public, entrenched interests block changes to the rules of the game that promote greater equality and political reform (*The Economist*, 2018). In spite of the fact that many people might confuse (ordo)liberal ideas with business-led interests, support for a liberal European economic order will further vanish if consumers feel that they do not have an equal say in setting the rules of the economic game (the paradigmatic example is the negative public reaction to the negotiations of the Transatlantic Trade and Investment Partnership, TTIP, between the EU and the US). In practical terms, this requires reconsidering how nation states work together with the EU when setting the economic agenda and who is given a stake when pivotal economic policies in trade, finance, and industrial policy are negotiated.

A revitalization of ordoliberal thinking

In the aftermath of the last financial crisis, economic liberalism has lost popularity in Europe (*The Economist*, 2018). One reason for this decline might be a narrow understanding of what constitutes liberal economics. Many liberals (including ordoliberals of the second and third generations in Germany) became complacent and simply repeated the ideas of their intellectual forefathers. In addition, they often focused on a business-led agenda of economic policymaking and the justification of existing market institutions (Braunberger, 2016; Posner & Weyl, 2018). A common belief was the mantra that socioeconomic imbalances were tolerable considering the unprecedented wealth generated by market economies and the ability of existing social safety nets to absorb drastic hardship. Furthermore, economic theory became more technical and narrower in the second half of the 20th century, delegating the 'social question' (i.e. of distributional justice) to its neighboring disciplines. Many economists today would want to draw a sharp distinction between the 'positive' science of economics and normative evaluations (Hausman, McPherson, & Satz, 2016, p. 337).

In light of the previous discussion, it is clear that these interpretations of economic liberalism and economic theory will not provide the requisite strategies to tackle the current crisis of the liberal order. A revitalization of

Ordoliberalism and beyond 259

ordoliberalism will also not provide definitive answers (e.g. on the distributional issue of how to weigh the returns to high- vs. low-skilled labor); nor will it provide a definite set of policy proposals. However, we think that this book has reflected upon the manifold ways in which ordoliberalism provides a constructive way of thinking about the interdependence of social orders, one that brings together various systems of logic (the economic and the social, the positive and the normative, the theoretical and the practical, etc.). This can help us understand the multifaceted nature of our current crisis. It also provides us with a normative vision that harnesses the social radicalism inherent in free, open, and competitive markets while being sensitive to power imbalances and collective action problems.

The ordoliberals of the first generation (Eucken, Böhm, Rüstow, Röpke, Müller-Armack and others) lived in a world that was in many ways different from our times. Yet, they faced many similar challenges. In their view, the economic and political system of the first half of the 20th century was ill-prepared for the transformations in technology, demographics, and cultural life that accompanied the transition of traditional societies into modern mass societies. They were well aware that economic theory had to be embedded in a broader theory of social orders for it to be relevant. In addition, they were all concerned with questions of social justice and social security. We think that a twofold approach to economic liberalism (i.e. broadening the scope of economic theory *and* embracing the social core of liberal values) is necessary to deal with the ubiquity of transformative processes (globalization, digitization, mass migration) that are currently changing the equilibrium between the economic and other social systems. In times of dynamic structural changes, a revitalization of ordoliberal thinking can contribute to a deeper understanding of the transformative powers at work and give us guidance in implementing an appropriate institutional framework (Zweynert, Kolev, & Goldschmidt, 2016).

Ordoliberalism explicitly addresses the normative foundations of applied political economy. In spite of recurrent criticism of its value-laden nature, the normativity of ordoliberalism (its explicit political–philosophical underpinning) can be regarded as an argumentative advantage in the public debate about potential solutions to the crisis: in addition to the presentation of convincing empirical evidence, arguments for a liberal economic order have to be ultimately won on moral and political grounds through the art of persuasion. The implementation of policies needs to be supported by the European citizenry whose approval of reforms will not only rest upon economic efficiency concerns, but depend upon moral arguments that go to the heart of what it means to live together as a 'European community.' Hence, ordoliberalism can bring back political and normative thinking into a discourse that has mostly become dominated by economic technicalities.

Strengthening the PPE legacy

Modern economics is built on the idea of academic specialization. Differentiation of disciplines is fundamental to scientific progress and the accumulation of knowledge over time. However, the division of labor between disciplines becomes problematic when the sociology of a profession (i.e. career incentives, norms for publication, the nature of conferences, workshops) narrows down the set of methods and questions that its members are allowed to deal with. In economics, interdisciplinary research has become difficult and a risky career choice for young scholars (Naidu, Rodrik, & Zucman, 2019). Many economists consider research on 'social justice' and 'inclusive prosperity' external to the discipline. They would respond with a laconic: "This is not economics!"

Today's economics provides us with ideas (e.g. well-defined property rights, contract enforcement, macroeconomic stability) that are associated with efficiency and generally assumed to be conducive to growth. Yet, these ideas are compatible with a vast array of institutional arrangements, each with different effects on the freedom of individual market participants and the overall distribution of goods and services. Economics helps us explain behavior under these alternative institutional frameworks and predicts their pecuniary opportunity costs. However, thinking in comparative terms does not solve the deeper question of the desirability of the standards of comparisons themselves. Economics typically relies on efficiency standards based on the utilitarian notion that social welfare is maximized when more consumer preferences are satisfied by means of economic growth (Hausman et al., 2016, p. 109). When confronted with the task of renewing economic liberalism, this form of economic thinking is not satisfactory. The right value standard for evaluating social welfare (including non-pecuniary sources of well-being), the distribution of outcomes (and not simply the average income level), and questions of social justice (from health care to climate change to political rights) are all issues that many citizens regard as central to current policy debates. All too often, economists suppress these complex, normative issues in order to provide rough-and-ready policy advice. But as Hayek rightly pointed out in his Nobel prize speech, applied economic thinking without a political–normative discourse portrays a naïve belief in quantification that narrows the political vision to variables that can easily be quantified (Hayek, 1975).

As we have argued in this chapter (in line with other authors in this book), ordoliberalism opens economic thinking to philosophical and political questions on what kind of society we want to live in and which 'preferences' and 'values' we want to prioritize. In doing so, it embraces the idea of PPE (Philosophy, Politics, and Economics). We are currently witnessing a reintegration of these disciplines in the form of a convergent research agenda based on the insight that tools and methods of all three disciplines are necessary to make progress on many social problems (Gaus, Favor, Lamont, 2010, p. 3). There is a growing number of workshops and conferences on PPE-

Ordoliberalism and beyond   261

related topics and the International PPE Society is now entering its fourth year. Many leading colleges and universities around the world offer PPE programs. Research and teaching in PPE are guided by a twofold conviction: on the one hand, normative analysis is utopian and unhelpful if it ignores economic knowledge. Empirical research is crucial to support theoretical hypotheses and discipline ideological policy advice.[16] On the other hand, economics becomes irrelevant for many debates if it does not take account of the moral and political dimension of economic choices.

This book has shown that ordoliberalism cannot live by its gloried past. We therefore propose that contemporary ordoliberals advance their thinking in connection with international discussions in PPE. Bringing these three disciplines together provides the tools to open the black boxes of 'politics' and 'institutions' that are degraded to background assumptions in many top-tier economic journals. A PPE-oriented ordoliberalism helps analyze *and* advocate the implicit normative assumptions of economic policy advice (e.g. what kind of welfare criterion is assumed or how can a proposed change in rules be legitimized).[17] If ordoliberals try to copy Anglo–Saxon-style economics, they will lose their comparative theoretical advantage which lies in their capacity to address normative questions within a positive politico-economic theory of rules. With this proposal, we do not wish to suggest that ordoliberals abandon reasoning about legal rules. Quite the contrary: we see the prime task of contemporary ordoliberalism as applying methods and tools from PPE to legal and institutional questions.[18]

Finally, the ambition of contemporary ordoliberalism cannot only be the provision of policies for given economic ends. Rather, ordoliberals have to ask themselves how to organize and improve the quality of public reasoning on the ends themselves. Only when people themselves agree on a liberal economic agenda will nativist and populist movements lose their attractiveness. In order to contribute to a more informed democratic debate, contemporary ordoliberals should be empirically oriented, open to normative arguments, and equipped with a decent amount of humility to recognize the limits of their own knowledge. Only then can ordoliberalism become a *living* tradition.

Notes

1 Eucken emphasized that theorizing is pointless (even dangerous) if economists do not carefully consider the institutional realities and practical constraints of time and space (1992, pp. 41–44). Unlike proponents of the historical school, Eucken didn't deny the importance of theory. However, he emphatically stressed the importance of 'reality-embedded theorizing.' For an excellent discussion of the substantive core of ordoliberalism, see Kolev (2015, pp. 424–427).

2 For an in-depth discussion of the development of the notion of a 'strong state' in the ordoliberal tradition, see Berghahn and Young (2013).

3 Besides the state, Eucken and Röpke both acknowledge the importance of societal players for the implementation and enforcement of social and legal rules. On this point, see Kolev (2015, p. 431).

4 See Eucken's 'constitutive principles' for a competitive order (1952, pp. 254–291): open markets, freedom of contract, private property, liability, a functioning price system, a sound currency, and constancy of economic policy. Note that a contemporary ordoliberalism might be compatible with the ideas of 'radical markets' propagated by Posner and Weyl (2018). Exploring complementarities and differences between Posner and Weyl's agenda and contemporary ordoliberalism is an interesting avenue for future research.

5 In recent years, the self-enforcing mechanism between economic and political power has gotten substantial attention in the literature on political capitalism and captured democracy; see, e.g., Zingales (2017), Krieger and Meierrieks (2016), Gilens and Page (2014), and Acemoglu and Robinson (2008).

6 We do not want to imply that the Green Party is in the same category as the far left and the far right. However, its rise in the last 20 years is another sign of the declining appeal of the centrist parties that formed the political and social fabric of post–World War II Germany.

7 While it is hard to show that the preferences of the economic elite define economic policies, Gilens and Page (2014) and Page, Bartels, & Seawright (2011) find that (for the US) the preferences of the rich are more likely to determine public policy outcomes than the preferences of the majority.

8 Posner and Weyl (2018, p. 8) estimate that 60% of the income of the top 1% of earners comes from profits attributable to monopoly power and returns on capital as opposed to wages.

9 Empirical evidence indicates that the likelihood to vote, make a financial contribution to political campaigns, actively participate in campaigns, and other forms of political activity all rise with income and education (Bénabou, 2000).

10 Countries with greater levels of income inequality tend to have lower levels of intergenerational mobility – a phenomenon coined the "Great Gatsby curve" (Corak, 2013). Besides the political economy argument, unequal access to financial resources for higher educational attainment plays a central role in the different degrees of intergenerational transmission of human capital (Jerrim & Macmillan, 2015).

11 Van der Weide and Milanovic (2018) find that inequality is negatively associated with subsequent growth rates among the poorer income percentiles and positively among the higher percentiles.

12 Krieger and Meierrieks (2019) provide a comprehensive account of the challenges of domestic and transnational terrorism to the European Union.

13 For an in-depth discussion of 'struggle-type competition,' see Dold and Krieger (2017c). For the original ordoliberal literature on 'prevention competition' (*Behinderungswettbewerb*), see Böhm (1937, pp. 123–127) and Eucken (1952, pp. 358–359).

14 A detailed discussion lies beyond the scope of this chapter. For further reading on this topic, see Posner and Weyl (2018, ch. 5) and Dold and Krieger (2017a, 2017b).

15 Research on culture and institutions indicates that trust and open-minded attitudes of citizens are necessary conditions for the effectiveness of economic reforms (Alesina & Giuliano, 2015).

16 We think that there is no lack of empirical research in current economics – especially since economics has become significantly more empirical since the 1990s (Angrist, Azoulay, Ellison, Hill, & Lu, 2017).

17 For a thorough discussion of the conceptualization of PPE, see Anomaly, Brennan, Munger, and Sayre-McCord (2016).

18 Examples of this type of integrative research program are *new institutional economics* (see, e.g., North, Wallis, & Weingast, 2009; Williamson, 2000; Ostrom, 1998), *constitutional political economy* (see, e.g., Buchanan, 1987; Vanberg, 2005), and the *law and economics* tradition (see, e.g., Calabresi, 2016; Cooter, 2002).

Ordoliberalism and beyond 263

Bibliography

Acemoglu, D., & Robinson, J. A. (2008). Persistence of power, elites, and institutions. *American Economic Review 98*(1) 267–293.

Alesina, A., & Giuliano, P. (2015). Culture and institutions. *Journal of Economic Literature 53*(4) 898–944.

Algan, Y., Guriev, S., Papaioannou, E., & Passari, E. (2017). The European trust crisis and the rise of populism. *Brookings Papers on Economic Activity 2017*(2) 309–400.

Angrist, J., Azoulay, P., Ellison, G., Hill, R., & Lu, S. F. (2017). Economic research evolves: Fields and styles. *American Economic Review 107*(5) 293–297.

Anomaly J., Brennan, G., Munger, M. C., & Sayre-McCord, G. (2016). *Philosophy, politics, and economics: An anthology.* Oxford, UK: Oxford University Press.

Autor, D., Dorn, D., Katz, L. F., Patterson, C., & Van Reenen, J. (2017). *The fall of the labor share and the rise of superstar firms* (No. w23396). National Bureau of Economic Research.

Bénabou, R. 2000. Unequal societies: Income distribution and social contract. *American Economic Review 90*(1) 96–121.

Berghahn, V., & Young, B. (2013). Reflections on Werner Bonefeld's "Freedom and the strong state: On German ordoliberalism" and the continuing importance of the ideas of ordoliberalism to understand Germany's (contested) role in resolving the eurozone crisis. *New Political Economy 18*(5) 768–778.

Böhm, F. (1937). *Die Ordnung der Wirtschaft als geschichtliche Aufgabe und rechtsschöpferische Leistung.* Stuttgart, Germany: W. Kohlhammer.

Böhm, F. (1960) *Reden und Schriften,* Karlsruhe, Germany: Müller.

Braunberger, G. (2016). Ordnungsökonomik ist nicht genug. Unsystematische Betrachtungen eines Wirtschaftsjournalisten. In J. Zweynert, S. Kolev, & N. Goldschmidt (Eds.), *Neue Ordnungsökonomik* (vol. 69) (pp. 252–237). Tübingen, Germany: Mohr Siebeck.

Buchanan, J. M. (1987). The constitution of economic policy. *Science 236*(4807) 1433–1436.

Buchanan, J. M., & Congleton, R. D. (1998). *Politics by principle, not interest: Towards nondiscriminatory democracy.* Cambridge, UK: Cambridge University Press.

Calabresi, G. (2016). *The future of law and economics: Essays in reform and recollection.* New Haven, CT and London, UK: Yale University Press.

Collier, P. (2018). *The future of capitalism: Facing the new anxieties.* London, UK: Penguin.

Cooter, R. (2002). *The strategic constitution.* Princeton, NJ: Princeton University Press.

Corak, M. (2013). Income inequality, equality of opportunity, and intergenerational mobility. *Journal of Economic Perspectives 27*(3) 79–102.

Dao, M. C., Das, M. M., Koczan, Z., & Lian, W. (2017). *Why is labor receiving a smaller share of global income? Theory and empirical evidence.* Washington, DC: International Monetary Fund.

Der Spiegel (2018, June 8). Liberal democracy is under attack: Rise of the autocrats, *24.*

Doepke, M., & Zilibotti, F. (2019). *Love, money, and parenting: How economics explains the way we raise our kids.* Princeton, NJ: Princeton University Press.

Dold, M., & Krieger, T. (2017a). Cyber-Security aus ordnungspolitischer Sicht: Verfügungsrechte, Wettbewerb und Nudges. *Wirtschaftsdienst 97*(8) 559–565.

Dold, M., & Krieger, T. (2017b). Informationelle Selbstbestimmung aus ordnungsökonomischer Sicht. In *Informationelle Selbstbestimmung im digitalen Wandel* (pp. 181–198). Wiesbaden, Germany: Springer.

Dold, M. & Krieger, T. (2017c). Competition or conflict? Beyond traditional ordoliberalism. In C. Joerges, & J. Hien (Eds.), *Ordoliberalism, law and the rule of economics* (pp. 245–260). Oxford, UK: Hart.

Dyson, K. (2017). Ordoliberalism as tradition and as ideology. C. Joerges, & J. Hien (Eds.), *Ordoliberalism, law and the rule of economics*. Oxford, UK: Hart.

Economist, The (2018, September 13). The Economist at 175: Reinventing liberalism for the 21st century (print ed.), pp. 45–54.

Eggert, W., & Krieger, T. (2009). Home ownership als Substitut für Sozialpolitik. *Wirtschaftsdienst 89*(6) 390–396.

EU (2016/679) Regulation of the European Parliament and of the Council of 27 April 2016 on the protection of natural persons with regard to the processing of personal data and on the free movement of such data, and repealing Directive 95/46/EC (General Data Protection Regulation), http://data.europa.eu/eli/reg/2016/679/oj.

EU Council (2000). Schlussfolgerungen des Europäischen Rates Lissabon 23./24.03.2000.

Eucken, W. (1948) On the theory of the centrally administered economy. An analysis of the German experiment, parts I and II. *Economica 15*(58) 79–100; *15*(59) 173–193.

Eucken, W. ([1952] 2004). *Grundsätze der Wirtschaftspolitik* (7th ed.). Tübingen, Germany: Mohr Siebeck.

Eucken, W. ([1950] 1992). *The foundations of economics: History and theory in the analysis of economic reality* (2nd ed.). Berlin, Germany: Springer.

Fuest, C. (2018). The third type of inter-system competition: Europe and the rise of China. ifo Viewpoint No. 200.

Gaus, G., Favor, C. & Lamont, J. (2010). *Essays on philosophy, politics, and economics: Integration and common research projects*. Stanford: Stanford University Press.

Gerber, D. J. (1994). Constitutionalizing the economy: German neo-liberalism, competition law and the "new" Europe. *American Journal of Comparative Law 42*(1) 25–84.

Gidron, N., & Hall, P. A. (2017). The politics of social status: Economic and cultural roots of the populist right. *British Journal of Sociology 68* S57–S84.

Gilens, M., & Page, B. I. (2014). Testing theories of American politics: Elites, interest groups and average citizens. *Perspectives on Politics 12*(3) 564–581.

Guiso, L., Herrera, H., Morelli, M., & Sonno, T. (2017). Demand and supply of populism. CEPR Discussion Paper DP11871.

Haucap, J., & Heimeshoff, U. (2014). Google, Facebook, Amazon, eBay: Is the Internet driving competition or market monopolization? *International Economics and Economic Policy 11*(1–2) 49–61.

Hausman, D., McPherson, M., & Satz, D. (2016). *Economic analysis, moral philosophy, and public policy*. Cambridge, UK: Cambridge University Press.

Hayek, F. A. v. (1975). The pretence of knowledge. *Swedish Journal of Economics 77*(4) 433–442.

Inglehart, R., & Norris, P. (2017). Trump and the populist authoritarian parties: The silent revolution in reverse. *Perspectives on Politics 15*(2) 443–454.

Jerrim, J., & Macmillan, L. (2015). Income inequality, intergenerational mobility, and the Great Gatsby curve: Is education the key? *Social Forces 94*(2) 505–533.

Khan, L. M. (2016). Amazon's antitrust paradox. *Yale Law Journal 126* 710.

Kolev, S. (2015). Ordoliberalism and the Austrian school. In P. J. Boettke, & C. J. Coyne (Eds.), *The Oxford Handbook of Austrian Economics* (pp. 419–444). Oxford, UK: Oxford University Press.

Kolev, S., Goldschmidt, N., & Hesse, J. O. (2019). Debating liberalism: Walter Eucken, F. A. Hayek and the early history of the Mont Pèlerin Society. *Review of Austrian Economics* doi:10.1007/s11138-019-0435-x.

Krieger, T., & Meierrieks, D. (2016). Political capitalism: The interaction between income inequality, economic freedom and democracy. *European Journal of Political Economy 45* 115–132.

Krieger, T., & Meierrieks, D. (2019). The economic consequences of terrorism for the European Union. Discussion Paper No. 2019–02, Wilfried-Guth-Stiftungsprofessur für Ordnungs- und Wettbewerbspolitik, Freiburg, Germany.

Mudde, C., & Kaltwasser, C. R. 2017. *Populism: A very short introduction.* New York, NY: Oxford University Press.

Munger, M. C., & Vilarreal-Diaz, M. (2019). The road to crony capitalism. *Independent Review 23*(3) 331–344.

Naidu, S., Rodrik, D., & Zucman, G. (2019). Economics for inclusive prosperity: An introduction. *Econfip.*

North, D. C., Wallis, J. J., & Weingast, B. R. (2009). *Violence and social orders: A conceptual framework for interpreting recorded human history.* Cambridge, UK: Cambridge University Press.

OECD. (2017). *Bridging the gap: Inclusive growth 2017 update report.* Paris, France: OECD, www.oecd.org/inclusive-growth/Bridging_the_Gap.pdf

Ostrom, E. (1998). A behavioral approach to the rational choice theory of collective action: Presidential address, American Political Science Association, 1997. *American Political Science Review 92*(1) 1–22.

Ostrom, E. (2000). Crowding out citizenship. *Scandinavian Political Studies 23*(1) 3–16.

Page, B., Bartels, L., & Seawright, J. (2011). Democracy and the policy preferences of wealthy Americans. Paper presented at the annual meeting of the American Political Science Association, Seattle, Washington, DC, August 31–September 4, 2011.

Posner, E. A., & Weyl, E. G. (2018). *Radical markets: Uprooting capitalism and democracy for a just society.* Princeton, NJ: Princeton University Press.

Rajan, R. (2019). *The third pillar: How markets and the state leave the community behind.* London, UK: Penguin.

Richter, W. F. (2004). Delaying integration of immigrant labor for the purpose of taxation. *Journal of Urban Economics 55*(3) 597–613.

Rodrik, D. (1998a). Why do more open economies have bigger governments? *Journal of Political Economy 106*(5) 997–1032.

Rodrik, D. (1998b). Has globalization gone too far? *Challenge 41*(2) 81–94.

Rodrik, D. (2018). Populism and the economics of globalization. *Journal of International Business Policy* 1–22.

Van der Weide, R., & Milanovic, B. (2018). Inequality is bad for growth of the poor (but not for that of the rich). *The World Bank Economic Review 32*(3) 507–530.

Vanberg, V. (1997a). Die normativen Grundlagen von Ordnungspolitik. *ORDO: Jahrbuch für die Ordnung von Wirtschaft und Gesellschaft 48* 707–726.

Vanberg, V. (1997b). Subsidiarity, responsive government and individual liberty. In B. Steunenberg & F. Van Vught (Eds.), *Political institutions and public policy* (pp. 189–203). Dordrecht, Germany: Springer.

266 Malte Dold and Tim Krieger

Vanberg, V. (2005). Market and state: The perspective of constitutional political economy. *Journal of Institutional Economics* 1(1) 23–49.

Weichenrieder, A. J., & Busch, O. (2007). Delayed integration as a possible remedy for the race to the bottom. *Journal of Urban Economics* 61(3) 565–575.

Weiss, C. R., & Wittkopp, A. (2005). Retailer concentration and product innovation in food manufacturing. *European Review of Agricultural Economics* 32(2) 219–244.

Williamson, O. E. (2000). The new institutional economics: Taking stock, looking ahead. *Journal of Economic Literature* 38(3) 595–613.

Zingales, L. (2017). Towards a political theory of the firm. *Journal of Economic Perspectives* 31(3) 113–30.

Zweynert, J., Kolev, S., & Goldschmidt, N. (2016). *Neue Ordnungsökonomik* (vol. 69). Tübingen, Germany: Mohr Siebeck.

Index

academic specialization 260
ACLI *see* Associazioni cristiane dei
  lavoratori italiani (ACLI)
acquis communautaire 178, 183
Acton, John 98
Acton–Tocqueville Society 98
Adenauer, Konrad 65–6, 68, 101, 133,
  177
Ahlen: manifesto 66; Program 81
Albert, Michel 75
Alesina, A. 181
Allais, Michel 96
Allies 76–8, 85, 132–3
Almunia, Joaquín 2
Amazon 74
American capitalism 74
Angeloni, I. 181
Anglo–American capitalism 75
Anglo-Saxon economics 110–11,
  114–17, 153, 261
"Anglo-Saxon–Latin pragmatism" 223
Anglo-Saxon neoliberalism 62
Arbeitsgemeinschaft Erwin von
  Beckerath 62
Archbishop of Cologne 82, 84–5
aristocratic liberalism 98
Associazioni cristiane dei lavoratori
  italiani (ACLI) 67
aus dem Moore, N. 240
Ausschuss für Makroökonomik 111, 117
Austrian Catholic Vogelsangian 65
Austrian-Hungarian Empire 192
Austrian School 27, 30
Austro-Marxists 27
authoritarianism 223

Baccaro, L. 59
Bachmann, Rüdiger 11
Banca d'Italia 97

bankruptcy 138, 142, 146, 155, 171–2,
  199, 202
Barbier, H. 109
Basic Law of the Federal Republic 77–8,
  83
"Basic Outlines of the Morality of the
  Stock Market" 85
'battle of methods' 23, 26, 31
Bauhaus movement 39
BdA *see* Bundesvereinigung deutscher
  Arbeitgeberverände (BdA)
Beck, T. 224–5
Becker, Gary 28
Becker, Johannes 12
benevolent dictator 238
Berghahn, Volker 10–11
Berthold, Norbert 13, 113
Beveridge, William 27
Biebricher, Thomas 13, 223
Bild 139
Bildung 84
Bismarckian welfare-state provision 42,
  68, 101
BKU *see* Bund Katholischer
  Unternehmer (BKU)
Blankart, Charles 113
Bloomington School 34
Blüm, Norbert 70
Blyth, Mark 8, 223
Böckler, Hans 86
Bofinger, P. 113
Böhm, Franz 1, 29–30, 63, 99, 113, 126,
  195, 208, 226, 227, 237
Böhm-Bawerk, Eugen von 26–7, 30
Bon, Gustave Le 192
Bonhoeffer, Dietrich 62
Bonhoeffer Kreis 62
Bononi, Paolo 66
Borchardt, K. 41, 47

268 *Index*

Braunberger, G. 112
Brennan, G. 43
Bresciani-Turroni, Costantino 94, 96–7
Bretton Woods currency system 88, 93, 97, 102–3
Breuning, Bernharda von 84
Brexit 230, 233
Briefs, Götz 94
Brüning, Heinrich 48, 115, 226
Brunnermeier, M.K. 8, 151, 224
Buchanan, James 34, 43, 93, 95–6, 182, 210, 227, 239
Bülow bloc 44
Bundesbank 102, 131–4, 136, 181, 202
Bundesvereinigung deutscher Arbeitgeberverände (BdA) 83
Bund Katholischer Unternehmer (BKU) 81–3
Burckhardt, Jakob 98
Burda, Michael 8, 159
Burke, Edmund 226

Cannan, Edwin 27
CAP *see* Common Agricultural Policy (CAP)
capitalism 53, 63, 199, 229, 254; American 74; corporatist 68; market 39; Nell-Breuning on 84–8; organized 41; and socialism 51; varieties-of- 59–60, 75
Capitalism and Freedom (Friedman) 33
Carli, Guido 97, 103
Carter, Jimmy 74
cash-for-clunkers program 109, 114
Catholic Centre 44
"The Catholic Entrepreneur in the Coming Economic Order" 81
Catholicism and Protestantism 10; impact of 66–70; reactions in socioeconomic concepts 61–6
Catholic University of Milan 65
CDU *see* Christian Democratic Party (CDU)
centralization and harmonization 128–9
Chicago, neoliberalism in 24–9, 31, 33
Chicago School 25, 28, 92–3, 95–6, 101–2, 153
Chirac, Jacques 141
The Christian Democrat Enrico Mattei 67
Christian Democratic Party (CDU) 63–9, 78–9, 83, 101
Christian Democratic Union/Christian Social Union (CDU/CSU) 224

Christian humanism 99
Christianity 30, 53
Christian Socialism 63–5
Christian Social Sciences 83
Christian Social Union (CSU) 101
circoli (social organizations) 67
citizen sovereignty 239, 249–50; and contemporary ordoliberalism 253–4
Coalition Agreement 224
Cochrane, John 110
codetermination 87
Cohesion Policy 14
Coldiretti 67
Colloque Lippmann 226
Colloque Walter Lippmann (CWL) 24–5, 31–3
Common Agricultural Policy (CAP) 178, 182–3
Communist Party 47
competition policy framework 257
competitive market 248; and economic and legal context 225–9
concentric circle approach 129
Conference of Bishops 80
Confessing Church 99
Confindustria 67–8, 76–8, 85, 132–3
Congress of Vienna 49
consensus on constitutional interests 209–11
conservatism 248
constituent principles 51
constitutional economics 239; and consumer sovereignty 240; and methodological individualism 239; and normative individualism 240; positive approach to 242
constitutional interests 210; consensus on 209–11
constitutionalism 43, 45–6
Constitution of Liberty (Hayek) 42
constitutive principles 238
consumer sovereignty 26, 240, 249–50
contemporary ordoliberalism 246–7; consumer and citizen sovereignty 249–50; core ideas of 247–50; dispersion of power 248–9; responses 253–8; rules of the market 247–8; socioeconomic hazards, protection against 249
continental economist 27
Coolidge, Calvin 226
coronation theory 4
Corporatism 66
corporatist capitalism 68

Council of Economic Advisers 111
countercyclical national fiscal policy 169
credibility 91–2, 94, 97–8, 103
CSU *see* Christian Social Union (CSU)
cultural political economy 58–61
CWL *see* Colloque Walter Lippmann (CWL)

DC *see* Italian Democrazia Cristiana (DC)
debt ceiling 140
De Gasperi, Alcide 65–6
de-homogenization 29
Delors, Jacques 134
Delors Report 102
democracy, and ordoliberalism 39–53, 98; liberal prewar economic order 41–6; overview 39–41; permanent crisis in Weimar State 46–8
democratic legitimacy 144–6
democratic market economies 210
Deutsche Bundesbank 133
Deutsche Gewerkschaftsbund (DGB) 66, 81–2, 86
DGB *see* Deutsche Gewerkschaftsbund (DGB)
Die Gesellschaftskrise der Gegenwart (Einaudi) 97
Die Tatwelt 98
digital economy 252–3
Director, Aaron 28
disciplinary revolution, in Europe 98–9
distributional struggles among social groups 251
D-mark 131–6, 155
Dold, Malte 15
Dollfuss, Engelbert 85
Dörr, Julian 14
Dossetti, Giuseppi 65–6
Draghi, Mario 146, 196
dualism 43, 46, 75
Düsseldorfer Leitsätze 78
Dyson, Kenneth 10, 250

ECB *see* European Central Bank (ECB)
ECJ *see* European Court of Justice (ECJ)
econometrics 241
Economia (Fanfani) 68
Economic and Monetary Union (EMU) 6, 8, 11–13, 94, 98, 102–3, 129, 131–2, 135–6, 198–9
"The Economic Conditions of Interstate Federalism" 175
economic crisis 5, 39, 48–53, 61–6, 87,

103, 141, 147; Catholicism and Protestantism 61–70; and cultural political economy 58–61
economic efficiency and social equity 209–11
economic nationalism 50, 114
economic orders 39–47, 50
economic policy 8–10, 13–15, 23, 33, 42, 48–9, 51–2, 63, 94, 99, 108–17, 126, 141, 147, 151, 153–4, 156, 168–9, 173, 177, 194–5, 200, 217–18, 223–5, 228, 237–8, 240–1, 249, 254, 258, 261
economic regulations, and business-led agenda 251–2
economic stagnation 47–8, 51, 74
ECSC *see* European Coal and Steel Community (ECSC)
EEC *see* European Economic Community (EEC)
Einaudi, Luigi 93–4, 96–8
Einführung in die Wirtschaftstheorie 112
embeddedness, of ordoliberalism 95–8
EMS *see* European Monetary System (EMS)
EMU *see* Economic and Monetary Union (EMU); European Monetary Union (EMU)
ENI *see* Ente Nazionale Idrocarburi (ENI)
Enlightenment 97
ENP *see* European Neighbourhood Policy (ENP)
Ente Nazionale Idrocarburi (ENI) 67
Erdsiek-Eucken, Edith 76
Erhard, Ludwig 33, 63, 68, 78, 85, 88, 99–102, 115, 126, 133, 163, 177–8, 231
Erhard method 100
ERM *see* Exchange Rate Mechanism (ERM)
"Ersatzwirtschaftspolitik" 217
ESM *see* European Stability Mechanism (ESM)
An Essay on the Nature and Significance of Economic Science (Robbins) 28
EU *see* European Union (EU)
Eucken, Irene 75–6
Eucken, Rudolf 75, 98
Eucken, Walter 1, 10, 24, 28–30, 32–4, 41–3, 47–9, 51, 61–2, 75–80, 88, 92, 94–6, 99–100, 113, 115, 126, 133, 153, 192, 193–4, 202, 208, 209, 223, 225–9, 237, 238–9; and concept of privilege-free order of competition 208–9; interdependence of orders 240; on socioeconomic hazards 249

270 *Index*

Eucken Association 98
Eucken School 92–3
EU Commission 215, 217, 225
The Euro and the Battle of Ideas
(Brunnermeier) 224
euro currency 131–6; commitment
problem 142–4; democratic legitimacy
144–6; institutional failure 139–42;
liability and control 147–8; promise
and disappointment 138–9; reforming
eurozone 148–9, 160–3
Europe: heterogeneous economic
cultures 208; inequality in 207;
ordoliberalization of 192–9; political
and monetary–economic integration
3–6; social Europe 230–3
European Banking Union 161
European Central Bank (ECB) 12, 102,
104, 114, 131–2, 134, 136, 138, 144,
154–6, 158–60, 168–70, 190, 195–6,
199–200, 229
European Coal and Steel Community
(ECSC) 101
European Commission 2, 4, 101, 142,
155–6, 173, 177–9, 190, 196, 201,
257
European Council 4, 142
European Court of Justice (ECJ) 2, 128,
178, 230
European Deposit Insurance Scheme 129
European Economic Community (EEC)
101, 177
European fascism 227
European integration 2–3, 175–86
European liberal order 250; and labor
market programs 255; and low- and
high-skilled workers 255; and social
groups 254–5; *see also* populism
European Monetary Fund (EMF) 161,
172, 201, 233
European Monetary System (EMS) 134
European Monetary Union (EMU) 116,
151–2, 155, 157–8, 162–3, 167–73,
181–2, 233
European Neighbourhood Policy (ENP)
185
European *Ordnungspolitik* 208
European Parliament 4, 128, 131, 173
European Pillar of Social Rights 15, 225
European Regional Development Fund
215
European Semester 196
European Senate for Political
Competition 129

European Social Fund 215
European social market economy:
capability as key element of modern
social policy 212–14; consensus on
constitutional interests 209–11;
economic efficiency and social equity
209–11; Eucken and concept of
privilege-free order of competition
208–9; EU Cohesion Policy 214–18;
inequality and political acceptance
211–12; overview 207–8; participation
as element of modern economic and
social policy 212–14; social Europe
embedded within 230–3; *Vitalpolitik
for Nations* 214–18
European sovereign debt crises 224
European Stability Mechanism (ESM)
103, 149, 160–1, 172, 191, 199–201,
232, 233
European Structural and Investment
Funds 215
European Subsidiarity Court 129
European Union (EU) 3–4, 92–3, 96,
144–6, 167–8, 197, 215, 233, 254–8;
centralization and harmonization
128–9; Cohesion Policy 208, 214–18;
and European integration 175–86; and
ordoliberalism 126–7
eurozone crisis 6, 8–14, 23, 34, 145;
commitment problem 142–4;
Germany's role in 155–60;
management 223–4, 229; and
ordoliberalism 190–202; reforming
148–9, 160–4; ten commandments for
167–73
Exchange Rate Mechanism (ERM) 97,
102–3
external constraint *(vincolo esterno)* 97, 103

Fabian Society 27
Fanfani, Amintore 66, 68
Federal Republic of Germany 77–9,
81–3, 88, 132
Federal Reserve Model 100
Feld, Lars 8, 15, 111–12, 163
financial crisis 5–9, 59, 108, 110, 143,
154–6, 190, 207, 257–8
Financial Times 8, 116
Fiscal Compact 232
Fiscal Pact 200
The Foundations of Economics (Eucken) 30,
194
Frankfurter Allgemeine Zeitung 108–9, 113,
116

Freedom and the Economic System (Hayek) 28
"'Free' Enterprise and Competitive Order" 32
free market economy 248; constitutive principles of 238
Freiburg circles 30, 62, 99
Freiburger Denkschrift 62
Freiburg School of Economics 10, 29–31, 33, 75–80, 92–3, 125, 153, 175, 192, 195, 208, 212, 223, 237; and ordoliberalism 1–2; and Viktor Vanberg 239–40
Freud, Sigmund 192
Friedman, Milton 28, 33, 153, 226
Frings, Joseph 82–4, 87
"From Being Free of Values to Being of No Value" 108
Fuest, Clemens 12, 111–12

Galli, G. 67
Gasset, José Ortega y 98, 192
Gaulle, Charles de 96
General Data Protection Regulation 257
Geneva, and neoliberalism 29–31
Gentile, Panfilo 97
German austerity culture 223
German Bundesbank 223
German Central Bank 168
German Council of Economic Advisers 111, 129, 132
German Council of Economic Experts 111
German oddity 9, 23, 25, 29, 33
German ordoliberalism: competitive market order and economic and legal context 225–9; critique of 238–40; France and Germany, battles between 229–30; future development of 241–2; future viability of 243; introductory comments 223–5; new German *Methodenstreit* 240–1; overview 237–8; social Europe embedded within European social market economy 230–3
German 'Reich' 192
German Social Democrats (SPD) 167
Germany: battles between France and 229–30; GDP of 39, 41, 59–60; and governance of EMU 152–5; macroeconomics 108–18; reunification 69; role in eurozone crisis 155–60
Gestapo 76, 80
Gewerkschaftliche Monatshefte 86

Gide, Charles 24
global financial crisis 207
Gocht, Robert 102
Goethe, Johann Wolfgang von 98
Goldschmidt, N. 14, 240–2
The Good Society (Lippmann) 29, 32, 95, 226
Google Ngram 24
Google Scholar 59
Gothenburg summit 2017 225
Great Depression 27, 39, 50, 80, 92–3, 95, 152–3
Great Recession 156
Great War 41, 50
Green, Thomas H. 27
Großmann-Doerth, Hans 1, 30, 195, 226–7
Group Psychology and the Analysis of the Ego 192
growth model 59–60
Grundlagen der Nationalökonomie (Eucken) 76
Grundsätze der Wirtschaftspolitik (Eucken) 78, 92, 153, 225, 228
Grundsätze (Eucken) 42–3

Haberler, Gottfried 31
Habilitation (Höffner) 76, 80
Hall, P. 59, 75
Hallstein, Walter 2
Handelsblatt (German business daily) 108–9
harmonization and centralization 128–9
Hartmann, Nicolai 98
Hartz reform 157
Hawtrey, Ralph 96
Hayek, Friedrich August von 9, 24, 27–9, 31–3, 42–3, 93, 98, 128, 175–6, 178, 180, 228, 260
Hegel, Georg Friedrich Wilhelm 115
Heidegger, Martin 76
Hesse, Jan-Otmar 112
Hien, Josef 10, 229
Historical School 29–31
Hitler regime 76, 85, 153
Hobhouse, Leonard T. 27
Hobson, John A. 27
Höffner, Helene 79
Höffner, Joseph 79–85, 87–8
Höffner, Paul 79
Holocaust 76
Hoover, Herbert 226
'house-in-order' approach 96
Huizinga, Johan 98

272 *Index*

Hume, David 24
Husserl, Edmund 30, 76, 98
Hüther, Michael 109
hyperinflation 39, 41, 132, 152

ideational approach 60–2
Ifo Institute 112
IMF 217
Imperial Germany (Kaiserreich) 40, 42–3, 46
incentive-compatible harmonization 256
individual economic anxiety 251
individualism: methodological 239; normative 240
inequality and political acceptance 211–12
inflation 52, 93, 100, 103, 110, 114, 131–2, 134, 143, 155, 157–60, 170, 199
Institute of Christian Social Sciences 81
institutional economics 125
institutional weakness 139–42
International Monetary Fund (IMF) 141, 172, 190
International PPE Society 261
interstate federalism 175–6
IRI *see* Istituto per la Ricostruzione Industriale (IRI)
Iron Curtain 157
Istituto per la Ricostruzione Industriale (IRI) 67
Italian Democrazia Cristiana (DC) 65–7
Italian Liberal Party 97

Jahrbuch für die Ordnung von Wirtschaft und Gesellschaft 77
James, H. 151
Jena University 75
Joerges, C. 229
Journal of Public Economics 112
Juncker, Jean-Claude 167, 173, 179, 225, 233
The Juncker Commission 201

Kantian idealism 98–9
Kaufmann, F.-X. 63
Ketteler, W.E. von 85
Keynes, J.M. 27–8, 47, 96
Keynesian and Beveridgean welfare state 62
Keynesianism 110–12, 114, 116–17, 153–4
Kindleberger, C. 50
Kirchgässner, Gebhard: critique of

ordoliberalism 238–9; German *Sonderweg* 241; public choice theory 238–9
Knight, Frank 28, 95–6
Köhler, Ekkehard 15
Kolev, Stefan 9–10
Kolping, Adolf 85
König, Heinz 113
Kotz, H.H. 224
Krämerseele 116
Krelle, Wilhelm 112
Krieger, Tim 15
Kroes, Neelie 2
Kronberger Kreis 113
Krüger, Dirk 109
Krugman, Paul 8

labor: 'distributive struggle' between low- and high-skilled 255; division and sociology of a profession 260; institutional neglect and populist movement 252; market programs 255
Labor Law and Morality (Nell-Breuning) 85
laissez-faire liberalism 1, 25–6, 28, 33, 62, 77, 95, 99, 125, 193, 226–7, 231
Landau, J.-P. 151
Landmann, Oliver 13
La Pira, Giorgio 65
Lazzati, Giuseppe 65
Lehman Brothers 138, 142, 155
Leistungswettbewerb 1, 78, 197
Leitsätze, Düsseldorfer 66
Le Monde 100
Lenger, Alexander 14, 242
Leo XIII 64
liability and control 147–8
liberalism 9, 11, 15, 23–5, 27–8, 32, 40, 48, 52–3, 91; aristocratic 98; cross-national disciplinary revolution in 91–104; economic, for twenty-first century 246–61; laissez-faire 1, 25–6, 28, 33, 62, 77, 95, 99, 125, 193, 226–7, 231
liberal prewar economic order 41–6
Liefmann-Keil, Elisabeth 113
Lippmann, Walter 29, 32, 95, 226
Lippmann Colloquium 93, 95–6
Lisbon Agenda 217
Lisbon Treaty (TEU) 12, 126, 135, 230
lobbying 47
Locke, John 24
locomotive theory 4
London, neoliberalism in 24–9, 31, 33

London Debt Agreement of 1953 100
London School of Economics and
Political Science 27
long-term investment 51
L'ordre sociale (Rueff) 96
Ludwig-Erhard-Stiftung 109, 113
Lutheran Church 99
Lutheran Protestantism 79, 99
Lutz, Friedrich 95

Maastricht Treaty 5, 7, 12, 97, 102, 104,
126–7, 134–5, 140–1, 154–6, 163,
168, 201, 230, 232
McKinsey effect 110
Macroeconomic Imbalances Procedure
(MIP) 103
macroeconomics 6–7, 11, 13, 23, 27, 91,
98, 103, 108–17, 136, 151–6, 158–64,
196, 215, 225, 240
Macron, Emmanuel 151, 168, 170, 224,
233
Magna Carta 173
Majone, Giandomenico 197
Malthus, Thomas 226
Maritain, Jaques 65
market capitalism 39
Marshall Aid 100
Marxism 86
Mendès-France, Pierre 100
Menger, Carl 26–7
Merkel, Angela 70
Methodenstreit 115
Methodenstreit (2009) 110
methodological individualism 239
Meyer, Fritz 112–13
Miert, Karel Van 2
Miksch, Leonhard 32, 100, 113
Mill, John Stuart 24
MIP *see* Macroeconomic Imbalances
Procedure (MIP)
Mises, Ludwig von 27, 31–3
modern economic and social policy:
capability as key elements of 212–14;
participation as key element of 212–14
"modern economic state"
(Wirtschaftsstaat) 42, 49
modern institutional economics 125
Mommsen, Theodor 44
monetary policy 12, 23, 52, 91, 93, 95,
100, 102, 104, 110, 114, 132–6,
143–4, 148, 152, 154, 158–9, 161–2,
168–9, 172, 181, 198, 226, 248
monetary union club 181–2
Monti, Mario 2, 230

Mont Pèlerin Society (MPS) 24, 28–9,
31–4, 95
Mounier, Emmanuel 65
MPS *see* Mont Pèlerin Society (MPS)
Müller-Armack, Alfred 1, 14–15, 23, 29,
62–4, 78, 87–8, 94, 99, 113, 126, 225,
226, 231–2
multi-speed concept 129
Münchau, Wolfgang 8
Müncker, Theodor 80
Mussler, W. 4

national economic policy 169
Nationalökonomie 194
Nationalökonomie wozu? (Eucken) 194
National Socialism 30, 33
Naumann, F. 43–4
Nazis 76–7, 80, 96, 114–15, 133, 152–3
Nell, Arthur von 84
Nell-Breuning, Oswald von 65, 79–81,
84–8
neoclassical synthesis 153
neoliberalism 23–34; birthplaces of 25–9;
and Colloque Walter Lippmann
(CWL) 31–3; Freiburg and Geneva
29–30; and Mont Pèlerin Society
(MPS) 31–3; multiple meanings of
24–5; overview 23–4
NEP *see* New Economic Policy (NEP)
Neuer Methodenstreit 109
'New Chicago School' 28
New Deal 28, 95, 115
New Economic Policy (NEP) 40
new German *Methodenstreit* 240–1
normative constitutional economics 242
normative individualism 240
North German Federation 42
North–South conflict: Catholicism and
Protestantism 61–70; overview 58–9;
and political economy 59–61

OCA *see* optimum currency area (OCA)
OECD 207
OECD countries 251
'Old Chicago School' 28
open market 248
optimum currency area (OCA) 104
Ordnung der Wirtschaft (order of the
economy) 227
Ordnungspolitik 43–4, 175, 178, 191
ORDO articles 77–8
ordoliberal governmentality 195
ordoliberalism 211, 223; alternative
subsidiarity-linked concepts of

274 Index

ordoliberalism *continued*
  integration 129–30; and "battle of
  ideas" 151–2; centralization and
  harmonization 128–9; critique of 238;
  and democracy 39–53; description
  237; economic liberalism for twenty-
  first century 246–61; and EU 126–7;
  and Europe 192–9; and European
  integration 2–3, 175–86; and eurozone
  crisis 190–202; and financial crisis 6–9;
  and Freiburg School of Economics
  1–2; Germany and governance of
  EMU 152–5; and governance of EMU
  152–5; as modern institutional
  economics 125; and neoliberalism
  23–34; normativity of 259; political
  and monetary-economic integration
  3–6; Protestant 58–70; rules 125–6;
  sociological form of 247; and US-style
  macroeconomics 108–18; *see also*
  German ordoliberalism
Ordoliberalism: A German Oddity? (Beck
  & Kotz) 225, 229
ordoliberal thinking 258–9
ordoliberal tradition: disciplinary
  revolution in Europe 98–9; embedded
  nature of 95–8; nature of 92–5;
  overview 91–2; significance of 100–4
Ordo Manifesto 63, 225, 227
Ordungspolitischer Einspruch 109
organic policy 241
organized capitalism 41
Ostrom, Elinor 34
overlapping integration areas 129–30

Pantaleoni, Maffeo 24
"Parisian Panama corruption" 45
paritätische Mitbestimmung 81–3, 87–8
parliamentarianism 40, 43–5
partial membership approach 129
Paulssen, Constantin 83
'perfect competition' *(vollständiger
  Wettbewerb)* 77
performance-based competition 254
performance competition 240
"Perspectives of Economic Policy" 169
Pesch, Heinrich 65
Phillips curve 113
Piettre, André 100
Pius XI (Pope) 79, 85–6
Poincaré, Raymond 97
political authority 249
political economy, cultural 58–61
populism 250; current rise of 251; and

economic regulations 251–2; and
institutional neglect of labor 252; and
self-interested motivation 253; and
technological progress 252; and urban
land 251; *see also* European liberal order
positive constitutional economics 242
"A Positive Program for Laissez Faire:
  Some Proposals for a Liberal
  Economic Policy" 28
PPE (philosophy, politics, and economics):
  oriented ordoliberalism 261; programs
  261; strengthening of 260–1; workshops
  and conferences on 260
praxeology 28
"Prices and Production" lecture series 28
principle of subsidiarity 254, 256
Principles of Economic Policy (Eucken) 194,
  202
privileged interests 210
privilege-free order of competition:
  Eucken and concept of 208–9
Prodi, Romano 141
productivity 47, 50, 146, 251–2
"Property and Co-determination" 87
protectionism 44, 49–50, 53, 181
Protestant Church 30
Protestant ordoliberalism 10, 58–70;
  Catholicism and Protestantism 61–70;
  overview 58–9; and political economy
  59–61
public choice theory 238–9
public programs 256

Quadragesimo anno 40, 63, 65–6, 68, 79,
  85–6
"qualitative freedom" 213

raising rivals' costs 128
Rathenau, Walter 39
Rawls, J. 46, 243
Raymond, Walter 83
Reagan, Ronald 24, 74, 230
"Rebuild German Economics According
  to International Standards" 240
redistributive policies 147–8
Reformed Protestant 99
reforming eurozone 148–9, 160–3
Regional and Structural Funds 178
Reich Economics Ministry 76
Reichstag 40, 43–4
Renaissance 97
reunification 69
Rheinischer Merkur (Catholic weekly) 84,
  109

Rhenish capitalism 75
Rhenish Catholics 79, 84
Ricardo, David 226
Rist, Charles 96
Ritter, Gerhard 76
Road to Serfdom (Hayek) 28, 98, 175–6
Robbins, Lionel 27–8, 31
Rodrik, Dani 155, 164, 237
Romer, Paul 237
Röpke, Wilhelm 1, 24, 28–34, 45, 48–9, 94, 97–100, 126, 176–80, 193, 226
Rossi, Ernesto 97
Rougier, Louis 93–6, 98–9
Rueff, Jacques 93–4, 96, 99
Ruhr industries 82
rule of law 126
Rüstow, Alexander 1, 29, 32, 34, 49, 62, 94, 126, 193–4, 208, 211–12, 214, 218, 226, 241

Sachverständigenrat (German Council of Economic Advisers)111
Samuelson, P. 153
Santayana, George 98
"Save Economic Policy in the Universities" 240
Schäfer, Wolf 12
Schäuble, Wolfgang 9, 70, 110, 202, 223–4
Scheler, Max 98
Schiller, Karl 102
Schmidt, C. 240
Schmidt, Helmut 113–14, 144
Schmoller, Gustav 29, 45
Schneider, Erich 112
Schneyder, Werner 143
Scholz, Olaf 224
Schröder, Gerhard 70, 141
Schroeder, Wolfgang 86
Schuknecht, L. 181
Schwarze Null 198
Seelisberg meeting 32
self-enforcing power mechanism, digital economy 252
self-interested motivation 253
Sen, Amartya 14, 208, 212
SGP see Stability and Growth Pact (SGP)
Simons, Henry 28–9, 95
Single European Act (1985) 178, 230
single market club 181
Sinn, Hans-Werner 169, 241
Six-Pack 191, 196, 200, 232
SME see social market economy (SME)

Smith, Adam 1, 24, 240
social Catholicism 10–11, 64–6, 70, 75, 79, 83–5
Social Democratic Party (SPD) 44, 47, 85, 113, 224
social echo chambers 251
"The Social Encyclical" 85
social equity, and economic efficiency 209–11
social Europe 230–3
social groups: and European liberal order 254–5; systematic and persistent disadvantage of 254
socialism, and capitalism 51
Socialist Calculation Debates 27–8
social market economy (SME) 64, 125–6; Eucken and Freiburg School of Economics 75–9; Höffner and 79–84; and Nell-Breuning 84–8; overview 74–5
Society of the Friends of the Arts of Jena and Weimar 76
socioeconomic concepts 61–6
socioeconomic hazards 249
sociology of a profession 260
Soskice, D. 59, 75
sovereign debt crisis 223
sovereignty: citizen 239, 249–50; consumer 240, 249–50
Soviet centralized socialism 227
Soviet communism 226
Soziale Marktwirtschaft 134, 225, 231
Sozialkommissionen der Christlich-Demokratischen Arbeitnehmerschaft 79
Spann, Othmar 115
SPD see Social Democratic Party (SPD)
Staatswissenschaften 115
Stability and Growth Pact (SGP) 96, 103–4, 135, 141, 201, 232
Stability Pact 141
stabilization period 41
Stark, Jürgen 202
Stiftung Marktwirtschaft 111, 113
Stigler, George 28
Streeck, W. 59
Streit, M.E. 4
"Structural Change of the State and the Crisis of Capitalism" (article) 41
Sturzo, Dom Luigi 94, 97
subsidiarity: alternative concepts of integration 129–30; centralization and harmonization 128–9; and ordoliberalism 127–8

276 *Index*

subsidiarity principle *see* principle of
  subsidiarity
subsidies *(Osthilfe)* 48
Süddeutsche Zeitung 109
Svallfors, S. 59

TEU *see* Lisbon Treaty (TEU)
"Teutonomik" 159
Thatcher, Margaret 24, 230
Theoretische Ausschuss 112
Third Reich 81
Third Republic 43
Thirty Years War 58
time-consistency theory 91–2, 94, 97–8,
  103
totalitarian fascism 226
trade policy 44–5, 49, 186
Transatlantic Trade and Investment
  Partnership (TTIP) 258
transfer union 103, 147, 155, 160–1, 171
Treaty of Rome (1957) 2, 101, 177
Treaty on Stability and Growth 190
Trichet, Jean-Claude 138, 145–6
Trier Seminary 81
Trippen, Norbert 79
Troika 58, 146–7, 190, 195–6, 200
Tsarist Russia 192
Tullock, G. 182

Uber 74
Uhlig, Harald 109
unemployment rates 6, 13, 41, 69, 80,
  93, 113–14, 146, 149, 152, 154, 157,
  167, 170–1, 207, 216, 226, 232, 256–7
University of Cologne 23, 108–9, 112,
  240
University of Freiburg 226
urban land 251
urban property owners 251
US-style macroeconomics 108–18

Vanberg, V.J. 109, 180, 227–8, 239–40
varieties-of-capitalism approach 59
Varieties of Capitalism (Hall and Soskice)
  59
Vaubel, Roland 116
'veil of uncertainty' 210
Veit, Otto 99
Verein für Socialpolitik 29, 111, 112,
  117
Vermeersch, Artur 79
Vestager, Margrethe 2
Vienna, neoliberalism in 24–31, 33

Vienna Circles 27
Viennese Privatseminar 27
Villeroy & Boch 83
Viner, Jacob 28, 31
Virginia School 34
Vitalpolitik for Nations 211–12, 214–18
Voigt, S. 242
Volksverein für das katholische
  Deutschland 86
voluntary consent 210
von Mises, Ludwig 226

wages 24, 42, 47, 59–60, 64, 103, 128,
  140, 146, 157–8, 169–70, 180, 193,
  199, 212, 223, 230, 249, 251–2
Walter Eucken Institute 8, 109, 112,
  198
Watrin, Christian 108–9, 112, 113
Wealth of Nations (Smith) 27
Weber, Max 28–31
Wegner, Gerhard 10
Weidmann, Jens 202, 223
Weimar Constitution 46
Weimar State 10, 39–43, 46–8, 51, 53,
  152, 193–4
Weltanschauung 7, 225
Welty, Eberhard 81
Werner Plan 102
Wieland, Volker 111
Wieser, Friedrich von 26, 30
Wilhelmine state 41–2
Willgerodt, Hans 108–9, 112
Wirtschaftsordnungen (economic orders)
  115, 227
Wirtschaftsstil paradigm (economic styles)
  115
Wirtschaftstheoretischer Ausschuss 117
Wirtschaftswunder 115, 126, 157, 163
Wissenschaftliche Beirat beim
  Bundeswirtschaftsministerium 113
Wohlgemuth, Michael 13
Works Constitution Act (1952) 82
World Bank 217
World Economic Conference 50
World War I (WWI) 10, 39, 42–3, 75,
  77, 192
World War II (WWII) 11, 32–3, 42, 48,
  52–3, 61, 67, 131, 225, 231
Wyplosz, Charles 169

Young, Brigitte 14
Youngest Historical Schools 29
Young plan 41

Printed in the United States
By Bookmasters